Russia's Social Gospel

Russia's Social Gospel

*The Orthodox Pastoral Movement in
Famine, War, and Revolution*

Daniel Scarborough

THE UNIVERSITY OF WISCONSIN PRESS

The University of Wisconsin Press
728 State Street, Suite 443
Madison, Wisconsin 53706
uwpress.wisc.edu

Gray's Inn House, 127 Clerkenwell Road
London ECIR 5DB, United Kingdom
eurospanbookstore.com

Copyright © 2022
The Board of Regents of the University of Wisconsin System
All rights reserved. Except in the case of brief quotations embedded in critical articles and reviews, no part of this publication may be reproduced, stored in a retrieval system, transmitted in any format or by any means—digital, electronic, mechanical, photocopying, recording, or otherwise—or conveyed via the Internet or a website without written permission of the University of Wisconsin Press. Rights inquiries should be directed to rights@uwpress.wisc.edu.

Printed in the United States of America
This book may be available in a digital edition.

Library of Congress Cataloging-in-Publication Data

Names: Scarborough, Daniel, author.
Title: Russia's social gospel : the Orthodox pastoral movement in famine, war, and revolution / Daniel Scarborough.
Description: Madison, Wisconsin : The University of Wisconsin Press, [2022] | Includes bibliographical references and index.
Identifiers: LCCN 2021040742 | ISBN 9780299337209 (hardcover)
Subjects: LCSH: Russkai͡a pravoslavnai͡a t͡serkovʹ—History. | Orthodox Eastern Church—Russia—History. | Social gospel—Russia—History. | Church and social problems—Russkai͡a pravoslavnai͡a t͡serkovʹ. | Pastoral theology—Russkai͡a pravoslavnai͡a t͡serkovʹ. | Russia—Church history.
Classification: LCC BX491 .S27 2022 | DDC 281.9/47—dc23/eng/20211116
LC record available at https://lccn.loc.gov/2021040742

ISBN 9780299337247 (paperback)

For
Olesya, Nicholas, and Victoria

CONTENTS

	Acknowledgments	ix
	Introduction	3
1	The New Kind of Pastor	20
2	War, Revolution, and Famine	44
3	Revolt in the Seminaries	65
4	The Church as a School	83
5	The Parish Crisis	106
6	The Pastor as a Political Actor	136
7	Revolution in the Church	158
	Conclusion	190
	Notes	199
	Selected Bibliography	241
	Index	255

ACKNOWLEDGMENTS

This book is based on research that was made possible by numerous individuals and institutions. As a graduate student at Georgetown University, I was awarded a non-service fellowship by the department of history that supported my first, extended research trip to archives in Russia. This allowed me to build the foundation for my project and apply for larger research grants. I then successfully applied for a Fullbright-Hays Fellowship that allowed me to spend a year in Russia. As a postdoctoral fellow at the Havighurst Center at Miami University, I was given a free semester to conduct further research. Additional research and the final stages of this project were supported by a "social policy" research grant from Nazarbayev University.

I am grateful for the guidance, advice, and friendship of many remarkable people, who have helped helped me with this book. My graduate mentor, Catherine Evtuhov, first encouraged me to pursue my interest in Church history. Her advice to explore regional archives and local history helped me approach this project from a unique perspective. Scott Kenworthy has been a mentor throughout the writing process and has provided invaluable guidance and encouragement. Randall Poole has been a great friend and intellectual resource. Curtis Murphy has been a great friend and colleague through every stage of this book's development. I am grateful to Eric Lohr, Michael David Fox, David Goldfrank, and the late Richard Stites for their generous help and guidance, especially in the early stages of the project. My colleagues at the Havighurst Center offered me their advice and encouragement during my time as a postdoctoral fellow: Steve Norris, Zara Torlone, Venelin Ganev, Neringa Klumbyte, Dan Prior, Ben Sutcliffe, Ted Holland, Ivan Grek, and the late Karen Dawisha. I am also grateful for the advice and feedback of my wonderful colleagues at Nazarbayev University, including Nikolay Tsyrempilov, Mikhail Akulov, Clare

Griffin, Simon Pawley, Elliot Bowen, Rozaliya Garipova, Halit Akarca, Daniel Beben, Niccolò Pianciola, David Moon, Alexander Morrison, and Beatrice Penati.

Many other friends and colleagues have contributed to the successful completion of this project. In particular, I would like to thank Paul Werth, Paul Valliere, Gregory Freeze, Martin Beisswenger, Alexander Mramornov, Roland Clark, John Corcoran, Allan Roe, Aileen Friesen, Francesca Silano, Isabella Kaplan, Erina Megowan, Maria Amelicheva, Anton Fedyashin, James Sweet, Henry Chance, Christine Curran, and William Harwood. I am also grateful to my friends in Tver', Liudmila Iuga, Nikolay Pogorelov, and Grigorii Dubovoi. Irina Paert and Patrick Lally Michelson offered brilliant advice for the final revisions to the book. Amber Rose Cederström at the University of Wisconsin Press helped me through all stages of the editing process. My copyeditor, Anna Paretskaya, paid meticulous attention to my manuscript and saved me from making many mistakes. I would like to thank my parents, Charles Scarborough and Sherry Stewart, for all their support and encouragement. Most of all, I want to thank my wife, Olesya Melnikova, and our children, Nicholas and Victoria. This book is dedicated to them.

Russia's Social Gospel

Introduction

THE BOLSHEVIK REVOLUTION marked a high point in the global subjugation of religion to secular forces. It seemed to confirm the prediction of many intellectuals that modern society would see the erosion of religious faith and the preponderance of secular thought. Yet religion was not displaced by Marxism or nationalism. Rather, religious practices developed in response to the changing conditions of the modern world and provided the impetus for such dramatic phenomena as the US civil rights movement and the Iranian Revolution.[1] By the end of the twentieth century, many scholars had begun to revise or reject the "secularization thesis" in recognition of the fact that religious practice remained a significant force in modern society.[2] On the eve of the Bolshevik dictatorship, religion in the Russian Empire was not a declining force but a prominent factor in the modernization process. A central aim of this book is to examine Orthodox Christian practices during the rapid social, economic, and political changes of the Russian Empire's final decades. Specifically, it examines the practices that were developed and promoted by the parish clergy in response to the humanitarian crises of the late nineteenth and early twentieth centuries, including two famines, two wars, and three revolutions. I argue that the pastoral activism of the parish clergy during this period shifted the focus of Orthodox devotional practice in Russia toward cooperative social engagement. This increase in importance of social activism for ecclesiastical life and administration altered the organizational structure of the Orthodox Church, which became more participatory and conciliar.[3] These developments established the Church as a source of trust and mutual aid at a time of disruption and crisis.

Modern Christianity emerged as a dynamic social force in dialogue with the challenges it faced in the wake of the "dual revolution" of the late eighteenth century.[4] The Industrial Revolution disrupted traditional communities through rapid demographic expansion, social dislocation, and urban poverty. Meanwhile, political revolution precipitated the integration of mass society around various iterations of the national ideal.[5] The churches of Europe found their cultural authority challenged or usurped by the new unifying myths of the nation-state. This cultural reconfiguration led many scholars to view religion as increasingly obsolete in the modern world. As Eric Hobsbawm put it, Christianity was "no longer (to use a biological analogy) dominant but recessive, and has remained so to this day."[6] Yet the assumption of religion's progressive decline in the modern world came under increasing scrutiny in the late twentieth century. Sociologists began to reconceptualize "secularization" as a process in which religion becomes differentiated from other spheres of society, such as the state and the market, but may continue to exert social influence in the public sphere.[7] Historians have reconsidered the influence of "public religion" on the culture, politics, and social structures of the modern world. Margaret Anderson argues that "not the secularization of Europe in the nineteenth, but only the secularization of scholarship in the twentieth century can account for the absence of the catholic revival from our research agendas for so long."[8] Recent scholarship has highlighted the importance of Orthodox Christianity in the formation of modern Russian identity.[9] Patrick Lally Michelson, for example, argues that the discourse surrounding the ideal of Orthodox asceticism informed the development of "ethnoconfessional" national identity in late imperial and émigré Russia.[10] Varieties of Christian thought and expression competed for influence in fin-de-siècle Europe and Russia.

A prominent feature of modern Christianity was church-based social activism in response to the traumas of economic transformation. Based on his research into religious practices in nineteenth-century Germany, Lucian Hölscher observes that declining rates of church attendance and the clergy's loss of political privilege were balanced by the growth of Christian social networks of charitable and civic associations. He calls this process the "sacralization" of civic life as a compensatory response to the "secularization" of modern society.[11] Other scholars have noted that, contrary to the traditional secularization thesis, industrialization sometimes catalyzed an expansion of religious practice, as in Britain and Belgium.[12] Church leaders and intellectuals articulated the social turn in Christianity in the late nineteenth and early twentieth centuries. Pope Leo XIII issued his encyclical *Rerum novarum* in 1891, bestowing papal sanction on the organization of labor unions among Catholics. In the same year, the Dutch Reformed pastor and theologian Abraham Kuyper delivered a speech in Amsterdam titled "The Social Question and the Christian Religion." Both men declared the moral duty of their respective churches to resist the exploitation of workers and help improve conditions for the poor.[13] Protestant intellectuals such as Adolf Harnack and Friedrich Naumann expressed the view that the principle of *Persönlichkeit*, or individual development in relation to God and human community, had to be expanded beyond a privileged elite to the population at large.[14] This focus on social conditions has often been attributed to small circles of Christian intellectuals with a naive faith in the power of the Church, as a community of human beings, to bring cultural and political progress to society—a theological perspective that was considerably undermined by the atrocities of the twentieth century.[15] Yet the Christian engagement with modern social concerns also found support from more conservative and broad-based perspectives. Prominent figures in the social gospel movement in the United States at the turn of the century, for example, were theologically conservative in their focus on individual redemption from sin, despite their commitment to a Christian reconstruction of society.[16] Moreover, according to Walter Rauschenbusch's 1917 book, *A Theology for the Social Gospel*, that movement emerged within the community before being defined theologically. "We have a social gospel. We need a systematic theology large enough to match it and vital enough to back it."[17] In Russia's Orthodox Church, social activism was a similarly "grassroots" development. It emerged from the work of rank-and-file parish priests among a largely peasant laity.

Orthodox social activism, while part of a global Christian dialogue with modernity, developed in the unique social context of late imperial Russia. Talal Asad's critical theory of "religion as an anthropological category" serves as a useful approach to the examination of this particular context. In his 1993 essay by this name, Asad describes religious traditions as encompassing a wide range of practices that vary over time.[18] Using Michel Foucault's concept of "discourse," Asad argues that particular practices are approved or excluded from a given religious tradition by an "authorizing discourse," which is formulated by religious authority: "The medieval Church did not attempt to establish absolute uniformity of practice; on the contrary, its authoritative discourse was always concerned to specify differences, gradations, exceptions. What it sought was the subjection of all practice to a unified authority, to a single authentic source that could tell truth from falsehood."[19] Religious authority itself, even in such a seemingly centralized form as that of the medieval Catholic Church, is also variegated and subject to change over time.[20] The "authorizing discourse" of a given religious tradition is, thus, formulated by a variety of authorities in dialogue with one another: "A practice is Islamic because it is authorized by the discursive traditions of Islam, and is so taught to Muslims—whether by an *'alim*, a *khatib*, a Sufi *shaykh*, or an untutored parent."[21] The authorizing discourse of Western Christendom, Asad argues, was fragmented by the Reformation and marginalized by the Enlightenment and the modern state. The idea of "religion" as a discrete and universal category, distinct from other categories of social activity, followed from this compartmentalization of religious discourse: "The insistence that religion has an autonomous essence—not to be confused with the essence of science, or of politics, or of common sense—invites us to define religion (like any essence) as a transhistorical and transcultural phenomenon. . . . This definition is at once part of a strategy (for secular liberals) of the confinement, and (for liberal Christians) of the defense of religion."[22] Thus, the project of formulating a universal definition of religion emerged from a specific, Western European discourse and cannot serve as a theoretical model for the study of all religious traditions, many of which cannot be compartmentalized within their social contexts. Asad concludes that "there cannot be a universal definition of religion, not only because its constituent elements and relationships are historically specific, but because that definition is itself the historical product of discursive processes."[23] This complication of "religion" as a category of analysis has inspired reconsideration of the kinds of practices that should be considered "religious" and their relevance to the modernization process.[24] Asad's concept of a shifting and multivalent "authorizing discourse" as guiding religious practice is particularly helpful for the present examination of Orthodox Christianity, which underwent a reconfiguration of its organizational structure and of the devotional practices that it "authorized" in late imperial Russia.

Orthodox Christianity was not a marginalized tradition in imperial Russia. In terms of church attendance and other devotional practices, the Orthodox laity in Russia were among the most observant Christians in late nineteenth-century Europe.[25] Orthodoxy served as the organizing principle behind many leisure and associational activities such as pilgrimages, temperance societies, and adult education.[26] Moreover, in contrast with the emergent nation states of nineteenth-century Europe, in which national allegiance was prioritized above religious identity, the tsarist regime identified the Russian nation with Orthodoxy. The official ideology of "Orthodoxy, Autocracy, and Nationality" was first articulated in 1833 by Sergei Uvarov, minister of education, as a conservative counterpoint to the revolutionary motto "Liberté, égalité, fraternité." This ideology posited a direct, spiritual connection between emperor and nation that was not to be adulterated by any limit to autocratic authority.[27] Yet this official narrative did not monopolize Orthodoxy's "authorizing discourse." Orthodox Russia experienced a dramatic increase in contemplative monasticism over the course of the nineteenth century, while Roman Catholicism experienced the opposite trend.[28] As Michelson explains, this resurgent asceticism generated competition among monks, theological academies, and the official hierarchy as rival claimants to "authentic Orthodoxy."[29] Through sermons, spiritual eldership, and publication, these rivals strove to shape the practice of Orthodoxy "beyond the monastery walls" and thereby reshape society as a whole.[30] Dissident activists sought social justice and political liberation within and through Orthodox tradition as well.[31] Orthodox Christianity encompassed a broad range of social relations that were changing rapidly by the late nineteenth century, and the Church responded to these changes through pastoral work.

The parish clergy's pastoral work formed a point of convergence for multiple forms of religious life, or "discursive traditions" in Orthodoxy. Parish priests served as the primary representatives of the institutional church for the vast majority of the Orthodox population. They guided the religious lives of their parishioners, endorsing some practices as Orthodox and discouraging others as superstitious or sectarian.[32] They also acted as representatives of the state. Priests communicated official decrees to their parishioners, such as the emancipation reform of 1861, which abolished private serfdom. At the behest of state authorities, they promoted public health by encouraging parishioners to receive vaccinations and instructing the population in hygienic practices during cholera outbreaks.[33] Pastoral work was also influenced by the intellectual climate of the nineteenth century, which animated the theological academies and seminaries with concern for social justice.[34] Due to their limited material and political resources, however, the parish clergy depended on the assistance of their parishioners for the success of their pastoral work. Priests, therefore, tended to disregard official directives that might alienate their parish communities, such as reporting crimes revealed during confession to the police.[35] On the other hand, priests embraced official initiatives that were likely to garner lay support, such as the promotion of literacy, care for orphans, and the organization of famine relief. This pastoral work was a form of "authorizing discourse" insofar as it was intended to establish and sanctify cooperative social activism as an important component of Russia's religious life. This discourse developed at the local level through dialogue between pastoral work and popular Orthodoxy. In this book, I refer to the parish clergy's collective efforts to recruit the support and participation of the laity in the Church's social mission as "the pastoral movement."

SOCIAL MISSION AND RELIGIOUS AUTHORITY

Although it emerged in response to the specific social and economic problems of the late nineteenth century, the pastoral movement was a modern expression of the foundational Christian practice of philanthropic social activism. Expressed in New Testament writings such as Christ's parable of the sheep and the goats (Matthew 25:31–46), the Christian injunction to render aid to the unfortunate is expressed as *philanthropia* throughout early patristic texts.[36] In his monograph *The Rise of Christianity*, Rodney Stark offers his theory that the Christian practice of serving God by serving humanity greatly contributed to the ultimate predominance of Christianity over other religious movements in the Mediterranean world. He argues that charity and social service enabled Christian social networks to survive the waves of epidemic disease that devastated the late Roman Empire. Non-Christian social networks fragmented as urban residents fled these epidemics, while Christian communities maintained their solidarity through care for the sick. Meanwhile, pagan survivors replaced their shattered social attachments by joining Christian networks that offered them care.[37] In 362, the anti-Christian Emperor Julian the Apostate remarked, "The impious Galileans support not only their poor, but ours as well. Everyone can see that our people lack aid from us."[38] Over subsequent centuries, philanthropic social activism remained an important means by which the Church would interact with and influence its social environment. For example, the Orthodox and "heretical" Arian hierarchies operated rival philanthropic institutions in fourth-century Constantinople to compete for the allegiance of the population. Church hospices and orphanages promoted Orthodox Christianity and the Greek language throughout the Byzantine Empire.[39] Social activism has served as an important instrument of the Church's "authorizing discourse" since the early centuries of Christendom, and control of the Church's social mission is an indicative feature of religious authority.

The Church's responsibility for the promotion of social welfare is a salient concern in early sources of canon law. The seventeenth rule of the First Council of Nicaea (325) decreed that hospitals should be erected in every city of the Roman Empire, and the eighth rule of the Council of Chalcedon (451) placed responsibility over shelters for the poor in the hands of the Church hierarchy.[40] Canon law, derived from the New Testament, Apostolic Canons, rules of the ecumenical councils, and certain statements of the church fathers, regulates both church governance and relations with secular authorities. For the Eastern Church, where the Roman Empire persisted long after its collapse in the West, canon law prescribed collaboration with the state in pursuit of the Christian social mission. While the Latin church fathers, since Saint Augustine (354–430), emphasized the tension between Christian society and the City of God, the politically stable Orthodox East was conceived as a reflection of the Kingdom of Heaven. The Byzantine church and state, therefore, were regarded as operating in harmony, or *symphonia*.[41] Eastern church fathers, such as Eusebius of Caesarea (263–339), developed a vision of the ideal Christian emperor as God's representative on Earth, possessing and practicing the virtue of *philanthropia*. This political narrative motivated the Byzantine state to support the church's philanthropic institutions, including almshouses, orphanages, shelters for the elderly, and hospitals, which far surpassed analogous institutions of Western Europe in scale and sophistication well into the medieval era.[42]

The Eastern Church's traditional role of supporting public welfare on behalf of the state persisted in the emerging Orthodox monarchy of fifteenth- and sixteenth-century Muscovy. The Abbot Iosif Volotsky, an influential codifier of Russian monastic practice and a theorist of Muscovy's theocratic monarchy, established the ideal of organized charity as an essential component of monastic life. In his *Monastic Rule*, Volotsky instructs his followers in the necessity of work, both to support monastic contemplation and to ease the suffering of the unfortunate: "And work not only for your own needs, but also for the lowly, the wandering, the enfeebled, and the aged, for such benevolence is a welcome offering to God."[43] Volotsky has been reviled by historians for providing religious justification for tsarist authority in order to secure protection for monastic property and wealth.[44] Yet he used that wealth to feed the poor and aid the peasantry. During a famine in 1512, he exhausted his monastery's grain reserves to feed the starving and support an orphanage and infirmary.[45] As it consolidated power over subsequent centuries, the Muscovite monarchy would continue to rely on the Church as a source of political legitimacy and social stability.

The collaborative relationship between church and crown ultimately degenerated into domination of the former by the latter, allowing the monarchy to regulate the Church's social mission. The church hierarchy reached the zenith of its power in the seventeenth century after the establishment of the Patriarchate of Moscow in 1589 and the temporary collapse of the monarchy during the Time of Troubles (1598–1613). Yet the crisis of Patriarch Nikon's liturgical reforms, and his deposition in 1667, dealt a severe blow to the Church's political independence.[46] In 1721, the patriarchs of Constantinople, Antioch, Jerusalem, and Alexandria acquiesced to Peter I's abolition of the Moscow Patriarchate, demonstrating the great influence that the Russian state now wielded over the Eastern Church as a whole.[47] The Spiritual Regulation, which replaced the patriarch with a state-supervised Synod, also directed the new ecclesiastical administration to reform the practice of charity in accordance with Peter's cameralistic strategy. Monasteries were instructed to provide support and shelter for certain groups of deserving poor, such as wounded soldiers, while able-bodied beggars were to be driven away and punished.[48] Finally, in 1764, Empress Catherine II secularized monastic lands, closed hundreds of monasteries, and reduced the remainder to fiscal dependence on the state.[49] Russian monastic spirituality would continue to occupy a prominent role in the Orthodox tradition in the nineteenth century, serving as a model for pastoral conduct as well as a refuge for parish clergy who became disillusioned with the priesthood.[50]

Nevertheless, Russia's once wealthy network of monasteries ceased to play a significant role in the management of social welfare.

The secular government delegated progressively greater responsibility for the Church's social services to the parish clergy. The Spiritual Regulation called for the establishment of seminaries in each diocese to train a more literate, skilled, and therefore useful parish clergy. By the early nineteenth century, graduation from a seminary had become a prerequisite for ordination.[51] The better-educated priests were used as inexpensive, auxiliary civil servants to augment the empire's thinly stretched bureaucratic infrastructure. They were expected to maintain church journals to record births, deaths, marriages, and local events of importance.[52] They were expected to establish parish schools to educate peasant children. They were called upon to aid in the implementation of vaccinations and potato cultivation. They had to be present in the event of a fire, look after midwives, and ensure the sanitary burial of bodies.[53] Priests in Siberia gathered statistical and ethnographic information for the Resettlement Administration.[54] As Jennifer Hedda points out, in ecclesiastical publications of the late nineteenth century, the parish priest was increasingly referred to as "pastor" (*pastyr'*), a term previously reserved for the bishop, rather than simply "priest" (*sviashchennik*), reflecting the parish clergy's more prominent role in the life of the Church.[55]

While the imperial Russian state subsidized seminary education and provided financial support for urban priests, most clergymen relied on the voluntary support of their peasant parishioners for the majority of their income. Other European states used the clergy of their official churches as auxiliary civil servants as well, but they compensated their priests and ministers for this work by compelling the population to tithe or by paying clergymen fixed salaries.[56] Russia's Orthodox priests were forced to pool their meager resources in order to maintain the poorly funded seminaries and to provide care for the widows and orphans of clergymen. In lieu of adequate financial support for this quasi-civil service, the imperial state tolerated extensive freedom of association among the parish clergy so that they could organize their own pension funds, charities for poor seminary students, and other forms of mutual aid within each diocese. This freedom, which was not extended to the celibate members of the Church hierarchy, allowed the parish clergy to develop one of the most extensive social networks in the empire, extending from the provincial capitals to remote parishes. Thus, the demands of the state contributed to the notorious poverty of the parish clergy but also allowed them to develop as an autonomous social and ultimately political force within the Church.

The parish pastorate's growing influence over the Church's social mission eventually presented a challenge to the synodal authority structure. The bishops who oversaw the dioceses were drawn from the "black" clergy who had received monastic tonsure and usually completed higher education at one of the empire's four theological academies. Unlike the "white," or parish, clergy, bishops received generous state salaries but did not have the freedom to form associations or to assemble independently of the synodal bureaucracy. While the secular officials who oversaw church administration could not simply depose uncooperative prelates, they could, and frequently did, transfer bishops from one see to another, thus weakening their ties with the communities under their pastoral care. Nevertheless, bishops were considered successors of Christ's apostles and endowed with "apostolic authority" over the parish clergy within their jurisdiction. In imperial Russia this authority was interpreted as nearly absolute. Bishops could defrock or incarcerate parish clergymen practically at will, and their personal blessing was required for any and all pastoral assemblies, initiatives, and expenditures of diocesan resources. As the parish clergy's diocesan networks assumed ever-greater responsibility for the Church's social mission, they came to resent the heavy-handed and often obstructionist oversight of these "diocesan satraps," as one dissident priest characterized the bishops.[57] An unintended consequence of the deployment of priests to ameliorate social conditions was that the parish clergy came to perceive the rigid authority structure of the Synodal Church, and of the autocracy, as obstacles to their own efforts to serve the material and spiritual needs of the people. The pastoral movement thus acquired a political dimension in the aspiration of many parish priests for the decentralization of ecclesiastical authority.

Meanwhile, parish clergymen were themselves confronted with the demands of laypeople for greater control over the resources they were asked to contribute to their parishes and dioceses. The increasingly literate and assertive Orthodox laity did not always appreciate their priest's use of parish resources for social services. In order to retain lay support for their mutual aid societies, educational institutions, and charitable associations, it was imperative for the parish clergy to transform the Church's social mission from a state-mandated enterprise into popular religious practice. The parish clergy, therefore, gradually integrated laymen and, eventually, laywomen into the decision-making structures of their diocesan networks.[58] Diocesan assemblies of clergy and laity became forums for debate over the distribution of ecclesiastical authority and resources, even as they carried out the work of humanitarian relief during the Russian Empire's final decades of war and revolution. Gregory Freeze has suggested that the weakening of clerical authority within the Church constituted "a powerful subversive factor in the revolutionary process leading to 1917."[59] Yet the contentious dialogue between clergy and laity that took place in parish assemblies and diocesan congresses resulted not in institutional collapse but ecclesiastical reform and exerted a powerful influence on the successful All-Russian Church Council (Sobor) of 1917–18.

The social networks that the parish clergy organized throughout the nineteenth century provided an effective means of political mobilization in the early twentieth century. Ever suspicious of their potential to challenge the existing hierarchy, church and state authorities nevertheless permitted the intermittent expansion of these networks in the hope that they would augment social stability and counteract political unrest. The hierarchy's capacity to restrain their activity evaporated with the tsar's abdication. Over the summer of 1917, diocesan congresses of clergy and laity convened in all sixty-seven dioceses of the former empire, deposing a number of bishops. These assemblies dispatched delegates to the All-Russian Congress of Clergy and Laity, which assembled in Moscow in June. This "ecclesiastical revolution" facilitated a reform of the Church's authority structure, including the introduction of the "electoral principle" (*vybornoe nachalo*) into the transfer of apostolic authority. It provided a popular mandate for the restoration of the Russian patriarchate at the Sobor, which followed soon after in August 1917, helping the Church survive the collapse of the empire and emerge as the only institution of tsarist Russia to remain intact after October 1917. This book will attempt to determine how the political discourse that emerged from the pastoral movement influenced the reform of Russia's Orthodox Church.

Voluntary Associations and Civil Society

The pastoral movement serves as an important example of voluntary association transcending estate, class, education, and other social barriers of late imperial Russia. Scholarship on this period is animated by the ongoing debate over whether civil society under the tsarist autocracy was "primordial and gelatinous."[60] Like the secularization thesis, "civil society" remains a widely referenced theoretical concept despite having undergone extensive revision. It usually refers to the sphere of voluntary associations, outside the realms of the state and the marketplace. In his classic account of the early United States, Alexis de Tocqueville argued that the capacity to form voluntary associations had enabled the American citizenry to preserve their democracy by protecting their rights and liberties against the encroachment both of their government and of the "tyranny of the majority."[61] Later theorists have observed that a vibrant civil society does not necessarily support liberal democracy and may even undermine it in the absence of a stable government.[62] The characterization of civil society as fully autonomous from and antagonistic toward the state has also been challenged, as scholars have pointed to collaboration and overlap between government and voluntary associations.[63] Efforts to pin down a normative model have resulted in the creation of decontextualized, idealistic visions of civil society. As one recent survey of the literature on civil society remarks, "civil society, not the state, is the bastion of utopianism in political thought today."[64] The incongruity of imperial Russian society with such a normative model of civil society is often referenced to explain its descent into civil war and totalitarian dictatorship in the twentieth century.[65]

The legal division of imperial Russian society into estates (*sosloviia*) and other groups based on confession or nationality is often cited as a primary impediment to the formation of civil society.[66] While internally cohesive, this view argues, estates became mutually exclusive, causing society as a whole to "break down into ever smaller constituents, each defining itself in the particularistic language long associated with estate solidarity [*soslovnost'*]."[67] For example, merchants excluded other professional groups from membership in their associations and were themselves internally divided by religion and ethnicity.[68] Some historians have argued that the tsarist regime deliberately perpetuated the estate system precisely to prevent the formation of a common "bourgeois identity" that could have presented a challenge to autocracy.[69] In his study of Russia on the eve of World War I, Wayne Dowler cites Ernest Gellner's theory of the "segmentary society," in which individuals who are closely identified with social units, such as estates or confessions, cannot foster a neutral and open sphere of truly free association: "The division of the population into legal estates, however unstable they had become, preserved in the empire the remnants of what Gellner calls a segmentary society, in which the individual is seen as an integral part of a social unit. Such a society precludes civil society, and its partial persistence in Russia slowed the transition to a new civic consciousness."[70] The extensive literature on this topic correctly identifies estates and other social and religious categories as barriers to the formation of a collective social identity on the model of the nation-state. It is, however, limiting to regard the Russian Empire through the lens of Gellner's theoretical dichotomy of modern, civil society versus "segmentary communities, cousin-ridden and ritual-ridden, free perhaps of central tyranny, but not really free in the sense that would satisfy us."[71] This model obscures the important role of those estate societies in facilitating the proliferation of voluntary associations that Dowler himself describes. The pastoral movement was one form of free association among many that emerged from specific "social units" within the Russian Empire.

While "civil society" does not necessarily facilitate a normative path of development toward liberal democracy, the capacity of a population to support networks of trust and cooperation empowers individuals to define and pursue common goals within modern, mass society. Penelope Ismay describes this process in her study of Christian mutual aid societies in eighteenth- and nineteenth-century Britain: "Friendly societies helped Britons negotiate the social space between a society based on birth and hierarchy to one based on risk and mobility in the same way they helped working men navigate the geographic space between rural villages and anonymous urban centers."[72] Voluntary associations played a similar role in late imperial Russia.[73] Peasants leaving the old communal system of agriculture to operate independent farms were aided by the fastest-growing cooperative movement in Europe.[74] Migrants to Siberia and Central Asia were greeted by societies for the provision of aid to needy settlers.[75] Old Believers formed charitable networks both to support their coreligionists and to ingratiate themselves to their neighbors so as to avoid persecution.[76] Wounded soldiers returning from wars in Europe and Manchuria were received at makeshift hospitals supported by the Orthodox communities. Soldiers' families received support from Muslim philanthropic associations.[77] By the beginning of World War I, more than six hundred associations were operating in Moscow, more than five hundred existed in Saint Petersburg, and many provincial cities had more than a hundred.[78]

Scholarship on the late imperial period has also argued that the considerable overlap between the public sphere and state service prevented the self-assertion of Russian civil society. Peter Holquist points out that bureaucratic reformers sought collaboration with "civil society," but only as a means of mobilizing public support for their own technocratic agenda.[79] Laura Engelstein argues that "the dream of civil society" never came true in the Russian Empire because of this close association with the state. Public life, in her analysis, was divided between the radical intelligentsia, which placed no value on autonomous social institutions, and educated society (*obshchestvennost'*). The latter aspired to civil society on the Western model but never achieved the requisite legal autonomy from autocratic authority. Thus, voluntary associations operated under the control of the tsarist regime—and ultimately collapsed along with it: "society, though mobilized, rallied on behalf of a regime that was digging its own grave."[80] Engelstein acknowledges that the Church "strengthened the fabric of informal associations through which society governed its own affairs, sometimes in concert with government efforts, sometimes on its own."[81] Nevertheless, she seems to underestimate the breadth and diversity of associational life in the Russian Empire, which extended far beyond educated society and exceeded the regime's capacity to control. By the mid-nineteenth century, the estates were being used not only to monitor and extract resources from the population but also to allocate responsibility for vital social services that the state could not provide.[82] A 1909 memorandum from the Ministry of Internal Affairs to the provincial governors reflects official anxiety at the growing autonomy of estate associations: "It is necessary to maintain constant surveillance on the activities of all institutions of petty credit, based on estate [*soslovnago tipa*]."[83] Yet state surveillance and intervention were inconsistent and indecisive because of the essential functions these associations had come to perform. The enlistment of the clerical estate to organize social services is one example of this phenomenon, and the growth of the pastoral movement is illustrative of the state's limited control over estate-based associations.

The concept of "civil society" was widely discussed among Russian intellectuals in the late nineteenth century. In his *Filosofiia prava*, first published in serial form in 1898–99, the liberal philosopher Boris Chicherin defined civil society (*grazhdanskoe obshchestvo*) as the diverse web of human interaction that occurs independently of the state. He considered the autonomy of this realm as essential to individual freedom: "For the human individual [*lichnost'*], for his rights and freedom, the autonomy of civil society is of the utmost importance, for by it he is protected from absorption into the whole."[84] Chicherin saw the integrity of civil society as contingent upon the willingness and ability of the state to safeguard the rule of law for all citizens, yet this was never the reality in the Russian Empire. Indeed, Chicherin was removed from his post as mayor of Moscow in 1883 because of his support for constitutional limits on autocratic authority. Randall Poole has argued that Chicherin and other Russian liberals articulated a particularly robust defense of human dignity precisely because it could not be taken for granted under the tsarist autocracy.[85] Chicherin saw civil society as the social foundation of self-determination and dignity, regardless of political circumstances: "In public life, corporate ties serve as a school of autonomy and self-reliance. Here, people learn to manage their affairs together, and at their own initiative. . . . The independence of corporate associations, while they remain subordinate to state power, must be firmly upheld, for it serves to ensure civil liberty."[86] A central question of this book is whether the pastoral movement achieved such a collective assertion of self-determination, despite its subsequent suppression under the Bolshevik regime.

Methodology and Plan of the Book

The lack of any comprehensive history in English or Russian of the parish clergy's diocesan institutions or the social networks that grew to support them has contributed to the scholarly neglect of the pastoral movement. The most comprehensive study of imperial Russia's Orthodox pastorate in any language remains Freeze's two monographs on the parish clergy in the eighteenth and nineteenth centuries.[87] In his now classic work, Freeze examines the efforts of state officials and church leaders to modernize and improve the social, economic, and professional status of the parish clergy, which he regards as an ultimate failure, or "reform manqué." With its empire-wide scope, Freeze's work tends to focus on the perspective of the reformers and their frustrated priorities, while paying less attention to the institutions of the parish clergy themselves and their work at the local level, such as their famine relief councils of 1891–92 and 1906–8, the parish councils for the provision of aid to soldiers' families in 1914–16, and the "revolutionary" diocesan congresses of 1917. A more recent book by Hedda on the radical priests of early twentieth-century Saint Petersburg has shed unprecedented light on the social turn in Orthodox Christianity in Russia.[88] This work explores the charitable work and social activism of the parish clergy of the capital as it developed around Saint Petersburg's Theological Academy. In its exclusive focus on the city of Saint Petersburg, however, Hedda's book neglects the social roots of the broader pastoral movement in the clerical estate. A large proportion of the capital's churches were attached to urban institutions rather than to their own parishes, rendering them "unfettered by the constraints of the existing parish system."[89] By tracing the history of the parish clergy's diocesan institutions from the mid-nineteenth century up to 1917, my aim is to examine the broader scope of the pastoral movement, including the social framework that supported it.

In addition to institutional history, which I derive primarily from church publications and official reports, this book relies on consistory, seminary, and synodal archives to examine the local development of the pastoral movement in the dioceses of Moscow and Tver'. Moscow hosted one of the empire's four theological academies and two seminaries. The Tver' diocese, Moscow's medieval rival and home province of Russia's first patriarch, contained the empire's largest seminary. In addition to the cities of Moscow and Tver', both dioceses contained smaller municipalities and large swaths of rural parishes. By the early twentieth century, the Church as a whole was divided into sixty-seven dioceses, the boundaries of which usually corresponded with those of the provincial administrations. The dioceses of Moscow and Tver' were unique in the success of their pastors at recruiting lay participation in the Church's social mission. Their clergymen were aided in this regard by the wealth of their respective capital cities. Moscow was heavily industrialized, containing 750 factories by 1910, more than twice the number operating in Saint Petersburg.[90] Tver' contained a large train-car factory, and 164 other industrial enterprises had been established throughout the diocese by 1909.[91] While the pastors of these dioceses faced extremes of both urban and rural poverty, they did not have to contend with the vast distances between villages that characterized many eastern territories or the unmitigated poverty that plagued some dioceses that were further removed from industrial centers. At the same time, they did not enjoy the extensive financial support that the state provided their colleagues in the western provinces to aid them in competition with the Catholic Church.

The parish clergy of Moscow and Tver' were, therefore, motivated to work among the laity that supported them and able to access the resources necessary to impact lay communities. The pastors of these dioceses, together with those of the imperial capital, achieved the greatest success in their efforts to mobilize lay support for the Church's social mission. A consequence of my decision to focus on these dioceses is neglect of pastoral activism in less favorable circumstances elsewhere. Yet this focus allows me to examine the pastoral movement in greater depth where it was successful, as it rose in prominence to influence the Church as a whole.

This book is divided into seven chapters, following a roughly chronological and thematic survey of pastoral work in Moscow and Tver'. Each chapter begins with a survey of the institutional context of clerical association and then focuses on specific events in the dioceses. The first chapter opens with an overview of the diocesan structure in which the clerical mutual aid networks developed. It traces the development of these networks from their establishment in the early nineteenth century up to their early use for pastoral work. The chapter then examines that work in Moscow and Tver', and the use of those networks, under the Synod's direction, for the coordinated transfer of resources to famine victims during the relief campaign of 1891–92.

The second chapter continues the institutional history of the parish clergy's diocesan networks from the period of the "counter-reforms" of the late nineteenth century up to the revolutionary crisis of 1905. This period witnessed the gradual weakening of state control over clerical organizations and the increase of lay participation in them. The chapter then focuses on the campaign to relieve victims of war, revolution, and famine from 1906 to 1908 in Moscow and Tver'. It also examines the correspondence of the Moscow and Tver' consistories with those of famine-afflicted dioceses, revealing a variety of responses to this crisis throughout the Church. It demonstrates that, as pastoral associations gained greater autonomy, certain clerical communities initiated the expansion of their social networks beyond the boundaries of their own estate.

The third chapter examines the seminary as a central institution of the pastoral associations, forming an important focus of clerical mutual aid to secure the education, ordination, and employment of the sons of parish priests. It examines the history of the protest movement that arose among these seminarian sons of clergymen when their access to secular universities was restricted in an effort to force members of the clerical estate to serve the Church. This chapter draws a distinction between the violent and radical component of this protest movement, which was hostile to the Church in general, and the petition movement, which expressed the wishes of much of the clerical community to extend the Church's service beyond the boundaries of estate.

The fourth chapter examines the parish clergy's educational work and promotion of literacy in collaboration with lay communities. Priests established schools in their parishes, in part, to provide employment for their adult children. Teaching was an important source of income for seminary graduates who were not yet ordained as priests. It was even more important for the orphaned daughters and widows of priests. Parishioners contributed to the construction of parish schools and the purchase of books and other necessities in return for the education of their children. This chapter argues that the partnership between the clergy and the peasantry played an important role in the spread of literacy, particularly for women. In addition to expanding the job market for female teachers from the clerical estate, parish schools provided access to education for peasant girls.

The fifth chapter evaluates the parish clergy's success at inculcating mutual aid into the religious life of Russia's parish communities. This pastoral work took place in the context of highly politicized debates over parish reform and conflicting attempts to co-opt the Orthodox parish for a variety of ideological agendas. This chapter demonstrates that clerical efforts to organize church-based philanthropic mutual aid within the parishes were, despite the political obstacles these efforts confronted, far more successful than most scholarship on "the parish question" has claimed. The chapter goes on to examine the Church's last major humanitarian relief campaign for the victims of World War I. The parish clergy in Moscow and Tver' succeeded in mobilizing unprecedented participation by many different communities in a common humanitarian relief effort for victims of the war on the home front. Yet the Church's support for the war effort created tensions with their lay supporters, and a bifurcation of relief efforts developed between the clergy's efforts to provide logistical support for the care of wounded soldiers and the more locally focused work of lay parishioners. These tensions rendered the Church vulnerable to the revolutionary crisis of 1917.

The sixth chapter focuses on the political consequences of the pastoral movement. It examines the history of the parish clergy's exclusion from secular politics until the early twentieth century. The parish clergy were permitted to participate in the Russian Empire's democratic experiment with a national parliament, or Duma. While censorship of church publications renders a general evaluation of political sympathies among parish priests extremely difficult, this chapter argues that the pastoral movement prepared the parish clergy to join politically with the rural and working-class voters whose collaboration they already sought for the Church's social mission. Thus, clerical deputies to the first two Dumas, from 1906 to 1907, were solidly leftist, despite intense pressure from the monastic hierarchy to abstain from dissident politics. The regime responded by altering election laws to confine clerical voters to a separate curia, in which their political activity could be monitored and controlled by the Synod. Meanwhile, the clergy were courted by right-wing, monarchist groups who sought to mobilize the clerical estate against democratic reform. The suppression of political activism among the clergy placed them at a disadvantage in competition with anti-religious radicals and other confessions. Yet no "clerical party" ever emerged within the clerical estate to support the reactionary, chauvinistic agenda of monarchist groups.

The seventh and final chapter of this book examines the general revolt against ecclesiastical authority that swept through the Church over the summer of 1917. It examines the diocesan congresses of Tver' and Moscow, both of which expelled their bishops, and the dialogue with the Holy Synod that followed. The Church survived this revolt and organized an All-Russian Church Sobor from September 1917 until August 1918, which reestablished the Patriarchate of Moscow and negotiated a reform of the Church's authority structure. The ultimate success of the reform process depended on the ability of the Church's various communities to forge a compromise in the midst of a political and ecclesiastical revolution. The pastoral movement played a critical role in molding this compromise—and the form that the Orthodox Church assumed as a result.

I

The New Kind of Pastor

In June 1852, in the village of Lisitsy, Tver' gubernia, a parish priest and a government surveyor stood, regarding the farmland of a community of state serfs. Four years prior, when the village was founded, the peasants had agreed to support their priest with a fixed payment. When they abruptly refused to continue making this payment, the priest, Father Dranitsyn, had complained to the local chamber of state domains (*palata gosudarstvennykh imushchestv*) that his parishioners were in breach of contract and that a share of their land, four *desiatiny*, should be carved out of the common field.[1] The surveyor allowed the priest to choose it himself. "Where, father, shall I mark your plot? Which land do you like the best?"[2] Father Dranitsyn chose the most fertile land, along the Volga River. The peasants stood aghast. "If the priest is going to do this to us, we will get him back. Lads, don't give him more than three silver kopecks for prayers and twenty-five for a wedding. We'll teach him."[3] The priest relented and chose a different plot near the forest. While Father Dranitsyn may at first appear as the exploiter and oppressor in this scenario, the peasants had the upper hand, and they knew it.

Improvement of the parish clergy's material condition was a central concern of church policymakers throughout the nineteenth century. One strategy for securing their livelihood was the state-mandated provision of land. In 1829, as part of the "Provisions for the Improvement of Conditions among the Clergy," the Orthodox laity were required to contribute a portion of farmland to their parish, the size of which depended on local conditions.[4] This practice had been carried out with less formality over the preceding centuries as the traditional means of supporting Orthodox priests, deacons, sacristans, and their families. In lieu of land, parishioners could agree with their priest on a regular payment of money and agricultural products, known as *ruga*. If a parishioner reneged on this payment, the clergy could claim a greater share of land, but the process was not always as easy as it was for Father Dranitsyn. In 1859, for example, in Volokolamsk district of Moscow gubernia, a landowner refused to pay the full *ruga* to his parish clergy, and their efforts to obtain compensation dragged on for decades.[5] Moreover, state serfs, like those of Lisitsy, would be emancipated in 1866, gaining personal freedom and collective ownership of their farmland, which would no longer be subject to seizure by the chamber of state domains. Even once they had secured a land allotment, parish priests could not properly cultivate it. By the nineteenth century, priests' pastoral duties were too demanding to allow them to concentrate on farming, while their sons were occupied with seminary training and could not serve as a labor force. Some priests, therefore, simply leased the land back to their parishioners. Yet this option did not always provide a secure income either, as illustrated by a 1905 letter from a village priest to the bishop of Moscow, complaining that his parishioners had not paid him full rent in years and that his final resort to a lawsuit had so spoiled his relations with them that he was forced to request a transfer to another parish.[6] Ultimately, there was no escape from material dependence on the laity for Russia's parish clergy. Even Father Dranitsyn's enserfed parishioners were well aware of his reliance on their good will.

Throughout the history of the imperial Orthodox Church, most parish clergymen derived the majority of their income from the voluntary contribution of their parishioners. These usually took the form of small monetary or in-kind payments in exchange for religious services. Accounts of parish life in rural Russia are replete with anecdotes, ranging from the amusing to the horrifying, of priests trying to squeeze resources out of their parishioners who, in turn, tried to shortchange their priests. In his autobiography, Metropolitan Evlogii (Georgievskii) of Paris recounted such scenes from his childhood in a clerical family near Grodno in the 1870s, as when one of his uncle's peasant parishioners handed him in the dark a dead crow instead of a chicken.[7] In his journal from 1852, Father V. F. Vladislavlev of Tver' recounted a fellow priest's psychological manipulation of a merchant's widow after performing the requiem service over her husband's body: "You sent me three silver rubles for the fortyday remembrance [*sorokoust*], but I did not accept them. It seemed strange to me that when your servant Dar'ia died, you sent me three, and then when your husband died, you also sent me three. You are mocking your husband, aren't you? He left you half a million."[8] It was another priest from Tver', I. S. Belliustin, who first publicly criticized the pastorate's dependence on the laity in a scathing critique of corruption and tyranny in the Church's leadership, which was published in Paris and then smuggled back into Russia in 1858. Belliustin argued that the necessity of constantly appealing to the laity for support had degraded the parish clergy and destroyed their religious authority: "Even when he has administered the sacrament of communion, he does not recoil in horror from money.... What moral influence can he exert on the parishioners when they understand perfectly the primary goal of all his actions? And, lacking in authority, what kind of pastor can he be?"[9] Belliustin expressed the sentiment of most Orthodox priests in the mid-nineteenth century when he argued that the only way to restore religious authority to the pastorate was for the state to provide adequate salaries to all parish clergymen.[10] Yet this was not to be.

The imperial state's efforts to use the Orthodox Church as a tool of governance were hampered by its inability to provide adequate financial support for the tens of thousands of parishes scattered throughout the empire.[11] Since the reign of Paul I, the state had provided salaries to a portion of the parish clergy and had periodically increased this funding over the course of the nineteenth century.[12] Higher salaries were provided for landless urban priests and for clergymen in strategically sensitive areas, such as the western provinces dominated by Catholic landowners.[13] But for the majority of parish clergymen, these salaries remained small and insufficient to satisfy even the minimum needs of the parish clergyman and his typically large family. In 1911, the Third Duma designated 14 million rubles for the support of parish clergy, which provided fairly insignificant norms of between 100 and 300 rubles a year. Such a salary was more of a grant to relieve poverty than a source of real support.[14] At the same time, the state demanded an increasingly diverse array of extra-liturgical duties from the parish clergy, in order to aid its thinly stretched bureaucracy in serving the needs of the growing and industrializing population. This work required training and resources, which the state could subsidize but not fully support. Instead, the parish clergy were granted increasingly extensive freedom of association to facilitate their organization of mutual aid societies, charitable institutions, and professional support networks. This freedom of association for the collective support of pastoral work endowed the parish clergy with an authority over the organization of religious life, different from the authority that Belliustin and others had hoped to gain from financial independence from the laity.

The present chapter traces the development of clerical associations from their initial formation as social support organizations to control poverty within the clerical estate through their expansion into pastoral networks for the provision of humanitarian relief to the general population during the famine of 1891–92. While these pastoral networks developed in dialogue with the priorities of both the imperial state and the Orthodox laity, they also achieved a significant degree of local autonomy. The parish clergy's assumption of responsibility for pooling their own resources to fund and organize pastoral work gave them some control over how to interpret and implement state-mandated tasks. Their continued reliance on the laity for material support, moreover, served to focus the pastoral mission of the parish clergy's associations on responding to the social problems that threatened to erode that support.

THE SYNODAL SYSTEM

The Synodal Church of the nineteenth century had become significantly more complex since its establishment in 1721. Both the monastic hierarchy and the parish clergy were far more educated than their eighteenth-century forebears, and they were tasked with managing a more elaborate system of religious schools, maintaining records of marriages, births, and deaths for a larger and more fluid population, and supervising a growing clerical estate. The lay bureaucracy had expanded both to address these extensive administrative duties and to buttress the Church's vertical authority structure. Yet this rigid hierarchy would prove impractical for the management of social realities in the nineteenth-century church, and the synodal system would become increasingly reliant on the delegation of responsibility for the Church's pastoral functions to the parish clergy at the local level.

The Spiritual Regulation augmented the religious authority of the monastic hierarchy in the interest of the state. The synodal roster (*shtat*) of 1819 called for seven clergymen to staff the Holy Governing Synod, the apex of the Church hierarchy: four bishops, two archimandrites, and only one member of the white clergy, an archpriest.[15] This membership varied over time but was always dominated by the episcopate, and was traditionally chaired by the metropolitan of Saint Petersburg.[16] Gregory Freeze has decisively discredited the long-held notion that the Church's authority was entirely subordinated to that of the secular state.[17] He points out that Peter's reform delineated a "spiritual domain" (*dukhovnaia komanda*), to be overseen by the Synod, which rendered that body's authority comparable to that of the Governing Senate over the separate and parallel "secular domain" (*svetskaia komanda*). Within the former, the synodal prelates developed separate systems of taxation and justice, which gave them more control over the Church's staff and budget than the Moscow Patriarchate had ever exercised.[18] Freeze also points out that the Synodal Church exerted greater control over certain spheres of social life, particularly marriage, than any other European church.[19] Yet the modernization of semiautonomous institutions is a common feature of "indirect rule" by imperial governments over subject populations, and the Russian state utilized the Orthodox Church as a conduit for its own authority among the people.[20] As stated in article 65 of the Svod Zakonov, the official digest of the Russian Empire's code of law, "Autocratic power acts in church administration through the Holy Governing Synod, which it established."[21] The synodal system was developed in order to prevent the authority of the Church hierarchy from conflicting with that of the autocracy.

The structure of the Synod ensured that the prelates' loyalty to the emperor could be enforced without directly violating the autonomy of the spiritual domain. A lay bureaucrat, the ober-procurator of the Holy Synod, represented the emperor at every synodal assembly. His official duty was to serve as the "eye of the emperor," by monitoring the legality and order of synodal proceedings. The influence and prestige of this official grew substantially over the nineteenth century, along with the expansion of the synodal bureaucracy. In 1839, an Economic Administration, a Religious-Educational Administration, and a Chancellery of the Ober-Procurator were all established within the synodal bureaucracy. The directors of these and all synodal organs answered directly to the ober-procurator. Beginning in 1835, he represented the Church at both the State Council and the Council of Ministers.[22] While the ober-procurator did not exercise the same authority over the Synod that the ministers wielded within their departments, he could regulate the activity of its members. For example, while he did not have the right to veto synodal resolutions, the ober-procurator was the only member of the assembly with direct access to the emperor and could therefore advise the sovereign against approving the prelates' decisions.[23] The metropolitans of Saint Petersburg, Moscow, Kiev, and the exarch of Georgia held permanent seats in the Synod, but the emperor could replace the other members at the ober-procurator's advice. Between 1881 and 1894, thirty-six different members passed in and out of the Synod.[24] Moreover, no form of assembly was permitted for the episcopate outside of the closely monitored Synod. An exception was made in 1884, when bishops were allowed to participate in the First All-Russian Missionary Congress in Kiev, with explicit instructions from the ober-procurator not to breach the topic of church governance.[25] It is little wonder that the Orthodox hierarchy, as M. E. Grabko observes, "were unable and, obviously, considered it impossible to take decisive steps, on the model of the Catholic Church, to ameliorate, much less eliminate, social tensions and anticlericalism."[26] The Church's leadership failed to sanction workers' unions, advocate for fair wage, or formulate any such policies in reaction to social changes because the synodal system confined their religious authority to the "spiritual domain."

At the diocesan level as well, the synodal system both elevated and circumscribed the authority of the Church hierarchy. The diocesan bishop exercised "apostolic authority" over religious life within his see. The practical extent of this authority was not clearly defined in canon law. Further delineation by synodal resolutions and government decrees afforded the bishop extensive personal authority, particularly over the parish clergy.[27] In theory, the bishop resolved all judicial cases for the clergy of his diocese, excluding those of a political nature. He received a constant stream of petitions ranging from petty requests to important financial issues, often couched in obsequious language: "Merciful Arch-pastor, and Father . . . casting myself at the feet of your Most Holiness, I give myself over to your mercy."[28] Harsh penalties for all manner of pastoral malfeasance and insubordination were meted out in the bishop's name, such as periods of monastic incarceration and temporary suspension of the right to perform the liturgy, during which the clergyman and his family would be left with no source of income.[29] The bishop received assistance with his substantial administrative responsibilities from the diocesan consistory, which consisted of five to seven clergymen, most of whom were priests and archpriests. By the nineteenth century, however, consistory business was increasingly managed by the diocesan chancellery, consisting of a lay secretary and his staff of scribes.[30] The diocesan secretary was appointed by the Synod and reported directly to the ober-procurator. He scrutinized every document that passed in and out of the consistory, giving him significant influence over consistory business, including the disciplining of the lower clergy.[31] Thus, the secretary and his staff provided essential administrative support for the bishop's personal control over his diocese, while also monitoring his actions on behalf of the Synod. Conflict with the ober-procurator, or even with the diocesan secretary, could result in a bishop's transfer to another diocese. The year 1892, for example, saw thirty transfers of bishops from one diocese to another.[32] Thus were the diocesan prelates tethered to the will of the Synod, and their ties to the parish clergy weakened.

As the Synod could not appoint lay bureaucrats to work alongside every priest, it instead strove to ensure that every parish clergyman was directly and exclusively accountable to the diocesan authorities for all his pastoral duties. In 1797, the right of parishioners to elect their priests was abolished in favor of direct appointments by the bishop. The Synod rejected proposals for the restoration of parish elections on the grounds that the bishop was morally responsible for the position of each priest.[33] The bishop also appointed a priest or archpriest to serve as "superintendent" (*blagochinnyi*) of every district (*okrug*) of ten to thirty parishes. By 1907, the city of Moscow was overseen by fourteen superintendents while the surrounding gubernia was overseen by sixty-three.[34] This office originated from the practice of electing clerical elders to represent the parish clergy, but in 1820 the superintendent was converted into an appointed office, answerable only to the diocesan bishop. The decree (*ukaz*) that effected this transformation referred to the superintendent as "the eye of the bishop in all affairs concerning church oversight."[35] He was responsible for monitoring all the activities of the clergy under his jurisdiction, including every sermon they delivered. In his account of the Russian Empire published in 1877, the British journalist Sir Donald Mackenzie Wallace was shocked to learn from a parish priest that "if I wish to preach a sermon—not that I often wish to do such a thing, but there are occasions when it is advisable—I am expected to show it first to the Blagochinny. . . . He acts as the spy of the Consistory, which is filled with greedy shameless officials, deaf to anyone who does not come provided with a handful of rubles."[36] Yet this power dynamic could not internally divide the parish clergy, who were linked by ties of kinship and mutual aid. Parish clergymen were disinclined to spy on one another for the consistory, as is indicated by the collected reports of the superintendents of the Tver' diocese for the volatile period of 1905–6, which contains not one denunciation for any infraction aside from several instances of public drunkenness, which had already been reported by parishioners.[37] Moreover, the Synod's efforts to control the pastoral mission of the parish clergy were undermined by its reliance on their capacity to perform their work autonomously, as well as in collaboration with one another.

While the synodal bureaucracy could neither fund nor monitor the parish clergy's work, it imposed far more extra-liturgical duties on them than on the monastic hierarchy. Arguably, the most important of these duties was participation in mutual aid within the clerical estate. The last resort of a parish clergyman who fell into desperate circumstances was to seek refuge "with his family in the clerical calling [*u svoikh rodnykh dukhovnago zvaniia*]," in the words of a Moscow deacon who took in a defrocked priest, suffering from a "nervous disorder."[38] Clerical mutual aid became an effective source of support for the training and social security of the pastorate because it was not difficult for parish clergymen to perceive care for the elderly, widows, orphans, and seminary students within their own estate as a component of their pastoral mission. Other duties that appeared to contradict that mission were neglected. For example, priests routinely concealed Old Believers living in their parishes from the authorities, shielding them from higher taxation, and priests almost never reported crimes revealed during confession to the police.[39] As the synodal bureaucracy grew, so did the variety of services demanded of the parish clergy. Some of these were virtually ignored, such as Count Nikolai Protasov's demand, during his tenure as ober-procurator (1836–55), that priests instruct peasants in agronomy.[40] Other duties, particularly those that directly benefited parishioners, were taken up readily. In an article from 1914, a priest from Tver' reflected on how this activity had altered the character of pastoral work among the parish clergy.

We can see that the modern clergy has become completely different from the clergy of former times. The old pastor of the Church was man of prayer, a zealous and diligent servant of God and the Church. He carried out his service quietly, on a spiritual plane, the visible sphere of which is the Church. ... In present times, there has arisen ... a new type of pastor. These pastors are social actors. They work as catechists in various religious and secular schools. They are representatives in higher legislative bodies, in the zemstvos, and in city administrations. They work in cooperatives. They are lecturers and writers in this or that field of social service, and so on. A type of pastor has appeared who, while not a social servant, is thoroughly occupied with the concerns of a practical and worldly worker. With what eyes should we behold this type of pastor and his social activities? Is there not in these activities something prejudicial and contradictory to the calling of a pastor?[41]

The author, Father Bazhenov, concluded that this social work "should not be viewed with reproach or disdain."[42] Behind it lay the "completely just demands, placed on the pastors of the Church by secular society itself."[43] Bazhenov and other clergymen did not view such work as incompatible with their pastoral duty because it had become a part of that duty. Clergymen performed such work not at the behest of the synodal bureaucracy but in response to the needs of "secular society." The "new type of pastor" emerged as the clerical community came more closely to identify itself with that "secular society."

The Clerical Network

By the early nineteenth century, the freedom to form mutual aid associations had become a practical necessity for the survival of the parish clergy within the synodal system. Peter I's initiative to build seminaries in every diocese had finally been realized by this time, and graduation from seminary became a prerequisite for ordination as a priest.[44] This placed added financial pressure on clergymen to secure a future in church service for each of their sons by sending them to the diocesan center for seminary training. Yet this education did not open new sources of income for the parish clergy. Ordained priests were barred from moonlighting in other professions, aside from teaching and farming.[45] Moreover, the clerical estate itself was growing faster than the number of parishes recognized in the official registry (*shtat*), which provided the primary source of income for this population. Parish farmland provided no long-term security for the families of these pastors because it did not belong to them but was attached to the parish itself. A priest and his family would, therefore, lose any investment he made into this land when he retired or was transferred to another parish.⁴⁶ In 1823, the Synod addressed an appeal to Emperor Alexander I to authorize, in light of the growing number of widows and orphans within the clerical estate, the establishment of mutual aid organizations to address the problem.⁴⁷ The emperor's consent initiated the growth of the parish clergy's diocesan network. The origins of this network, in semiofficial associations for controlling poverty within their own estate, allowed the parish clergy to develop their capacity for collective social action.

On August 12, 1823, the emperor recognized the establishment of the diocesan trusteeship for poor clergy (*popechitel'stvo o bednykh dukhovnogo zvaniia*). This institution was given semiautonomous status within the diocesan administration, "separate from the diocesan consistory." But it was also to operate "under the direct authority of the local prelate."⁴⁸ The central committee was to be composed of six members selected by the bishop from among the diocesan clergy, one of whom was to be a member of the consistory as well. Half of the committee was to be composed of permanent residents of the diocesan capital so that the trusteeship could meet monthly, while the other half could come from other places in the diocese and could "perform their work from their own localities."⁴⁹ Local committees were to perform the work of gathering and distributing funds throughout the diocese. The central committee was to collaborate with three representatives of the parish clergy in each county (*uezd*) of the diocese.⁵⁰ These local committees were required to submit annual reports to the superintendent in whose jurisdiction they were located, detailing all expenditures. The reports were then sent to the central committee.⁵¹ Despite the trusteeship's subordination to the bishop, and its supervision by his appointees, it had no coercive power over the parish clergy, relying entirely on their voluntary and informal collaboration, outside of the hierarchic chain of command.

The texts of the Synod's proposal and the foundational legislation indicate that the trusteeships were built on a preexisting culture of mutual aid among the parish clergy. In order to conserve the resources of the trusteeship, applicants for aid were encouraged to rely on kinship networks for support whenever possible: "If it happens that someone asks for aid who has children or close relatives nearby, the trusteeship, together with providing aid, will use its resources to convince the children and relatives, in the words of the Apostle: [But if any widow have children or nephews], let them learn first to show piety at home, and to requite their parents."⁵² Moreover, the trusteeships relied on kinship networks for information in order to scrutinize requests for aid and ensure that poverty relief was applied appropriately and effectively: "To ensure that aid is granted according to true need, it is necessary that the person receiving aid, if he is not well known, include in his request to the diocesan bishop:

1) whose son he is; 2) how old he is; 3) where and how long he has served; 4) does he have a family and if so who they are."[53] Having ensured that these kinship networks did not relinquish their responsibilities, as explained in the original proposal, the purpose of the trusteeship was to combine their activities and extend their collective reach throughout the diocese: "Specific knowledge of local conditions and of benevolent care will, without a doubt, open these sources [of charity], if not in all, then at least in some dioceses."[54] Thus, in an effort to manage the growing population of impoverished and destitute members of the clerical estate, the regime permitted the expansion of the clergy's social support networks to the scale of the diocese, the borders of which corresponded with those of the gubernia.

The freedom of the parish clergy to associate and cooperate was not formally extended again until Russia's era of social transformation known as the Great Reforms. This period began when the Edict of Emancipation, composed by Metropolitan Filaret (Drozdov) of Moscow, was read in churches and private estates throughout the empire in 1861, declaring the abolition of private serfdom. Subsequent reforms were driven by a combination of necessity and a shift in the ideology of the monarchy in favor of a more participatory society. The bestowal of personal freedom on more than twenty-three million peasants created an urgent need for local self-administration throughout Russia's countryside. The zemstvo reform of 1864, which established democratically elected local government assemblies, was followed by the introduction of jury trials, expanded freedom of the press, and the creation of municipal government bodies.[55] The clerical estate benefited unevenly from these reforms. Parish clergymen were not included in the judicial reform and remained under the jurisdiction of the diocesan consistory rather than juries of their peers.[56] Clergymen were also excluded from the right to vote and stand for election in local government until 1905.[57] Despite official ambivalence toward their engagement in public life, the pastorate took advantage of limited concessions during the reform era to increase their corporate autonomy and the scope of free association within the clerical estate.

The relaxation of press censorship in the early 1860s resulted in an initial torrent of criticism of the synodal system and monastic hierarchy, similar to Belliustin's scandalous diatribe.[58] While ecclesiastical censorship was tightened again the following decade, the more long-term consequence of press freedom for the clergy was a significant expansion of church publication. In 1863, Metropolitan Filaret led the creation of an association in Moscow, the Society for Lovers of Spiritual Enlightenment, dedicated to improving religious education and discourse. Its members, mostly Moscow clergymen, assembled a diocesan library, hosted public lectures, and launched Moscow's diocesan publication, the *Moscow Church Journal* (*Moskovskie tserkovnye vedomosti*).[59] Similar diocesan journals appeared throughout the empire, primarily for use by the clergy. *Diocesan Journals* (*Eparkhial'nye vedomosti*) usually included an "official section" for announcements from the consistory and Synod as well as information about clerical initiatives throughout the diocese. This resource greatly enhanced the parish clergy's capacity for large-scale cooperation by announcing charitable campaigns, praising contributors, and publicizing financial statistics. These journals also included an "unofficial section," containing articles, sermons, obituaries, accounts of parish life, and other writings by clergymen and lay intellectuals. Although subjected to varying levels of censorship, these journals provided a public forum for discussion and debate on pastoral work. As the pastoral mission took shape in the late nineteenth century, diocesan publications gave it intellectual substance.

The parish clergy gained their most important institution of voluntary association virtually by accident. In 1864, a seminar charter (*ustav*) established the parish clergy's right to elect a representative to serve on the pedagogical council of the religious school that would educate their sons. This election was to be carried out by a diocesan congress (*eparkhial'nyi s"ezd*), an assembly of elected representatives of the clergy—priests or archpriests—from each superintendent district. No other function was mentioned in the text of the charter. Yet the rights and responsibilities of these bodies gradually, and often unofficially, increased over the next decade to include the raising of funds for ecclesiastical schools and seminaries and the organization of mutual aid and charity. In 1867, the charter was revised to authorize local congresses as well, to be held in the districts (*okruga*) surrounding each ecclesiastical school.[60] The delegates to these district congresses (*okruzhnye s"ezdy*) would collect detailed information on the needs of their local schools and submit reports to the diocesan congress.[61] In the same year, the Synod issued regulations restricting permissible topics of discussion at these congresses to purely financial matters. Congresses were explicitly forbidden, for example, from discussing zemstvo affairs or amendments to the structure of diocesan administration.[62] Yet, in the words of one priest, Father Bogoiavlenskii, who submitted his master's thesis on the diocesan congresses to Kazan' Theological Academy in 1900, "diocesan congresses, by force of the demands of Russian church life, have expanded the sphere of their activities in the affairs of religious-educational institutions. They have engaged questions of the improvement of conditions for the clergy, especially questions of religious-moral character. Thus, naturally, they came to be guided not by synodal decrees alone but by the authority given them from the diocesan bishop, and this authority came to be as great and varied as the activity of the diocesan congresses."[63] Indeed, the Synod was unable to restrict clerical associations to narrowly utilitarian functions. In 1865, Archbishop Mikhail (Golubovich) of Minsk authorized the clergy of his diocese to meet at superintendent congresses (*blagochinicheskie s"ezdy*), the same assemblies that elected representatives to the district and diocesan congresses, to discuss religious life in their parishes and consider means of combating superstition, alcoholism, illiteracy, and other problems afflicting their parish communities. Over subsequent years, more and more diocesan bishops followed Mikhail's example and formally recognized all levels of the parish clergy's congresses as "pastoral assemblies."[64]

These new forms of association bore tangible results for the parish clergy. For example, delegates to the diocesan congresses of Moscow and Tver' organized pension funds to support retired clergymen and seminary teachers, as well as their widows and orphans, in 1867 and 1878, respectively.[65] These funds were established with the investments of clergymen and clerical teachers throughout the diocese at an average rate of thirty rubles a year as well as more sizeable contributions of some wealthier archpriests and prelates. The Moscow congress resolved that the money would revert to the diocesan trusteeship if the venture failed.[66] Sufficient investment was achieved and the fund was maintained, in part, by informing clergymen about the opportunity through the diocesan journal.[67] The parish clergy also managed to raise more diocesan funds for their seminaries, ecclesiastical schools, and other purposes by investing in the construction of ritual candle factories. On December 21, 1870, the Synod decreed that a candle factory should be built in each diocese, the profits from which should be used to support clerical schools.[68] Official support for this project went no further than the decree, and it fell to the clerical congresses to finance the project. The Moscow clergy built their factory in 1879. Like everything in the diocese, this institution was under the "direct authority of the bishop," but it was run by the diocesan congress, which elected a priest to serve as the factory's manager.[69] The success of this venture was contingent upon the willingness of all parish priests to purchase candles exclusively from the diocesan candle factory rather than sparing their individual parish coffers by purchasing cheap alternatives, and the diocesan journal played an important role in informing clergymen of their common interest in this regard as well.[70] Similar projects substantially improved standards of living and education in dioceses across the empire. Yet the benefits for the parish clergy were not only material. The reintroduction of the electoral principal (*vybornoe nachalo*) into diocesan administration and the right of clergymen to participate in church administration through representative assemblies elevated the dignity and social status of the parish clergy.[71] Congresses continued to call for greater local autonomy for their associations. Some prelates began to grant the requests of their diocesan congresses to convert the office of superintendent into an elected representative of the clergy.[72] In 1877, for example, Archbishop Savva (Tikhomirov) of Tver' accepted and promulgated rules developed by his diocesan congress for the election of superintendents.[73]

Clerical institutions of association came to play an increasingly important role in the life of the Orthodox Church, in part, because of their culture of accountability. The priest, deacon, and sacristan of each parish divided up all donations they collected, reserving only a portion for themselves, and allocated the rest to parish needs, such as church renovations, and diocesan needs, such as funding for the seminary, pension funds, shelters for the elderly, and so on.[74] While embezzlement of parish funds was not unknown, corruption was rare among the clergy because of its disastrous consequences for both individual priests and clerical community as a whole. A letter to the Moscow consistory from 1899, signed by a church elder and twenty parishioners, illustrates these consequences: "Father Orlov . . . giving himself over to temptation, has behaved to the detriment of the church and the parishioners. He has harmed the financial and social standing of the church."[75] Not only was a corrupt clergyman likely to lose his position and livelihood, but he also threatened to erode the support of the lay community for the pastorate as a whole. For this reason, the clergy actively guarded against corruption in their own ranks. In his memoir, Metropolitan Evlogii (Georgievskii) described an attempted theft after a religious procession in Kholm. A sacristan collecting donations slipped a coin into his boot but was noticed by a deacon: "The sacristan was dismissed and the deacon commended. The people were poor, but gave generously."[76] Moreover, the clergy's accountability to one another was crucial to the survival of the diocesan network, and they often proved to be more effective at monitoring their own taxation and budget than the consistory bureaucrats. One representative to Tver's diocesan congress in 1901 devised a standardized form on which each priest could report his church's income, the amount of land attached to his parish, and the number of his parishioners in order to facilitate budget consideration at the congress.[77] When diocesan taxes on parishioner donations fell short of what was required to support a school or the clerical poor of a certain district, assembled clergymen regularly pledged additional funds from their own pockets to cover the shortfall.[78] The expansion of civil liberties that followed the 1905 Revolution allowed the clerical network to grow further, and the petitions of parish priests for still greater freedom of association reveal a perceived connection between the effectiveness of their associations and their right to self-administration. In 1907, for example, a priest wrote to the metropolitan of Moscow, arguing that the participation of more clergymen in more local congresses would make diocesan tax evasion less likely: "Are there significant sums that parishes do not reveal? Is the tax levied on profits from candle sales just? ... In order to resolve these questions effectively, the clergy must hold preliminary discussions at assemblies within their superintendent districts, which have more of a familial and domestic character. Since educational concerns affect everyone equally, priests as well as deacons and sacristans, it would be just to invite all members of the parish staffs to these assemblies and to grant them equal voting rights."[79] While this request to extend participation to deacons and sacristans was not granted, the pastorate's capacity for large-scale cooperation was certainly a major factor in the hierarchy's tolerance of their semiautonomous associations. It also attracted participation from other estates in clerical associations.

Voluntary association was largely segregated among Russia's different estates. Because of the state's apprehension of public activity by the rising professional classes, groups with non-estate ties were forbidden to form permanent associations.[80] Only the nobility had the privilege and wealth to organize large-scale associations through provincial noble assemblies. The peasantry had little opportunity to do so beyond the level of the township (*volost'*), and they lacked the resources to establish robust mutual aid societies. Thus, as Adele Lindenmeyr notes, mutual aid was most poorly developed in the strata of the population that needed it most.[81] Yet the regime was less threatened by association under the auspices of the official Church. Certain clerical associations, therefore, such as Moscow's Society for Lovers of Religious Enlightenment, could accept nonclerical members.[82] The Church's lay population began turning to the parish clergy and their substantial social infrastructure to facilitate a variety of initiatives, from building churches, to supporting education, to managing poverty. The clerical network came to provide a sphere of free association for the Orthodox population as a whole.

The Orthodox laity was first invited to form associations through the Church during the Great Reform period, with the revival of Orthodox brotherhoods. These associations were first organized among the Orthodox population of the Polish-Lithuanian Commonwealth in the sixteenth and seventeenth centuries. They used mutual aid as a means of protecting church property and supporting religious education, especially after the defection of six of their eight bishops to union with Rome in 1596.[83] In 1862, Metropolitan Arsenii (Moskvin) of Kiev sponsored the restoration of the brotherhoods in their place of origin, Ukraine. New brotherhoods were established in Belarus and Saint Petersburg the following year. In 1864, Minister of Internal Affairs P. A. Valuev established the Fundamental Rules for the creation of these associations, which granted retroactive state recognition to existing brotherhoods. They authorized the voluntary association of Orthodox Christians from all estates. The synodal prelates primarily viewed the brotherhoods as a means of mobilizing popular support for the official Church in competition with other confessions.[84] A 1901 synodal report on church affairs called the brotherhoods "a wonderful manifestation of popular participation in the assertion of Orthodoxy."[85] In fact, the scope of a brotherhood's activities was determined by its members and could involve a wide variety of church-related initiatives, which had to be drawn up in its charter and submitted for approval by the bishop. Interest in the brotherhoods was quite uneven throughout the empire. Aleksandr Papkov, a lay Orthodox intellectual and author of numerous studies on the Church, conducted an empire-wide survey of brotherhoods in 1893 and reported their number to be 159 with 37,642 members in possession of an estimated 1,629,707 rubles.[86] These were concentrated in certain dioceses, particularly in the former territories of the Polish-Lithuanian Commonwealth, such as Mink, where twenty-two brotherhoods operated. Papkov observed the second-largest number of brotherhoods in the dioceses of Moscow, Riga, and Podol'sk, each of which contained eight. He found six operating in the capital and only two in Tver'.[87] Archival records of smaller brotherhoods in Moscow, not mentioned in Papkov's report, suggest that these numbers must have been higher.[88] Church-based association through brotherhoods, therefore, seems to have developed unevenly, and in some instances on the foundation of its historical roots in the western part of the empire where these organizations had first emerged.

Orthodox brotherhoods took several different forms, and the parish clergy played a central role in each of them. The largest brotherhoods consisted of hundreds of members, including bishops, provincial governors, and even members of the imperial family. These brotherhoods supported a variety of charitable causes within their dioceses.[89] Their agendas were, of course, formulated by their most powerful members, often focusing on religious education as a source of political order or on missionary activity as a means of imperial expansion in the empire's borderlands.[90] These large-scale operations relied on the social network of the parish clergy both for the implementation of charitable services and as a source of information on local needs for these services.[91] Many of the smaller brotherhoods were dominated by membership of parish clergymen, with the prelate as a nominal member, and served as extensions of the clergy's mutual aid network. In 1890, for example, the clergy of one rural Moscow district presented a donation of forty rubles to the Brotherhood of Saint Nicholas, along with a statement of gratitude for that organization's support for the education of their children: "Now even the largest and poorest clerical families need not despair over the education of their sons."[92] Localized, lay-dominated brotherhoods often focused on the construction and renovation of churches. These smaller associations often depended on the contributions of a wealthy patron or patrons, as peasant members could not always meet their financial commitments.[93] The recruitment of local gentry, merchants, or urban patrons for small brotherhoods was usually accomplished by parish priests, who also encouraged members to support social services, similar to those performed by the clerical network. Of the 159 brotherhoods recorded in Papkov's 1893 report, 78 claimed to be engaged in some kind of charitable activity.[94] The pastorate, therefore, influenced religious association through their work within the brotherhoods, facilitating cooperation across estate boundaries and promoting social support as a cooperative religious activity.

POBEDONOSTSEV

The terrorist bomb that killed Alexander II in 1881 abruptly ended Russia's reform era and effected the transition of power to a new tsarist administration that was deeply suspicious of free association, viewing it as an infringement on the uniquely Russian bond between autocrat and *narod*.[95] An important figure in the "counter-reform" administrations of both Alexander III and Nicholas II was Konstantin Pobedonostsev, who began his twenty-five-year tenure as ober-procurator of the Holy Synod in 1880. Pobedonostsev served as personal tutor to both of Russia's last two emperors, and his ideological influence over their reigns prompted contemporaries to refer to him as the "gray cardinal" and the "Russian Torquemada."[96] While Pobedonostsev's role in shaping government policy may have been exaggerated, there is no question that he wielded more influence over church administration than any previous ober-procurator. This state bureaucrat became a towering figure within the ecclesiastical sphere and significantly influenced the course of Russian Orthodox history.

Pobedonostsev reinvented the office of ober-procurator. While the post was previously intended to maintain a supervisory agent of the state within the church hierarchy, Pobedonostsev used it to promote his vision of Orthodoxy as the vital link between the tsar and the people. His immediate predecessor and new minister of internal affairs, Count Aleksandr Tolstoi, complained that Pobedonostsev was "the delegate of the priests or, more accurately, of the monks before the government, and not of the government before the Church. The power of the synodal ober-procurator in the clerical sphere is not thus defined."[97] Pobedonostsev succeeded in imposing new religious laws on the population to increase the Church's prestige. In 1881, theatrical productions were forbidden during the great fast. In 1885, it became illegal to sell alcohol near churches or monasteries. After 1893, factory owners could no longer demand work from their employees during religious holidays or on Sundays.[98] While despised by liberals and dissidents as a reactionary, Pobedonostsev provided great impetus to the pastoral movement by encouraging the parish clergy's engagement in society through educational and humanitarian work. His promotion of this work was not driven by the cameralistic ideology of some of his predecessors but by his conviction that the Church should play a central role in the social life of the Orthodox population. He decried the modern compartmentalization of religion in his 1901 essay "Church and State": "When was it decided that the Church exists only to produce ascetics, to fill monasteries, and to perform the poetry of its rituals and processions in the churches? No, all of this is only a small part of the Church's goal. . . . Her task is to instill respect for law and authority in the people, and to instill respect for human freedom in the authorities. And they say the Church has no business in society!"[99] The ober-procurator viewed the clergy's pastoral work as a force of social harmony and political stability.

Pobedonostsev envisioned Orthodox social engagement as being animated and guided by the authority structures of church and state. The brotherhoods conformed to this vision because of the widespread participation of prelates and state officials in many of them. Pobedonostsev encouraged their work and hosted the Saint Petersburg Brotherhood of the Holy Mother of God in his own home.[100] Yet he viewed self-organized local initiatives as products of an alien ideology, imported from Europe and harmful to the organic unity of native Russian society. This rendered the parish clergy's associational network incompatible with Pobedonostsev's vision: "The system of a 'free Church in a free state' is founded on abstract, theoretical principles; not of faith, but of religious indifference. . . . In this abstract system, the fruit of the new rationalism, the Church is presented as an abstract political institution with determinate goals or as a private society that is organized for determinate goals, just like any other corporation that is recognized within the state."[101] Thus, Pobedonostsev's tenure would be marked by the simultaneous encouragement of pastoral activism and suppression of local autonomy and initiative.

From the outset of his tenure as ober-procurator, Pobedonostsev worked to reign in freedom of association among the parish clergy. In 1880, he managed to persuade the reformist Tsar Alexander II to abolish the clerical elections of superintendents, which were being held in some form in about half of the empire's dioceses.[102] In the course of redrafting the seminary charter in 1884, he was able to abolish all clerical congresses below the diocesan level and reiterate the official restriction of the issues discussed at diocesan congresses to financial matters.[103] Now all joint initiatives of the parish clergy had to pass through the diocesan administration, ostensibly under the archpastoral guidance of the bishop but in reality under the supervision of chancellery bureaucrats. It was under these circumstances that the parish clergy encountered one of Russia's greatest humanitarian catastrophes of the nineteenth century.

The Famine Relief Campaign

During the autumn and winter of 1891, drought combined with a series of hard frosts led to massive crop failure across seventeen provinces of European Russia by the summer of 1892. The small harvest of 1891 led to an increase in grain prices and a decrease in wages for rural labor, exacerbating an already desperate situation for an affected population of approximately six million people.[104] Epidemics of typhus and cholera soon combined with the crisis of starvation, leading to the deaths of an estimated 400,000 people by the end of 1892.[105] In his study of the famine, Richard Robbins documents the frantic attempts by the central government to address the disaster. Challenging the narrative of a callous and complacent regime presented in Soviet historiography, Robbins argues that the central government's relief work warded off mass starvation and economic collapse.[106] He attributes the high death toll to the empire's lack of infrastructure, which presented a major obstacle to the government's attempts to identify communities in greatest need and supply them with appropriate amounts of relief grain. The zemstvo network of each province penetrated the countryside only as far as the district, and government agents such as police and tax collectors maintained no permanent presence in peasant villages.[107] As in the past, the state called upon the clergy to supplement its thinly stretched bureaucracy by identifying affected communities, verifying the honesty of applications for aid, and spreading information on hygienic practices to limit the spread of cholera.[108] In 1891, however, the now highly developed clerical networks would allow the clergy to organize a proactive humanitarian relief campaign that would have lasting consequences for the Church's social mission—and for the parish clergy's influence over that mission.

If use of clerical mutual aid networks to facilitate pastoral work had been nascent in previous decades, it became systematic during the famine of 1891–92. While the brotherhoods did participate in the organization of famine relief, their role was marginal compared to that of the clergy's own social networks.[109] These diocesan networks set into motion from the outset of the crisis because clergy living in affected communities were starving along with the peasantry. Pobedonostsev described their circumstances in his annual report to the emperor.

> The crop failure could not but degrade the material condition of the parish clergy in particular. The condition of the lowest members of the parish staffs, those with large families and those in poor parishes, became truly harsh. The clergy already found themselves in very difficult circumstances after the initial, tragic results of the crop failure. When the disaster reached its full proportions,

most rural parishes fell into desperation. Due to the universal impoverishment of the population, parish income—the voluntary payments of parishioners for religious services—which had been meager in previous years, shrank to an absolute minimum in some places and ceased altogether in others. . . . With nothing to live on but government salaries, which not all parish clergy receive, and soon to be left with nothing, many clergymen and other servants of the Church were forced to sell their livestock and other remaining possessions for very little, literally in order to avoid starvation. The impoverishment of some lower members of parish staffs became so complete that they found themselves without a crust of bread and were forced to live by begging.[110]

This account illustrates both the extent to which the parish clergy depended on their parishioners for support and the inability of the central church and state authorities to replace that support. The Synod issued a grant of 2,500 rubles for the relief of starving clergy, and Pobedonostsev personally donated 1,000 rubles to relieve the particularly hard-hit clergy of Kazan'.[111] Yet it was the trusteeships for poor clergy that averted disaster by distributing these funds effectively and by raising more throughout the crisis. Pobedonostsev realized that the clergy could use this mutual aid infrastructure to assist the starving population in general. This agenda was expressed in the Synod's instructions to the diocesan consistories: "Requests [for aid] by parishioners are to be satisfied according to the same reckoning and in the same way as requests by clergy, i.e. through the trusteeships for poor clergy."[112] Thus, the clerical networks were officially enlisted to participate in general famine relief.

The diocesan consistories were instructed to organize their relief work along strictly hierarchical lines, in accordance with the regime's deep aversion to independent association. The Synod's first decree (*ukaz*) on famine relief was issued on August 21, 1891. It instructed the parish clergy to begin holding collections for famine relief at every church service. Strict accounts of these donations were to be maintained. Those priests who served parishes affected by the famine were to accept requests for aid and to identify famine victims such as orphans who could not apply for aid on their own. The decree instructed each bishop to organize and preside over a diocesan committee, composed of clerical and lay members for the oversight of the entire process. The large Moscow diocese was divided between two committees, each headed by a vicar bishop.[113] The initiative for collection was to pass from the central committee down to the parishes. The committees ordered the superintendents to gather money from their parishes. The superintendents were to order the priests under their jurisdictions to obtain this money in the form of donations from their parishioners. These resources were all to be passed back up to the diocesan relief committees, overseen by the bishops. In dioceses unaffected by the famine, such as Tver' and Moscow, these donations would be passed to the committees of those dioceses that were experiencing starvation. Yet actual distribution of funds in affected dioceses was often handled by the trusteeship for poor clergy, now operating as a general relief organization. Moreover, the synodal decree conceded that "in cases of special need," temporary committees of parish clergymen and parish elders could be organized in district centers for the collection and distribution of funds as well.[114] From the outset of the campaign, therefore, the parish clergy regained a small measure of their local autonomy, belying their official role as mere executors of their prelate's will.

By securing sovereignty over the Church's famine relief campaign for the synodal hierarchy, Pobedonostsev also freed the clergy from the oversight of the state bureaucracy. This independence allowed the clergy to organize their campaign with greater efficiency than the zemstvo network. The provincial zemstvos had always been forbidden from cooperating with their counterparts across the boundaries between gubernias, which meant that during the famine they were forced to communicate through the governors. This could render cumbersome the process of receiving and distributing famine relief, especially if the governor was uncooperative. For example, the governor of Vyatka imposed a ban on grain exports from his province, supposedly to prevent speculation, thereby preventing the Vyatka zemstvo from sending aid to famine-stricken provinces.[115] The diocesan committees, on the other hand, were permitted to communicate with one another directly. In December 1891, the committee of the famine-stricken Ryazan' diocese sent 4,000 rubles that it had raised internally to the committee of Tver', which used the money to purchase grain from the less desperate peasants in its diocese. The Tver' committee then shipped the food back to the Ryazan' committee for distribution among its starving population.[116] Some diocesan committees took advantage of the Synod's permission to establish district committees, "in special cases," to free up their internal lines of communication as well. These committees were organized throughout the dioceses and were usually chaired by a priest or archpriest. They were typically composed of ten to twenty members, most of whom were parish priests, joined by monastic clergymen, local officials, and merchant-philanthropists. District committees were established in both Moscow and Tver' and were given the responsibilities of coordinating the collection efforts of all the superintendent districts under their purview and of organizing the storage and shipment of grain collected or purchased within the district. They were also authorized to establish collection points at railroad stations and along roads.[117] By contrast, the Ministry of Internal Affairs decreed on September 1, 1892, that private citizens could organize no charitable collections without the permission of the provincial governor, who was to determine the parameters of the membership and activities of any such organization.[118] The "spiritual domain" (*dukhovnaia komanda*) sheltered an unbroken network of communication from the parish to the inter-diocesan level.

Even within the context of the synodal administration, the campaign itself was not the top-down process outlined in the Synod's 1891 decree. The Church's relief efforts involved the transportation of large sums of money and supplies of grain over great distances and among many different hands, and this was not accomplished by the oversight of the bishops and their diocesan committees alone. Indeed, the logistical work involved in the storage and transportation of resources was performed by the "temporary" district committees rather than by the diocesan authorities. Moreover, archival records in Tver' indicate that irregularities were identified and corrected at the district level, not by diocesan overseers. On March 10, 1892, for example, the committee of Novotorzhskii district informed the Tver' diocesan committee that their contributions of rye, flour, and dry bread had been overestimated in the diocesan committee's January report. Another letter on March 27 presented the diocesan committee with a detailed account of the district committee's actual contributions since its creation.[119] In another case, in November 1891, the Bezhetskii district committee called the diocesan committee's attention to conflicting reports on their last shipment of bread, one claiming that it was sent to Penza and another claiming that it was sent to Voronezh.[120] The parish clergy's culture of accountability, developed through an increasingly sophisticated network of mutual aid, had now been extended to large-scale, charitable operations as well. It is perhaps due to this diligence on the part of clerical organizers that neither the Moscow nor the Tver' consistory archives contain evidence of the kind of fraud and embezzlement of famine relief resources that took place in the zemstvos.[121]

Still more crucial to the success of the Church's relief campaign was the willingness of parish clergymen to provide aid to the hungry from their own resources. Despite the rigorous oversight of all relief activity, outlined in the Synod's decree, church authorities could not coerce the parish clergy to participate. The majority of the Church's contributions to famine relief were drawn from the same well that supplied the parish clergy's livelihood, the largesse of peasant parishioners. This well could run dry, as illustrated by the explanation of one priest to his superintendent regarding the paucity of his parish's contribution to the relief effort in May 1892: "I have the honor of explaining to Your Blessedness that I ordered the church elder to hold a door-to-door collection for the starving after the Easter prayers. . . . Yet the peasants have always provided for the salaries of the church watchmen and communion bread baker on this very holiday and, in light of this collection, none of the peasants of these three villages, which compose two-thirds of the parish, displayed any desire to contribute anything to the starving."[122] In sending donations to the district or diocesan committee, a priest was further dividing his parish's resources, which were already divided among the lower clergy, church servants, and a variety of diocesan institutions. Priests had every incentive to de-prioritize the collection of famine relief, especially in dioceses like Moscow and Tver' that were not directly affected by the famine and were only exporting relief funds to other communities. The committees pressured the superintendents, who in turn pressured the priests to come up with more donations. Yet, as another priest explained, no amount of pastoral admonition could change local conditions, which determined how much parishioners could contribute.

> As I am well acquainted with the conditions of daily life in the village of Chizhev, I did not expect better results from this collection in the parish. Because of their shortage of land, our Chizhev peasants are forced to buy their own bread almost year-round, and themselves suffer from frightful want of money, bread, and fodder for livestock. . . . Under these conditions, no amount of pastoral council and exhortation to elicit donations for victims of crop failure in other provinces could stir Christian sympathy in the hearts of our hungry and unhappy parishioners.[123]

The diocesan authorities had little knowledge of the resources available in rural parishes beyond the number of parishioners, or "souls," assigned to each church. In the event of perceived shortfalls in donations, the Church's relief committees could do little more than demand explanations. In light of these circumstances, it is remarkable how much aid did flow from the parishes. For example, the superintendent district that encompassed sixteen parishes, including those of the priests quoted above, contributed 396.87 rubles from September 1891 to February 1892. This was no mean sacrifice for a rural district, which, as the superintendent explained, had just experienced a poor harvest itself.[124] In rural parishes, moreover, clergymen often supplemented the kopeck donations of their parishioners with contributions of one to five rubles from their own pockets, as indicated on the signed donation sheets collected by the Novotorzhskii district committee.[125] Donations obtained at the parish level were further supplemented at the committee level, which attracted the contributions of monasteries, local merchants, nobles, and officials. In the month of December 1891 alone, aside from donations of grain, the fourteen district committees and single diocesan committee of the Tver' diocese collected a total of 12,711.75 rubles in donations.[126] Over the previous month, by comparison, the Ministry of State Domains had contributed 10,655 rubles for famine relief, and the Ministry of Internal Affairs 272,121 rubles.[127]

The continued tolerance of the clerical networks' de facto administrative independence up until the official cessation of famine relief may have reflected tacit recognition of the Church's valuable contribution to the overall effort. On November 17, 1891, the emperor announced the formation of a Special Committee under the chairmanship of his son, the future Nicholas II, which would consolidate the various organizations that had arisen to address the crisis. The move was officially intended to better coordinate the collection and delivery of aid and to impose broader oversight to prevent waste and theft.[128] According to Robbins, the Special Committee was to establish affiliates in each province to replace the separate committees organized by the governors, the Red Cross, and, over Pobedonostsev's protests, the clergy as well. A similar merger was to be carried out at the district level.[129] The reality, at least in Moscow and Tver', was that the clerical relief networks remained largely intact. The district committees continued their operations as before. They continued to address their contributions to the "diocesan committee." They continued to organize and fund the transportation of grain donations, by river and by rail, to the diocesan centers.[130] The only difference was that the diocesan committees now passed their collected funds on to the affiliate of the Special Committee and ceased their direct collaboration across diocesan boundaries.[131] The extent to which the Special Committee may have usurped the Church's aid delivery efforts in famine provinces must be evaluated on the basis of local research in those areas. Yet Robbins notes the continued role of the parish clergy in famine-stricken provinces of receiving applications for aid and identifying the communities in greatest need.[132]

The clergy continued their work until July 18, 1892, when the Synod ordered all committees to cease collection, submit all remaining funds and documents to the diocesan administration, and disband.[133] From the beginning of its operations until that point, the Tver' committee had collected an estimated total of 69,167.32 rubles, as well as 16,449 *pudy* and 32 *funty* (about 297 tons) of grain.[134] The two main committees from the much larger and wealthier dioceses of Moscow reported cumulative donations by the end of July at 150,119.08 rubles and 138,551.15 rubles, respectively.[135] The portion of these sums and of those collected by other diocesan committees after December 1891 became part of the 2.5 million rubles that the Special Committee received from various institutions. This was a small fraction of the overall 13 million rubles raised by the Special Committee, the bulk of which, Robbins reports, came from the proceeds of two charitable lotteries.[136] The scale of the Church's monetary contribution does not, of course, reflect the valuable logistical support that the clergy provided for the relief effort—or the opportunity for free association that it had opened for the Orthodox laity. While the quantitative contribution of rural parishioners was small in comparison with that from the urban centers, their participation in the relief campaign had demonstrated the possibility for the widespread, voluntary cooperation of Russia's far-flung communities in the interest of self-help and recovery from disaster. This was a significant development both for the Church and for Russia's nascent civil society.

Conclusion

The famine relief campaign altered the Church's position in late imperial Russia. As Pobedonostsev had intended, the Church's contribution to famine relief had enhanced its social presence and revived its status as a guardian of general welfare. Yet Pobedonostsev had not intended or expected the campaign to reveal the indispensability of the parish clergy's social network to the tasks that he had called upon the Church to perform. In his report to the emperor on the famine relief campaign in 1893, Pobedonostsev acknowledged that the clergy's diocesan congresses, of which he disapproved, had been convened out of necessity so that representatives of the parish clergy could agree to contribute their own pension funds toward famine relief.[137] The parish clergy's right to convene district congresses (*okruzhnye s"ezdy*) was officially restored in 1896.[138] Use of their own mutual aid networks to transfer resources to the starving had demonstrated the utility of clerical associations for the Church's capacity to influence society. Subsequent crises would result in further concessions to their freedom of association in the coming years.

The parish clergy's social network did not provide the financial independence from the laity that Belliustin had demanded, but it did afford them a different kind of authority over the corporate religious life of the Orthodox population. The associations that the parish clergy had developed to address their own economic problems were developing into a framework for church-based association for all estates. They provided logistical support for state welfare, leadership for the brotherhoods, and trust for private donations to charitable causes. This gradual transformation was accomplished by the collective willingness of the parish clergy to perform the uncoerced and uncompensated work of transferring resources, which sustained their own communities, back to the peasantry. Their motives for performing this work were, in part, quite practical. By helping the laity, pastors preserved the social basis for their own economic support and the autonomy of their associations. Yet the scale of the clergy's participation in humanitarian relief in 1891–92 suggests a more expansive motivation. By incorporating the clerical estate's practice of association beyond the immediate community into pastoral work among the laity, "the new kind of pastor" was changing the practice of Orthodoxy in the Russian Empire.

2

War, Revolution, and Famine

In his short story "The Nightmare," Anton Chekhov describes a young parish priest, Father Iakov, through the eyes of a rural zemstvo board member, Kunin, who has agreed to collaborate with the priest in the establishment of a parish school. Kunin is at first annoyed by Father Iakov's squalid appearance and timid behavior, until he realizes the extent of the priest's poverty. Father Iakov confides in Kunin that he and his family suffer from hunger because he gives most of his meager income to other people.

> I get a hundred and fifty rubles a year from my parish, and everyone marvels at where this money must go. But, I'll tell you honestly. I contribute forty rubles a year to the ecclesiastical school for my brother Petr. . . . Besides that, I must give Father Avraamii at least three rubles a month. . . . Father Avraamii was the priest in Sinkino before me. . . . Where can he go? Who will feed him? Though he's old, he needs a corner, bread, and clothes. I cannot allow him, as a priest, to go begging for alms. . . . I know if I were to beg and to bow down, everyone would help, but . . . I cannot! I am ashamed. How can I beg of the peasants? . . . How can one beg of a beggar?[1]

Kunin's revelation of the extent of rural poverty, of which he had been naively unaware, is his "nightmare." Chekhov's story portrays the awkward tension that prevailed in rural parishes between the clerical estate and the peasant parishioners who were asked to support it. Father Iakov's shame expresses the clergy's awareness of the burden that their mutual aid networks presented to the Orthodox laity. As the clerical networks expanded in scope and complexity, consciousness of their debt to parishioners motivated parish priests to avail the laity of the resources and associational benefits that these networks provided.

The parish clergy's enhanced organizational autonomy facilitated greater lay involvement in their expanding network of associations. It also presented the clergy with the choice of whether to use their collective resources for the benefit of their own estate or to expand their social networks to other communities. This dilemma was not unique to the parish clergy. By the mid-nineteenth century, members of the middling urban estate (*meshchanstvo*) had developed their own charitable associations to cope with poverty in the growing, industrializing urban centers. But these associations reserved their pooled resources for needy members of their own estate—and sometimes for a particular profession.[2] The state exacerbated social barriers by restricting association across estate boundaries. For example, industrial workers of the peasant estate were segregated from the rest of the urban population, which prevented their guild organizations and mutual aid societies from collaborating with other urban associations.[3] Much of the scholarship on this period has identified estate isolation as an ultimately insurmountable obstacle to an inclusive civil society. This isolation of imperial Russia's emerging communities, the argument goes, converted their corporate vitality into violent radicalization.[4] The pastoral movement presents a counterexample to this narrative. Confronted in 1905 with the multiple crises of war, revolution, and famine, the parish clergy did not retreat into a defensive estate isolation. The clerical networks of Moscow, Tver', and other dioceses voluntarily and independently extended aid to other communities.

The progressive transformation of the parish clergy from a service estate into an independent pastorate owed much to Konstantin Pobedonostsev's tenure as ober-procurator. Under his influence, both the Synod and the government repeatedly called upon the parish clergy, as auxiliary civil servants and liturgical functionaries, to confront social problems more directly. In 1900, for example, an imperial decree granted "unhindered access for Orthodox parish priests to industrial enterprises within their parishes for pastoral discussions with workers" in the hope that their pastoral influence would mitigate the spread of socialism.[5] They were also enjoined to combat alcoholism, illiteracy, and poverty.[6] The ober-procurator's vision of a more proactive pastorate, however, had proven to be incompatible with the restrictions he imposed on the clergy's corporate organizations. An unintended consequence of Pobedonostsev's instigation of pastoral activism was a gradual increase in the clergy's organizational autonomy, which increased over the decade after the famine relief campaign with the approval of most diocesan bishops. As Pobedonostsev had feared, this corporate autonomy created a sense of collective dignity and entitlement to freedom of association. Clerical pride and self-assertion did not lead to their social atomization, which Pobedonostsev associated with the foreign fashion of democratic organization. Rather, the parish clergy continued to promote and reinvent the Church's social mission. As Russia was enveloped in the chaos of 1905, and Pobedonostsev's regime of surveillance and regulation evaporated, the parish clergy organized multiple, decentralized humanitarian relief campaigns.

Expansion of the Clerical Network

Archival records of the Moscow and Tver' dioceses from the early twentieth century exhibit far more instances of lay participation in associations and institutions organized by the parish clergy than in the preceding decades. Much of this collaboration took place within the context of the growing Orthodox brotherhood movement. A report from a brotherhood in the town of Sokolov, for example, listed seven clergymen and thirteen laymen on its central committee in 1899. This association was organized around a school for girls, where it provided material support for religious instruction and charitable aid for poor students and teachers.[7] Education provided the most common focus for clerical-lay collaboration, but it could coalesce around a variety of initiatives. One brotherhood, founded in a rural parish in Tver' in 1901, provided financial support for a local clinic and a firefighter society.[8] In addition to their increasing participation in brotherhoods, many Orthodox laypeople had come to benefit from clerical mutual aid institutions, extended to them by their pastors. An obituary for one Moscow priest in 1903, for example, mentions that he administered a shelter both for elderly servants of the Church and for the poor in general.[9] The expansion of the clerical networks to lay communities depended both on the organizational initiative of the clergy and on the willingness of the laity to support these networks financially. The need to maintain the latter undoubtedly served as an important motivation for the former, yet clerical initiative was also driven by a changing perception of the pastoral office (*san*) as a position of social leadership.

Lay participation in clerical associations was encouraged by trust in the reliability of clerical institutions as conduits of philanthropic aid, which the famine relief campaign had helped establish. As the population became more mobile with the growth of urban centers, this participation came to transcend both estate and geographical boundaries. Moreover, it was not only nobles and merchants who entrusted the clergy with their charitable contributions to the lower classes. Peasantry and townspeople had also begun to use the clerical networks to engage in philanthropy beyond their immediate communities. The clergy helped groups and individuals send donations from urban centers to rural parishes and even across provincial boundaries. The case of a donation in 1909 by two Moscow townspeople (*meshchane*), formerly peasants, for the welfare of their old parish in Tver' serves as an example.

For the use and salvation of souls close to ours, those most in need, we have decided to make a donation to the parish church where we were once parishioners, of a government bond certificate at 4% interest for one thousand rubles. . . . We ask the Tver' consistory to comply with our wishes as follows: . . . The interest earned from the bond should be used to help poor parishioners of this church, especially old women who cannot work, widows with young children, and victims of natural disasters, fires, and floods. These allowances should be granted by the local church council and especially by the priest and church elder. An annual report should be presented to the consistory on the distribution of allowances.[10]

The letter reveals the donors' trust in the clergy's integrity and competence to administer their grant. This trust was inspired by the clergy's reliable custodianship over such endowments. In 1902, for example, the Tver' consistory received a complaint regarding a shelter for elderly women that a parishioner had established in the city of Staritsa in 1890. The complaint alleged that the priest who administered the shelter was neglecting its seven residents and, more importantly, refused to surrender the shelter's funds to the founder's family, of whom the complainant was a member. This resulted in two visits to the shelter by priests, which uncovered no evidence of neglect. The local priest and his wife continued to maintain the shelter by purchasing supplies, storing them, and preparing three meals a day for its residents.[11] Both voluntarism—the willingness of pastors to perform social services for little or no compensation—and vigilance against corruption were necessary for the attraction of lay participation in the expansion of the clerical network.

As their network grew, the parish clergy found Pobedonostsev's synodal administration increasingly oppressive. As discussed in the previous chapter, the synodal system provided the pastorate with protection (one could use the modern Russian term *krysha*) from the secular bureaucracy. Yet the Synod had its own lay bureaucracy that tied ecclesiastical administration to the imperial state. The examples above illustrate the potential benefits of the ecclesiastical bureaucracy. The consistory could provide oversight of charitable operations, accept complaints of pastoral malfeasance, and conduct investigations, all of which enhanced the parish clergy's credibility in the eyes of the laity. The strict subjugation of all pastoral initiatives, however, to the oversight of consistory bureaucrats, acting in the name of the bishop's apostolic authority, obstructed much of the clergy's work. To cite one example, the brotherhood of Mary Magdalene in the town of Ruza applied to the Moscow consistory for permission to purchase a building to provide better accommodations for a parish school, then housed in a run-down structure. The request was rejected on the grounds that property ownership was not included in the brotherhood's charter.

Thus, another application was submitted to revise the charter. The entire process of revision and reapplication took almost two years.[12] Pobedonostsev's policy of restricting all unsupervised collaboration among clergymen had further inhibited the effectiveness of the clerical network. In September 1892, delegates to Moscow's diocesan congress complained to their prelate, Metropolitan Leontii (Lebedinskii), that they had insufficient knowledge of the relative financial needs of the ecclesiastical schools throughout the diocese because of the 1884 abolition of district congresses. The metropolitan, nevertheless, denied the delegates' request to hold these assemblies, replying that written reports from school administrators should be sufficient.[13] Pobedonostsev's own reinstatement of the district congresses in 1896 amounted to a tacit acknowledgement of local initiative as necessary for his own vision of the Church as a prominent social force.

The partial restoration of the clergy's reform-era freedom of association was clearly linked to the accomplishments of the clerical networks in the early twentieth century. The district congresses not only facilitated more informed decisions by the diocesan congresses but also allowed the parish clergy to form new associations at the level of the school district. In July 1905, an article in *Tserkovnyi vestnik*, a journal published by the Saint Petersburg Theological Academy, reported the organization of mutual aid societies, shelters, and charities by local congresses throughout the empire.[14] District congresses submitted reports to the diocesan level of the formation of various local societies, such as life insurance cooperatives.[15] Clerical assemblies at all levels continued to organize cooperative institutions for all estates, including shelters for the elderly, charitable funds, parish schools, and libraries.[16] This work altered the clergy's perception of their social position. If the Tver' priest I. S. Belliustin had expressed a half century earlier the frustrated desire of most clergy for the government to secure their pastoral authority by remunerating their service to the state, the parish clergy of the early twentieth century now called for the freedom to help themselves. A parish priest's 1907 letter to Metropolitan Vladimir (Bogoiavlenskii) of Moscow typified this attitude. The priest argued that funding shortfalls in the diocese's schools necessitated a diocesan congress. "It is an unavoidable truth that if we ourselves do not come up with the funds to improve our appalling educational conditions, then no one else will give them to us."[17] This new understanding of the parish clergy and their work was shared by much of the monastic hierarchy.

By the early twentieth century, most bishops perceived the diocesan congresses and other clerical associations as effective institutions of ecclesiastical administration. Many prelates used their personal authority within their episcopal sees to entrust the diocesan congresses with a broader array of responsibilities than the financial matters to which they were confined by synodal decree. Some even endowed the congresses with formal authority. The bishop of Vladivostok institutionalized the congresses as "an accomplice of the diocesan authorities in carrying out all the principles on which the life of the clergy and the parish should be based.... In light of their significant position, the decisions of the diocesan congress, upon confirmation by the diocesan authorities, assume legal status for the entire diocese."[18] Other prelates, however, perceived a challenge to their own apostolic authority in the diocesan congresses and routinely obstructed their activity so as to "put them in their place."[19] These prelates forbade the assemblies from assuming responsibilities that were not specifically assigned to them in the seminary charter. The parish clergy of Vyatka became so frustrated with their bishop's suppression of their congresses that they sent a delegation to Saint Petersburg in 1907 to petition the Synod to endorse their right to assemble and overrule their bishop.[20] While this action was, of course, unsuccessful, it reflected a growing perception among the parish clergy of their right to assembly and collaboration as an essential component of their pastoral status.

Community leadership through voluntary associations was coming to be recognized throughout the Church as an integral component of pastoral work rather than simply the convenient method of diocesan administration to which it had been reduced under Pobedonostsev's leadership. The first revival of "pastoral assemblies" took place in the capital, under the auspices of the Society for Moral and Religious Enlightenment, an organization founded in Saint Petersburg in 1881 to help the city's clergy to compete with the Protestant missionary and Baron of Radstock, Granville Waldegrade, and his followers among the educated classes in the capital. The society sponsored lectures, gatherings, and charitable initiatives similar to those organized by the "Pashkovites," named after Vasilii Pashkov, one of the Protestant leaders. In 1895, Metropolitan Palladii (Raev) successfully petitioned the Synod for a modification of the Society's charter to specifically permit its members to host conferences for all the clergy of the city. The scope of discussion at these conferences was to include the general state of religious morals among parishioners, social problems affecting these morals, sectarian religious movements, and pastoral measures to be taken in response to these issues.[21] While the Saint Petersburg conferences set an important precedent for the official recognition of pastoral assemblies, they were confined to the urban clergy of the capital. A more extensive revival of this practice took place at the initiative of Metropolitan Flavian (Gorodetskii) of Kiev, who convened a pastoral assembly for all the clergy of his diocesan capital in September 1903. He then drew up his own statutes for subsequent assemblies in which he stipulated that they would be open to all clergy of the diocese. At his encouragement, expressed in an article in Kiev's diocesan press, subsequent assemblies were held in superintendent districts throughout the diocese.[22] In his declaration of the commencement of pastoral assemblies, Flavian identified collaborative pastoral work as a form of clerical mutual aid.

> Pastoral work now presents demands, which not every pastor can meet, regardless of his energy or knowledge. Does not the struggle with sectarianism, for example, demand the close cooperation of pastors? Does not the development of common measures through which to better influence parishioners demand discussion and brotherly agreement among pastors? Does not care for the poor and sick, for the material and spiritual aspects of their lives, demand such cooperation, not to mention the general need for a brotherly exchange of ideas, views, and experience among pastors? If pastoral mutual aid [*pastyrskaia vzaimopomoshch'*] is ever appropriate and applicable, it is in matters of the enlightenment of the popular masses among all classes in the light of Christian faith.[23]

Flavian's words tied the mutual aid practices of the clerical estate to the religious duty of the pastoral office. The political upheaval of the next years would solidify this perception of pastoral work as a collaborative project throughout the Church.

Pobedonostsev's bureaucratic intransigence ultimately provoked a temporary alliance among the parish clergy, monastic hierarchy, and even members of liberal society in favor of greater independence of the Church from the state. In 1901, an article appeared in the Orthodox journal *Vera i razum* written by a "former clergyman," who declared that the Church had been subjugated by the Russian state since the reforms of Peter I. This journal was overseen and censored by Bishop Amvrosii (Kliucharev) of Kharkov and its publication of this article amounted to a declaration of dissent on his part.[24] Other publications overseen by the hierarchy and the theological academies began to relax censorship on criticism of the synodal system, and subsequent years saw increasingly bold denunciations of the Church bureaucracy and of Pobedonostsev himself throughout the Church's extensive media empire.[25] Diocesan periodicals openly criticized official infringement on the independence of both black and white clergy, including the transfer of bishops between dioceses and the censorship of priests' sermons.[26] A pastoral assembly convened in Saint Petersburg in early 1905 to formulate a proposal for the convening of an All-Russian Church Sobor, which could bring about church reform independently of the state. This Group of Thirty-Two Saint Petersburg Priests, as they came to be known, brought their proposal to Metropolitan Antonii (Vadkovskii), who shared their view that the synodal bureaucracy was holding the Church back from its pastoral mission.[27] Antonii, in turn, found an ally in Count Sergey

Witte, then chairman of the Council of Ministers, who submitted a proposal for church reform to the council in February. Pobedonostsev was able to transfer this discussion to the Synod on the grounds that church reform lay beyond the jurisdiction of the Council of Ministers, in other words beyond the "secular domain," despite the fact that reform was meant to free the Church from state control.[28] In July 1905, Pobedonostsev issued Circular 3542 to all Orthodox bishops, soliciting their opinions on church reform, in the hope that they would support the synodal structure, in which they occupied privileged positions. To his surprise, their responses demonstrated nearly unanimous support for the reform or dismantling of the synodal system, possibly in favor of restoring the patriarchate.[29]

Pobedonostsev became a political casualty of the 1905 Revolution, but the synodal system did not. War and unrest served as pretexts to delay the proposed Sobor, which did not take place until after the fall of the Romanov regime in February 1917. The most significant structural change that the Church experienced after 1905 was the lifting of restrictions on the parish clergy's freedom of association. While bishops remained wary of the potential challenge that clerical assemblies presented to their ecclesiastical authority, many responses to Circular 3542 recognized the diocesan congresses as pastoral institutions. Metropolitan Vladimir of Moscow, for example, stated that "in regard to the affairs that fall under the purview of the congresses, it is desirable that their scope be broadened beyond the limits of mere economic issues so that the congresses may concern themselves with pastoral work as well."[30] On November 18, 1905, the Synod authorized all parish priests, with their bishop's approval, to hold pastoral assemblies at the superintendent district, regional district (*uezd*), and diocesan levels, and to include laity in these assemblies. It also authorized priests to invite up to twelve of their adult parishioners to form a parish council (*tserkovno-prikhodskii sovet*) to promote closer collaboration between clergy and laity. The Synod's decree was prefaced with the following explanation: "In these difficult days of great sorrow for the Russian realm, when the fatherland is betrayed and law and order are trampled upon, there arises a great and urgent need for close unity of pastor with parishioner and for constant collaboration among pastors."[31] After years of restriction and regulation, the Synod was now calling upon the parish clergy to expand their networks of free association in order to carry out the Church's social mission in the midst of the First Russian Revolution.

YEARS OF CRISIS AND FREEDOM

From 1905 until as late as 1908, the Russian Empire experienced a conjunction of several crises that nearly brought about its collapse. The first decade of

Nicholas II's reign had been marked by rising political tension, agrarian uprisings, urban strikes, and political assassinations. Upon his ascension to the throne in 1894, he immediately rebuffed the proposal of a group of liberals from Tver' for an expanded role for the zemstvos in Russia's governance as "senseless dreams," a phrase taken from Pobedonostsev, and asserted his unwavering commitment to autocracy.[32] This speech, together with repressive measures against local government, incensed zemstvo activists, who began holding informal meetings and illegal congresses in Moscow with the aim of organizing a national zemstvo assembly.[33] Meanwhile, the regime suffered a series of devastating defeats in the 1904–5 war with Japan that the public and the world had expected Russia to easily win, which encouraged political defiance on many fronts. The catalyst for open revolt came from the Church. Father Georgii Gapon, a Saint Petersburg pastor who had organized a workers' association tolerated by the authorities, led a church procession (*krestnyi khod*) to the Winter Palace on January 9, 1905, bearing a petition to the emperor. The petition's humbly and religiously worded pleas for political freedom and workers' rights appealed directly to the regime's own ideology of "Orthodoxy, Autocracy, and Nationality."[34] This made the subsequent disaster seem all the more of a betrayal by the monarchy of its own people. Troops deployed to contain the marchers panicked and fired upon the crowd at various points along the procession, inflicting more than one hundred casualties. News of the massacre, later dubbed "Bloody Sunday," spread quickly, fueling public outrage and an escalation of urban, rural, interethnic, terrorist, and random criminal violence.[35] Finally, severe food shortages in the countryside of the Central Black Earth region developed into an outright famine by the spring of 1906, completing the multifaceted humanitarian crisis.[36] Nicholas II managed to retain his throne only though political concessions, including the creation of Russia's first national parliament and the extension of religious freedom for the confessional minorities of the empire.

For the parish clergy, the 1905 crisis brought both hardship and opportunity. Violence and food shortages affected all servants of the church, many of whom had only the clerical networks to turn to for help. Moreover, the state once again called upon the clergy to divert their own resources to ease the suffering of the population by sheltering wounded soldiers and providing famine relief to peasants. Yet the pastorate's standing within the synodal system had changed significantly since 1891. The prelates publicly condemned Father Gapon immediately after his procession to the Winter Palace.[37] At the same time, leading bishops used the regime's instability to challenge the authority of the synodal bureaucracy over the Church. Pobedonostsev called the hierarchs "Gaponites" for their insistence on reform but ultimately resigned as ober-procurator on

October 19, 1905.[38] The official lifting of restrictions on pastoral assemblies took place a month later. Thus, the clerical networks were far less subject to centralized direction in the early twentieth century than they had been in 1891. The response of the clerical networks to the multiple crises of war, revolution, and famine, therefore, provide important insight into the understanding of the Church's pastoral mission throughout the ranks of the parish clergy.

WAR IN THE EAST

From Japan's surprise naval bombardment of Port Arthur on February 8, 1904, until Prime Minister Witte's official surrender of the Liaotung Peninsula and half of Sakhalin Island to Japan at Portsmouth, New Hampshire, on August 29, 1905, the Russian empire suffered an estimated 125,000 combat casualties.[39] The massive westward flow of wounded soldiers along the newly constructed Trans-Siberian Railway throughout the conflict put enormous strain on the empire's infrastructure. In the first year of the war, the government called on the Church to serve in its customary capacity as an auxiliary civil service. On April 29, 1904, the Synod decreed that all bishops within the military regions of Siberia, Kazan', Moscow, and Saint Petersburg should collect information from within their dioceses regarding the availability of beds and medical personnel in and around clerical institutions within comfortable distance of regional centers for the care of sick and wounded soldiers, evacuated from the Far East.[40] In formulating this decree, Pobedonostsev had acted at the request of Minister of War Viktor Sakharov for church facilities to house less seriously wounded soldiers in order to reduce overcrowding and to utilize local resources available for their support. Sakharov's letter to the ober-procurator stated that "if care for sick and wounded soldiers [by the Church] is not provided for by charity, then the treasury will provide compensation for this care."[41] As in 1891, Pobedonostsev pressured the bishops to place their diocesan communities at the state's service. Yet the war minister's appeal to pastoral charity implicitly recognized the clergy's ability to withhold their resources. In fact, the clerical networks did not enthusiastically support the highly unpopular war effort in the Far East.

The Moscow consistory circulated questionnaires on the availability of space for soldiers' clinics together with Sakharov's appeal on May 18. All respondents provided detailed information regarding the availability of doctors and hospitals in their localities and their exact distances from the railroad. Many of these facilities were attached to clerical schools, but some forms mention zemstvo, military, and private hospitals and doctors as well.[42] The appeal for charity elicited a much less consistent response. Many of Moscow's monasteries agreed to provide care and shelter for between ten and one hundred soldiers without compensation. These included Sergiev Posad, Bogoiavlenskii, Spaso-Andreev, Vysokopetrovskii, Znamenskii, Danilov, Pokrovskii, and Sretenskii monasteries.[43] Some institutions of the parish clergy also offered what they could. The Zvenigorod ecclesiastical school, for example, offered to house and support soldiers in two hospital rooms and four classrooms when lessons ended for the summer.[44] The parish staff and church elder of the cathedral church of the town of Bronnitsy offered the use of a building that was then being rented out at twenty-five rubles a month. They offered to provide fifteen beds, bedclothes, heating, and two changes of clothes for each patient. For food, medicine, and the cost of laundry, they requested financial aid.[45] In some less wealthy parishes, priests and parishioners offered the use of their own houses and what little they could provide for sick or wounded soldiers.[46] The majority of responses from parishes and clerical schools, however, included only the requested information and occasionally cited a lack of space and funds to support patients.

The participation of Moscow's pastorate in the evacuation of wounded soldiers demonstrated a growing distinction between their duties as auxiliary civil servants and their pastoral mission. The parish clergy would continue to perform state-mandated duties on a routine basis, such as this information-gathering task, and other basic social services, such as instructing parishioners in proper sanitary measures to prevent the spread of cholera.[47] Yet parish priests were now taking control of their own pastoral mission to society. They were defining that mission themselves, in dialogue with the lay communities on whose support and collaboration that mission relied. In the context of the war relief effort, the pastoral mission was typified by one priest in a parish of the town of the Bronnitsy district. In his report, Father Lebedev claimed to have initiated his relief project for soldiers before receiving the Ministry of War's appeal. He had assembled a diverse group of "good people," who agreed to fund and support a field hospital for the housing and care of six soldiers. These included a Moscow merchant, a zemstvo representative, the local train station administrator, four local shopkeepers, peasants from three villages, and the director of a local factory. In addition, the wife of a mechanic had donated linens, and two schoolteachers had agreed to serve as nurses.[48] Lebedev's work epitomized the clergy's voluntary performance of the kind of social activism that Pobedonostsev had encouraged and the potential for collaboration that such autonomous initiatives provided for members of all estates. In the context of the war effort, however, his actions were the exception. Most of the Moscow pastorate had accepted the Ministry of War's appeal as a civil service task. Their refusal to dedicate resources to the evacuation of soldiers demonstrated the emancipation of the pastoral mission from state control.

REVOLUTION

The clergy's response to another crisis of 1905, revolutionary violence, exemplified the blurring distinction between the mutual aid function of the clerical networks and their role as instruments of the pastoral mission. The anti-religious ideology of revolutionary activists directed violence against the Church in 1905. Clergy and church property across the empire became targets of vandals and terrorists during the height of the revolutionary frenzy.[49] Political agitators preached to the Orthodox population against their clergy, calling priests gendarmes, agents of the regime, and enemies of the people, and beseeching parishioners to cease all support for the Church.[50] A priest in Tver' reported an attempt on his life in October 1905, in which "a bullet missed him by an *arshin* [an arm's length]."[51] The hardship that this violence caused for the clergy was, for the most part, absorbed by the clerical networks. Destruction of clerical property was always a possibility, and the diocesan trusteeship existed to shelter clergymen from destitution in such circumstances or to provide care for their widows and orphans.[52] The concern was raised in the Synod, however, that victims of anti-religious violence on the margins of the clerical networks would not receive the support they needed, particularly church watchmen and their families. This position was often given to poor members of the clerical or peasant estates as a means to support themselves. A committee was formed in 1908 to find housing in orphanages for all children of church watchmen and "other lower servants of the Church who died at the hands of anarchist-thieves in the line of duty."[53] The parish clergy of Moscow diocese were ordered on June 13, 1908, to collect information on any cases fitting this description. Yet this initiative proved to be ineffectual. The Synod's criteria were overly narrow and based on a misperception of the effects of anti-religious violence on the Orthodox community.

Reports submitted to the Moscow consistory in response to the Synod's directive did not confirm the scenario that its authors had envisioned. Priests reported a small number of cases of murdered watchmen who left behind adult and elderly family members and suggested that funds be allocated for their support. One priest reported that a peasant who was killed defending a church from burglars was survived by an unmarried thirty-six-year-old daughter who "supports herself at this time through day labor. [She] Galkina has no inclination to live in any shelter for orphans, but would like some kind of grant to ease her material hardship."[54] Another priest reported the death of a peasant who served as a caretaker of monastery property, who was killed in a riot, leaving behind a widow and two small children.[55] This case fit neither the stipulation of having died "in the line of duty" nor that of children in need of an orphanage. Two other priests reported similar murders and the presence of family members who required aid but had no desire to give their children up to orphanages. Moscow's consistory submitted all this information to the ober-procurator on September 4.[56] There is no record of the Synod's response to these requests for aid.

The relief efforts initiated by Moscow's parish clergy themselves presented a striking contrast to the Synod's ineffectual response to anti-religious violence. Four archpriests and one layman formed Moscow's diocesan committee for the relief of victims of broadly defined "disturbances" in January 1906. This committee solicited donations from all the parishes and monasteries of the dioceses. These donations were consolidated in superintendent districts before being forwarded to the committee and totaled 142,839.16 rubles by October 1908. Parish priests, meanwhile, interviewed applicants for aid and recorded the circumstances in which they had been disabled or lost the head of their family to revolutionary violence. By the end of the campaign, the committee's funds had been distributed to 195 different families, most of which were identified as peasants or townspeople.[57] With this campaign, the Moscow clergy demonstrated the effectiveness of their networks at delivering humanitarian aid on the basis of local knowledge. The campaign also demonstrated the transfer of a substantial amount of money for use outside of the clerical community, at the initiative of clergy themselves. The departure from mutual aid exclusive to the clerical estate may have elicited more lay support for this initiative by presenting anti-religious violence as a common problem for both clergy and laity. This transition within the clerical networks from mutual aid for servants of the Church to more universal philanthropic care was evident on a much broader scale in the response to the largest humanitarian disaster of 1905.

FAMINE

Widespread crop failure and hunger directly affected a far greater proportion of the empire's population, including the clerical estate, than any other crisis of the revolutionary years. The parish clergy confronted the crop failure with the same autonomy as in the aforementioned relief campaigns. The Synod issued a directive on October 7, 1905, for all parish priests to begin holding weekly collections for donations for the families of wounded soldiers and to grant the Red Cross access to their churches to hold parallel collections for the relief of those stricken by crop failure for a period of one year.[58] The parish clergy, for the most part, disregarded these instructions and initiated independent relief campaigns in numerous dioceses for victims of the famine. Immediately after the Synod issued its instructions, Metropolitan Vladimir issued his own decree, establishing a diocesan relief committee in Moscow with famine relief as its primary focus.⁵⁹ The clergy of Tver' also initiated a famine relief campaign. Neither Tver' nor Moscow experienced substantial crop failure, yet the pastors of both dioceses organized the transferal of substantial sums of money from their own communities to famine victims in other dioceses.

The records of the famine relief effort in Moscow and Tver' reveal a decentralized humanitarian aid movement organized around local leadership. Whereas the parish clergy involved in famine relief in 1891 had been made to surrender control of aid distribution to a government committee in November of that year, the clerical committees that began relief work in 1905 retained control of their own distribution and were therefore free to choose the communities they wished to help. There were never any restrictions on communication between committees of different dioceses or between clerical and lay committees. Even local committees could bypass their own diocesan committee and send their donations directly to other provinces.⁶⁰ Clergymen could send their parishioners' contributions to their superintendent, to a local committee, or directly to the diocesan committee. Local committees were never ordered to disband and continued to operate into 1909, when they stopped receiving donations.

The relief efforts in Moscow and Tver' were also decentralized in terms of their impetus, deriving momentum from the clerical networks themselves. Again, in contrast to the 1891–92 campaign, the diocesan leadership did not demand reports or exert pressure on individual parishes to increase their collection of donations. Instead, the relief effort seems to have been driven by collective pressure. For example, the occasional publication of contributions in the diocesan press exposed the level of each parish's participation to the scrutiny of the diocesan community.⁶¹ Individual clergymen also drove the effort at the local level, from parish to parish, both soliciting donations from parishioners and leading by example. Donation records show that parish priests often supplied the largest individual donations among their parish's overall contributions. Poorer members of the clerical community such as deacons, sacristans, and communion bread bakers also contributed donations.⁶² By assuming collective leadership over this major relief effort, the parish clergy also guided its priorities. Records of the collaboration between the pastors of Moscow and Tver' with those of other dioceses reveal these priorities to have varied between a narrow focus on the clerical estate and a more universally philanthropic effort.

The clergy of some affected dioceses used their networks to channel outside aid to the sections of their own community that were most severely affected by the famine. Bishop Arkadii (Karpinskii) of Ryazan', for example, addressed a letter to Moscow's Vicar Bishop Serafim (Golubiatnikov), chairman of Moscow's relief committee, explaining that a requested sum of 1,500 rubles would be distributed to those people who were "most in need of material aid, due to their poverty and large families, for relief from the effects of the 1905 crop failure. These people have received no support either from the government or from the zemstvos." There followed a list of the names, positions, and parishes of 172 clergymen and orphans and widows of clergymen, grouped according to their superintendents for the collection and distribution of aid.[63] In his presentation of a similar list of needy clergy, the bishop of Tula surprisingly, and perhaps disingenuously, claimed that "the diocesan administration has no information on the needs of individuals outside of the spiritual domain."[64] The bishop of Orel simply asked that 1,500 rubles be donated to the trusteeship for poor clergy in his diocese.[65] It is not surprising that bishops and other members of diocesan consistories would concern themselves primarily with the plight of their parish clergymen and the orphans and widows of clerical origin. As Bishop Arkadii explained in another letter two years later, the peasantry would have to complete their own recovery from the crop failure before they could begin supporting their pastors again. In the meantime, these pastors and their families would have to get by somehow.[66] At the same time, the fact that Bishop Lavrentii (Nekrasov) of Tula felt compelled to explain his exclusion of the laity from the list of famine victims as the result of a lack of information suggests the expectation that the Church's efforts would be more universal.

The clergy of some dioceses used their networks to identify and deliver aid to remote or marginalized famine victims among the laity. Bishop Innokentii (Beliaev) of Tambov, for example, submitted a list of twenty peasant land societies (*sel'skie obshchestva*) across two rural districts "in greatest need of urgent help." He provided the names and addresses of eight different superintendents who could receive and distribute aid to those communities.[67] Clergy who chose to serve the laity thus employed the same kind of precision in allocating small but effective grants as they did in the distribution of aid within their own communities. In at least one case, priests provided relief for rootless urban poor, driven from the countryside by famine and bereft even of the support that a peasant commune could provide. One priest from Saratov, Father Chetvernikov, described his committee's use of a 500-ruble grant from the Moscow committee in a letter of thanks addressed to the latter.

> The money was received during Holy Week, at the most critical moment. That very week had marked the end of the city's drainage work, which had provided wages all winter for several hundred people from famine-stricken areas. All of these workers, together with their families, were left in Saratov without any means to support themselves, having been deprived of the pittance of 25 kopecks a day that the city had paid them. . . . In order to distribute aid grants more

effectively, the committee decided to directly collect information on those without work by sending members, usually parish priests, to visit their apartments. In doing so, members collected information on other impoverished people in this or that parish. They learned of an entire sea of poverty in the city of Saratov, huddled among ravines of Glebuchev and Beloglinskii. The following impressions, gathered by a committee member, present a clear picture of this poverty. 1) Potap Meshcheriakov is an unskilled worker with a family of six small children who gather wood chips from the ravines for kindling and rags to sell. Sometimes they beg alms. His wife is sick. She is unable to earn any wages, watch her small children, or support her family in any other way. Their home is a shanty without a bench or a bed. They owe 16 rubles for this dwelling. They were given a grant of 10 rubles. 2) Kirill Kuznetzov has a wife who is mentally ill, four children, and lives in terrible and depressing conditions. 3) Evgeniia Romanova is 40 years old, unmarried, and missing one arm. She has a 9-year-old girl and an infant. They live in indescribable poverty. They have no linens, only one dress, and no change of clothes. Their apartment is empty and cold, and the rent has not been paid for two months. She was given three rubles. . . . All the unemployed were issued grants from the committee of one to five rubles. More was given in cases of exceptional need or large families. The committee granted a total of 673 rubles and 6 kopecks to 192 families. 50 rubles were sent to one of Saratov's villages for the construction of a soup kitchen and a nursery. . . . In addition to grants of money, the committee rendered aid in kind (linens, shoes, clothes), paid rent on apartments, etc.[68]

The case of Saratov, in particular, demonstrated a transcendence of the mutual aid function of the clerical relief organizations. Unlike the peasantry, the urban poor had no economic relationship with the diocesan clergy, and their recovery, or at least survival, would render no material benefit to their parish priests. It was Saratov's Bishop Germogen (Dolganev) who called attention back to the needs of his clergy. In April 1908, he requested more aid from Moscow for seven clergymen, nine clerical widows, one former diocesan clerk, and four laymen whom "the diocesan committee has not been able to help."[69] Thus, the initiative to channel diocesan funds away from the clerical community seems to have originated among Saratov's parish clergy.

The clergy of unaffected dioceses, such as Moscow and Tver', had the choice of linking their relief efforts to the clerical networks of other dioceses or striving to organize a more universal relief campaign. For the clergy of Moscow, who occupied urban parishes and enjoyed access to wealthy donors, the contribution of aid to their fellow pastors in the hinterland of the diocese was a well-established duty. They were frequently reminded of this duty by Moscow's clerical mutual aid societies through the diocesan press: "We can only hope that the older and more prosperous members of the great family of Moscow clergy will show sympathy for the great needs of the rural clergy, their lesser brothers . . . in consideration of the enormous difference between their material and living conditions from their own."[70] The obligation of supporting poor clerical communities at a distance from their own was well established among the Moscow pastorate, and the extension of aid to lay communities was an outgrowth of that practice. An article in Moscow's diocesan press from February 1906 encapsulates the complexity of motivations behind the clergy's relief campaign. The author was a Moscow priest who related his observation of conditions in the famine-stricken dioceses of Samara and Kazan'.

> At a ceremony for the opening of a temporary children's shelter to feed and care for orphans, I heard one priest, almost unable to contain his anxiety, ask the assembled circle [of clergy] who ran the shelter if his children might be permitted to eat in the shelter's cafeteria that was supported by private donations. How can the clergy support themselves when those who support them, the peasants, have nothing for themselves! . . . Is it not our holy duty to provide them with support in their helpless sorrow and terrible need, and not only support through sympathy but also through the material relief of their difficult circumstances?[71]

In this appeal to his fellow pastors, the author pointed to the direct link between the material condition of the clergy and that of the peasants who supported them. He also described how a charitable institution, organized and run by the clergy for parishioners, could potentially support clerical families in desperate times. Yet the article's audience of Moscow priests had no more direct material connection to the communities in question than did their parishioners, who were much more likely to support a more universal relief effort. This "holy duty," therefore, was related but not confined to estate solidarity. While Moscow's priests funded relief efforts in Ryazan', Orel, and Tula that were limited to fellow clergymen, they also funded relief efforts for laity and gave two grants of 2,000 and 1,000 rubles to the all-zemstvo organization for famine relief in April 1908.[72] Cooperation with secular institutions demonstrated a conscious decision on the part of the Moscow clergy to extend the Church's relief effort to the whole of society.

For reasons that are not clear, the clergy of Tver' adopted a much more deliberate approach than their colleagues in Moscow to the question of whom their diocesan funds should be used to support. Almost every donation sent to Tver's diocesan committee came with instructions for its use. Shortly after the diocese launched its campaign in 1907, the consistory began issuing forms to every parish priest on which to record famine relief donations and to specify their intended use: for clergy or for laity. The recipients of Tver's donations in other dioceses were asked to honor these designations. In June 1907, for example, Kazan's diocesan committee reported to its counterpart in Tver' that, in accordance with the latter's specification, the funds it received had been divided between the trusteeship for poor clergy and a lay committee organized by Kazan's Academy for Women.[73] The records of the donations that flowed into the diocesan committee for the duration of the relief campaign are consolidated and remarkably complete. They provide an intriguing picture of Tver's entire relief campaign from January 1907 until December 1909. Over this period the committee received a total of 1,314.28 rubles for clerical communities and 1,873.09 rubles for lay communities in areas affected by crop failure.[74] Per capita, clerical famine victims received more relief from this contribution than non-clergy, the latter comprising a vastly larger portion of the population.[75] Nevertheless, more than half of the funds raised by clerical associations were diverted toward the relief of the nonclerical population. The details that emerge from these records suggest that local collaboration among parish clergymen and some parishioners served as the decisive factor in this outcome.

Tver's donation records do not suggest that the diocesan leadership drove the campaign to help the laity. Beyond his formal role in the collection of donations, the involvement of Tver's Bishop Aleksii (Opotskii) in the campaign was inconspicuous. He contributed two personal donations of 20 rubles for clergy and 24 rubles for laity. This sum, together with sixteen separate donations from the seminary rector, monasteries, and convents around the diocese brought the monastic clergy's overall contributions to 126.60 rubles for the clergy and 240.65 rubles for the laity, or 10 and 13 percent, respectively, of the diocese's total relief funds.[76] Moreover, there is no evidence that the diocesan leadership applied any pressure to the parish clergy to designate funds for the laity. On the contrary, the diocesan committee followed the instructions that were included with donation submissions even when, as in the case of the Kashin town committee, those instructions favored the clergy. When donations were submitted without instructions, the diocesan committee divided them evenly.[77] The decision of where donations were to be sent was made at the parish and district levels.

Influence over the relief campaign from the other end of the diocesan spectrum is harder to evaluate, as peasant parishioners left few documents expressing their wishes. Parishioner donations comprised the largest share of the Church's famine relief contributions, just as they composed the largest share of diocesan funds in general. The designation of tithes for use within the parish was agreed upon by the priest and the church elder, the parishioners' elected representative.

Yet parishioners had no platform from which to express their wishes regarding the use of church funds at the diocesan level. The fifty-nine individual parishes that sent their donations directly to the diocesan committee collectively designated 291.06 rubles for the relief of clerical communities affected by the famine and only 266.33 rubles for the relief of lay communities.[78] Yet the donation records may also reflect the beginning of a new assertiveness on the part of parishioners who expressed their wishes through parish councils, the lay assemblies that the Synod had authorized together with pastoral assemblies on November 18, 1905.[79] In 1907, three such councils contributed sums of 163.75 rubles, 157.75 rubles, and 6 rubles, all of which were designated for the laity.[80] When parishioners ceded authority over their contributions to a single church elder, priests were inclined to designate a slight majority of the relief funds they collected toward their fellow clergymen and their families. Yet, where parishioners engaged with their pastor regarding their donations, perhaps with the help of a parish council, the priest would likely have been obliged to respond to the priorities of his flock, such as the support of starving peasant communities.

The superintendent committees tipped the scales in favor of contributions to lay communities. The fifty-six contributions from superintendent districts amounted to 657.07 rubles for clergy and 1,093 rubles for the laity.[81] Although no further specification is given, the identification of a certain superintendenture as the source of a sizable contribution would seem to indicate that the surrounding parishes had consolidated their donations in the center of their district, the same administrative center that had been designated for pastoral assemblies. If individual priests seem to have been inclined to channel their parish's donations toward clerical communities, why would the superintendent have collectively designated such a large sum for the relief of the laity? One possible explanation is that these designations were made through consultation among pastors who had gathered to consolidate their parishes' donations, in other words, by pastoral assemblies. After 1905, moreover, these assemblies were permitted to include lay parishioners in their meetings. It may have been a combination of the mission that the pastoral councils promoted and the influence of lay representatives that prompted the superintendent committees to designate almost twice as much of their collective contributions for the relief of lay communities than for fellow clergymen, lending Tver's overall response to the famine a more universal character. This scenario suggests that broader and more diverse participation in clerical associations contributed to their transcendence of estate boundaries.

The parish clergy's main contribution to the 1905–9 famine relief effort was not purely quantitative. The significance for Tver' pastorate of the 3,187.37 rubles that the diocese collected for famine relief from 1907–9 may be grasped by comparing this figure with the financial statement submitted by Tver's diocesan administration to the Synod for the year 1906: 6,883.76 rubles of income from parish taxation.[82] The combined monetary contribution of all the diocesan committees was surely diminutive in comparison with the Second Duma's famine relief expenditures of 39.5 million rubles in 1907.[83] For more than a century prior, the parish clergy had relied on similarly limited resources, consolidated through social networks, to provide social security, education, and disaster relief for the poorest members of their estate. The freedom of Russia's first revolutionary years allowed those networks to expand and to formulate their own goals on the basis of discussion and cooperation at the local level. This freedom of association, a long-held desire of the parish clergy, elevated their status within the Church from obedient servants of the synodal hierarchy to community leaders. The pastorate expressed this new autonomy through multiple philanthropic initiatives, motivated in part by awareness of their continued reliance on the support of the Orthodox laity, for the continued existence and autonomy of their social networks. By extending humanitarian aid universally to those in need, clerical leaders may have hoped to elicit more active support and participation in their social networks from the laity. Famine relief and other pastoral initiatives that grew out of 1905 thus further expanded church-based free association beyond the confines of the clerical estate.

Conclusion

Pobedonostsev's two and a half decades as ober-procurator of the Holy Synod were formative years for the Orthodox pastorate. He envisioned a socially engaged pastorate, capable of fortifying Russia's traditional social order against the political trends that were infecting Russia from Western Europe. For Pobedonostsev, autocratic authority was the most honest form of government for Russia and the true source of solidarity among subjects of the emperor, while foreign trends such as parliamentarianism (*parlamentarizm*), the formation of interest groups, and elected representation were alien, hypocritical, and divisive.[84] Yet, by tasking the parish clergy with confronting the social traumas of modernization in order to curb these tendencies, Pobedonostsev inadvertently empowered them to aspire to those very freedoms to which he objected. In order to meet the responsibility of organizing communities to resist poverty and disaster, the parish clergy required the freedom to form voluntary associations capable of collective action through democratic decision-making. These were practical measures to strengthen the Church's influence throughout society that were based on the clerical estate's own system of mutual aid, not foreign models. However, when conservative bishops endorsed the use of pastoral assemblies and parish councils to calm the restive population in 1905, they implicitly acknowledged a shift in leadership of the Church's social mission from the direction of the Synod to the decentralized, collaborative organization of the parish clergy.

While church reform was driven by the common desire among both parish and monastic clergy to break free of Pobedonostsev's stifling regime of surveillance and control, the ober-procurator's contribution to the pastoral movement should not be overlooked. The expansion of the parish clergy's social support networks to benefit other estates was a natural consequence of their material dependence on the laity. Yet Pobedonostsev's promotion of pastoral activism converted that gradual process into a movement. His initiation of the 1891–92 famine relief effort, together with other philanthropic campaigns, established the parish clergy as community organizers. These campaigns built public trust in the clergy's charitable networks and increased lay participation in them. These developments created a change in the nature of pastoral work. Rather than performing their various duties in exchange for the passive contributions of parishioners, parish priests began to seek their active collaboration. As in 1891, the parish clergy carried out the philanthropic campaigns of 1905 voluntarily and without compensation. Whereas the former was directed by the Synod, the multiple campaigns of 1905 were organized around collaborative initiatives with lay supporters. While the aims of these initiatives were varied, the data from Tver' suggests that more active participation by parishioners contributed to a more universal philanthropic focus. All these initiatives expressed the common goal of the pastoral movement to establish sustained lay participation in clerical associations as a regular religious practice in Orthodox Russia.

3

Revolt in the Seminaries

On December 7, 1906, the inspector of Moscow Seminary received a phone call from the Third Tverskoi Police Precinct of Moscow. The The caller, a student of the seminary's fourth grade named Aleksandr Druzhinin, had been arrested at a performance of Nikolay Gogol's *Government Inspector* at the Malyi Theater. The national hymn had been sung before the performance, after which some in the audience shouted "Again! Again!," and others shouted "Enough!" As part of the latter group, the young man had been apprehended for "disturbing the peace." In their recorded deliberations for submission to the Holy Synod, the inspector, rector, and other members of the seminary's pedagogical assembly made numerous arguments in the student's defense. They quoted a synodal decree from 1881, urging the utmost caution and consideration before expelling a student "in light of the difficult circumstances to which a student will be exposed outside the school walls upon expulsion from seminary." The assembly said nothing in favor of expelling the student. After building their case in his defense, they made note of Druzhinin's expulsion.[1] The impetuosity of clerical youth often resulted in tragic consequences for them and their families, especially when the political implications of their behavior removed them from the jurisdiction and protection of the spiritual domain. In some cases, however, the youthful protests of seminary students gave voice to the political aspirations of the entire clerical community.

Even as the parish clergy led the Church's response to the calamities of war, revolution, and famine, their own sons took part in the widespread social protest of 1905. In October and November of that year, seminary students throughout the empire began a general boycott of all classes and studies. The Church's entire seminary network was shut down until January 1906. This strike was both a component of the 1905 Revolution and a continuation of decades of seminarian dissent. Unrest had grown out of the squalid and often brutal environment of the Church's school system. By the late nineteenth century, it had coalesced into a movement in opposition to the restrictions that the Synod placed on the seminary, particularly the prohibition against seminary graduates from enrolling in secular universities as well as the ban on students from nonclerical estates from entering the seminaries. Radical political ideology influenced and inspired many seminarians, some of whom embraced materialist philosophy and turned against the Church entirely. Seminarians were particularly active in the Populist movement of the 1870s and 1880s.[2] Yet seminarian protests also expressed the priorities of the entire seminary community and sometimes received support from clergy and faculty. The 1905 seminary strike provided the broader clerical community with the opportunity to demand greater autonomy for clerical schools and the associations that supported them as well as the right to choose one's membership in either. The reforms that followed weakened the estate boundaries that circumscribed the clerical community and contributed to the redefinition of pastoral work as voluntary and inclusive.

This chapter begins with an examination of the seminary as an institution at the heart of the clerical community. The seminary formed the original focus of the clerical network, the collective efforts of which shaped pastoral work as profoundly as the education that it existed to support. The clerical networks of Moscow and Tver' supported two of Russia's largest seminaries. During the 1905–6 academic year, Moscow Seminary and Tver' Seminary contained 593 and 625 students, respectively, making Tver' Seminary the largest in the empire. Moscow diocese also supported Bethlehem Seminary, with 282 students.[3] These schools were located near the center of the seminarian protest network, Moscow Theological Academy being the site of the seminarian union's third empire-wide congress. This chapter considers the specific policies of the "counter-reform" era that gave rise to the grievances behind the seminarian movement. It then provides an overview of seminarian protest as an empire-wide phenomenon, from its origins up to the formation of an organized movement. It outlines points of agreement between the seminarian protestors and the clerical community and the results of their temporary convergence in 1905. Finally, this chapter examines the influence of radical ideology on seminarian protest, including its eventual alienation of the movement from the broader seminarian and clerical communities through terrorism.

Estate and Education

The provision of seminary education for their frequently numerous sons constituted the primary financial concern for most parish clergymen since without this education clerical offspring could hope for neither ordination nor secular employment other than agricultural labor. In his autobiography, Metropolitan Evlogii described the humiliating experience for his father, a parish priest, of going into debt with a local *kulak*, or rich peasant, in order to send his son to seminary in 1877.[4] Since the reign of Peter I, the tsarist regime had subsidized the seminaries so as to elevate the general level of education among the Orthodox pastorate. Yet, because state support was never sufficient to meet all the seminary's needs, the clergy of each diocese were forced to pool their meager resources in order to compensate for funding shortfalls and to secure a future for their children. The archival records of Moscow and Tver' reveal the variety of necessities to which these pooled resources were dedicated. These included the compensation of instructors for teaching the growing number of students whose basic tuition was not funded by the state in "parallel classes." These funds provided room and board for students whose families could not afford it, paid the salaries of the medical staff of the seminary clinic, and purchased books for the seminary library.[5] In a report to the emperor, the ober-procurator estimated that the clergy of Moscow and Tver' paid, respectively, 52 and 26 out of the 260 and 164 rubles spent on each seminary student in their dioceses in 1907.[6] The parish clergy provided all funding for the ecclesiastical schools (*dukhovnye uchilishcha*) that prepared children for seminary. In order to retain these pooled resources for the Church, in 1826 the Holy Synod restricted the admission of boys from nonclerical families into the seminary system.[7] This act marked the legal segregation of the clergy into a hereditary estate. It exacerbated the frequently lambasted "caste isolation" of clerical families from the rest of society.[8] These legal boundaries were porous, however, and subject to fluctuation. A more formative influence on clerical identity than estate was the seminary— and the culture of mutual aid that sustained it.

The seminary was, itself, a mutual aid society. As of 1884, seminary teachers received 700 rubles a year for up to twelve weekly lessons during their first five years of service, after which they received 900 a year.[9] An article in *Pravoslavnoe obozrenie* on the material conditions of seminary and church school teachers in 1885 estimated their cost of living in the provincial capitals to be significantly higher than what this salary could support, "no less than 1,460 rubles a year."[10] Teachers depended on bonuses to their salaries, obtained from charitable contributions, as a form of social support, and these bonuses were often redistributed in cases of great need. In November 1908, for example, the Moscow pedagogical committee resolved to grant a portion of the yearly bonus money, 239 rubles, to a former teacher to ease his poverty and chronic illness, meaning that there would be three instead of four bonuses to be given out at the end of the year.[11] Such grants were also extended to seminary employees, such as the school's medical orderly, and to the families of deceased teachers, all in cases of extreme need and at the cost of faculty bonuses.[12] This culture of mutual aid was not confined to the "clerical caste." A percentage of the faculty, usually teachers of science and mathematics, as well as other seminary employees, came from outside the estate.[13]

Collective support was also extended to poor students. Parish clergy and faculty members organized charities to provide poor seminarians with food and clothes and to pay for their transportation from rural parishes to the provincial capitals where the seminaries were located.[14] Widows of clergyman usually had no trouble obtaining full support in ecclesiastical schools and seminaries for their numerous children.[15] The mother of one Moscow seminarian was given 25 rubles after she exhausted her own resources in the attempt to treat his ultimately fatal illness.[16] Wealthier priests with good positions in the city and members of the monastic hierarchy could donate significant sums. The yearly 38 rubles of interest from a 1,000-ruble donation from a Moscow archpriest, for example, was designated for the poorest members of the graduating class of Moscow Seminary in 1907.[17] In 1912, the widow of a Moscow archpriest presented the seminary with 300 rubles, "only to be spent on the needs of poor students."[18] In 1914, Archbishop Nikon (Rozhdestvenskii), a member of the Synod and the State Council, donated 5,000 rubles to Moscow Seminary to aid poor students. He remarked, "I consider myself indebted, both morally and materially, to my native seminary."[19] Indeed, the moral and material components of this education were connected. The system of collective support that permeated the seminary profoundly influenced the moral and religious culture of the pastorate that it trained.

The estate isolation of the parish clergy came under critical scrutiny during the reform era, as did much of imperial Russia's social structure. While this system had been effective at encouraging mutual aid, critics argued that the parish clergy should not be composed of young men who chose ordination for lack of a better alternative. Since Peter I's ecclesiastical reform, male members of the clerical estate who could not find employment in church service were periodically conscripted into the military or reassigned to the poll tax–paying peasantry. By the early nineteenth century, enough seminaries had been established to make graduation from one of them a prerequisite for ordination.[20] While the occasional Mikhail Speranskii was recognized among seminarians for his talent and accepted into state service, most seminary graduates competed for the limited number of clerical positions in order to escape material hardship. In 1861, Petr Valuev, minister of internal affairs under Alexander II, initiated discussion of church reform, including abolition of the clerical estate as a means of raising the social status and morale of the parish clergy. In 1867, the Synod passed a new seminary charter, which authorized the enrollment of students from all estates in the hope of training a more diverse pastorate. At the same time, access to secular universities without passing an entrance exam was opened to students who completed at least four out of six years of seminary education.[21] Meanwhile, a joint commission of church and state officials tasked with church reform deliberated the estate question until 1869, when it submitted legislation to the State Council granting the status of "personal noble" to the sons of priests and of "honored citizen" for the sons of unordained sacristans, allowing them to seek careers outside of church service without fear of social demotion into the tax-paying peasantry.[22] In provincial towns, after only two or three years of seminary education, the sons of clergymen could seek employment in post offices, city administrations, courts, and schools.[23] In anticipation of a smaller number of students enrolling in seminary to pursue ordination, government funding was reduced. Funding for "parallel classes" as well as for the ecclesiastical schools that prepared boys for seminary would now have to come from parish collections and from the parish clergy's own resources.[24]

The net effect of the 1860s church reforms was not to convert the seminary into a smaller institution focused on the pastoral calling but to expand it into a more general educational institution that was even more reliant on mutual aid. The many clerical sons who chose to pursue secular careers after the reform were not balanced by equivalent numbers of students from other estates (*inososlovnye*) who felt called to the pastorate. Occasionally peasants entered the seminary in order to pursue ordination, but the life of a parish clergyman was not attractive for most nonclerical families.[25] How, then, could priests ask parishioners to continue making contributions to the diocesan seminary, whose function was no longer exclusively to train clergymen? One solution was to make the seminary a source of education for impoverished children. In 1877, for example, a widowed peasant from Arkhangelsk gubernia sold all her possessions and took her only son to Moscow to stay with relatives before dying the same year. The boy was enrolled in Moscow's Bethlehem Seminary on a full scholarship and later became a teacher of catechism.[26] Such charitable enrollments played a role in the Church's humanitarian relief campaigns, such as the acceptance of the orphans of soldiers who died in the war with Japan into seminaries throughout the empire.[27] Scholarships were offered to students who were already in the Church's care, such as the ten "children from impoverished families" who were accepted into Moscow Seminary in 1908 from the synodal school of liturgical singing.[28] Charity was also extended to foreign students, such as one Serbian seminarian in Moscow who could not support himself.[29] These enrollments put additional strain on the clergy's educational resources, which were already stretched by the reduction of state funding. Yet they also allowed the seminary to perform a charitable function for those lay communities that had provided those resources to begin with. Like the delivery of humanitarian relief to lay communities, the acceptance of poor children from other estates into the seminary was a means of involving the Orthodox laity in the diocesan mutual aid network. These efforts were expressions of the pastoral movement to instill cooperative social support into popular religious practice.

In August 1906, a law student from Moscow University wrote to Metropolitan Vladimir, asking for permission to take a seminary exam for ordination as a priest: "Having completed my course of study at First Moscow Gymnasium this year, I became a student at Imperial Moscow University. But I feel a greater calling to the clerical profession and want to serve the Church of God as a priest. I therefore dare to ask Your Most Holiness to permit me to take the necessary exam for the right to seek ordination as a priest at some rural church under Your administration in the Moscow diocese."[30] Those very few students of means who wanted to be priests could forgo seminary altogether. They were educated in Christianity at more comfortable secular schools and had only to prove their qualification for ordination by taking a seminary exam. Moscow Seminary administered only six such exams between 1906 and 1909. Four other university students and one professional artist left secular careers for more difficult lives as priests.[31] The vast majority of Russia's Orthodox pastors would continue to be drawn from the clerical estate and recruited from the seminaries. The reforms of the 1860s made ordination more of an individual choice for seminary graduates. This individual choice, however, was inextricably linked with the broader clerical and lay communities and their voluntary support for the seminary.

Oppression and Counter-Reform

The Synod, and through it the state, regulated seminary life in order to mold pastors into reliable agents of central authority. Since plans for the seminary were laid out in Peter I's Spiritual Regulation, successive emperors and empresses had supported the institution in the belief that it would train a more useful and loyal pastorate.[32] To ensure this outcome, state authorities closely monitored the seminaries for any sign of political dissent. The police and the Ministry of Education routinely submitted lists of "politically unreliable" seminary graduates to the diocesan consistories with instructions to bar those individuals from employment in church service.[33] Collective punishment could also be inflicted on entire seminaries. All students of Vologda and Saratov Seminaries were denied access to the theological academies and any other institutions of higher education in 1869 and 1875, respectively, after recent graduates of these institutions were convicted of engaging in radical propaganda.[34] These political offenses could be as petty as an incautious comment, such as in the case of a young seminary graduate who was overheard, while onboard a train, criticizing General Kuropatkin's performance in the war against Japan and was barred from the priesthood forever.[35] Like many government policies, this did not produce the desired effect. The efforts of the state and synodal authorities to control the social and intellectual resources of the seminary provoked resentment and resistance. The clerical community typically offered passive resistance to unpopular policies, such as concealing the infractions of seminarians from the Synod.[36] The clerical youth, however, were prone to more open forms of protest.

The synodal authorities regulated the intellectual life of the seminary, often to suit the priorities of the state. This was the case during the tenure of the domineering Count Nikolai Protasov as ober-procurator (1836–55), who pushed through a reform of the seminary curriculum to emphasize "practical subjects," such as medicine and agronomy, at the expense of philosophy and theology.[37] The reading material available to students was regulated according to the priorities of successive synodal administrations, but tight censorship was the norm. In reaction to these restrictions, clandestine student groups were formed in almost every seminary for the purpose of self-education in forbidden materials, and these groups were often unofficially tolerated by the seminary faculty. Metropolitan Evlogii, who served as inspector of Vladimir Seminary from 1895 to 1897 and rector of Kholm Seminary from 1897 to 1902, expressed sympathy in his autobiography for those students who maintained secret libraries: "I understood why they took up Uspenskii, Zlatovratskii, and so on. In illegal literature they found at least imaginary satisfaction of their desire for a just and bright existence."[38] Intellectual revolt was not confined to any particular political orientation. Some illegal seminarian libraries were found to contain a variety of illicit material, such as the religious writings of Lev Tolstoy and the historical lectures of Vasilii Kliuchevskii, together with socialist-revolutionary tracts.[39] Intellectual dissent became ingrained in the seminary system and was not confined to the student body.

In the final decades of the nineteenth century, the Synod moved to reclaim control over the resources and administration of the seminary that it had partially relinquished in the 1860s. Concern over the departure of many clerical youth from church service prompted Ober-procurator Aleksandr Tolstoi to revoke in 1878 the right of seminarians to enter secular universities without passing an entrance exam.[40] He was replaced the following year by Konstantin Pobedonostsev, who was determined to counteract the secularization of the seminaries. Pobedonostsev pushed through another seminary charter in 1884, which reformed the curriculum to focus on religion. It tightened censorship of unapproved literature and made religious observance mandatory.[41] This curricular reform would make it more difficult for seminarians to transition to secular education. Pobedonostsev was also determined to reconstitute the clerical population as a service estate for the Church. In 1898, his educational commission in the Synod proposed that the number of students of nonclerical origin in the seminaries should be reduced, arguing that these students from other estates were merely exploiting the Church's school system to escape military service and obtain a free education. The Synod passed a decree in March 1900 that limited the maximum number of non-clergy in any seminary to 10 percent of the student body and obliged these students to pay forty rubles a year in tuition.[42] These "counter-reforms" in the Church were converting pastoral service back into a caste obligation.

Pobedonostsev's counter-reforms minimized the participation of the clerical community in seminary administration and concentrated power in the hands of the bishop. The 1884 charter was drawn up in less than a month by a closed committee chaired by Metropolitan Ioannikii of Moscow. This was in stark contrast with the 1867 seminary charter, which was composed after years of debate and solicitation of opinions from parish clergymen throughout the empire.[43] The rector, a member of the monastic clergy, and the lay inspector, who was responsible for supervising student behavior and morals, were no longer to be elected by their colleagues but appointed instead by the bishop. The rector chaired the pedagogical council, which consisted of the inspector, two clergymen elected by the diocesan congress, and three teachers appointed by the bishop. The seminary's governing structure, therefore, was made accountable to the diocesan bishop and Synod rather than to the faculty or clerical community. Moreover, as discussed in chapter 1, the 1884 charter restricted the function of the diocesan congresses to financial matters and abolished local congresses altogether.[44] The seminarians were not the only ones, therefore, with cause to resent the system imposed on them, and their revolts sometimes expressed broader, clerical discontent.

SEMINARIAN PROTEST

Seminary protests were an empire-wide phenomenon, the roots of which stretched back to the early nineteenth century, well before the "counter-reforms." Violence in the seminaries was a byproduct of the poverty that the parish clergy struggled to manage in the education of their children. Upon leaving home for the first time at age fourteen, young seminarians found themselves in overcrowded and even filthy conditions.[45] Overwhelmed supervisors often controlled clerical youth with violence or left younger students at the mercy of the older. Conditions outside the dormitories could be even worse. An inspector's report from Tver' Seminary in 1848 complained that drunks and brawlers infested one street on which students lived and that supervisory visits to these residences were dangerous for the inspector himself.[46] Violence from outsiders, among seminarians, and from teachers created an environment that occasionally produced physical protest against the seminary. In 1830, Tver' Seminary students attempted to ambush and shoot their bishop in retaliation for him having imposed strict disciplinary policies during their exams.[47] Over subsequent decades, these revolts received guidance from a variety of political influences.

Policies to reestablish estate boundaries and force clerical youth into church service galvanized seminarian protest into a movement. The first terrorist bombing took place in Voronezh Seminary in 1879, immediately after the closure of easy access to secular universities for seminary graduates.[48] In 1901, dissidents were able to coordinate simultaneous riots in the seminaries of Tula, Kaluga, Orel, Ryazan', Irkutsk, and Kazan'.[49] This growing movement was drawn in many different directions by the political ideologies of the time. Bombings in Tiflis Seminary between 1886 and 1905 were connected with the Georgian nationalist movement.[50] Riots in Poltava Seminary in 1900 were associated with Ukrainian nationalism.[51] In 1900, some seminarians in Tver' attended Marxist readings and carried out agitation among textile workers.[52]

Alongside the more destructive expressions of seminarian discontent, there arose a petition movement that seems, in some cases, to have been supported or even guided by faculty or clergy. The first formal articulation of grievances by the seminarian movement was drawn up by a charitable organization for poor seminarians in Tula. In 1900, its members wrote a letter to the Synod that identified the source of disturbances in Tula Seminary to have been oppressive regulations, especially the prohibition of seminary graduates from entering secular universities. Tula's bishop, Pitirim, endorsed this letter.[53] In 1901, a police report on the students of Tver' Seminary provided a list of mischievous deeds, including breaking windows and mailing high-ranking church officials caricatures of themselves, but also the submission of a petition to the seminary administration asking that living conditions be improved.[54] Seminarians began organizing clandestine assemblies in 1901, which drew up petitions for submission to the Synod with threats to call a general strike if their demands were not met. Parish clergymen participated in the composition of at least some of these petitions, most notably in Yaroslavl' and Samara.[55] While radical groups carried out violent attacks against the seminaries, the petition movement expressed practical and political aspirations of the entire clerical community. For this reason, the petition movement attracted broader and more lasting support.

The student petitions, composed at both individual seminaries and inter-seminary conferences, displayed similar features. Typical demands were more lenient discipline, easier access to universities, and a general secularization of the curriculum to include greater emphasis on modern languages, mathematics, and the natural sciences.[56] Yet theology was also included in the desired curriculum, indicating that petitioners continued to identify the seminary as a religious school. Moreover, many of the petitioners' typical demands expressed the priorities of the entire seminary community. These included the right of students to form their own mutual aid societies and the restoration of access to the pedagogical council for the students' parents.[57] A demand that was common to all petitions was an end to the caste isolation of the seminary: "Entry should be open to all without restrictions on estate (soslovie) or racial origin."[58] The elimination of estate criteria for enrollment was demanded in one of the first inter-seminary petitions, drawn up at Tambov Seminary in 1901.[59] The first all-seminarian congress, held in Vladimir in June 1905 and attended by representatives from Astrakhan, Vladimir, Vyatka, Don, Irkutsk, Mogilev, Perm', Saratov, and Tver', also cited "caste isolation" as a grievance.[60] This consistent demand for unrestricted access to the seminaries did not serve the petitioners' immediate interests but was motivated by the desire to elevate the dignity of the clerical estate. One underground seminarian journal from Saratov published a satirical portrait of the life of a parish priest in 1906, which lampooned his dependence on the laity: "And see, sometimes you have to squeeze the last bit of money out of a peasant. But what's to be done? . . . Volodia away at seminary needs so much, and he's already worn out his coat. . . . I'd go out and talk to the peasants from my soul, but they flat out take me for some kind of sponger and not a human being."[61] Even seminarians who chose to leave church service continued to identify with the clerical community of their parents, and the isolation of that community into a seemingly parasitical estate was, for many, a humiliation.[62] The right of the clerical community to accept and support nonclerical students was almost as important to seminarian protestors as their own freedom to pursue a secular calling, because it elevated their social identity above that of a service caste. Estate integration was also desirable from the perspective of the pastoral movement because it drew lay communities into the clerical networks as beneficiaries as well as contributors.

Demands for Reform

The protestors received the greatest support from faculty and clergymen when their petition movement culminated in an empire-wide strike. On November 1, 1905, before their students had even joined the strike, which had already spread to about one-third of the empire's seminaries, the Moscow Seminary administration formed a delegation of the inspector, two priests, and one lay teacher to travel to the capital and urge the Synod to concede to the students' demands, particularly expansion of the seminary curriculum and access to universities.[63] They were joined by delegations from other seminaries that also urged concessions to the petitioners.[64] The delegation from Tver' Seminary was the boldest. Led by a history teacher, Vladimir Kolosov, this delegation proposed that the 1884 seminary charter should be reformed by an empire-wide congress of seminary teachers, who would be elected by secret ballot. Kolosov also envisioned a permanent organization, the Union of Teachers in Church Educational Establishments, which would serve as an empire-wide mutual aid society to participate in the renewal of the seminary system.[65] The Synod rejected Kolosov's proposal, but it did authorize congresses within individual dioceses. The parents of students from Moscow's Bethlehem Seminary proposed a conference of faculty and clergy to discuss the situation. The Synod authorized such a conference for the entire diocese and appealed to those parents whom it had excluded from seminary administration since 1884 for help in ending the strike.[66] This involvement by the entire clerical community in Moscow and elsewhere allowed the Synod to save face even as it gave in to the demands of the strikers, as it could claim that "seminary reform will be based on the principles of recognized church authority, and will be determined with the help of the pedagogical authorities of the spiritual domain, and will by no means be the result of this or that desire expressed by immature school children."[67] On December 20, the emperor granted the seminarians' first demand by ordering the minister of education to authorize their admission to all universities in the empire.[68] Further concessions followed.

Classes resumed in 1906, after the Christmas holidays. The journals of Moscow's pedagogical assembly reveal a concerted effort by the administration to take advantage of subsequent reforms to improve the academic and intellectual quality of the school. On February 8, 1906, the Synod authorized the expansion of seminary student libraries, the organization of vocal concerts, and more time for students outside the seminary before dark.[69] In December, the assembly resolved that students should be taken on excursions around the city so as to better acquaint them with the "monuments of old Moscow." While the suggestions of the faculty delegation from Tver' were not adopted, the diocesan clergy were given a slightly larger role in seminary administration. Teachers were to designate specific times to meet with parents and relatives of students to discuss their children's education.[70] In January 1908, the rector of Moscow Seminary, Archimandrite Feodor, declared that students should be exposed to a broader range of ideas, including radical thought, so that they would be less vulnerable to socialist propaganda. In May of that year, the seminary purchased new books for the library with titles such as *The History of the German Social-Democratic Party, Socialism in England, The Agrarian Question and Socialism,* and *The Christian-Socialist Movement in England*.[71] Such a collection would have been unthinkable before the protest movement.

The seminary faculty and broader clerical community consistently supported the seminarians' demand for the admission of students from all estates to the seminary. The faculty delegations to the Synod endorsed this demand in 1905.[72] Fifty-four percent of respondents to Pobedonostsev's Circular 3542 to diocesan bishops on church reform argued that religious education for future pastors should be provided without regard for estate.[73] The Pre-Sobor Commission (*predsobornoe prisutstvie*) of prelates, parish clergy, and lay professors, which assembled in 1906 to discuss the anticipated All-Russian Church Sobor, also endorsed the admission of all estates to the seminary.[74] In August 1906, the Synod finally decreed that more than 10 percent of students enrolled into a seminary could come from other estates, with the permission of the bishop.[75] In 1914, another decree specified that no limitation whatsoever was to be imposed on the admission of students on the basis of their estate.[76] This reform did not serve the material interests of the clergy. Pobedonostsev's enrollment cap and tuition fee for non-clergy had relieved the diocesan networks of the burden of supporting nonclerical students and reduced the competition for merit-based scholarships as well as financial aid. Moreover, if the admission of students from other estates was intended to recruit more young men to the pastorate, as Aleksandr Mramornov remarks in his book on the seminaries, this priority was contradicted by the demand that seminarians be admitted to universities.[77] How, then, can the persistent demands of seminarians, faculty, and clergy for the elimination of estate barriers be explained?

The unified call for an end to estate isolation reflected a new understanding of the clerical profession. The reforms of the 1860s had encouraged young men of the clerical estate to view pastoral service as a calling rather than a hereditary obligation. As Laurie Manchester points out in her book on the sons of priests, some seminary graduates considered their secular careers in government or teaching to be a worldly form of pastoral service.[78] The freedom to choose ordination or leave church service had elevated the dignity of the clerical community. Yet both seminarians and clergymen understood this dignity to be contingent upon the support of the Orthodox laity. The pastoral movement developed in the understanding that lay communities would have to benefit from and participate in the mutual aid networks that they were asked to support. This was equally true of the seminary system, which the clergy hoped to maintain as a common educational endeavor. The seminaries continued to offer charity and free education for the poor of both clerical and lay communities until the Bolshevik Revolution.

Radicalization and Decline

In the wake of the 1905 Revolution, the seminarian movement lost its focus on the priorities of the clerical community. While violence had always been present within the movement, it became the dominant form of protest after 1905. Between 1906 and 1907, the seminary inspectors of Chernigov, Tiflis, and Penza were all shot, the last one fatally, and two rectors of Tambov Seminary were shot in succession.[79] Terrorist bombings also became more common. At the same time, the movement became less unified and less capable of coordinated action. One likely explanation for this fragmentation into random violence is that the lull in mass protests after the satisfaction of many of the petitioners' demands allowed political radicals to gain influence over the movement. What was left of a common seminarian organization then drifted away from the goals of the petition movement in favor of more ideological agendas.

Radicalization began at the level of the inter-seminarian congresses. Representatives from eighteen seminaries to the second all-seminarian congress, which took place in Vladimir in February 1906, jointly declared their support for the Liberation Movement, an inclusive organization founded by zemstvo liberals. The third and final seminarian congress exhibited an extreme shift to the left. Twenty delegates convened on Christmas night of 1906 within Moscow's Theological Academy and worked for three days. Attended by a representative of the Social Democratic Party, the congress declared the movement's support for the overthrow of the tsar and the boycott of Duma elections.[80] Having adopted a radical atheistic agenda, the seminarian movement could no longer appeal to the seminarian community as a whole.

Intercepted correspondences among seminarians suggest that the movement's Central Committee began losing influence over affiliate organizations after the final congress. The overshadowing of the seminarian movement by radical political agendas certainly played a role in this decline. A seminarian newsletter intercepted in April 1907, for example, noted that in Yaroslavl' Seminary, "propaganda is carried out among the seminarians, but at the initiative of [political] parties and not the Central Committee. The Socialist Revolutionary organization has the greatest influence over the seminary."[81] Radicalization may have contributed to the general decline in underground activity among seminarians, which is described in an undated letter, sent to the Central Committee with the address defaced, from the "Social Democratic Organization of Chernigov Seminarians": "If, for some reason, the Central Committee cannot in good conscience lead the all-seminarian movement, it should have informed all seminarians of this long ago through normal correspondence."[82] A more specific failure of the Central Committee was its appeal in April 1907 to all seminarians to boycott their final examinations.[83] Most students ignored this appeal, preferring not to ruin their academic standing, and isolated activists resorted to bombings to accomplish their goal. This proved to be the last significant action initiated by the all-seminarian movement in most dioceses. The unfolding of these events in Tver' and Moscow illustrates this precipitous decline.

On April 4, 1907, a member of the faculty of Tver' Seminary discovered a Hammond typewriter, the first issue of a radical student journal, radical poetry, a manifesto of the Organization of Tver' Seminarians, and unspecified bomb-making chemicals, all hidden in an unused cloakroom. A bank booklet from the Tver' post and telegraph office for one ruble was found to be made out to a student, Aleksandr Maslov, who later confessed to his involvement but refused to incriminate anyone else. Subsequent questioning of all students revealed three other students of the sixth class were considered members of the All-Seminarian Union, one of whom, Sergei Lebedev, was believed to have acted as a leader. After the young men were interrogated, the rector concluded that Maslov and his accomplices belong to a party of seminarians dissatisfied by the obligation to take final exams. When they had failed to organize a boycott, the rector and investigating gendarme speculated, they planned to use the chemicals to disrupt the exams and force their cancellation. As the amount of chemicals was too small to be used for a bomb, however, and as the radical literature that was printed on the typewriter was found not to have been distributed, the gendarme investigator concluded that criminal prosecution was unwarranted. Maslov and Lebedev were simply expelled.[84]

The literature discovered in Maslov's cloakroom revealed a confused organization. The first issue of the journal *The Student Paper* (*Uchenicheskii listok*) appeared to reproduce articles from other radical publications: "Socialist parties are going to the Duma to use it as an instrument of agitation . . . unite the popular masses around it, and eventually present them with the necessity of armed uprising."[85] Another article, perhaps an original work, rejected the seminary as a politically harmful institution: "The religious school is a weapon for the training of apologists for the economic and political enslavement of the popular masses."[86] At the same time, the manifesto declared, "History demonstrates that the Seminary, with each year, becomes more free from its years of oppression. We believe that soon the Seminary will cast off its yoke, be renewed, and become a free school."[87] The character and purpose of this renewed seminary is difficult to understand, in light of the organization's seeming condemnation of the seminary as a purveyor of opium for the people. The manifesto declared the purpose of the student union to be the organization of opposition to "reactionary elements," the organization of self-education, and the invitation to "members of socialist parties" to take part in this education. Yet the underground library that the students had assembled for this purpose, at a price of 46 rubles and 57 kopecks, was found to contain religious, philosophical, and political books, none of which were actually forbidden.[88] It is perhaps because of this confused vision that neither the Organization of Tver' Seminarians nor the decrepit All-Seminarian Union seemed to wield much authority among students. In response to the reimposition of testing requirements for seminarian applicants to secular universities in 1908,[89] seminarians of Tver', Kursk, and Nizhni Novgorod submitted letters to the liberal politician Pavel Miliukov, asking him to raise the issue before the Duma.[90] This would seem to indicate a reorientation of the political sympathies of some seminarian activists away from radical socialism.

The final collective protest to take place at Moscow Seminary was triggered by a tragedy. On April 7, 1907, a student of the third grade named Ivan Vishniakov, probably sixteen or seventeen years old, committed suicide. The seminary inspector confronted the boy, who had been on a two-day drinking binge, after which he left the seminary and threw himself in front of a train. Vishniakov's fellow seminarians blamed the inspector for his death. On the morning of April 9, the entire student body refused to go to class and demanded a requiem service for their classmate, a move out of character with the radical socialist affiliation of the seminarian organization. The faculty consented, but after the service the students gathered in the corridors and declared a strike. No specific demands were expressed. The administration sent the students home three days early for the Easter holiday with a warning that anyone who did not return to class after the break would be expelled.[91]

The revolt proved to be short-lived, and classes resumed after the Easter break. It was perhaps their inability to sustain the protest that prompted some radical students to resort to violence. On May 8, at three o'clock in the morning, a bomb exploded in the fork of a tree within the seminary grounds, setting it on fire. On the morning of May 9, a bomb exploded in the main seminary building while most students were attending liturgy. It destroyed the oven in which it was placed but caused no injury.[92] Moscow's mayor ordered a police raid of the seminary that evening, which found three students of the fourth grade to be in possession of the following documents: a lithograph appeal from the Central Committee of the All-Seminarian Union for all students to boycott exams, six copies of the same issue of Tver' Seminary's radical student journal *The Student Paper*, and a handwritten essay complaining about the seminary. Searches of student apartments in the city uncovered the protocols of the all-seminarian congress in the possession of six more students. Six of these students were expelled after completion of their exams, and three were allowed to stay.[93]

Another bomb was set off in Moscow Seminary on May 29, during a visit by Metropolitan Vladimir. The small explosion took place in a water closet and caused no injuries. The bomber was not identified.[94] By June, however, the seminary administration had identified nineteen students whom they suspected of having played prominent roles in the April strike. In their own defense, three of the older students claimed that by taking charge of the protest, they had prevented an outbreak of violence. Indeed, closure of the seminary would have ruined these students' chances of graduating. The police investigator and the pedagogical council came to the same conclusion that the bombings were the work of a small number of students, possibly with poor grades and no hope of graduating, who wished to terrorize the seminary administration, as well as their fellow students, in order to cause a boycott of the final exams.[95] On the basis of this theory, the pedagogical assembly reached a relatively mild verdict. Only three students of the first two grades were expelled for their defiant expression of solidarity with the Central Committee of the All-Seminarian Union. Two students were deprived of their free room and board, and the rest were given one point lower for behavior. The five graduating students were allowed to keep their diplomas.[96] With this verdict, the council isolated violent radicals from the majority of seminarians, most of whom continued to identify their interests with the seminary community.

The spring of 1907 marked the end of coordinated seminarian protests throughout the empire. In May, bombings took place in the seminaries of Nizhni Novgorod and Kaluga, and police raids uncovered the Central Committee's appeal for a boycott of the final exam in numerous seminaries.[97] But no boycott took place. Subsequent expressions of seminarian protest were limited to isolated acts of violence, such as the fatal stabbing of the inspector of Saratov Seminary in 1911.[98] In August of that year, police investigated rumors of a seminarian congress in Moscow but ultimately concluded that no such meeting had been organized.[99] The authorities had succeeded in identifying and arresting or expelling many of the most radical activists from the seminaries. Those radicals, however, had already alienated the movement from the seminary and the clerical community surrounding it.

Conclusion

The collaboration of protestors, faculty, and parish clergy in 1905 won greater access to the seminary administration for the clerical community and greater intellectual freedom for the seminary system. Yet they were unable to build upon these victories. The Tver' delegation's 1905 proposal for an empire-wide forum for intellectual and financial collaboration was blocked, despite Kolosov's pledge that the seminary teachers' congress would eschew political activism, and the seminary community's freedom of association remained confined to the diocesan level. Secular school teachers later organized interprovincial assemblies, such as the congress of the teachers' union that met in Moscow in March 1907, which was attended by forty-five delegates from nine gubernias, including Tver'. Yet the delegates' expression of solidarity with the Social Democratic and Socialist Revolutionary Parties precluded significant collaboration between the seminaries and the teachers' union.[100] Members of seminary faculties were unwilling or unable to press for greater concessions from the authorities outside the context of the student disorders. The Synod's tightening of censorship on the clerical press in November 1906 elicited no significant protests from the parish clergy or the seminaries.[101] The seminary rectors, all tonsured monks appointed by their bishops, played an important role in discouraging defiance of the Synod. The parish clergy in general were often silenced by the looming threat of defrocking or monastic incarceration. It is also clear, however, that the growing prominence of radical, anti-religious political parties played an important role in dividing the clerical community internally and alienating it from politically active social groups, such as secular teachers.

The limited reforms that followed the 1905 boycotts failed to attract substantial lay participation in the seminary as a common educational endeavor. Few young men from other estates took advantage of the opportunity to enroll in seminaries after the Synod abolished the 10 percent cap in 1906. In fact, overall enrollment of students from nonclerical families actually dropped from 19.3 percent in 1906 to 15.3 percent in 1914.[102] Russia's rapid industrialization over the first decades of the twentieth century created new employment opportunities, making the priesthood an increasingly unattractive profession in terms of its material compensation. Despite their emphasis on the provision of free education for impoverished students, the lay community was not generally persuaded to regard the seminaries as more than schools to train servants of the Church. Indeed, parishioners sometimes questioned their priests as to why they were being asked to provide support for schools that seemed to be producing radicals instead of pastors.[103] Nevertheless, the seminary did serve to develop the pastoral movement among students who were called to the priesthood, instilling in them the culture of mutual aid and the desire to include the laity in the Church's social mission.

In December 1917, the rector of Tver' Seminary drew up plans for the survival of the school after the seizure of all its funds and property for transfer to the Commissariat of Popular Education. The rector began by acknowledging the many years of common contributions to the seminary and presenting the loss of that wealth as a tragedy for the entire Orthodox community and not simply a loss for the institutional church: "This heavy loss for the Church amounts to millions in property, including buildings, inventory, libraries, investments, and other religious schools for girls and boys. In Tver' diocese this property was accumulated over the course of more than 150 years. Everyone contributed their small share: bishops, clerics, and laymen—rich and poor alike."[104] According to the rector's plan, Tver' Seminary could remain open, even without state support, if students began paying 100 rubles a year in tuition. He estimated that this income, together with the continued support of the parishes, monasteries, and brotherhoods of the diocese, could sustain the seminary and allow it to continue providing free education to "orphans and children from the poorest classes of the population."[105] The rector specified that theological training should be focused on older students who intended to pursue ordination. For the rest, he asserted that the seminary should continue to provide a broader and more philosophical curriculum than secular schools and do so at less expense.[106] The prioritization of these expansive services in the midst of such a crisis, including free education, reflected the broader educational mission that the seminary had undertaken. The seminary, which had provided much of the practical motivation for the pastoral movement among the clerical estate, eventually became an instrument of that movement for extending the educational resources of the clergy to the Orthodox laity—and especially to the poor.

4

The Church as a School

Nikolai Ostrovskii's socialist realist novel *How the Steel Was Tempered* opens with the description of a conflict between the young hero, Pavel Korchagin, and his tyrannical village teacher, "a bloated man in a cassock, with a heavy cross around his neck," who expels the protagonist from his parish school over a petty slight.[1] The priest-educator was a ubiquitous presence in late imperial Russia and a favorite target of socialist as well as liberal critics, who saw him as an instrument of the autocracy. The regime also regarded clerical teachers as agents of its authority and subsidized clerical teaching as a means of promoting political loyalty as well as modernization. On the empire's Central Asian frontier of Semirech'e, state funds were disbursed for the construction of parish churches with school rooms attached in order to maintain the Russian Orthodox identity of the colonial settler population.[2] After the war with Japan, advocates of parish schools argued before the Duma that clerical teachers could produce more educated and effective recruits for the army.[3] Yet clerical teaching was only partially and temporarily supported by the state. It relied on the participation of the Orthodox population in the mutual aid initiatives of the clergy for the support of parish schools. Despite the material deprivation they faced and the controversy that surrounded them, locally supported parish schools played an important role in the spread of literacy, particularly among women. They also contributed to the integration of mutual aid into the religious life of the parish.

The state subsidized the clergy's pedagogical work, as it did with much of their extra-liturgical activity, as a means of procuring a social service at low cost. Priests were not compensated for teaching parishioners, but state funds helped them construct school buildings and pay small salaries to assistant teachers, who were almost always recruited from the clerical community. Through uncompensated teaching, therefore, priests could procure modest state salaries for young men and women within the clerical network. Even at the height of state funding for parish schools, however, lay collaboration was essential for their survival and success. If parishioners were skeptical of the seminary as a useful institution, they clearly perceived the utility of the resource it produced, large numbers of well-trained teachers willing to provide basic education for little compensation. Orthodox laypeople were thus drawn into the clergy's mutual aid project of providing collective support for parish schools, teachers, and students. This collaborative relationship allowed the "new kind of pastor" to rally the parish community around education as a common priority, even as the modern world eroded his traditional authority.

The Clerical Teacher

The Orthodox clergy had served as an important educational resource since medieval Rus', but it was only by the late nineteenth century that the lower clergy began spreading literacy on a mass scale. The state played no small role in equipping and motivating pastors to work as teachers. By the early nineteenth century, Peter I's seminary initiative had finally reached the scale necessary to replace the illiterate priests, deacons, and sacristans of the previous century with a well-educated parish clergy. Together with demobilized soldiers and minor officials, the parish clergy comprised one of the only literate groups spread throughout the Russian hinterland. The reforms of the 1860s lent new importance to the literate clergyman as a social resource. From the moment of emancipation, government ministers instructed the parish clergy, through the Synod, to explain the abolition of serfdom to the peasantry and educate them in the use of legal avenues to resolve disputes.[4] From the perspective of state officials, the parish clergy represented a potential source of cultural continuity in the midst of alarming change. They could instruct their peasant parishioners in literacy and self-administration through traditional religious education that would stress moral behavior and political loyalty. Moreover, demand grew among the peasants themselves for the education that clergymen could offer once literacy became a commodity for social advancement. Since they were barred from engaging in commerce or working for wages, teaching was one of the few nonliturgical jobs clergymen could legally perform to earn extra income, and they presented an eager workforce to meet popular demand. Teaching also provided pastors with a means of influencing religious life among the laity.

After the abolition of serfdom, in a dearth of educational infrastructure, peasants organized "home schools" and hired any literate people they could find to teach in them.[5] Boris Veselovskii, the Menshevik historian of the zemstvo, compiled data on schools in one district of Tula gubernia in 1873. He found seven registered schools and forty-five unofficial schools, thirty-two of which were operated by clergymen.[6] In 1862, all official schools were required to employ an ordained clergyman appointed by the diocesan bishop to teach scripture and catechism.[7] Archives contain many letters from priests and deacons to their bishop requesting appointment to these salaried teaching positions.[8] Yet clergymen were hired to teach in zemstvo and state schools in nonreligious capacities as well. In a letter on February 8, 1908, an archpriest in Moscow district complained to the consistory that one sacristan under his supervision had been neglecting his liturgical duties after being hired as an assistant teacher at the Lazarevskii Institute of Eastern Languages. The sacristan sent his own letter requesting authorization for this position, arguing that "most sacristans perform such work on the side."[9] The service reports (*posluzhnye spiski*) that clergymen submitted to their diocesan consistory in support of various requests typically describe histories of both formal and informal teaching work throughout their careers. In 1908, for example, a Moscow deacon reported, "I first taught peasant children in my home. Since 1885 I have taught in a literacy school located in the church-watchman's house."[10] Thus, popular demand was at least as important a factor in the growth of clerical teaching in the late nineteenth century as state sponsorship.

Pedagogical work was not only a source of income for parish clergymen but also a pastoral duty. Clerical teaching became an important component of the Church's social mission in the nineteenth century, and an increasing number of priests opened schools for their parishioners, where they provided instruction in religion and basic education for their children for no direct compensation. In 1836, the Synod issued the first of many directives to the parish clergy to establish these schools, but no state funding was designated to support them. Parish schools were established and supported with the help of clerical mutual aid networks and the voluntary contributions of the laity. One Moscow priest described the process thus: "The clergy create schools from what? Well, from nothing. We have neither funds nor material. The priest goes from door to door, bows, and asks his parishioners to help him build the school in which their children must learn."[11] The official estimates of the Synod from 1881 indicate that the majority of support for parish schools came from the voluntary contributions of parishioners. In this year, empire-wide, monasteries contributed 20,632 rubles and zemstvos contributed 43,227 rubles to parish schools. Parish church funds, parish charities, private donations, and village councils contributed total sums of 2,186 rubles, 26,338 rubles, 27,245 rubles, and 111,350 rubles, respectively.[12] Even with the free teaching of their priests, peasant parishioners could not equip a large network of schools with teaching space, books, food, medicine, and so on. By one estimate, there were a modest 4,488 parish schools with 119,740 students throughout the empire in 1880.[13] Yet these numbers would increase dramatically over subsequent decades through state support.

A Branch of the Clerical Network

After considering the idea for the better part of the nineteenth century, the Synod and Council of Ministers resolved to provide support for the clergy's widespread teaching work and create a new network of religious schools under the supervision of the Synod. The unanimous decision in the Council of Ministers to subsidize parish schools in 1881 with a small annual sum of 55,000 rubles was driven by two main arguments. The first, championed by Oberprocurator Konstantin Pobedonostsev, was the need to increase the clergy's role in popular education in order to reestablish religious piety and political loyalty in the population. This view garnered much support after the assassination of Emperor Alexander II in the same year.[14] The second argument came from the Christian pedagogue and former professor of botany at Moscow State University Sergei Rachinskii. Motivated by his perception of ineffective pedagogical practices in primary schools in Tver', Rachinskii established his own school in 1875, which he used to develop a program of religious education.[15] He felt that a religious perspective would make basic education more accessible and interesting to the peasantry. Rachinskii took part in the committee within the Council of Ministers that drew up a statute for a new system of parish schools in 1884. The result was the Regulations for Church Parish Schools, which removed parish schools from any accountability to the Ministry of Education and placed them under the direct and exclusive jurisdiction of the Church. The Regulations established a School Council in the Synod, which was to oversee a network of diocesan school councils, each headed by the diocesan bishop. This network was augmented in subsequent years to include district sections of the diocesan councils with their own salaried inspectors.[16] While he had previously answered to the provincial school council administered by the nobility and under the jurisdiction of the MNP, the priest was now solely responsible for his parish school, reporting only to his bishop and the diocesan school inspector. Emperor Alexander III approved the Regulations on July 13, 1884. He wrote to Pobedonostsev, "I hope that the parish clergy prove worthy of their high calling in this important task."[17] In fact, the entire clerical estate would transform parish schooling into a major source of basic education.

With an average of 1,400 parishioners for every priest, clergymen could not perform this task alone.[18] Government support for the schools, which peaked at 10.3 million rubles in 1902, supplied both teaching materials and salaries for teachers to work under the supervision of each priest.[19] This support gave priests the opportunity to establish salaried positions for relatives and family members. According to the statistics of the Synod's School Council, there were 42,882 salaried teachers working in parish schools throughout the empire in 1907. Most of the 1,913 teachers working in the four-year, "two-class" parish schools earned 300 to 360 rubles a year. The 28,269 working in the two-year, "one-class" schools usually earned about 240 rubles a year. The 12,700 teachers who worked in the small and often poor "literacy schools" only earned about 120 rubles a year.[20] These figures are mirrored by a 1901 report on pay levels for parish school teachers in Moscow diocese.[21] In the estimation of one archpriest and member of the Moscow parish school council, expressed in a letter he addressed to a diocesan congress in 1909, the median wage of 20 rubles a month was the equivalent of what an illiterate groundskeeper could earn in the city of Moscow.[22] This level of pay was too low to attract many secondary-school graduates who were qualified to teach. For seminarians, however, it was a practical option for a number of reasons.

For seminary graduates who wanted to become priests, parish school teaching was the most convenient way to support themselves and their families while waiting for ordination. A seminary graduate could not legally be ordained until the age of thirty, and the chronic shortage of parish positions for the ever-expanding clerical population could force aspiring priests to wait even longer. Although seminary graduates could work as sacristans, this position had become associated with the less educated strata of the clerical community.[23] For seminarians who had been unable to graduate, often due to some kind of hardship, teaching at a parish school provided a reliable source of income and the likelihood of becoming a sacristan as well. Moreover, a position in a parish school provided continued access to clerical social support networks after leaving the seminary community.[24] In a letter to a 1908 diocesan congress in Moscow, an archpriest and member of the diocesan parish school council argued for the necessity of establishing a charitable society to improve the living conditions of the "hungry army" of parish school teachers throughout the diocese. His letter reveals the identification of this "army" with the clerical community: "Since the matter closely and immediately affects the clergy of the entire diocese and their children, then one must assume that the Moscow clergy will offer its complete sympathy and support to the development of such a society."[25] The parish school system, thus, became an important branch of the clergy's social support network.

While teaching positions were open to anyone, statistics indicate that most of the parish school workforce came from the clerical estate. Diocesan seminaries administered certification exams for parish school teachers, although seminary graduates were not required to pass them. The exam covered catechism and church history on the first day, Russian grammar and composition on the second, arithmetic on the third, history, geography, and more arithmetic on the fourth. Each section had both oral and written components, and the examinee was required to give observed lessons in the seminary's own parish school on the last day.[26] Between 1900 and 1905, Moscow Seminary administered 140 of these exams, 38 of which were failed. Fifty-three of these exams were given to seminary dropouts. Seventeen were given to clerical youth who had only graduated from a primary ecclesiastical school. Eighteen were administered to sacristans, and one former monk took the exam. Of the nonclerical examinees, there were thirty-six peasants, seven townsmen, four nobles, one Cossack, and one man identified as a palace servant.[27] In September 1908, teachers at Moscow Seminary complained that "experience has shown that examinees for certification as parish school teachers often have no intention of serving in this capacity, but take the exam to obtain a more profitable position in society. Some examinees have revealed that they hoped this certification would garner them positions as private tutors . . . others hope to obtain the privileges of government service, since a teaching certification is held in higher regard than a diploma of graduation from an institution of primary education."[28] In order to discourage frivolous applications for certification, the pedagogical council decided to begin charging five rubles per exam, except for applicants living in poverty.[29] Statistics bear out the committee's impression about who was teaching in the parish schools. For example, completed questionnaires from parish school teachers in Bronnitsy district, sent to the Moscow diocesan consistory in 1906–7, reveal that of twenty-four non-ordained male teachers, seventeen had completed or dropped out of clerical educational institutions, six had themselves graduated from parish schools, and only one had graduated from a secular gymnasium.[30]

By the end of the nineteenth century, teaching work in a parish school had become a kind of obligatory stepping-stone for seminary graduates before they could be ordained.[31] The work allowed future priests to establish contacts in the diocesan community and possibly attract the notice of the consistory, which granted ordination and appointment to a parish. For example, in 1905, the Moscow consistory received a letter signed by thirteen parishioners from a village in Zvenigorod district praising their parish school teacher of seven years, Aleksei Beliaev, and requesting that he be ordained to replace their aging priest and marry the priest's daughter so that their beloved pastor could die in his own home.[32] The parishioners' request was not granted, perhaps because of the prohibition against marrying into a parish, but the letter must have made an impression as Beliaev was ordained and assigned to another parish in the same year.[33] Most seminary graduates tried to avoid teaching for as long as

Beliaev did. A parish school inspector's report from 1901 complained that many teachers left their posts too early and viewed teaching work as a temporary situation while concentrating most of their energy on finding positions as priests or in the bureaucracy.[34] Another report from the same year found that of 827 parish school teachers in the Moscow diocese 365 had taught for less than three years.[35] A less transient parish school teaching force was composed of young men who had fewer prospects than seminary graduates.

The parish school network came to serve as an important safety net for seminarians who could not graduate. Lack of academic success, family circumstances, illness, and poverty were some of the reasons given for withdrawal from seminary, and mention of a student's withdrawal in the journals of the seminary's pedagogical committee was almost inevitably followed by that student's request to take the qualification exam for parish school teaching certification. For these former students, work in a parish school provided a small salary, exemption from military conscription, and a path to appointment as a sacristan. These modest benefits also attracted peasant youth who had graduated from parish schools themselves. Thus, the parish school network served as an important source of employment for future priests, as well as for the lower strata of the clerical estate and members of other estates who became attached to it. The most important segment of the parish school teaching force, however, was neither transient future priests nor partially educated peasants and sacristans. The backbone of the parish school network was composed of clerical women.

EPARKHIALKI: DIOCESAN WOMEN

By the end of the nineteenth century, female members of the clerical estate, the wives and daughters of clergymen, served the parish school network as a large teaching force that was both more permanent than seminary graduates and better educated than seminary dropouts and peasant teachers who had merely passed the parish school exam without attending seminary. If teaching work served as an important source of income for clerical men, it was even more important for clerical women who could not perform liturgical rites. Clerical women often assisted their fathers and husbands, working the plot of land attached to the parish and assisting in pastoral work by, for example, serving as orderlies in the parish shelter for the elderly. In addition, clerical women had traditionally secured support for their aged parents by marrying the successor to their father's parish. The Synod decreed an end to this practice in 1867, but it continued unofficially, as the above-mentioned case of the teacher Beliaev suggests.[36] When a clerical woman was widowed or orphaned, she had few options by which to escape poverty. A letter from a thirty-two-year-old, unmarried daughter of an elderly priest to the Metropolitan of Moscow illustrates such a situation.

> Your Holiness, Merciful Father and Archpastor! My father is an elderly, retired priest who now lives in the Aleksandrovskii Polstovskii shelter due to his ill health. As Your Holiness knows, I am not permitted to live in such a shelter. Because I received no secondary education, I can find no work. My situation at the present time is exceedingly desperate, as I have no means on which to live. Hoping for Your Archpastoral mercy, I am so bold as to ask Your Holiness to appoint me to a position as a communion bread baker.[37]

Such positions for impoverished members of the clergy were not plentiful. As the letter indicates, education was essential for clerical women who had to support themselves, and possibly their children, alone.

The first educational institution for clerical women was established in 1843, in Tsarskoe Selo, at the initiative of the noble ladies Nadezhda Shultz, Elizaveta Shipova, and Grand Princess Ol'ga Nikolaevna, who wrote the school's charter and designed its curriculum. Nadezhda Shultz served as the head administrator. The school was intended to produce educated brides for priests from among the clerical estate and from orphanages, without instilling in them the desire to attend the theater or balls, or mingle in high society. The focus of its modest curriculum was on basic literacy, practical handicrafts, and piety.[38] By 1866, there were eleven such institutions, all under the patronage of Empress Maria Alexandrovna. They all received funding from the Synod, and the headmistresses were approved by the empress. These schools attracted the enthusiastic support of the local clergy. For example, a school established in Simbirsk in 1847 was staffed entirely by the nuns of the Spasskii Convent, who taught the girls handicrafts and housekeeping for no compensation. Local clergymen volunteered to teach the girls reading, writing, and liturgical singing. In addition, several seminary teachers offered the bishop to teach the girls for free. The seminary doctor and pharmacist treated the girls and provided them with medicine for free.[39] The clergy soon built on the foundation that the Saint Petersburg noblewomen had laid, making the project their own.

The clergy took over the project entirely after 1867, when the Synod forbade clergymen from marrying into parish positions. Deprived of this traditional practice, the clerical estate was now under more pressure than ever to secure employment for their female members. A common charter (*ustav*) was approved for clerical women's schools on September 10, 1868. Unlike the seminaries and the eleven schools patronized by the empress, these new clerical schools would receive no government support. They were essentially private institutions, funded entirely by diocesan resources, which were designated for that purpose at the annual diocesan congresses.

Meeting this financial burden often constituted the main order of business at diocesan congresses.[40] Charities for students of these schools joined the ranks of the clergy's now ubiquitous mutual aid societies. In an article on the activities of one such society, founded to aid the Moscow Filaret School for Girls in 1898, the author wrote: "Who is unacquainted with the bitter demands of the upbringing and education of the children of our parish clergy? Who is unaware of the enormous burden of supporting a son or daughter at school on the modest means of a parish sacristan, deacon, or priest? It is often the case that fifteen or twenty-five rubles of aid can prevent a poor sacristan from having to sell his cow and sacrificing the health of his small children."[41] Through cooperation, the parish clergy of Moscow, Tver', and most other dioceses shouldered this burden, and the number of diocesan schools for girls grew. In 1886, there were thirty-nine; in 1890, forty-six; in 1896, fifty-one; in 1907, fifty-three; and in 1914, seventy-seven.[42] In a speech before the diocesan cathedral in Poltava in 1897, the provincial governor remarked that "the Poltavo clergy have enabled even their poorest members, including sacristans and widows, to hope that their daughters will complete a full education and be prepared for life. No other estate has achieved this."[43]

Despite being open to girls of all estates since their establishment, the diocesan schools for women consistently educated clerical youth who usually found employment as servants of the Church. This was the case for some of the same reasons, described in the previous chapter, that the seminaries remained solidly clerical in their social makeup. Like the seminaries, the diocesan schools offered free education and scholarships to the needy to cover the cost of food and lodgings. The clerical style of education was stronger in the humanities and weaker in math and science than the gymnasium education.[44] The curriculum included: catechism, Russian, Slavonic, geometry, physics, geography, history, handwriting, and liturgical singing. Pedagogy was also taught, and practice lessons were given in a parish school attached to the institution. Because of the absence of dance, drawing, and modern foreign languages in the curriculum, clerical graduates were less desirable as tutors for children of wealthy families. This market was dominated by graduates of institutes for noble girls. Teaching work in secondary schools was usually given to graduates of higher courses for women. Like seminarians, diocesan women could only enroll in secular higher educational courses after passing exams that were based on the gymnasium education. Moreover, few clerical families could afford to pay for room and board in the cities where these courses were held. Graduates of the six-year course of study at a diocesan school for girls earned the title of "teacher," giving them the right to teach in primary schools or parish schools, garnering the least pay and least prestige of all.[45] For these reasons, few outsiders wanted to send their daughters to a diocesan school. In 1903, out of 819 total students in Moscow's two diocesan schools for girls, 78 came from outside the clerical estate. Of the 433 students in Tver's one diocesan school, 26 were nonclerical. Of the 20,178 diocesan students empire-wide, only 1,812 were nonclerical in 1903.[46] The need for these clerical women to take on work in primary schools proved a great boon to the Church's parish school system.

The diocesan schools for women began training the daughters of clergymen in pedagogy around the same time that the Ministry of Education granted unmarried women permission to teach in primary and secondary schools in 1871. According to contemporary reports, the patriarchal peasantry typically regarded urban-educated female teachers as cultural outsiders and treated them with suspicion.[47] Christine Ruane has argued that such reports were usually written by male teachers and administrators who were motivated to cast aspersions at the professional competence of their better-educated female colleagues, with whom they were in competition for work. In fact, Ruane argues, peasants often perceived their female teachers as *staritsy*, the celibate wise women who traditionally worked as educators of children as well as spiritual advisors.[48] Yet neither of these characterizations applied to the female educators of the clerical estate, many of whom were related or married to the priest in charge of the parish schools.[49] The *matiushka*, or priest's wife, and her daughters were more integrated into the parish communities than the *baryshnia*, or "lady" teaching in the ministerial school, who was usually the daughter of a nobleman or civil servant.[50] Reports on the extra services that female teachers provided at the parish schools, such as free adult literacy classes, suggest that these women often acted as parish community leaders as well as pedagogues.[51] A report from a parish school in Moscow district in 1904, for example, describes classes in reading, writing, and arithmetic that a priest, his wife, and another female teacher taught on Sundays in the school house for 106 women, and their efforts to retain these students despite the significant demands of rural domestic life: "Of the twenty-six students who left the school, three did so after getting married, and the rest due to situations at home or lack of success, in spite of the teachers' efforts to convince them to stay."[52] The parish school system became an important source of security for clerical women and of basic education for Orthodox women in general.

The female contingent of the teaching force became increasingly important to the parish school network over the first two decades of the twentieth century. In 1903, there were 18,964 women and 25,094 non-ordained men teaching in

44,000 parish schools.[53] By 1914, female teachers were in the majority, with 28,944 women versus 18,328 laymen teaching in 37,528 parish schools throughout the empire.[54] This increase in female teachers can perhaps be explained by the reduction in state funding for parish schools after 1906, prompting much of the less permanent male workforce to seek employment elsewhere.[55] While men had more opportunities to perform liturgical services or leave church service altogether, women remained committed to the parish school system as a reliable source of income. Clerical women augmented the teaching force in secular schools as well and contributed to other sectors of society. The request of a deacon for financial aid from Tver' Seminary for his son in 1916 serves as a vivid example of the capacity of the clerical networks to provide education for the numerous daughters of even the poorest clergymen and of the variety of work these women could perform as a result. This deacon had eight daughters and claimed an annual income of only 350 rubles: "Elizaveta, 28 years old, teaches in a Moscow city school. . . . Valentina, 20 years old, manages a shelter for refugees in the city of Astrakhan. Pavla, 18 years old, teaches at Inal'tsevo Zemstvo School. . . . Elena, 10 years old, studies in the first class of the Kaliazin private gymnasium for girls at her parents' expense. Aleksandra, 9 years old, studies in the parish school. Mariia, 6 years old, Tamara, 5 years old, and Ol'ga, 2 years old, stay home with their parents."[56]

The Parish School Community

The active participation of parishioners was a crucial element in the success of the parish school project. The Synodal journal, *Tserkovnyi vestnik*, estimated in 1909 that irregular voluntary donations had accounted for half of the parish schools' overall collective income that year.[57] The need to attract this support can partially account for the prodigious efforts that priests and their families invested in their parish schools. It was not uncommon for priests and even sacristans to contribute their own money to provide students in their parish schools with food and extra reading material.[58] To compensate for funding shortfalls, clerical school councils sometimes imposed taxes on the income that clergymen derived from pedagogical work outside the parish school system.[59] In 1904, for example, the Vyshnevolotsk district branch of the Tver' diocesan school council imposed such a tax on the income that twelve local deacons derived from teaching in secular schools in order to purchase insurance for one parish school building and to hire an additional teacher.[60] In addition to such individual and collective material sacrifices, clergymen contributed their time to providing extra services in their parish schools such as adult literacy classes, public readings, and craft workshops. "Extraordinary dedication to parish school affairs" and "exemplary service as a parish school administrator" were among the most frequent commendations mentioned in nominations of clergymen for awards and promotions.[61] This dedication was more effective than any verbal persuasion at inspiring similar work and similar sacrifices from the parish community as a whole.

No matter how diligent a priest may have been, the survival of a parish school was always contingent on the participation of parishioners. In a 1909 letter to their bishop requesting a synodal decoration for their pastor, the parishioners of a poor Moscow church attributed the success of their parish school to their priest's leadership in obtaining such participation: "Our parish school was opened through his zeal and has been sustained for almost ten years through resources he has obtained from charitable contributors."[62] As the letter indicates, parish school operations depended on such "charitable contributions." In-kind contributions were sometimes as crucial as monetary donations just to support the teaching staff. The Moscow diocesan parish school inspector published an account in 1906 of a teacher in a remote parish who lived on a salary of 16 rubles and 66 kopecks a month, half of which went to support her mother. While the priest occasionally gave her money, she survived on "village products" that the peasants brought to her free of charge.[63] Yet parishioners were under no legal obligation to contribute anything to their parish school.[64] The clergy could only obtain their support by drawing the peasantry into the school project as a community endeavor.

The parish school had to become more than an institution of basic education in order to be the focus of community participation. A parish school education provided access to jobs that required basic literacy, such as office work at the local railroad station.[65] Yet not all parishioners were interested in these opportunities. Clergymen and teachers drew more of the peasant community to the parish school by volunteering their time to teach adult classes during nonworking hours and by organizing instructional workshops in leatherwork, carpentry, tailoring, and other crafts so that, in the words of the Moscow diocesan school inspector, "the population might come to see the school as a place where not only children, but adults as well might learn something useful and necessary, where they could spend their free time not in empty entertainment, but in productive activity; in short ... to strengthen the perception of the school as a genuine source of all possible enlightenment and education."[66]

Some members of the clergy had experience in trades such as beekeeping to impart to their parishioners, and policymakers had always encouraged clergymen to obtain such practical skills that would be of interest to the peasantry.[67] Realistically, however, the clergy were much more qualified to offer literacy instruction and lectures on religious topics. Peasant parishioners were themselves most capable of providing instruction in handicrafts, and many contributed to the parish school system as teachers as well as material supporters.

Instruction in basic crafts was provided in parish schools since their inception. The cooperative production of food and the performance of free services began out of necessity in some remote parish schools and led to the development of these activities in parish schools in larger communities as well. Since 1887, Pobedonostev urged the Council of Ministers to provide grants of state land to sustain remote parish schools in the Far North. The State Council finally passed such legislation on May 12, 1897, which authorized priests to apply for small grants of state land "for the economic and pedagogical needs of the schools and of the teachers and students in them." By 1901, 7,979 schools had been granted a total of 10,341.3 *desiatiny* (about 27,921.51 acres) of land, which was typically used to grow food for students and teachers.[68] In 1906, the Moscow inspector published an account of an unusually large parish school, with more than 120 students in Moscow's Preobrazhenskii factory district, in which parishioners volunteered their time to teach gardening as well as bookbinding, barbering, and shoe repair. Some students went on to practice the trade they learned in this school, and all of them benefited from the communal garden that supplied the students with vegetables and from the services they and their parents provided one another.[69] According to synodal statistics, from 1897 to 1903, trade skills such as bookbinding, joinery, and metal work were taught in 517 parish schools. In 1907, basic crafts such as knitting, tailoring, and shoe repair were taught in 5,121 parish schools.[70]

The parish school initiative contributed more than literacy and basic skills to Orthodox communities. It created mutual aid networks among the laity, similar to those that the clergy had built for themselves. In addition to the support they offered to the teaching staff, members of parish school communities supported one another. In 1906, the Moscow inspector observed a case in which the students of one parish school in the Moscow district had brought food for a poor classmate throughout the year.[71] Such local charity sometimes assumed larger proportions. In 1903, a charitable society was organized among numerous parish schools in Zvenigorod district, and it attracted the support of both clergymen and parishioners. It provided clothes and food for poor students in fifty different schools that year.[72] The voluntarism of clerical organizers encouraged and facilitated these and other mutual aid activities by laypeople, such as the teaching of crafts and the performance of services for parish school communities. The clergy's success at drawing peasants and other laypeople into the parish school project did not merely serve to generate social support for the clerical estate. It also helped establish participation in mutual aid associations beyond the confines of the immediate community as a part of religious life among the Orthodox population.

The Internal Mission

The economic processes that created demand for parish schools also disrupted traditional religious life in the Orthodox parish. The growth of urban employment drew parishioners and resources out of the villages, bringing them into contact with urban vices and radical ideas. Migrant workers returned to the villages having abandoned the complex cycle of fasts and saints' days that ordered life in the parishes. By the early twentieth century, village priests were reporting acts of anti-religious hostility, such as drunken jeering during icon processions.[73] One priest lamented, "Life in the village is like life in a monastery. Life in the capital cities is like life in Babylon. . . . As water from the mountain travels to the valley, so does immorality flow from the capitals to the villages. That is why our ancient and pious traditions and customs begin to weaken."[74] The "monastic" piety of the village was particularly vulnerable to the challenges of modern society. In 1906, one priest in Tver' diocese observed that the faith of his peasant parishioners was uninformed: "While they harbor no doubts about their faith, their customs and convictions are unexamined and unexplored. Their knowledge of their faith is limited to a number of prayers, which they do not understand. That is why superstition frequently distorts their meager understanding about God, belief, life, and nature."[75] Such an unchallenged faith was vulnerable to the challenge of radical anti-religious thought, which was disseminated throughout Russia's rural environment during the industrialization process by migrant workers as well as political activists. In a 1906 consistory report, one priest described the speeches of Social Democratic and Socialist Revolutionary orators in the rural communities of Tver': "[The revolutionary orators] described extreme political teachings at their assemblies. They called the people to armed insurrection, to seize the property of others, to rebel against authority, to refuse taxation. They vilified the entire structure of parish life. Some parishioners, especially young people, were seduced by the evil speeches of these agitators."[76] By the late nineteenth century, clergymen and church publicists began calling upon the pastorate to conduct an "internal mission" among the Orthodox believers in order to fortify the faith against such ideological challenges.[77] Articles in the diocesan journals focused on education and extra-liturgical discussion as the primary tools of the internal mission.[78] Yet the effectiveness of these tools would depend on the collaboration they elicited from the laity. Like the parish school initiative, this internal mission would rely on the appetite for education of an increasingly mobile and inquisitive population for its success.

Many priests found that they could influence the laypeople's understanding of faith and the modern world more effectively in an educational rather than a liturgical setting. This was due in part to the Synod's regulation of sermons delivered in parish churches. As prescribed in an 1885 digest of synodal decrees, the priest was expected to preach "about submission to authority, and especially to the authority of the tsar, about the obligations of every rank, and try to uproot superstition and instill fear of God."[79] To prevent deviation from this formula, all priests were required to submit their sermons in written form to their superintendent for approval prior to delivering them. When delivering these pre-approved sermons, priests were forbidden to gesticulate, cry, or laugh.[80] This censorship stymied the effectiveness of the sermon. As one superintendent reported to the Tver' consistory in 1906, "The delivery of sermons . . . written in a fairly academic style, is not very useful and is even sometimes boring for the listeners. The clergy are almost never permitted to give lively sermons on current themes 'without notes.'"[81] Yet the report went on to say, "The clergy do not neglect discussion with the people about current events, such as the war with Japan and the revolutionary disturbances in our Fatherland. But this takes place more often in private discussion than from the pulpit."[82] Priests could hold discussions with larger groups of parishioners in educational contexts, particularly "public readings." On April 16, 1869, the Synod authorized all clergymen to hold, with the permission of the civil authorities, public readings on religious themes in schools, administrative buildings, or in the open air.[83] They were intended to explain the significance of the liturgy, encourage reading, and impart moral edification. The decree also permitted parishioners to pose questions to the reader, in which case the event became an "extra-liturgical discussion," or *beseda*. The participation of parishioners in such discussions allowed for considerable deviation from the official program of a "reading," as illustrated in a 1906 report on public readings held in Tver's Otroch Monastery: "The program does not exclude the interlocutors from independently choosing this or that subject for discussion, especially if it involves circumstances from contemporary life."[84] The clergyman's ability to persuade and instruct his parishioners was, therefore, often contingent upon their engagement in discussion with him.

These readings were held regularly in most parish schools. In fact, failure to hold them could earn a priest a public rebuke in the diocesan press.[85] With the use of image projectors, choir singing, and the selection of entertaining and useful material, readings became a popular form of entertainment. In some cases, authorization was obtained to hold large-scale readings among several parishes, and talented orators from among the clergy were invited to conduct them. The readings and discussions held in the Otroch Monastery in Tver' reportedly attracted audiences of at least 250 people every Sunday in 1905.[86] Factories provided the most convenient locations to attract large audiences, and the urban clergy found them to be an effective setting in which to involve workers in the parish community. The Moscow diocesan leadership began funding "readings for workers" in 1902, providing free literature and image projectors at numerous locations throughout the city. Metropolitan Vladimir delivered readings himself at Moscow's Historical Museum. These readings included practical, nonreligious themes to broaden their appeal. During the 1907–8 academic year in the city of Moscow, clergymen delivered 238 readings on theology, 140 on law, 118 on history, 42 on literature, 30 on geography, 16 on hygiene, 9 on physics and astronomy, 5 on music, and 4 on agriculture.[87]

While Russia's growing industrial centers loomed over the clergy as threatening sources of impiety, some priests found new opportunities for educational work in cities and factories. Clergymen were not subjected to the same restrictions on their pastoral work in urban centers that they faced in rural parishes. Collaboration between rural parishes, separated by miles, required lengthy authorization procedures and were not always approved.[88] Parish associations were often approved on the condition that they comply with a synodal decree of 1893, which stipulated that they be "associated exclusively with the parish church and not extend [their operations] outside the boundaries of the parish."[89] Urban parishes, by contrast, could not be segregated from one another and often served transient populations from numerous provinces. Some pastors felt alienated by such parishes. A priest who served a parish in the city of Tver' complained in 1905 that "939 workers from the train wagon factory came to my church for confession and Holy Communion. They were not my parishioners, but new arrivals . . . [from sixteen different provinces]. . . . How, I would ask, could I consider these peasants from so many different towns as my parishioners?"[90] In the same year, however, a military priest who served a battalion of soldiers stationed by the railroad near Tver' began delivering public readings for the same factory. He also met with workers individually and organized a choir. The factory administration was so pleased with his work that it paid for the construction of a church for the priest and applied to the consistory to authorize the creation of a new parish to include its workers: "While the factory administration could submit a list of workers who want to be parishioners in the new regimental church, it sees no reason for this, as these workers can leave the factory at any time and be replaced. Consequently, after every change of workers and demand for lists of them, it would be necessary to constantly apply for the opening of a parish around the regimental church without any hope of success."[91] The text of the petition, which the consistory rejected in any case, revealed the superfluity of a separate factory parish. The fluidity and anonymity of the urban environment allowed parishioners to move more easily between churches, as well as confessions, rendering ecclesiastical jurisdiction less meaningful. The challenge of appealing to large crowds of workers was also an opportunity for priests to build larger social networks among Orthodox laity and bring the "internal mission" to more of the population.

Another form of pastoral education that the urban parishes facilitated was the distribution of literature. In previous decades, the village priest had often served as the main conduit of current information to his illiterate parishioners by reading newspapers to them, and this remained the case in some parishes into the twentieth century.[92] Yet, with the spread of literacy and access to printed material, the clergy were forced to compete with other sources of information. One priest described the bewilderment of his peasants by radical articles published in newspapers: "The people, trusting in the printed word, were confused by all the indecent references to the servants of faith and authority. They took all kinds of lies to be the truth."[93] Priests attempted to influence their parishioners' consumption of literature by compiling church libraries. Yet libraries were expensive for rural parishes, and many church elders would not agree to the expenditure of their tithes for the purchase of books.[94] Official restrictions on inter-parish collaboration also limited the capacity of rural parishes to establish common libraries. Yet parish schools could receive donations from diocesan brotherhoods as well as from parishioners for the acquisition of literature.[95] Moreover, urban parish schools served larger communities and attracted more donations to compile libraries for adults as well as children. The frequent migration of peasant workers back to their villages allowed for the broader circulation of books from such libraries. Moscow's parish school inspector's account of the Preobrazhenskii parish school library illustrates the capacity of an urban parish to distribute literature among numerous, smaller communities.

> Books were gathered in a variety of ways and, if necessary, repaired and rebound, so that the library contains more than 2,000 books at this time. . . . First of all, the books are used by students of the school, who take and exchange books every day at five o'clock, both for themselves and for their parents. . . . The parents also take books directly for themselves, usually before their departure to their villages for Christmas, Easter, and at other times. They can take one, two, three, or more at a time, and always return them with gratitude. Large numbers of books, fifty,

one hundred, and even two hundred at a time, are lent to various mills and factories for workers to read. In 1898, books were lent to twenty-one different places. The readership can already be numbered in the thousands.[96]

The parish clergy made the same use of the urban centers as their radical socialist opponents to overcome the isolation of rural communities and circumvent government restrictions on association.

Parish clergy were part of the processes of growing literacy and social change that many of them viewed with trepidation. The pastorate influenced the laity most effectively by eliciting their participation in clerical initiatives, usually on the basis of common priorities, and education was possibly the most salient of such priorities. For the parish clergy, however, education was not merely a practical basis on which to build parish communities. It was an essential component of the Orthodox faith in the modern world. In reports on conditions in the parishes, priests frequently credited the spread of literacy with the persistence of "true faith and piety."[97] Priests noted that this more literate faith of many parishioners was also less subject to traditional authority: "With the development of literacy we also see more conscientious observance of religious duties. Yet with this conscientiousness comes criticism and the erosion of simple, meek faith."[98] A more critical and questioning faith was, however, essential to the parish clergy at the turn of the century, as almost every component of pastoral work required active collaboration rather than passive acceptance, including the *beseda* replacing the sermon.

Criticism of the Parish Schools

By the end of the nineteenth century, parish schools had become the focus of criticism, especially by liberals and socialists. Proponents of zemstvo schools portrayed parish schools as institutions of the state (*kazennye*). They were, therefore, a threat to local autonomy as well as to secular education.[99] Parish schools were first attacked in the press. After the 1905 Revolution, Nicholas II's "October Manifesto" established Russia's first, elected legislative body, the Duma, which served as a new forum and legal avenue through which to attack the schools. The parish clergy were generally accused of using the schools "to arrange positions for their children and relatives."[100] In a 1908 speech in the Duma, one leftist peasant representative argued that the parish schools "do not so much serve the interest of popular education as the material and official interests of their managers and instructors."[101] As many on the political Left considered the clergy to be servile agents of the regime, they argued that the parish school system served as an obstacle to free thought and political self-assertion. The perception of the parish schools as a tool of reactionaries in the government to enrich a parasitic clergy and stifle independent thought has been echoed by historians up to the present.[102]

How did the parish school system become the focus of such widespread hostility? As Ben Eklof points out, the curriculum of the parish schools differed little from that of their zemstvo counterparts: "The official programs of the Church schools (1886) and zemstvo schools (1897) were virtually identical; again and again, studies of time allocation showed that Church and zemstvo schools spent almost the same proportion of the day devoted to each subject; at most, the Church schools gave more attention to Church Slavonic."[103] Yet the clergy were charged not only with attempting to monopolize popular education but also with striving to indoctrinate students in political and moral subservience to the regime. Pavel Miliukov, leader of the Constitutional Democrats (Kadets) and one of the most articulate opponents of the parish schools, expressed this position in a 1908 speech in the Duma: "Defenders of parish schools do not conceal the meaning of the 'religious-moral' education that they expect from them. It is a way to paralyze the political danger that can arise from educating the people in secular schools. Secular schools aim to free the individual, and parish schools aim to limit the individual."[104] In the absence of any institutional justification, such claims were based on the assumption that the parish clergy themselves were agents of the central authorities. This perception was reinforced by some church leaders, like Bishop Mitrofan, who, in his 1908 Duma speech, bellowed that all the empire's schools should be under the authority of the Synod.[105] Far more damaging to the reputation of the parish schools, however, were government policies that seemed to confirm perceptions of the clergy as government agents. Clergymen who taught catechism in secular schools were officially required to monitor the faculty for any signs of impiety or disloyalty. Such regulations rarely had any effect in real life. In secular schools, the clergyman who taught catechism was outnumbered by his lay colleagues and had no real authority over them. The ministerial inspector was much more likely to report a school for fostering disloyal or impious activity than was the priest, who needed the institution to provide him with a salary.[106] Nevertheless, widespread hostility toward the parish schools created an organizational rift between the religious and secular school systems that actually complemented one another's practical efforts at spreading popular education.

A frequent argument that liberal critics leveled at the parish school system was that the Church's cheap system of primary education should make way for the better conditions and better trained teachers that zemstvo taxation could fund. This view was expressed at the outset of a 1901 article, published in the prominent liberal journal *Vestnik Evropy*, which claimed that parish schools were now acting as obstacles to the expansion of the zemstvo school system.[107] This argument ignored the fact that the parish clergy's method of funding their schools had laid the foundation of basic education before the zemstvos even took this task upon themselves and that clerical educators had helped the zemstvos to get their school system up and running. Eklof's research indicates that zemstvo funding for peasant schools amounted to little more than nominal subsidies before 1890, at which point the central government assumed financial responsibility for jails, courts, and other administrative needs, allowing the zemstvos to designate more funding for education.[108] Even after this point, there remained significant overlap between zemstvo and parish education. A number of provincial zemstvos, including Tver's, chose to transfer a large portion of their schools, due to funding shortages, to the diocesan parish school system before 1903.[109] The Tver' zemstvo also opened new schools in collaboration with the diocesan school council during this period.[110] Once the zemstvo system was on its feet, it had the advantage of obligatory taxation. Peasants who had to pay taxes to support a zemstvo school became much less willing to support a parish school voluntarily.[111] Reports from the diocesan inspector appeared by the second decade of the twentieth century regarding the closure of small parish schools due to the opening of new zemstvo schools.[112] If, therefore, parish schools became an obstacle to the expansion of zemstvo education, they were competing at a disadvantage.

It seems likely that the zemstvo and parish school systems continued to cooperate at least as much as they competed, even after the former became well established in most provinces. While literacy was no longer a rarity in peasant communities by the early twentieth century, the problem of illiteracy remained widespread. The "universal system of education," which was being discussed in the Duma, would have had to deal with both huge numbers of illiterate children and large distances between isolated rural settlements. The economical parish schools with smaller numbers of teachers and students could serve communities that their larger zemstvo and ministerial counterparts could not reach. An article from 1901 on the opening of a parish school in a rural Moscow district described such a situation: "Because of the great distance [from the zemstvo school], few children from the village have been able to go to school, and those who go are mostly boys. No more than three to five girls are usually able to attend, which is a tiny number from a population of more than one hundred households."[113] This article reveals another important function that the parish schools had assumed by the beginning of the twentieth century, the education of girls. Synodal statistics indicate that the empire-wide enrollment of boys in parish schools began to slow during the first decade of the century and declined from 1,300,183 in 1910 to 1,297,334 in 1911.[114] Yet the number of schools and overall enrollment increased steadily up to 1914 (the last year statistics were taken) because of the continual increase in the enrollment of girls, which grew from 718,270 in 1913 to 779,749 in 1914.[115] Many zemstvo workers who were directly engaged in popular education, rather than in political campaigns to shape policy, were aware of the continued importance of parish schools in the twentieth century. Thus, in 1907, 58 percent of district zemstvos in thirty-four different provinces voluntarily subsidized parish schools. The representatives of the Tver' and Olonetsk zemstvos spoke in favor of continued support for parish schools at the 1911 Zemstvo Congress on Popular Education held in Moscow.[116]

Ideological opponents of the parish schools charged that clerical education posed a threat to the political and social independence of provincial communities. In 1905, the journal *Russkoe slovo* reported the following resolution of a conference of zemstvo activists: "Popular education should be reorganized on the principles of freedom, democratization, decentralization . . . with the exclusion of the religious element."[117] Yet, as we have seen, parish schools were at least as beholden to their communities as they were to the diocesan authorities and much less beholden to the central government than was the zemstvo school system. Eklof points out the irony of the Duma campaign by advocates of "decentralization" to eliminate the independence of the Church's parish school system by uniting all the empire's schools under the authority and funding of the Ministry of Education.[118] According to a law passed on May 3, 1908, the ministry assumed a large share of the cost of zemstvo school funding and increased the number of inspectors supervising these schools.[119] Opponents of the parish schools succeeded in cutting off funding to the "literacy schools," the smallest and most poorly funded of the parish schools. Yet the Synod retained jurisdiction over parish school funding until June 20, 1917, when the Provisional Government cut off all funding to the Synod for education.[120] Despite the closure of thousands of literacy schools after 1908, parish schools continued to increase in overall number and enrollment up to 1917 thanks to sustained and voluntary local support. Institutionally, they remained more independent of the central government than any of the secular schools.

The parish school controversy serves as a particularly vivid example of the ideological fragmentation of the emerging public sphere of late imperial Russia. The tsarist regime played a central role in aggravating such political rifts during the Duma era. By driving wedges between interest groups in a vain attempt to prevent the coalescence of rival centers of authority, the regime undercut its own social foundation and exacerbated the violence that would characterize the final decades of the Romanov dynasty. By attempting to use clerical educators as spies as well as propagandists, the regime both discredited the parish school system and exposed the clergy themselves to revolutionary violence.

Conclusion

The clerical estate contributed enormously to the spread of literacy in late imperial Russia. The question remains as to how those communities that received education from the clergy and not from any secular institution were uniquely influenced by that education. As we have seen, clerical education was a thoroughly cooperative endeavor. The role of parishioners was so pervasive throughout the entire system of clerical education that it is difficult to portray clerical educators as an army of propagandists for the tsarist regime shoving a doctrine of political conformity down the throats of an oppressed peasantry. This picture reveals more about the liberal ideologues and publicists who painted it based on their perception of the peasantry as inert and passive. The conservatism that intellectuals found so disagreeable about the parish schools was more likely a reflection of the conservatism of the peasantry than of the clergy. Indeed, the congregation of one rural parish reacted with horror to the seminarian revolts in 1905–6 and threatened to stop tithing for the diocesan seminary because it was producing radicals.[121] In places where the peasants were influenced by political radicalism, parish schools were sometimes afflicted by the same violent disorders as the zemstvo schools.[122] Yet the clergy were not passive either, and they provided the leadership behind the enormous project of funding and organizing parish and adult education through association, cooperation, and mutual aid. Herein lay the distinguishing characteristic of clerical education.

On October 18, 1909, in the town of Saratov, Father Sofinskii conducted a *beseda* on the recent suicide of a young man, who had killed himself after his family could no longer pay for his education at the gymnasium. His prepared remarks were published in the diocesan press.

> A young life has ended—for what? Because of nonpayment for the right to study. This is what is happening before our very eyes. And this is at a time of enlightenment, when commerce and industry are being developed. In Saratov we have many factories and mills, many people with incalculable wealth.... We see such examples of indifference on the part of the rich to human needs in other centers of manufacture as well. Next to wealth and luxury huddles desperate need. Are these the Christians of this time of enlightenment? How can we explain these sad facts if not by a lack of Christian teaching, if not by a lack of Christian enlightenment. Only this can teach the rich the gospel of love.[123]

The priest's words reflected the rapid economic changes affecting the Russian Empire, the growing importance of education in this environment, and the parish clergy's response to these developments. While the priest went on to lament the foolishness of the act, his first priority was to condemn the situation that supposedly caused the student's desperation. The greatest expense in every clerical household was the education of their children, and the most important function of most clerical mutual aid societies was to help those who could not meet it. The "Christian enlightenment," which was the clergy's task to impart, was the culture of charity and mutual aid through which the clerical estate had built its own system of diocesan education.

5

The Parish Crisis

IN JANUARY 1906, a sermon that one Father Vinogradov had delivered in his parish church appeared in Moscow's diocesan journal. The priest began by paraphrasing the Epistle of James: "Our faith, if not manifested in works, is a dead faith." He went on to urge his parishioners to manifest their faith by supporting the poor in their parish.

> We, here in this church, are the parish. We have come here to pray to God as a parish, and when the service is over we go home to tend to our own affairs. That is the extent of our parish life. . . . Brothers! When you leave the temple, stop at the threshold and look upon the hands stretched out to you. . . . Those are your brothers and sisters who grew up with you. You know them as your neighbors and now they have fallen into poverty. Is it not painful for you to see them in need? . . . If you want the temple of God to be in order and in grace, form a parish trusteeship. . . . Then we would gather under the blood of our mother— the Church. We would discuss how to satisfy the needs of our temple, and we would think of how to provide alms for the poor of our parish.[1]

Father Vinogradov's sermon reflected the efforts of many parish clergymen to introduce philanthropic mutual aid into the religious practices of their parishioners through admonition, example, and organizational leadership. The preceding chapters of this book have explored the parish clergy's efforts to elicit lay collaboration in the transfer of charitable and educational resources from the official Church back to the lay communities that provided them. The individual parish community was the primary target of this pastoral movement.

Orthodox laypeople were unequal partners in the collaborative relationship that the pastoral movement sought to establish between pastor and parishioner, as the clergy retained ultimate authority over church resources. Once a layperson contributed money to her parish church, it became official church property and the clergy determined its allocation. Control over these resources allowed the clergy to support seminaries, charitable funds, and other diocesan institutions and initiatives without the explicit consent of their parishioners, who were often more interested in local priorities, such as maintaining their parish church. Their exclusion from the management of the Church's resources hindered the laity's involvement in church-based social initiatives and provoked protests against the clergy's confiscation of parish resources. One solution to the laity's alienation from the Church's social mission, beginning in the reform period of the 1860s, was the formation of parish-based associations, such as Father Vinogradov's proposed trusteeship, which would raise their own funds and operate in partnership with the pastorate.

The Orthodox parish of the late Russian Empire has long been scrutinized, far more closely than clerical networks, brotherhoods, and other forms of Church-based association. Contemporary intellectuals argued that the exclusion of the Orthodox people from the management of their own parish resources had engendered a religious crisis in Russia. Modern historians have maintained this assumption and argue that the ultimate failure to carry out comprehensive parish reform resulted in the clergy's loss of influence over popular religiosity. Aleksei Beglov, for example, argues that the laity took little interest in the humanitarian campaigns that priests asked them to support: "Parishioners, especially peasants, were indifferent to the lion's share of these collections."[2] As a result, Beglov observes, pastors diverted the regular contributions of their parishioners toward their own social initiatives to the detriment of local priorities, causing parish churches to fall into disrepair. Scholars have also argued that the compromise solution of promoting parish associations among the laity did little to heal the rift with the work of the pastorate.[3] Certainly, the religious priorities of the laity often differed from those of the clergy. Yet this scholarly focus on the "parish crisis" has obscured the pastoral movement's impact on religious life. As discussed in previous chapters, lay collaboration in clerical social work was prominent in the parish school movement as well as in multiple humanitarian relief campaigns. Moreover, the growth of parish associations was more significant than critics have claimed. Tension over control of parish resources provoked dialogue between clerical and lay religiosity. The clergy's promotion of parish associations was a part of that dialogue, and the response of the laity was gradual but robust. Parish associations collaborated with clerical and secular organizations to achieve common goals. Imperial Russia's "parish crisis" engendered an expansion of voluntary association across social boundaries of estate and class.

The Origins of the Parish Question

The exclusion of the laity from the governance of their own parishes occurred as a direct result of Peter I's initiative to develop an educated parish clergy. Before the eighteenth century, most parishes coincided with the rural commune, and candidates for the priesthood were elected by parishioners. Peter I initiated the consolidation of these parishes into larger units, sacrificing their social cohesion so that clergymen could draw on the support of larger numbers of parishioners to fund the education of their sons. Candidates for the priesthood came to be drawn from a hereditary estate rather than from the communities they served and were selected by the bishop on the basis of their education.[4] The right of parishioners to elect their priest was formally revoked in 1797.[5] In the early nineteenth century, a reform project for the expansion and improvement of clerical education resulted in the 1808 Instructions to Church Elders, which decreed that all revenue from ritual candle sales, a major source of parish income, should be sent to the diocesan center for the support of clerical education.[6] The church elder, an elected representative of the parishioners responsible for the joint management of parish funds with the clergy, would no longer report parish expenditures to his community. While still elected by his fellow parishioners, the elder would now present accounting statements to the clerical superintendent alone.[7] One contemporary equated this act with Peter I's Spiritual Regulation and Catherine II's secularization of monastic lands in terms of its impact on church life in Russia.[8]

The disenfranchisement of parishioners deprived the laity of any meaningful organ of assembly at the parish level. After the 1808 reform, the parish assembly (*prikhodskoe sobranie*) served almost no purpose other than the election of the church elder and often went for years without meeting. It lacked even the authority to compel its own members to contribute to parish maintenance. After the abolition of serfdom, this task was performed more effectively by the village council (*sel'skii skhod*), several of which typically fell within the boundaries of the parish. This body, established in 1861 to administer the rural commune (*obshchina*), was empowered to levy minor taxes to meet local necessities, including those of the parish. While its members did not assemble as parishioners, the village council often assumed the task of financing the parishes, together with redistributing communal farmland and collecting redemption payments.[9] It is not surprising that this arrangement failed to generate enthusiasm for parish life and led to chronic shortfalls in support for the parish clergy and their schools. The partial withdrawal of the gentry from the countryside after emancipation, moreover, deprived many parishes of wealthy patrons and exacerbated clerical impoverishment.

A solution to the decline of the parish became a target of the 1860s reformers. I. S. Belliustin's scandalous exposé, together with signs of "socialist aspirations" among some parish clergymen, brought the poor condition of the parish clergy to the attention of church and state leaders.[10] In 1861, Minister of Internal Affairs Petr Valuev submitted a proposal for church reform to the emperor. Many within the Church hierarchy viewed this initiative as a brazen intrusion into the spiritual domain by the state. Nevertheless, Valuev's proposal resulted in the formation of a joint commission of synodal prelates and state ministers, chaired by Metropolitan Isidor of Saint Petersburg, to draw up a program for church reform. The commission's work, which began in January 1863, stumbled over the conflicting priorities of church and state leaders. State officials resisted any resolution to obtain government funding for the project, preferring to enlist the support of parishioners to improve the conditions and status of the parish clergy. The reformers hoped to obtain this support by empowering the laity to play a more active role in parish life through new "civil privileges."[11] The prelates, however, refused to relinquish any authority over the parish or its resources in order to prevent their confiscation by the bureaucracy, the zemstvos, or the peasantry. The final outcome of the commission's work was the establishment on August 2, 1864, of the parish trusteeship (*prikhodskoe popechitel'stvo*) as a compromise solution. This was to be a voluntary association, chaired by the priest, and open to all adult members of a particular parish. Membership was mandatory for other clergymen working in the parish, sacristans and deacons, as well as for the church elder. The official purpose of the association was "to care for the economic development and welfare of the parish church and clergy, primary education for children, and charitable activities within the bounds of the parish."[12] In pursuit of these goals, however, the trusteeships were not permitted to access their parish church's funds. They were legally segregated from the Church and had to raise their own donations separately from regular church collections.

For those who took it, the trusteeships presented an opportunity for laypeople to assume control over the collection and allocation of religious donations. The initial response was underwhelming. By 1864, only 20 percent of the empire's parishes had established trusteeships.[13] Even at this early stage, however, the trusteeships presented a challenge to clerical authority. In 1870, the Synod received a stream of petitions and applications from many parishes and a number of provincial zemstvo assemblies for the resolution of disagreements with parish clergy over the right of the trusteeships to control their churches' finances. In response, the Synod reiterated that these associations only had the right to dispose of those funds that they had collected themselves.[14] In the same year, the trusteeships that had been established throughout the empire collectively spent 85 percent of the funds they had raised on church construction and renovation, versus 11 percent and 4 percent on charity and support for the clergy, respectively.[15] The hope that this reform would improve conditions for the parish clergy, therefore, had been dashed. These results also demonstrated that if parishioners were given control over parish resources, they were likely to divert funding away from seminaries and other diocesan institutions. This realization further entrenched the hierarchy's resolve to retain control of parish resources. At the same time, the trusteeships had presented the laity with the prospect of a greater voice in church affairs, and many among the Orthodox population would press for more.

Dreams of the Parish

The various solutions proposed for the parish question were often premised on utopian visions of what the parish should be. The proper organization and function of the parish within the larger Church structure were open to debate in the nineteenth century because of the "lack of a uniform, official ecclesiological vision in Russian Orthodoxy."[16] This ambiguity encouraged competition among rival claimants to authority over the parish as a religious community. A variety of interest groups articulated proposals for parish reform on the basis of both theology and social policy. Many of these proposals disregarded the actual religious priorities of the Orthodox laity and their pastors, while taking for granted the community's support for a particular ideological agenda.

The imperial state had acted as the main social engineer of the parish since the reforms of Peter I. State promotion of clerical education and pastoral services yielded a parish network that collected information and provided civil services and was largely supported by the population itself. During cholera outbreaks, for example, priests received orders from the provincial governor, passed through the consistory, to instruct their parishioners in proper sanitary practices and to supplement the work of the police by monitoring compliance with those instructions. The clergy of Moscow and Tver' received such orders as late as 1908 and 1910, respectively.[17] The resources necessary to educate and support the clergy continued to come from parishioner tithes, subsidized but not replaced by government funding. This burden grew along with the clerical population, and organizing support for the growing numbers of impoverished members of their estate became an official as well as a social obligation of parish priests. In 1901, Moscow's priests were reminded in their diocesan journal of their official duty to oversee the care and supervise the behavior of poor members of the clerical estate living within their parishes.[18] A superintendent report from Tver' in 1905 illustrates the magnitude of this responsibility: "There are eight male orphans and sixty-two female orphans in the district. Forty-two of them receive aid from the diocesan trusteeship. Several receive a pension from the diocesan pension fund and live in houses left to them by their families. One lives in a rented apartment for lack of her own. All the orphans behave honestly."[19] The use of parish resources to support the clerical estate as a parallel society and auxiliary civil service meant that pious donations were being diverted to institutions and services that many laypeople saw as irrelevant to their religious lives.

It is ironic that many zemstvo leaders envisioned a similarly utilitarian role for the parish in local government, even as they pressed for its emancipation from the burden of supporting the clergy. In 1880, the assembly of the Moscow zemstvo submitted a petition to the Ministry of Internal Affairs, calling for recognition of the parish as an independent "legal entity" (*iuridicheskoe litso*) with ownership over its own property. The petitioners reasoned that the parish could provide social welfare and education for the local population on behalf of the zemstvo if it were granted this status. Moscow's governor blocked the petition on the grounds that it exceeded the zemstvo's competence, but the zemstvos of Saint Petersburg, Voronezh, and Poltava added their support to the petition the following year. It was finally submitted to the ministry in 1883 and then forwarded to the Synod, which rejected any changes to the legal status of the parish on the grounds that this would result in spiritually divisive court disputes over parish property.[20] Over subsequent decades, zemstvo leaders continued to advocate the transformation of the parish into a "small zemstvo unit" (*melkaia zemskaia edinitsa*) with powers of taxation and administrative responsibilities.[21]

The liberal wing of the zemstvo movement saw the parish as a form of civil society (*obshchestvennost*'). In their eyes, the parish clergy were often perceived not as leaders or even members of civil society but as hired functionaries, representing officialdom rather than their community. Tat'iana Leont'eva points out, for example, that Pavel Miliukov ignored the role of the pastor in his *Notes on the History of Russian Culture*, when he attributed the growth of primary education in Russia to civil society. As Leont'eva argues, "Without that object of liberal disdain, the parish priest, civil society could not have gotten the project moving."[22] Members of the first zemstvo assemblies of Moscow, Tver', Saint Petersburg, and Tambov petitioned, unsuccessfully, for the exclusion of clergymen from service as elected representatives on the grounds that they paid no zemstvo dues and that worldly interests should be "completely foreign to members of the clerical station."[23] In fact, parish clergymen would take on a variety of responsibilities within the zemstvos over subsequent decades. In 1914, the bishop of Tver' wrote the following comments in his letter to the oberprocurator: "The great majority of the clergy should be considered zemstvo workers. . . . They work as teachers of catechism in zemstvo schools, as attendants in zemstvo hospitals, shelters for the elderly, orphanages, and jails. They participate in small zemstvo credit unions, cooperatives, and grain banks. They work as statisticians, providing the zemstvos with data on births, marriages, deaths, infectious and epidemic diseases, and harvests. They participate in zemstvo fire brigades."[24] Zemstvo boards frequently recommended priests for diocesan commendations for these uncompensated services.[25] At the same time, zemstvo leaders sought to limit the pastorate's influence over rural society. In 1879, one church publication described a Kulturkampf being conducted against the parish clergy by zemstvo workers (*zemtsy*).[26] In the same decade, the zemstvos of Pskov, Chernigov, Perm', and Odessa proposed their own assumption of responsibility for the support of the parish clergy with levied taxes in place of parishioner emoluments. The Synod as well as the parish clergy rejected the plan, as it would have converted the pastorate into zemstvo employees, subject to discipline and control by the zemstvo boards.[27] By 1905, having failed to incorporate either the parish or the clergy into their administrative structures, the zemstvos of certain gubernias, including Tver', began levying taxes on property attached to rural parishes and occupied by clergymen, their families, and their widows, adding to the financial burden of the pastorate.[28]

The Slavophile movement provided theological justification for parish autonomy within the Church. The main founder of Slavophile thought, Aleksei Khomiakov (1804–60), claimed that the Orthodox Church derived its unity from an internal collective bond, which he identified with the peasant commune (*obshchina*). The cohesion of the lay community was, according to Khomiakov, no less important to the Church's integrity than the authority of the hierarchy. Absent this internal bond, hierarchic authority imposed a purely external and compulsory unity, which is how Khomiakov characterized the Roman Catholic Church.[29] For Khomiakov's intellectual followers, the parish was the ecclesiastical expression of the Orthodox community. Dmitrii Samarin (1831–1901), brother of the more prominent Slavophile Iurii Samarin, composed a series of articles in 1867–68, which compared the parish to a living cell in the body of the Church. Samarin argued that the exclusion of laypeople from the management of parish finances amounted to the "bureaucratization" of this fundamental unit of religious life and later initiated the Moscow zemstvo's 1880 petition for parish reform in an effort to emancipate this living cell.[30] Like many zemstvo activists, Samarin assumed that the liberated parish community would voluntarily contribute its energy and resources to social welfare in collaboration with local government. For their part, Orthodox peasants rarely identified even their worldly interests with their local zemstvo and were unlikely to have turned to this institution for the regulation of their religious lives.[31]

Aleksandr Papkov (1852–1920), governor of the Finnish province of Hämeenlinna and latter-day Slavophile, envisioned a more radically independent parish community than most of his contemporaries. Through his prolific writings, from the 1890s up to 1917, Papkov described the parish as a self-contained religious community on whose autonomy the life of the Church depended: "We can only awaken from this pernicious, death-like sleep when we begin to rouse each other and enter into close, brotherly contact with one another and with our pastors. This can best be achieved on the foundation of the parish. That is why it is essential that we rid this foundation of all obstacles, barriers, and alien elements, and that is why the question of the Orthodox parish . . . is so important."[32] Papkov was unique among advocates of parish reform in that he sought parish autonomy for its own sake and not in the interest of state services or representative government. He therefore opposed all bureaucratic intrusion into parish life, including state subsidies to support the parish clergy.[33] Papkov argued that by consolidating all their skills and resources for the care of their community, parishioners could achieve self-sufficiency and obviate the intervention of "alien elements" into parish life. He based this claim on an idealized conception of the medieval Russian parish.[34] Yet his vision of the parish was modern. Papkov argued that the participation of women as educators and organizers in the parish community was essential to its success: "Everyone knows the prominent and beneficial role played by women in the Christian world, as well as their propensity and sensitivity for educational and charitable work in the Christian spirit."[35] Once realized, moreover, Papkov's ideal parish community would be capable of supporting the parish clergy as well as the urban poor. He quoted a speech by the historian Mikhail Pogodin to express this hope: "'Faith without works is dead,' said the apostle. . . . In different European cities and in Saint Petersburg, there are various charitable societies that take upon themselves the obligation of helping the needy . . . but we in Moscow can do this in the parishes much more easily and expeditiously."[36] Papkov was deeply involved in most negotiations for parish reform up to and beyond 1917. His zeal for parish autonomy stemmed, it seems, from his deep faith in the potential of the local Orthodox community.

The Church's prelates viewed the parish question from a "macroeclesial" perspective, as Vera Shevzov puts it. They identified the Church's unity with their own authority as successors to the apostles rather than with the internal bond of the parish community.[37] According to their scenario, the parish priest served as an extension of the bishop's apostolic authority at the parish level. While the bishops recognized the laity's alienation from parish life as a problem, most were more concerned by the danger of bankrupting the dioceses if control over parish resources were transferred to parishioners. In his 1906 commentary on church reform, Moscow's Metropolitan Vladimir (Bogoiavlenskii) said: "Despite the undeniable benefits that we could expect for the revival of parish life by involving parishioners in the management of their church's finances, it seems to me that this issue demands extreme caution. It could come to pass that all the church's resources would be spent on the parish with nothing left for the Church or for vital Church institutions such as clerical schools."[38] For the revitalization of the parish community, the bishops placed their hopes in the leadership of the parish clergy as agents of their own authority. As Metropolitan Vladimir went on to say, "The dedication of one pastor can accomplish much in this regard. . . . And it is still better if the entire parish gathers around its pastor and its church to form a close community, the members of which live one life with common interests."[39] As the preceding chapters of this book have argued, the Synod permitted the formation of a diverse array of associations for the parish clergy in order to facilitate pastoral leadership over strong Orthodox communities. Yet the bishops simultaneously restricted the parish clergy's ability to organize community initiatives by maintaining administrative oversight over all diocesan property. To quote Vladimir again, "Church funds and property are holy possessions, which by apostolic law are subject to the authority and disposal of the bishop."[40] What this meant in practice was that not even the pastor could make a managerial decision of any significance without the explicit approval of the prelate, the attainment of which involved a cumbersome application process. The result, as Papkov lamented in a 1902 publication, was that a parish priest could never make a quick bid on a potential property acquisition for his parish; he always lost out to other buyers or had to pay more than the initial asking price.[41]

The case of a property acquisition by a parish trusteeship in Tver' diocese illustrates this situation. In 1909, one Father Nikol'skii wrote to the Tver' consistory, asking for the bishop's permission to finalize the purchase of an estate by his parish's trusteeship. This purchase had in fact been concluded in 1898 when his predecessor had taken out a loan through the trusteeship to purchase an estate of 222 *desiatiny* (about 599.4 acres) from a noble family for 16,000 rubles. While a local notary had approved this purchase, the senior notary in the city of Kashin had refused to confirm it until the bishop's approval was obtained. Father Nikol'skii openly admitted that his now deceased predecessor "knew why the senior notary did not confirm the purchase and perhaps even knew that he would never confirm it. But, he did not petition the diocesan authorities because he knew that they would not allow the trusteeship to take out such a sizable loan."[42] However, the Senate had passed a law on January 31, 1900, that authorized all charitable associations affiliated with the Church to purchase property without prior authorization. Citing both this law and the fact that the trusteeship had paid off all but 2,708.41 rubles of its debt for the purchase, Father Nikol'skii requested that his trusteeship be confirmed as owner of the estate. The consistory took three years to respond. In January 1912, Tver's bishop signed a decision that the original purchase had been illegal and could not be retroactively confirmed. However, in light of the fact that the trusteeship had paid most of its debt through timber sales and parishioner contributions, the purchase could now be confirmed under the new law, an apparently meaningless distinction.[43] Like many of their ideological opponents, the synodal prelates were willing to sacrifice the parish community's viability in order to preserve their authority over it.

Their common priority of empowering the parish community proved an insufficient basis for compromise among the self-appointed defenders of the parish. On March 6, 1906, in the wake of revolution and Konstantin Pobedonostsev's resignation as ober-procurator, Nikolai II convened the Pre-Sobor Commission at Alexander Nevskii Monastery. This body was tasked with preparations for an All-Russian Church Sobor, which was expected to overhaul the synodal system of church administration and possibly restore the Patriarchate of Moscow. The commission's fourth section, out of seven, focused on parish reform. This section included Papkov and other church scholars but was dominated by representatives of the parish clergy. It drafted a proposal for the division of parish property and finances into three different categories: Church, parish clergy, and parishioner. The guardianship of each category would constitute a separate legal entity (*iuridicheskoe litso*). The third category would be governed by elected bodies of parishioners and given broad authority over parish property and religious education. This compromise solution provoked controversy in the general assembly of the commission but also attracted supporters, including some prelates such as Archbishop Sergei (Stragorodskii) of Finland, the future Patriarch of Moscow. Yet the commission concluded its work in December, and the Sobor was delayed indefinitely, allowing the Synod to seize control of the reform process. By September 1908, the Synod had approved its own reform project, produced by an internal commission, which included no members from the parish clergy. The Synod's proposal was to divide the parish into two entities, rejecting legal autonomy for the parish clergy. Parishioners would manage a truncated sphere of local concerns but would be entirely excluded from "church property," which would remain under the authority of the Synod. This project came under intense criticism from the Council of Ministers for the diminutive role it proposed for the parish community and was ultimately withdrawn.[44] Over subsequent years, the Duma also formulated a number of reform projects. In 1911, for example, the Third Duma designated 14 million rubles to relieve poor laypeople of the burden of supporting their clergy. When distributed among the many impoverished parishes of the empire, however, this subsidy provided salaries of only 100 to 300 rubles a year for some priests, which did not eliminate their reliance on parishioners for support.[45] Moreover, the Synod systematically rejected the structural reforms proposed by the Duma, most of which involved the transfer of control over parish property to the laity. Although bishops as well as priests serving in the Duma participated in the drafting of these proposals, the Synod designated them "illegal, uncanonical intrusions into the internal administration of the Orthodox Church."[46] The initiative for parish reform never escaped this stalemate among its competing advocates.

The parish clergyman, often sidelined in the public debates over the proper organization of the Orthodox parish, remained the leading activist for the renewal of parish life on a practical level. While various interests found charity and mutual aid within the parish communities useful or ideologically appealing, it was primarily the pastoral work of the parish clergy that provided an "authorizing discourse," to use Talal Asad's terminology, for these practices as devotional activity in the context of Orthodox Christianity. As we have seen, moreover, this work was performed despite the chronic intervention into parish life by the competing interests of Church, state, and educated society. The clerical perception of these influences on the parish was expressed in an article, published in Moscow's diocesan journal in 1906, which related the comments of one priest at a pastoral assembly. The writer praised the stoic dedication of the parish priest to his work, despite these intrusions: "Why is he not affected by those influences that have destroyed our parishes; the pressure of the secular and ecclesiastical authorities, material deprivation, the union of Church and state, and so on? It is obvious that these influences are not important and cannot hinder the work of a priest."[47] Despite the failure of parish reform at the institutional level, pastoral work over the late nineteenth and early twentieth centuries focused on the organization of new parish associations through which to elicit the collaboration of laypeople in the management of the Church as a society.

Voices from the Parish

At least as early as the reforms of the 1860s, when they gained the necessary freedoms of association and expression to perform such work, parish clergymen had made efforts to rally their parish communities around institutions of charity and mutual aid, similar to those that existed in the clerical community. Father Gumilevskii established Saint Petersburg's first two charitable brotherhoods in his parish in 1863.[48] He also published a journal with three other priests, *The Spirit of a Christian*, in which he expressed his ideas on pastoral service. In an 1862 issue of this journal, Gumilevskii argued that "the most common form of religious community in Russia is the parish. The parish represents the local community in its religious sense, and the parish clergy represents the local ecclesiastical administration. The priest should be present in all corners of parish life and hear all the groans of real poverty. The parish, as a Christian community, penetrated by the love of Christ, is obligated to care for its poorest members and for the orphans and widows of its clergy."[49] Gumilevskii expressed the outlook of other pastors of his time that the parish should serve the social needs of parishioners as well as clergy. In 1862, one other priest in Saint Petersburg and four priests in Moscow established charities to care for poor parishioners.[50] These forerunners of the pastoral movement, whose efforts preceded the Special Commission's establishment of the parish trusteeship by two years, strove to extend the mutual aid culture of the parish clergy into the parish communities in order to sustain both. These efforts were directed at a population that was increasingly resentful of its marginalization within the Church and occasionally hostile to the clergy.

The pastoral movement acquired a sense of urgency by the early twentieth century, when the 1905 Revolution released a surge of popular resentment against the Church. Beginning in January 1906, parishioners across the empire began refusing to support their clergy, contribute to parish collections, or pay rent for the parish land they had leased.[51] These boycotts were even more alarming to the clergy than the acts of anti-religious violence that also took place, because they presented an existential threat to the clerical community and its institutions. Reports identified the immediate cause of these boycotts to be radical agitators delivering speeches in taverns, schools, and outside churches during services, urging peasants to throw off the yoke of the greedy clergy.[52] This radical mood subsided in most dioceses after a month, but reports by priests on the state of their parishes that year expressed great concern over the laity's alienation from the diocesan economy. A superintendent in Tver' diocese reported that "recently, the peasants have become more and more dissatisfied with the clergy in many districts of our diocese. . . . I know that in three parishes, in a district outside of my jurisdiction, the parishioners have composed proposals for a reduction in payments for [religious] services. Such a proposal, unexpected by the clergy, was raised in a parish council in Novotorzhok district, and was followed by political discussions regarding the general lack of rights, the unlimited authority of the police, and of the hard lot of the peasant."[53] As the report suggests, parishioners had begun to equate their marginalization within the ecclesiastical structure with their political marginalization within the state. In response, the clergy's efforts to integrate parishioners into the clerical system of mutual aid assumed the character of a crisis response. In a 1907 contribution to Moscow's diocesan journal, for example, a priest explained his intentions in organizing a parish trusteeship: "I wanted to show the peasants, at least on a small scale, the concern of the Church for their needs. After all, the peasants have become accustomed always and everywhere to view the Church as an institution to which they must give."[54] In order to create a more collaborative relationship between clergy and laity, the pastoral movement sought to reshape the devotional culture of the population.

This devotional culture is expressed in the plentiful records of complaints and commendations of clergymen by the increasingly literate laity in the early twentieth century. The Orthodox believers of Russia remained extremely devout, and they valued their pastor's dedication to maintaining their ancestral church and performing the ancient liturgy.[55] While most parishioners were not opposed to charitable work, this was not typically the main quality they sought in a parish priest. Letters to the diocesan consistory from parishioners in praise of their pastor, usually nominating him for a cross of honor, almost invariably begin with praises of his maintenance of their church and performance of liturgical services. The organization of charity is often mentioned as a corollary to the pastor's effectiveness as a steward of the tradition. The accompanying endorsement of the parishioners' letters, written by the local archpriest-superintendent, expressed the religious values of the clergy and usually presented a mirror image of the original commendation. The superintendents typically emphasized the pastor's charitable work and mentioned church maintenance along with sobriety as merely expected prerequisites of a worthy clergyman.[56]

It was not only peasant parishioners who prioritized the ritual component of pastoral work over social activism. In an articulate letter to the metropolitan of Moscow from September 1905, a group of urban parishioners complained that their priest refused to perform the commemoration of the dead on Sundays. In compliance with his orders from the diocesan authorities, he performed this rite on weekdays, when parishioners were too busy to attend: "The prayers of our pastor alone, to which we cannot join our prayerful sighs, do not satisfy us and do not give us complete spiritual comfort." The parishioners threatened defection to other parishes and warned that some among them might "convert to various sects," which would impoverish the parish. Such an outcome would be a shame, they remarked, as their parish is already short of money "as a result of extensive charitable activity."[57] Here again, the organization of charity is referenced as a peripheral benefit, rather than an essential duty, of a functional pastor. The challenge of the pastoral movement, therefore, was to integrate mutual aid into the traditional life of the parish.

Lay and clerical priorities converged in the organizational work of the pastor. For the maintenance of traditional ritual features of parish life, parishioners relied on their priest's skills at organizing contributions of resources and work. The letters of parishioners to the diocesan consistories often credit their pastors with providing the initiative and organization behind church renovations. Beyond mere fundraising, parishioners valued pastors who could galvanize their scattered communities into a cohesive parish: "His reverent services and preaching of the word of God have attracted parishioners, despite our parish's dispersal across various places around Sergiev Posad, to visit the temple of God and to unite into one common flock."[58] This quality was especially valued in the early twentieth century because of the crisis of faith that laymen and laywomen felt as acutely as their clergymen. The decline of religious observance, the appearance of urban vices in the villages, and the spread of radical ideology, all concomitants of rapid industrialization, led many of the Orthodox faithful to feel that their world was under attack. Participants in icon processions during Orthodox holidays were subjected to the drunken jeers of young factory workers who had lost their faith while away from the village.[59] Residents of several parishes in Tver's Novotorzhok district were afraid to attend service on Easter Sunday of 1905 because pamphlets had been circulated threatening to set off bombs in their churches on that day.[60] The Orthodox faithful appreciated the innovations of their parish clergy to attract young people back to the Church. In this sense, the cultural upheaval of the early twentieth century presented the clergy with an opportunity to rebuild and reshape their parishes.

The sobriety society may have been the most versatile association available to priests to strengthen their parish communities. Clergymen first began opening parish sobriety societies in the 1880s, and they achieved great popularity in the early twentieth century.[61] Sobriety societies fell under the supervision of the Ministry of Internal Affairs, represented by the provincial governor. Membership was open to people living within a society's designated sphere of operations, usually one parish, but sometimes an entire city. Students, soldiers, and ex-criminals were forbidden to join, and the societies were subject to immediate closure should the governor learn of criticism of the state by its members. Nevertheless, this institution helped the parish clergy to bypass official restrictions on association because almost any activity could be justified in a sobriety society for the sake of providing parishioners with a recreational alternative to drinking. Members could engage in recreational activities such as chess, billiards, plays, concerts, and public lectures with projected images, all of which helped to restore the parish as a center of social life.[62] Organizers retained the devotional focus of these associations by incorporating liturgical singing and icon processions, as well as offering spiritual guidance to parishioners struggling with alcoholism. In a report on his society from 1906, one Tver' priest demonstrated particular sensitivity to alcohol addiction, recognizing the likelihood of relapses: "An oath can too strongly affect people of weak spirit (as alcoholics are). It shakes their very being and, if a person cannot keep his vow (as is often the case), it weighs heavily on his conscience as a grave sin. The Troitse-Viazniki society handles the matter more simply: An inductee into the sobriety society must listen to a prayer to the local icon, the Iverskaia Mother of God. During the prayer, the inductee must kiss the icon, Gospel, and cross, making an internal oath."[63] The sobriety societies thus provided pastors with a means of combining devotional practices with social activism.

Establishing a social problem such as alcoholism as an appropriate focus of parish life allowed pastors to emphasize parishioners' personal responsibility toward one another. In addition to supporting common efforts at sobriety, members were encouraged to sponsor the participation of those who were too poor to pay society dues. One priest explained the arrangement thus: "Each person inducted as a full member contributed 1 ruble and 20 kopecks for the Society, of which 1 ruble is used for routine expenses, and 20 kopecks are invested in a special fund to aid particularly needy members."[64] Members were also encouraged to extend such social support beyond the confines of the societies. The organization of charitable contributions for poor members of the parish was almost always included among the activities of any parish sobriety society. In 1906, one society in Tver' diocese spent 121.06 rubles on clothes, shoes, books, livestock, food, funerals, and marriages for poor parishioners.[65] The priest who organized this society stressed that such contributions, and membership dues in general, were strictly voluntary, in order to avoid accusations that the association existed for his profit, rather than for the community. "Collective donations or the contributions of some members for use by the society are taken as payment. . . . [Otherwise] Suspicions could arise that the society was established only in order to increase the priest's personal income."[66] Many of these sobriety societies thus resembled the clergy's own diocesan institutions of mutual aid. Pastors incorporated charity and mutual aid into these associations not just to provide community support for the common endeavor of sobriety but also to instill these practices into the religious life of their parishes. By the twentieth century, many sobriety societies had more than one thousand members.[67]

While sobriety societies, parish schools, choirs, and brotherhoods helped parish clergymen incorporate mutual aid into the practice of Orthodox Christianity, these parish-based associations were usually organized for specific goals such as education or missionary work, for which philanthropic activity served as a means of support. For all its faults, the parish trusteeship remained the best institution available to the parish priest to inculcate mutual aid as an essential devotional practice and a proper focus of parish life.

The Parish Trusteeship

The prelates and ministers of the Special Commission had primarily intended for the trusteeships to ameliorate clerical poverty and to maintain the parishes. In 1868, in response to requests from a number of parish trusteeships for clarification as to how they should allocate the funds they collected, the Synod issued the following statement: "The purpose of establishing the trusteeships is to render aid to the government and to the Church in maintaining the beauty of the parish church and in providing for her servants."[68] As Tat'iana Pankrat points out in her study of the parish trusteeships, "Charity was far from the first priority here."[69] It was the parish clergymen tasked with organizing the trusteeships who shifted their focus to the needs of the laity. In an article from 1907, one priest from Moscow expressed his embarrassment at the official rules of the trusteeships, which encouraged participants to designate funds for the support of their clergy, and avoided reading them to his parishioners.[70] Clergymen elicited participation in parish trusteeships as a form of religious observance, which included devotional practices to which parishioners were accustomed, such as icon veneration and singing, but incorporated engagement of the material concerns of the parish community.[71] As noted above, the trusteeships received a lukewarm response from most parishioners when they were first introduced. Gregory Freeze concludes that "in fact most parishes refused to establish a council [trusteeship] and, even when they did, the new organ accomplished little indeed."[72] Over time, however, the trusteeships grew in number and exerted a greater social and cultural impact on Orthodox Russia than such dismissive assessments suggest (see tables 1 and 2).

By 1902, approximately half of all parishes in the empire had established a trusteeship.[73] The majority of their resources, about 75 percent according to empire-wide statistics, was dedicated to the construction and renovation of parish churches, while only around 20 percent, or 735,563 rubles, was dedicated to education and charity.[74] Nevertheless, this figure represented an important source of social support for certain communities, especially in the absence of effective state welfare. In 1905, for example, "the townships and communes of all fifty provinces of European Russia spent only 1.9 percent of their entire budget on aid to the needy (1.4 million rubles)."[75] Moreover, the trusteeships of certain dioceses were heavily focused on mutual aid. In 1913, the trusteeships of thirteen out of the empire's sixty-four dioceses dedicated the majority of their resources to charity and education. These included Moscow, Tver', Saint Petersburg, Warsaw, Vladimir, Voronezh, Kaluga, Perm', Pskov, Riga, Ryazan', Stavropol', and Yaroslavl'.[76] A survey of expenditures by the trusteeships of Moscow and Tver' during the empire's final decades suggests a sustained increase in the

Table 1. Trusteeships: Tver' Diocese, 1884–1913

				Allocation			
Year	Parishioners	Trusteeships	Total expenditures	Support for clergy	Church establishment	Charity/ eduction	Avg per cap.
1884	1,623,720	155	1,707.09	654.77	668.57	383.75	.001
1894	1,711,578	164	1,455.06	332.44	362.32	760.30	.001
1905	1,889,864	182	3,081.19	0	538.75	2,542.44	.002
1907	1,898,540	190	4,969.51	0	1,267.14	3,702.37	.003
1913	1,904,672	220	10,605.84	0	1,348.41	9,257.43	.005

Source: *Vsepoddanneishie otchety Ober-prokurora Sviateishago Sinoda po vedomstvu Pravoslavnago ispovedaniia za 1884, 1894–95, 1905–7, 1913.*

Table 2. Trusteeships: Moscow Diocese, 1884–1913

				Allocation			
Year	Parishioners	Trusteeships	Total expenditures	Support for clergy	Church establishment	Charity/ eduction	Avg per cap.
1884	1,495,708	54	30,676.07	0	2,365.97	28,310.10	.021
1894	1,561,327	66	58,759.20	0	277.35	58,481.85	.038
1905	1,721,962	124	81,175.65	0	221.44	80,954.21	.047
1907	1,776,754	136	80,006.03	0	283.61	79,722.42	.045
1913	1,826,691	189	72,669.42	0	377.19	72,292.23	.040

Source: *Vsepoddanneishie otchety Ober-prokurora Sviateishago Sinoda po vedomstvu Pravoslavnago ispovedaniia za 1884, 1894–95, 1905–7, 1913.*

importance of philanthropic mutual aid in the religious lives of parishioners in those dioceses. While parish trusteeships did not provide significant financial contributions to social support per capita, they served specific needs, often in cooperation with other institutions. In 1909, for example, parish trusteeships of Tver' maintained nine shelters for the elderly and infirm while the zemstvos supported seven.[77]

Where they could be established, parish trusteeships provided efficient and appropriate responses to immediate needs, based on local knowledge. Reports and articles on the work of trusteeships frequently mention aid for victims of emergencies such as fires and floods.[78] Even those with scant resources could stand ready for emergencies, such as one trusteeship in rural Tver' with only 200 rubles in 1906, "from which parishioners distribute grants in cases of great misfortune."[79] Larger trusteeships were able to provide regular services for local needs. One sizable trusteeship in a rural parish of Moscow delivered crucial support for the parish school and aid to needy peasants and protected the dignity of poor families by caring for their dead. In 1903, its priest reported the following expenditures: "Burials for the poor—22 rubles. Given to the poor on holidays—129.64 rubles. Salaries for parish school night watchman—77 rubles. Given to the victims of a fire in Pokrovskaia village—57 rubles. Payment for insurance on the parish school—30.40 rubles. For the purchase of food for pupils in this school—45.92 rubles. For the construction of drainage ditches around the cemetery—23.65 rubles. Other expenses—32.35 rubles."[80] Clerical organizers prevented waste and misuse of their limited resources by investigating requests for aid. Many reports detail investigations in order to determine the proper distribution of aid. A 1903 report from one Moscow parish describes such investigations.

> Grants from the trusteeship are given exclusively to poor residents of the parish from all social backgrounds, both families and individuals. They must be in true need of help and known for their poverty, industriousness, and honest behavior. Grants are also distributed to those unable to work because of sickness. Among those receiving grants, some are blind, deaf, paralyzed, and so on. In order to investigate the circumstances of those applying for aid, the parish priests, Fathers Beliaev and Pomerantsev, visited their apartments and beheld sad sights of desperate need, poverty, and sorrow.[81]

This careful and efficient use of limited resources resembled the work of the clergy's own charitable associations.

Clerical reports indicate that the absence of trusteeships in many parishes was not necessarily indicative of apathy toward mutual aid on the part of the laity. One superintendent from Tver' reported in 1906 that "no parish trusteeships have been opened in the churches of this district [*okrug*] because of the poverty of the parishioners." Yet parishioners were "sympathetic and charitable to all who are in need and who ask for help."[82] Some pastors were able to organize mutual aid activity even in such parishes that were too poor for a trusteeship. One priest from Arkhangelsk described a small credit association that he had established for his parishioners, who could collectively contribute no more than a few rubles a month.[83] Trusteeships, however, usually required an initial investment into capital or real estate, which could provide the organization with a more substantial source of income than members' dues.[84] Dedicated parishioners could sometimes make the necessary collective sacrifice for such an investment. A peasant commune in one Moscow parish, for example, invested 4,000 rubles for their trusteeship.[85] Such an investment was usually too difficult for peasant parishioners, however, and required the contribution of wealthy philanthropists from outside the parish. In 1887, for example, one Moscow merchant donated 23,000 rubles to be divided among trusteeships throughout the diocese as 100-ruble contributions.[86]

The solution to the underdevelopment of poor parishes should have been the same that was employed by the clergy to save their poorest communities from destitution: cooperation among all parishes in the diocese.[87] Parishioners, unfortunately, lacked such institutions as the clergy's diocesan trusteeship or the diocesan congress that could have coordinated such inter-parish cooperation. There are some records of collaboration between neighboring parishes. In a report from 1906, for example, one priest explained that when his parishioners ceased contributions to the parish trusteeship, under the influence of revolutionary agitators, the institution had been kept alive by a sobriety society in a neighboring parish, whose members contributed donations until his own parishioners were persuaded to resume their support.[88] Yet the physical distance between most parishes and the sparse population and resources of rural Russia made such collaboration relatively rare. Rural trusteeships could easily disintegrate as a result of the loss of an important patron or of pastoral leadership due to illness, or a disagreement among parishioners.[89]

Inter-parish collaboration was much easier in Russia's cities because of the physical proximity of urban parishes to one another and the fluidity of their congregational membership. In 1909, the deans of seven different churches in Moscow's Kitai Gorod district submitted a request to the consistory for approval of a "seven-parish trusteeship."[90] This circumstance, along with access to a larger pool of wealthy donors, allowed parish trusteeships to play a much larger role in the religious life of Russia's cities than they did in the countryside. Some urban trusteeships were able to establish complex charitable operations by extending their services beyond the limits of their own parish and earning the support of patrons throughout the city. In 1901, a trusteeship on Moscow's Arbat Street opened an almshouse, a parish school, and inexpensive housing, all in one three-story building that it erected on parish land.[91] Examples of collaboration among the charitable associations of different parishes were found not only in capital cities like Moscow and Tver' but also in smaller towns such as Torzhok in Tver' gubernia.[92] Yet trusteeships played a particularly important role in the social support systems of industrial centers because of the dire needs of migrant workers, who had left behind their social support networks in their villages.

By the beginning of the 1890s, parish trusteeships were functioning in thirty-nine churches, or every sixth church, in the city of Moscow.[93] Many of these trusteeships were organized explicitly, as declared in their founding charters, to care for industrial workers. In 1904, a trusteeship in Moscow's Tverskaia-Iamskaia district housed fourteen impoverished families on the top floor and twenty male orphans on the bottom floor of a building it had purchased to shelter impoverished industrial workers and their families.[94] The scale of charitable aid that Moscow's parishes could offer to the urban poor was much less than that of state-sponsored organizations, such as the City Trusteeship for the Poor that provided meals for 1,500 unemployed people every day.[95] Parish trusteeships were valuable, however, because of the sustainable and targeted aid they could organize in collaboration with communities and smaller mutual aid associations. The trusteeship of the Cathedral of John the Baptist in Moscow's Presnenskaia district, for example, contributed 276 rubles a year to help a worker's consumer collective to purchase food.[96] Moreover, the local knowledge of priests and parishioners helped to both minimize the exploitation of charity by professional beggars and address the hidden poverty of those unwilling or unable to apply for aid by themselves.[97] The parish networks of some urban centers, therefore, used some of the same advantages as the diocesan networks that supplied their leadership.

The success of parish trusteeships in urban centers demonstrated their value for the Church's social mission—and for lay-clerical relations. The financial exclusion of the laity and their trusteeships from "church property," however, effectively segregated these urban parishes from the diocesan network and limited their ability to establish ties with members of other parishes in a religious context. Urban parishioners did extend their philanthropic contributions to rural congregations, but they required the mediation of the diocesan bureaucracy. In 1909, for example, two Moscow townspeople (*meshchane*) entrusted the Tver' consistory with a 1,000-ruble government bond for their former parish in a rural district of that diocese.[98] By 1914, the diocese of Moscow contained 194 parish trusteeships.[99] One hundred eight of these were supported by 112 parish churches in the city of Moscow, accounting for almost half of Moscow's 252 urban parishes.[100] Yet the remainder were far more sparsely distributed among the remaining 1,120 parish churches of the diocese.[101]

While the laity would never gain autonomous control over parish property under the synodal system, the Synod did attempt to integrate parishioners into the diocesan networks of their clergy. On November 18, 1905, the Synod issued a "decree on the organization of parish life and pastoral assemblies," which authorized priests to invite up to twelve of their adult parishioners to form a parish council (*tserkovno-prikhodskii sovet*) "to participate in the management of church finances."[102] The nature and extent of this participation were vague. But it was clear that the Synod wished to expand the activity of parish associations such as trusteeships: "A Christian's first community, beyond the limits of the family, forms around the church and near the pastor. ... And now devout people find the realization of this community in brotherhoods and parish trusteeships, uniting for mutual aid, charitable works, faith and piety, and presenting a strong spiritual bulwark against external currents in opposition to faith and true Christian freedom. But such trusteeships and brotherhoods do not exist everywhere."[103] While the decree granted the parish clergy broad freedom to convene pastoral assemblies at all levels of the diocese, as discussed in chapter 2, it also encouraged the participation of laypeople in these assemblies: "The Holy Synod blesses the convening, according to need, of pastoral councils within the boundaries of the superintenditure, the district, and the diocese for the discussion of questions of pastoral work, with the proposal that laymen from among the members of parish councils, parish trusteeships, and brotherhoods be invited, should the need arise, to take part in these councils."[104] Despite renewed calls from the Kadet Party for the parish to be granted independent legal standing with control over tithe funds, the decree of November 18 preserved the parish's status as part of the spiritual domain.[105] Yet the synodal administration clearly hoped to integrate parish community leaders into the management of both the parishes and the dioceses. While ultimate authority lay, as always, with the diocesan bishop, the parish priest was given the role of initiator and supervisor over this process of inviting parishioners to take part in the management of church assets.

Meanwhile, parish clergymen initiated another way to integrate laypeople into their diocesan networks. In his 1906 report to the Tver' consistory, one archpriest argued that only by including church elders in the diocesan congresses could the clergy relieve the growing demands from parishioners that their parish contributions be accounted for. Another priest brought this idea before Moscow's 1908 diocesan congress, suggesting that the inclusion of church elders as well as lower clergymen in congresses could create more effective church taxation for the benefit of the entire diocesan community.[106] The Synod finally issued a decree on this matter in response to pressure from the Duma in 1909. In drafting funding legislation for the support of the parish clergy, a Duma committee had argued that if parish clergymen were to receive some relief from their financial burdens, parishioners should be given a voice in "questions of church economy" through inclusion of the elders in local and diocesan congresses. In the decree that resulted, the Synod explained that this practice had been taking place in eight dioceses since 1906 and now should take place in all of them.[107] Moscow's clergy seem to have preempted the Synod's decree, as "several church elders" were in attendance at their diocesan congress on the same day that the decree was issued.[108]

The integration of laypeople into the diocesan networks was gradual. A discussion at the 1914 diocesan congress in Tver' on the difficulty of traveling to district centers to attend pastoral assemblies indicates that church elders were less keen than clergymen to bear the expense and inconvenience of this duty, but that some of them did participate with equal voting rights: "If in some, relatively small superintendent districts no more than half the local clergy and barely a fourth of church elders appear at local assemblies, then those districts that are spread out over eighty or hundred versts make it even more difficult to convene."[109] Parish councils were organized in some localities and seem to have encouraged greater lay participation in the management of their parishes.[110] As mentioned in chapter 2, three parish councils took part in Tver's famine relief effort of 1907–9 and contributed to the campaign's designation of more funding for lay communities stricken by famine than for clerical victims.[111] Clerical assemblies seem to have been influenced by the assertion of lay priorities. At a 1914 meeting of the Bezhetsk district assembly, for example, delegates resolved to reduce salaries for employees of their ecclesiastical school in order to spare parishioners the expense: "The deputy fathers, in consideration of the difficult situation of the clergy in some places and the rebukes of parishioners regarding the overtaxation of their churches . . . have deemed it just and appropriate to reduce church collections [for the ecclesiastical school] by 1 kopeck, and to collect six kopecks from each parish soul, instead of seven."[112] The limited voice that the laity achieved in church governance, therefore, seems to have influenced the distribution of diocesan resources.

This trend can be observed on a larger scale by comparing expenditures of the diocesan trusteeships for poor clergy with the cumulative expenditures of the parish trusteeships during the Russian Empire's final decades (see graph 1). In 1894, diocesan trusteeships for poor clergy throughout the empire spent a total of 4,668,518.76 rubles to support the social needs of clerical communities, while parish trusteeships collectively spent 2,801,991.28 rubles on parish needs. Twenty years later, in 1914, this ratio was inverted. Diocesan trusteeships spent a total of 1,979,416.78 rubles, while parish trusteeships spent a total of 4,894,458.92 rubles.

It is likely that the progressive transfer of resources from the clerical estate back to the parish communities was the result of pressure exerted by an increasingly assertive laity, both indirectly and through the positions they obtained within clerical assemblies. Moreover, the regular budgets of parish churches were

Graph 1. Relative expenditures of diocesan and parish trusteeships, 1894–1914

Source: Vsepoddanneishie otchety Ober-prokurora Sviateishago Sinoda po vedomstvu Pravoslavnago ispovedaniia za 1894–95, 1896–97, 1898, 1899, 1900, 1901, 1902, 1903–4, 1905–7, 1908–9, 1910, 1911–12, 1913, 1914. The total expenditures of diocesan trusteeships were not included in the reports for 1905–7, 1910, and 1911–12.

not depleted to meet the needs of the clergy. In 1913, for example, only 1.65 percent of parish churches' income, empire-wide, was spent on clerical schools and "diocesan taxation." The rest was spent on church upkeep, communal wine, candles, and other ritual-related expenses.[113]

One consequence of the progressive transfer of control over parish resources to the laity was that more resources were dedicated, in Freeze's words, "to that traditional popular fetish, church construction."[114] In 1913, only 19.4 percent of all parish trusteeship expenditures, or 953,689.02 rubles, were dedicated to education and charity.[115] Yet the empowerment of laypeople to allocate more of their parish contributions to the beautification of sacred space was not necessarily detrimental to the pastoral movement. The agency of parishioners in the distribution of parish funds allowed them to both oppose the decisions of their pastor and freely collaborate with him. The support of laypeople for the social initiatives of the pastorate was becoming more of a voluntary collaboration and less of a passive tax payment. Unfortunately, this relationship would not have the time to develop further.

The Church at War

In 1914, the Church faced the outbreak of war and the development of yet another all-embracing social catastrophe. Total war and the humanitarian crises that it engendered soon grew beyond the tsarist regime's capacity to manage, and Russia's civil society rose to fill the vacuum. The Church worked together with communities and associations such as the Red Cross and Union of Zemstvos to supply the army, care for wounded soldiers, and support their families.[116] Yet Russia's robust home front in the early years of the war exhibited social divisions that would widen under the trauma of modern warfare. This was true of the Church as well. Initially, the humanitarian relief campaigns of both Moscow and Tver' exemplified the true capacity of the diocesan networks to consolidate the voluntarism of a diversity of associations and communities for common social support. At the same time, the Church's relief campaign became bifurcated between the efforts of the parish communities and those of the clergy. The former focused on supporting the local families of soldiers, and the latter on supporting the military, particularly on providing care for wounded soldiers. This divergence of their specific goals weakened the cooperative relationship between the clerical and lay networks at a critical moment, on the eve of the political and social collapse of the Russian Empire.

On July 20, the day of the declaration of war on Germany, the Synod issued a pronouncement commanding that the Imperial Manifesto of War be read in all churches before the liturgy and calling upon "all monasteries, churches, and Orthodox congregations to contribute donations for the care of wounded and sick soldiers and for the support of families of those serving in the war."[117] The Synod issued a separate declaration on the organization of aid in the parishes, which prescribed the establishment of trusteeship councils in each parish for the care of families of individuals serving in the military. Trusteeship councils (*popechitel'nye sovety*) were elected bodies that served as executive organs for some parish trusteeships. The 1914 decree stipulated that these councils collect information on all families of soldiers residing in their parishes and organize collections for their support. Moreover, if adequate support could not be obtained through collections, "the parish and church elder should allocate the council a grant from their church's funds in an amount that is possible according to the state of the parish's finances and up to 50 rubles, without applying for permission from the diocesan leadership."[118] Once again, the Synod had offered the laity a small inroad to church resources in the hope of soliciting their cooperation in a time of crisis. Aside from this minor concession, the synodal leadership played a diminutive role in the Church's war relief efforts. In September 1914, one unidentified bishop asked the Synod for clarification as to where his diocese should send the donations it collected. The reply, published in the Synod's journal, was that all donations collected during church services should be sent to the Synod's economic department, to be passed along to the Red Cross.[119] Yet archival records from Moscow and Tver' contain no evidence of funds being sent to the Synod during the relief campaign. The extent and focus of each parish's participation in the relief effort would be determined by the pastor and by the parish community.

Due to minimal oversight by the ecclesiastical authorities, the parish-level relief effort was poorly documented in most dioceses. The Tver' consistory archive presents an exception to this rule thanks to the work of a "central committee" that compiled the reports of clerical superintendents. These reports indicated that at least half, and often all, of the parishes in most districts had established a parish trusteeship council by the summer of 1915. Tver's parish priests expressed joyful surprise at the population's support for this initiative. As one priest reported to his superintendent: "I cannot fail to remark on the joy that was felt in carrying out collections. Despite the extreme poverty of the parish, the population met the collection with great sympathy and willingly contributed what they could. The council that organized the collection counted on no more than about 30 rubles. In fact, they received almost 48 rubles and 40 rubles in kind. The heavy feeling of timidity that at first oppressed those carrying out the collection soon changed to joy."[120] The trusteeship councils carried out relief efforts in the context of regular devotional practices, during liturgical services and through door-to-door collections by icon-bearing processions.[121]

The relief campaign also recruited the collaboration of communities and associations outside the parishes. This created a larger network for the exchange of information, which maximized the effectiveness of aid distribution. For example, some of Tver's zemstvos asked trusteeships to provide aid for particular families with no other source of support.[122] The trusteeship councils, in turn, provided zemstvos with information about relatives of soldiers who were not receiving the state aid for which they were eligible.[123] They also withheld funds in numerous cases when military families were already receiving support from a zemstvo or local factory.[124] The trusteeships also coordinated the traditional mutual aid practices of the peasantry to benefit a larger proportion of the rural population. Relatives and members of rural communes had always assisted families that were temporarily unable to work their own fields or bring in their own harvest.[125] With so many families in this situation during the war, clergymen and parishioners worked together to determine who was receiving such assistance during the summer harvest and who was not. One superintendent reported that the trusteeship councils in his parishes had convened their village assemblies in order to determine how many families were still in need of assistance.[126] Parish trusteeship members throughout the diocese volunteered to help military families in their fields. Other trusteeships provided funds to hire field hands for those families with no other sources of help.[127] The popular response to this crisis, both church-based and otherwise, proved that the social isolation of Russia's rural communities could be overcome through free association.

As always, the parish clergy provided organizational leadership for these parish-level relief efforts. Priests delivered sermons in which they "beseeched and exhorted relatives and neighbors to extend what help they could to the needy families of soldiers."[128] Clergymen participated in relief efforts as individuals. One priest, a widower without children, housed and fed two relatives of a soldier in his own home.[129] The clergy also provided the campaign with the collective support of their diocesan networks. In at least one case, the assembled clergy of a superintendent district provided funds for childcare so that soldiers' wives could leave their children and go to work.[130] Tver's Central Committee extended small grants to the trusteeships when local funds were not available to meet pressing needs.[131] Nevertheless, support for parish-level mutual aid was not the main priority of the clergy's diocesan networks, and the funds raised to support military families on the home front remained modest. Table 3 shows the highest donation figures in the diocese for June 2015.

The central superintenditure of the city of Tver' thus collected an average of 5.24 rubles for each military family for the month of June, and this was thanks to a 1,000-ruble donation from a member of the imperial family. Most of Tver's other superintendent districts collected between two and three rubles for each family. These contributions provided relief for families in greatest need, and they do not reflect the other sources of support for military families or the nonmonetary aid that parish trusteeships organized. Yet they do reflect a small proportion of the diocesan resources that were dedicated to war relief.

The parish clergy focused their own prodigious relief efforts on supporting the military and, especially, wounded soldiers. Their diocesan associations operated with less centralized direction than in any previous relief campaign, and they combined their efforts with those of the Red Cross, municipal administrations, and the zemstvos. Prominent parish priests in Moscow organized one of the largest relief operations led by clergymen. On July 25, 1914, twelve out of seventeen of Moscow's urban superintendents assembled at the bishop's residence to establish a War-Charity Commission, chaired by Archpriest Ioann Vostorgov, dean of Saint Basil's Cathedral. Seized by patriotic enthusiasm, the assembled archpriests resolved that the commission would donate a portion of the funds it gathered directly to the armed forces, use

Table 3. Report of Tver''s first superintendent district for June 1915

Church name	Military families	Remainder from May	Rubles collected by parish trusteeships in June 1915			
			Monthly	One-time	Parish funds	Total
Diocesan Cathedral			2.15 r.			2.15 r.
Aleksandro-Nevskaia	99		102.75 r.			102.75 r.
Bogoroditse-rozhdestv.	57		40 r.			40 r.
Borisoglebskaia	22	138.39 r.	37.35 r.			175.74 r.
Vladimirskaia	42	3.30 r.	72 r.		15.18 r.	90.48 r.
Voznesenskaia	7	94.19 r.	20 r.			114.19 r.
Zhivonosn-istochnik	20	3.50 r.	56 r.	15 r.		74.50 r.
Il'insko-Znamenskaia	12	195.44 r.	37.90 r.			233.34 r.
Ioanno-Predtechenskaia	27		30 r.			30 r.
Mironosinskaia	18	155 r.	40 r.			195 r.
Nikolaevskaia	36		30 r.			30 r.
Nikol'skaia	17	2.63 r.	75.50 r.			78.13 r.
Pokrovskaia	31		40 r.			40 r.
Semenovskaia	31	83.14 r.	72 r.			155.14 r.
Smolenskaia	35		42 r.		13 r.	55 r.
Sretenskaia	30	200.90 r.	81.50 r.			282.40 r.
Troitskaia	44		65 r.	4.80 r.		69.80 r.
Khristorozhdestv. Convent	25		30 r.			30 r.
Khristorozhdestv. Monastery	15	96.51 r.	48.50 r.		4.35 r.	149.36 r.
Candle Factory			27.61 r.			27.61 r.
Committee of Princess Elizaveta Fedorovna				1000 r.		1000 r.
Total	568	973 r.	950.26 r.	1,019.80 r.	32.53 r.	2,975.59 r.

Source: GATO, f. 160, op. 1, d. 34461, l. 1–l. 2.

another portion for the care of wounded soldiers, and dedicate the final portion to the support of soldiers' families. Father Nikol'skii had already designated one apartment on the territory of Kazan' Cathedral, of which he was dean, to hold ten beds for wounded soldiers. The cathedral would provide them with food, clothing, and medical care. While initially confined to the capital, the commission soon drew support from parishes and monasteries throughout the diocese. "Several parishes," as reported in the commission's journal, sent donations directly to the army and navy until the city administration urged them to use this money to care for the wounded instead.[132] By the beginning of September, it had established forty-three clinics with six hundred beds, supplied with clothes and regular medical care, for which it contributed an initial sum of 40,000 rubles and a planned monthly payment of 25,000 rubles. More clinics were to be opened as well as a workshop to sew clothes and sheets for patients.[133] The clerical leadership of the War-Charity Commission determined that their efforts could be more effective if coordinated with other public organizations and decided to combine forces with the United Organization working under the umbrella of Moscow's municipal administration.[134] Other clinics in Moscow diocese were organized independently by rural superintendents. One sacristan complained to the Moscow consistory that his priest was trying to evict him from his parish apartment in order to house wounded soldiers there.[135]

The reports to the Synod on clerical contributions to war relief vary significantly in detail but generally present a picture of remarkable dedication and sacrifice. Tver's consistory, once again, provided some of the most detailed reports. In October 1914, one clinic was established at the residence of Tver's bishop and another in Tver' Seminary, the latter providing care for five hundred wounded soldiers. These clinics were supported by a long list of patrons, including at least seven associations of parish clergymen from throughout the diocese. These efforts were supplemented by smaller operations that some clergymen organized locally. The clergy of at least four of Tver's diocesan districts (*okruga*) opened their own clinics with up to forty beds for wounded soldiers. A further sixteen groups of parish clergymen, organized by district or parish, pledged monthly contributions of between 25 and 112 rubles for the support of zemstvo, Red Cross, and municipal clinics. The report specified that these groups made their contributions "from their own resources" (*iz svoikh sredstv*) or from their "salaries and incomes" rather than from collections among the laity.[136] The teaching staffs of some seminaries pledged 2 percent of their salaries to support military clinics.[137] Many clerical students pledged portions of their meager scholarship stipends for the same cause.[138] Numerous seminarians and young priests volunteered to serve in the army as soldiers or as military chaplains.[139] The clerical community was caught up in the wave of patriotic fervor that affected much of the empire in the first years of the war.

The participation of lay communities in the campaign to help wounded soldiers presents a striking contrast with their relief efforts for local military families. Tver's report to the Synod indicated that two trusteeship councils opened their own parish clinics with ten beds each. One brotherhood and one trusteeship council in the town of Kashin organized collections for the Red Cross. Finally, another trusteeship council promised a monthly contribution of 30 rubles to the clinic in the bishop's residence. With the exception of the work that these five lay organizations performed, parishioner participation in the effort to help wounded soldiers was limited to passive contributions in church.[140] This division of relief efforts between clergy and laity was, in part, the result of the continued division of parish resources between official church contributions and the funds raised separately by the trusteeships. Yet laypeople were not excluded from the diocesan assemblies that determined the allocation of relief funds. Church elders continued to participate in the clergy's diocesan congresses during the war, including Moscow's War-Charity Commission.[141] Moreover, the trusteeship councils used the power, which the Synodal decree had given them, to appropriate the savings of their parish churches for their own initiatives.[142] Parishioners, the great majority of whom were peasants, were far more concerned with the local impact of the war than with logistical problems facing the military and therefore chose to focus their philanthropic efforts on supporting local communities.[143]

The clergy's prioritization of support for the military must be considered from the perspective of 1914. In its initial stages, few could have imagined that the war in Europe would prove far more disastrous than the war, revolution, and famine of 1904–7, much less that it would bring down four empires and ignite two successive revolutions in Russia. In 1914, the population was less politically volatile than in 1905. Harvests were plentiful and the urban economy was expanding due to foreign investment and a stable currency. The state granted generous compensation to peasant households who lost their farm laborers to conscription.[144] On the other hand, as early as August 1914, tens of thousands of wounded soldiers were pouring into Moscow alone. Smaller clinics in the surrounding districts were used once the number of wounded in Moscow reached seventy thousand.[145] In rising to meet this challenge, the parish clergy joined forces with professional organizations, local government bodies, and other manifestations of *obshchestvennost'*. Ultimately, however, the clergy's continued support for the war effort drained the capacity of their social networks to address local needs and damaged their credibility among the war-weary population. In his study of the Church in Cheliabinsk in 1917, Patrick

Brown notes that the divide between clergy and laity continued to widen after the February Revolution around the issue of the war: "The diocesan paper revealed that the Church hierarchy was out of touch with the people when it announced its support for Miliukov, condemned the Cheliabinsk Soviet for pressuring the Provisional Government, and argued that Russia must see the war to its victorious conclusion."[146] In Moscow and Tver' too the diocesan networks descended into anarchy at the moment when they were most needed as a source of material and social solidarity.

Conclusion

The relative success of the pastoral movement at converting the laity's passive contributions to parish and diocesan coffers into voluntary participation in church-based mutual aid varied considerably among dioceses. By the early twentieth century, parishioners had far more direct influence over the management and allocation of diocesan resources than in the mid-nineteenth century, despite the inability of reformers to agree on an equitable division of authority at the parish level. This, together with the clergy's own impetus to help the population, contributed to the progressive transfer of resources from the clerical estate to the laity. While many communities directed these resources toward church beautification, their establishment of trusteeships for that purpose empowered the laity to assume control over their own parishes. In those dioceses where philanthropic mutual aid did become an important component of religious life, the parishes played a significant role in the mitigation of poverty and social dislocation, particularly in urban centers. The relief effort of the early war years demonstrated the full capacity of Orthodox social networks to organize charitable initiatives in collaboration with other organizations and serves as compelling evidence that the pastoral movement shaped Orthodox practice.

The bifurcation of the Church's war relief effort revealed the continued divergence of lay and clerical priorities, even in dioceses where mutual aid had become an established component of religious life. While most laypeople viewed their pastors as essential members of their religious communities, they also perceived the parish clergy as representatives of an alien officialdom. Despite extensive lay participation in the humanitarian campaigns of the diocesan networks between 1891 and 1917, laypeople continued to regard those networks as clerical institutions, which could threaten the interests of their own religious communities. This was, in part, a result of the failure of parish reform to facilitate an equal partnership between clergy and laity. Yet the outbursts of anticlerical resentment during the revolutions of 1905 and 1917 must also be attributed to the Church's close ties with the tsarist regime, which will be discussed in the next chapter.

6

The Pastor as a Political Actor

In a 1912 article that appeared in the liberal journal *Russkaia mysl'*, the Orthodox Christian philosopher and son of a village priest Sergei Bulgakov (1871–1944) recounted his observation of the parish clergy's participation in elections to the Fourth Duma.

> The authorities had assigned them to the "right-wing" bloc beforehand, and they were under the constant observation and influence of the bishop, both directly and through his agents. One must understand how great and unchecked the bishop's power over the clergy is in order to understand the fist that has been raised over the clergy's heads and the agonizing situation they have been put in. To show defiance and cast a "secret" vote, which was in fact observed at the voting box itself and, according to the vote count, was to consciously risk the loss of one's position and transferal to an inferior one or outright dismissal, i.e. complete ruination (and this was true at all stages of voting). One must be familiar with our clergy's large families and their age-old oppression, to put it mildly, their "apoliticality" in order to understand that for them, the elementary act of exercising political rights is to accept martyrdom.[1]

Bulgakov himself had attempted to establish a Christian Socialist organization in 1906, which ultimately failed to develop into a political movement. As Catherine Evtuhov explains in her book on Bulgakov, "whereas social Catholicism in Germany, Austria, or even France became a movement within the church itself and occasionally an instrument in the church's struggle for self-assertion against the state, Russia's religious radicals found themselves at odds with all the institutions that wielded power in the country."[2] In fact, Orthodox priests played a conspicuous role in the radical dissident politics of the early

Duma period. But, after the dissolution of the Second Duma and restructuring of voting laws, the clergy's freedom of political expression was drastically restricted, as Bulgakov observed. Ultimately, the Russian Empire never experienced a "clerical party" as did many other European countries by the turn of the century.[3] This political disengagement during the Duma era rendered the clergy dependent on the state to protect their own interests. Continued reliance on the state perpetuated the popular association of the Orthodox Church with the regime and rendered the clergy culpable for state oppression and social injustice.

This outcome is difficult to reconcile with the well-organized social networks that this book has examined as a defining characteristic of the pastorate. As Bulgakov's article explained, the diocesan bishops used their apostolic authority over these very networks to supervise the parish clergy's political behavior. This policy of surveillance and control was informed, in part, by the Church's tradition of abstinence from politics within the Russian Empire. The monastic hierarchy used this tradition of benevolent political neutrality to justify the manufacture of support for the political Right and the suppression of political dissent among the clergy. While individual clergymen participated in political movements on the Left and the Right, clerical associations were never collectively mobilized in support of any political party during Russia's experiment with parliamentary democracy. While this disengagement was partially imposed on the clergy, it was by no means the result of their inability to organize themselves politically. The parish clergy's reticence to act as a distinct interest group in competition with segments of the lay population precluded the development of a clerical party.

Symphonic Dissonance

While the Roman Catholic Church developed as a politically distinct institution that entered into occasional conflict with the secular powers of Europe, the Orthodox Church evolved in close partnership with the Eastern Roman Empire. The concept of *symphonia* is credited to Emperor Justinian (482–565), who claimed that "the priesthood ministers to things divine: the imperial authority is set over, and shows diligence in, things human; but both proceed from one and the same source, and both adorn the life of man."[4] This partnership rendered the Church vulnerable to state intervention, as in the case of the iconoclastic emperors in the eighth and ninth centuries. It also led to the sacralization of political power. John Strickland discusses an eschatological identification of the Christian emperor with the "kingdom of heaven on earth" in the political thought of the Eastern Roman Church. He also argues that iterations of this political eschatology arose throughout the history of the Orthodox

Church in Russia, including the concept of the "apostle-like tsar."[5] As discussed in chapter 1, the Russian emperor was expected to protect and enforce the Church's sovereignty over the "spiritual domain" (*dukhovnaia komanda*). This entailed protection of the Church from criticism and competition from other confessions, as well as draconian punishments for conversion away from Orthodox Christianity, including the seizure of property and even children from those deemed apostate from the official Church.[6] In return, Orthodox clergy were expected to refrain from any involvement in secular politics beyond public prayers for the health of the tsar and declarations of anathema against his enemies. Clergymen were accordingly subjected to a higher degree of censorship than most other segments of society. The clergy of no other religion endured such tight regulation of their sermons as did the pastors of the Orthodox Church.[7] Yet this policy of enforced political quiescence became increasingly untenable in the complex and volatile atmosphere of the early twentieth century.

The culture of fear and self-censorship that pervaded the parish clergy makes any generalization of political views among them highly speculative. "Political unreliability" could result in a priest being defrocked or a seminarian denied ordination. A single incautious remark could be enough to earn a clergyman this designation.[8] Young men and women of clerical origin were routinely blacklisted from employment in any educational institution as a result of political suspicion.[9] This looming threat to the livelihood of church servants severely limited freedom of expression in the Church's extensive network of print media. Authors rarely signed their own names, using initials or cryptic pseudonyms instead. This practice was so common that one priest saw fit to dismiss the article of a radical seminarian as an expression of youthful impetuosity, on the basis of the author's failure to hide his identity: "His [immaturity] is obvious from the fact that the satirical article is signed with the full name and surname of the author."[10] Within this stifling atmosphere, many priests clearly harbored illicit ideas, especially as Russia's social unrest and radical anti-religious politics demanded a dynamic pastoral response. In 1901, an article in Moscow's diocesan journal discussed Pope Leo XIII's encyclical *Graves de communi re*. The article outlined the theory of Christian political solidarity for the protection of workers' rights and then accused the Pope of "Jesuitical hypocrisy" for using this ideology to conceal his true power-mongering motives.[11] The author did not criticize the theory itself and may have been using this condemnation of Catholicism to mask an exposition of "Christian democracy." Such muted sentiments turned to open criticism of the state after panicked soldiers fired on the workers' procession led by Father Gapon in the streets of the capital on January 9, 1905. News of the brutal suppression of a peaceful religious procession severely damaged perception of the state as protector of the Church.

The partnership of Church and state was called into question before the 1905 Revolution, as a result of the 1904 decree by Nicholas II "On Plans for the Improvement of Public Order." In an effort to resolve various popular grievances, the emperor announced his intention to enact a series of vague reforms, including broader participation in the zemstvos, insurance for workers, relaxation of censorship, and a "revision of the legal rights of schismatics and of persons belonging to heterodox faiths and confessions."[12] Upon the announcement of this decree in the Council of Ministers, Metropolitan Antonii (Vadkovskii) of Saint Petersburg argued for a corresponding liberalization of the state's relationship with the Church. Otherwise it would be placed at a disadvantage in an openly multiconfessional society as the only religion with restrictions on sermons and other forms of expression. State tutelage, he argued, "renders the voice of the Church inaudible in both private and public life."[13] Although in favor of greater religious toleration himself, Metropolitan Antonii had called attention to the disintegration of the social contract with the state, which had required the Church to abstain from politics.[14] This process would culminate in the decree of April 17, 1905, "On Strengthening the Principles of Religious Toleration," which decriminalized apostasy from the Orthodox Church.

The scandal of Bloody Sunday weakened the capacity of censors to suppress discussion of church-state relations in the ecclesiastical press. On January 14, the metropolitans of Moscow, Saint Petersburg, Kiev, and Galicia jointly published an official condemnation of Gapon and his followers in which they accused the priest of having "insolently defied his holy vows."[15] Within a month, however, a group of cautious supporters of Gapon's efforts to improve conditions for workers, if not of his political methods, had assembled as the Group of Thirty-Two Saint Petersburg Priests. With Metropolitan Antonii's permission, this group began publishing articles critical of the synodal system. On March 17, one of their first articles appeared in the same journal of the Saint Petersburg Theological Academy that had published the prelates' condemnation of Gapon, *Tserkovnyi vestnik*. It began by hailing the forthcoming Edict of Toleration as a victory for Orthodoxy: "The immanent freedom of religious conscience from those external constraints, which have limited the faith of Old Believers and followers of other religions, cannot but be welcomed with spiritual joy by true sons of Orthodoxy, by zealots of the Church's holiness and purity." The article went on to echo, in more strident terms, Antonii's calls for a corresponding liberation of the Orthodox Church: "Limited in expression and self-determination, the voice of the Orthodox Church is enslaved to the worldly interests of the state. Will it be able to withstand the free, honest, and sincere voices of other faiths, Old Belief, and other convictions? Will it not be drowned out by these voices?"[16] Seven months later, the October Manifesto created a representative government in which the clergy could participate and officially relaxed censorship on the press, allowing the Saint Petersburg priests and their allies to express even bolder challenges to autocracy's influence over the Church in diocesan journals across the empire: "When it is even asserted from the church pulpit that the success of Orthodoxy is conditional upon the existing form of government and inseparable from it, we observe with horror how, because of age-old prejudice, the Church is trampled and humiliated."[17] Before full censorship was restored by synodal decree on November 25, 1906, the Church's alliance with the autocracy was debated on the pages of a relatively free ecclesiastical press.[18]

Many clergymen rose to defend the Nikolaevan formula of "Orthodoxy, Autocracy, and Nationality." As one parish priest put it in an article in Moscow's diocesan journal from February 1906, "faith in God remains strong in the true Russian person and can even be considered his characteristic feature. The other characteristic feature of the true Russian person is love for his tsar, whom he considers the anointed representative of God."[19] Strickland describes this ideology as "Orthodox patriotism," which supported the autocracy with an antidemocratic version of confessional nationalism. It conflated the Orthodox Church with the Russian nation, overseen and symbolized by an apostle-like tsar. Strickland argues that this ideology was sustained by the self-interested desire of many clergymen to retain the financial support and political protection of the autocracy for the Church and possibly revoke or curtail the tsar's promise of religious toleration.[20] Indeed, by the early twentieth century, some bishops received yearly salaries as high as 6,000 rubles.[21] Yet the great majority of clergymen did not experience such direct benefits from the Church's relationship with the state.

Despite their close identification with the autocratic order, many reactionary clergymen were highly cognizant of the need for a pastoral response to the economic hardships and social tensions afflicting the general population. For example, Metropolitan Vladimir (Bogoiavlenskii), Moscow's prelate from 1898 to 1915, was both an "Orthodox patriot" and a strong supporter of parish-based charitable and educational initiatives, particularly among factory workers. In 1902, he became head of the largest adult-education program for factory workers in the empire.[22] One of Vladimir's sermons, "To the Rich and to the Poor," was published in December 1905, in which the metropolitan argued that the Church should defend the poor while remaining aloof from the petty disputes of feuding parties.

> She [the Church] should not say that a worker should be assigned only eight hours of work every day, and not ten. Let the administrators and lawmakers

discuss that. But she must say that "It is unfair if someone collects millions from pennies [*groshi*] robbed from poor workers." It is not her task to say that laws are necessary against the keeping of workers, but she must say that "It is unjust to regard a worker as a living machine whom you use for your own profit before casting her out on the street."[23]

Vladimir expressed the outlook of many clergymen who were reluctant to engage in politics and believed that the pastoral movement required no explicitly political expression. Yet this "political neutrality" allowed conservative clergymen to remain in alliance with the autocracy during the Duma period.

Many among the clergy questioned whether conformity with the established power structure was compatible with the ideal of a universal Church, uniting all the faithful regardless of political interests. The regime's demand for silence or collaboration from the clergy in response to conditions that much of the population considered unjust, forced the latter into alliances with existing hierarchies against their own parishioners. For example, when performing the liturgy for factory workers, clergymen were required to pray for the health of the factory owner.[24] This undermined the Church's claim to political impartiality in the eyes of the general public and led priests to reinterpret their relationship with the political order. The author of one article in Moscow's diocesan journal from February 1906, signed "S. S. B.," included "monarchists" in a list of partisan interests to be avoided: "Our Russia will not be saved by the victory of the socialists, the constitutionalists, or the monarchists, but only by the strength of the Cross and the Gospels."[25] S. S. B. complained that at a time of great moral crisis many priests were motivated by professional self-interest rather than Christian inspiration to help and comfort the weak: "Is pastorship among us merely a profession by which to earn a living, which does not meet the needs of our inner convictions and of our hearts? We complain that seminarians do not become priests. But do they see in their fathers and brothers the image of a selfless fighter for Christian truth who exposes lies without fear, a friend of the poor, and defender of the destitute?"[26] He went on to argue that the clergy should win the young back from the revolutionaries by taking an equally radical stand against injustice: "Why not learn from the revolutionaries if to do so would be useful for us?! . . . From them we can learn selflessness, zeal, readiness to defend the poor, courage before the strong, everything that they use to attract the young! . . . Then the clergy will become the center of a Christian social movement. Joining neither parties on the Right nor parties on the Left, the clergy will call everyone to the Christian life."[27] Thus, social change and political unrest in the early twentieth century inspired a reappraisal, among the clergy, of the Church's relationship with the state. Even conservative prelates like Metropolitan Vladimir recognized the need for a more forceful pastoral response to injustice and exploitation. In fact, it was increasingly difficult for the Orthodox clergy to claim political neutrality by any measure, and this became particularly apparent within the Church itself.

THE DUMA ERA

On August 6, 1905, Nicholas II issued his manifesto on the establishment of the State Duma. The electoral law stipulated that the deans of parish churches could participate in the landowners' voting curia if their churches were assigned a sufficiently large plot of land.[28] The clergy had been explicitly forbidden to vote in elections for the zemstvo since 1890 and were now being thrown headlong into Russia's experiment with parliamentary democracy.[29] Yet the synodal leadership could hardly reject the opportunity to influence government policy through clerical deputies. Conservative clergymen resolved that the Church's new political role should be to uphold the autocracy. The monks of the Trinity-Sergius Lavra published their own "manifesto," in which they declared that all true Russians had been called upon to elect loyal Orthodox Christians to serve as advisors for the tsar: "We must be particularly wary of those who are alien to us in their faith and in their blood: if they find their way into the tsar's Duma, let us not deceive ourselves, they will care not for our needs, but for their own."[30] According to the August manifesto, the Duma was, indeed, merely intended to serve as a consultative assembly for the emperor. Yet the manifesto of October 17, 1905, promised a broadly representative Duma with the power to approve or reject all legislation and the right to form political parties. Much of the population learned of this development in church, from their parish priest. The Synod's official position on clerical participation in parliamentary politics was expressed in a resolution on January 15, 1906, that "a pastor of the Church should stand outside and above all parties. His relationship to politics and to the struggle of political parties should be analogous to that of a doctor or nurse to a state of war."[31] This resolution provoked requests for clarification from numerous dioceses. In February, Bishop Filaret (Nikol'skii) of Vyatka forwarded an objection from the members of his consistory that, while clergymen should remain aloof from politics as pastors, they should be allowed to participate as citizens, as they had been called to do by government decree, and moreover that the platform of the "Party of Legal Order" (*partiia pravovogo poriadka*) did not run contrary to Christian doctrine.[32] The Church thus entered the Duma era with no unified vision of "the pastor" as a political actor.

Parish clergymen greeted the new Duma with guarded enthusiasm. In late October, a "group of Moscow pastors" appealed to the public to abandon street violence so that their newly won freedoms could be established: "Life will establish a bright future through freedom of expression, conscience, assembly, and freedom from arbitrary arrest [*neprikosnovennost' lichnosti*], which have been granted us already!"[33] This anonymous endorsement of the emperor's concessions to society was thus presented as an expression of political loyalty and a call to order. Official reports to diocesan consistories in early 1906 were even more cautious and peppered with pledges of political moderation. As one superintendent reported to the archbishop of Tver', "All the clergymen of this district, without exception, are strictly conservative, as should be expected. With trust and gratitude, they greet these benevolent reforms in the realms of both politics and in the life of the Church. Yet they are not carried away by the contemporary trend toward revolution."[34] Some superintendents in Tver' expressed regret for the political speeches or writings of priests in their districts, and others claimed that the collective pressure of the local clergy had dissuaded the more politically minded among them from engaging in political activism. In one case, at a district assembly of clergymen, a group of sacristans was prevented from submitting a petition of complaint "somewhere or other."[35] In another, a priest was dissuaded by "the brotherly influence of neighboring priests" from attending an apparently conservative political meeting, organized by a land captain (*zemskii nachal'nik*) from the local gentry.[36] These priests and archpriests were obviously conscious of the threat that participation in the democratic process posed to their status and livelihoods. Yet their collective political caution would be turned to political mobilization when elections commenced.

Their extensive social networks provided the parish clergy with an effective means of political organization. In the aforementioned article from February, "S. S. B." called upon the clergy to organize a Christian social movement at "pastoral assemblies, diocesan congresses, and all-Russian Sobors!"[37] The Sobor would not be convened until 1917, too late to facilitate a Church-based movement on a national scale. But the parish clergy did make use of their professional assemblies throughout the dioceses to facilitate a high level of participation in the electoral process. Also in February, an archpriest reported to Tver's consistory that the clergy under his supervision had convened at pastoral councils and at a congress within his superintenditure, before assembling with clergymen from their district (*uezd*) at a preliminary election meeting in the town of Zubtsov. There, it was resolved to provide every priest with a list of all parish deans in the district and request that they mark twenty desirable candidates for the district electoral assembly. He concluded his report: "Now shall we begin local negotiation with minor landowners for mutual support at the elections."[38] The number of electors chosen from the clergy to serve on the electoral assembly of the landowners' curia was always small, as was the clerical proportion of the general population.³⁹ Yet the collective engagement of that population in the electoral process created the possibility for political discourse in the Church.

The content of political dialogue among the clergy is difficult to assess. In his report, mentioned above, the archpriest's only comment on the subject matter of the extensive pre-election discussions among the clergy of his district was that "material deprivation and dependence on parishioners are a sore spot among the clergy."⁴⁰ This concern, common to most parish clergymen, could not be addressed in isolation from other political agendas. Some priests supported monarchist and reactionary parties in the hope that a triumphant autocracy would provide for the Church. Others identified their interest with those of their working-class parishioners and became supporters of liberal or radical parties. Yet priests who publicly espoused partisan political views, especially those deemed "disloyal" by the police or provincial governor, risked severe punishments such as monastic incarceration or loss of their position.⁴¹ Many individual clergymen took that risk, and clerical publicists expressed pseudonymous political opinions in the press. Yet, because of collective self-censorship, clerical associations rarely expressed joint support for a specific political perspective.⁴² Numerous complaints in church publications that clerical assemblies were being used to organize support for the Constitutional Democratic (Kadet) Party suggest that these bodies were more political than they appeared: "We have already witnessed a pastoral assembly in one of the cities of our diocese at which a priest suggested that the clergy join this party of people's freedom [the Kadets]."⁴³ Whatever the prevailing political sentiment among the clergy may have been, the contribution of clerical deputies to the first two Dumas was decidedly on the Left.

Six priests were elected from the landowners' curia to serve in the First Duma, a small percentage of the five hundred deputies to that body.⁴⁴ Only one of them, Father Vozdvizhenskii from Tambov, described himself as "conservative." Father Kontsevich, elected in Volynia, joined the moderate Octobrist Party. All of the rest, from Bessarabia, Voronezh, Vyatka, and the Oblast of the Don Cossack Host, were directly or indirectly associated with the Kadet Party.⁴⁵ Father Afanas'ev, elected from the Don, had organized a series of political meetings ahead of the First Duma in support of the "Liberation Movement," for which he was placed under investigation by the police and the diocesan authorities.⁴⁶ As a deputy, Afanas'ev condemned as "anti-Christian" an initiative by the minister of internal affairs to forbid the clergy from "praying for the salvation of the lives and souls of those caught in rebellion against the authorities."⁴⁷ While these priest-deputies did not act as a united bloc, they all supported abolition of the death penalty and the redistribution of state, private, and church land to poor peasants. Even the conservative Father Vozdvizhenskii advocated for the redistribution of "all church land . . . if the urgent need arises to provide for poor peasants, I believe that none of our brothers would fail to support the measure, according to the dictates of their consciences."[48] When the emperor prematurely dissolved the First Duma on July 8, 1906, Father Ognev from Vyatka joined 220 other deputies, primarily Kadets and Trudoviks, in signing the Vyborg Manifesto, calling upon the population to protest through civil disobedience. The appeal failed to elicit a popular response but allowed the government to ban its signatories from voting or holding elected office, effectively disenfranchising the leadership of the Kadet Party and ending their predominance in the Duma. Father Ognev was imprisoned for several months, along with many signatories of the manifesto and suffered the additional punishment of being defrocked.[49]

The oppositionist behavior of the clerical deputies to the First Duma had come as a surprise to the authorities. On August 31, 1906, the Synod addressed a letter to all diocesan prelates calling upon them to unite the parish clergy around a policy of abstinence from partisan politics ahead of elections to the Second Duma: "It is incumbent on us, as the spiritual leaders of the pastorate, to spare no efforts to unite all the Church's pastoral forces. . . . Many will come and promise all the blessings of the earth to them and to the people, if only they give them their votes and those of their flock. And it will be difficult for the pastor to understand all their political disputes and party conflicts. It is for us to show them that they hold the highest and most indelible standard by which all human deeds are measured."[50] The synodal hierarchy resolved to increase the involvement of the diocesan bishops in the electoral process in order to impress this nonparty unity upon the parish clergy. Their plan was expressed in a synodal decree No. 11, issued on December 12, 1906, which called upon the diocesan prelates to admonish their parish clergy to support the tsar and to persuade lay voters to do the same. Priests were to lead prayers before every electoral assembly, and the bishop was to deliver a sermon before the final vote for Duma deputies in the provincial capital. The bishops were recommended "to provide additional guidance to the clergy under their jurisdiction by their own authority, if local conditions render it useful or necessary."[51] With such guidance, the Church hierarchy believed, clerical voters would act as a force of loyalty and stability in the Second Duma. Decree No. 11 also called upon the bishops to ensure that every eligible voter among the clergy appear personally at all electoral assemblies in order to maximize the clerical vote and increase the number of clerical deputies in the Second Duma. In late July, the official journal of the Synod published an article by a priest and future deputy to the Third Duma, Gepetskii of Bessarabia, that urged the parish clergy to scrupulously review all voting lists to ensure that every eligible priest was listed.[52] Unaware of the extent of dissident sentiment throughout the pastorate, conservative leaders believed that through force of numbers the clergy could counteract the influence of radical voters in the landowners' curia and act as a pro-government force in the Duma.

The campaign to increase the clerical presence in the Second Duma bore results, but this larger contingent of priest-deputies leaned even further to the Left than the first. Thirteen of the 520 deputies to the Second Duma were Orthodox clergymen. Two of them were prelates. Bishop Evlogii (Georgievskii) of the new Kholm and Lublin diocese was elected in Lublin and Sedlets gubernii and joined the moderate-Right faction. Vicar Bishop Platon (Rozhdestvenskii) of Chigirin was elected to the Duma in Kiev and joined the Right faction.[53] The other eleven clerical deputies were parish priests elected from Saint Petersburg, Orenburg, Yenisei, Perm', Poltava, Mogilev, Volynia, Podolia, Vyatka, Minsk, and Nizhni Novgorod. Five of them, including Grigorii Petrov, an original member of the Group of Thirty-Two Saint Petersburg Priests, supported the Kadets. In Vyatka, electors replaced the defrocked Father Ognev with the more radical Fedor Tikhvinskii, who joined the Trudoviks along with two other clerical deputies.[54] Konstantin Kolokol'nikov, elected in Perm', began his tenure as a Socialist Revolutionary and later joined the Kadets. Nikolai Pirskii of Poltava joined the moderate Right, and Viacheslav Iakubovich of Minsk joined the Octobrist faction.[55] Like their predecessors, the leftist priests in the Second Duma were united in their advocacy of peasant interests, including land redistribution, and strident criticism of the regime's brutality, particularly the use of field courts-martial to swiftly execute revolutionaries. In his memoirs, Evlogii recounted how Father Tikhvinskii publicly challenged him and Bishop Platon in a speech before the Duma: "One of the orators, the priest Tikhvinskii, did not speak but rather screamed from the rostrum: 'The death penalty, gentlemen, is terrible, it is horrible, it is inhuman revenge!' Further, addressing us, the two bishops (Bishop Platon and I): 'Prelates of God, step forward to this public platform and declare that the death penalty is abhorrent to Christ. Let no one dare to justify it in the name of our meek Savior. Gentlemen, it is better to be judged for being merciful than judged for being cruel.'" Evlogii responded that he agreed but that murders committed by revolutionaries were just as offensive to Christ.[56] Such political activism won priests like Tikhvinskii acclaim among workers and peasants and provoked alarm among the Church hierarchy.[57]

The issue of a foiled plot by a Socialist Revolutionary cell to assassinate the tsar provided the synodal leadership with an opportunity to bring the dissident priests to heel. A session convened on May 7, 1907, to discuss the plot was boycotted by leftist deputies, including the priests Grinevich, Brilliantov, Arkhipov, Kolokol'nikov, and Tikhvinskii. This scandal prompted a meeting of the synodal leadership, which resulted in a resolution on May 12, "On Priests, Acting as Members of the State Duma, Who Belong to Extremist Revolutionary Parties." The resolution asserted that by joining the boycott, the priests had openly refused to reject the ideas of the tsar's would-be assassins, which was incompatible with the office of an ordained priest. The Synod thus demanded that they publicly renounce membership in parties that called for a change to the existing authority structure.[58] When summoned before Metropolitan Antonii (Vadkovskii), the priests all denied formal membership in leftist parties, claiming that they merely joined factions as independent deputies. Antonii forbade them to cooperate with leftist parties and suggested they join the moderate Octobrists or voluntarily defrock. Grinevich complied, renouncing his affiliation with the Trudoviks. Yet Kolokol'nikov, Arkhipov, and Tikhvinskii refused either to change their political stances or renounce the priesthood. They, along with the Kadet-aligned Father Brilliantov who had refused to appear before Antonii, were forbidden to perform the liturgy and later defrocked.[59] Petrov was also defrocked after a period of monastic incarceration for having criticized the metropolitan.[60] Defrocking not only ended their careers as pastors but also barred the former priests from serving any longer as Duma deputies. By law, priests, along with civil servants, could neither vote nor run for office after being dismissed from service. Some of them adopted new professions and continued their political activism in other capacities. Petrov worked as an itinerant lecturer and was later restored to the priesthood by the All-Russian Church Sobor.[61] Tikhvinskii found work as a military doctor and later played a leading role in Tver's "diocesan revolution" over the summer of 1917.[62] In 1907, however, the defrocking of these deputies marked the end of free participation in the Duma experiment for the Orthodox parish clergy.

The political face of the Orthodox pastor changed after 1907, as did that of the Duma itself. The emperor dissolved the Second Duma on June 3, after it rejected a demand by the Minister of Internal Affairs, Piotr Stolypin, to expel fifty-five Social Democratic deputies who were suspected of plotting a violent uprising. He also signed a new electoral law, which would drastically reduce the representation of the peasantry, urban centers, and non-Russian nationalities and inflate that of the landowners in order to produce a more loyalist and compliant Duma. Once again, it fell to the priests to announce this new electoral law in their parish churches.[63] The "June 3rd system" was implemented in the Church by segregating voters from the clerical estate into a separate curia that could be insulated from radical elements outside of the clerical estate and more easily monitored. The clerical electors who would vote in the electoral assembly of each province and run for seats in the Duma would now be elected exclusively by other clergymen in superintendent assemblies and diocesan congresses. As illustrated by Bulgakov's observations quoted at the beginning of this chapter, this arrangement allowed the diocesan bishops to monitor and control the entire voting process. State and church authorities used the parish clergy's own social networks as a means of restricting their political expression.

Argyrios Pisiotis shed considerable light on clerical participation in the Third and Fourth Dumas in his dissertation, "Orthodoxy versus Autocracy." His research uncovered the reports of the Moscow priest Ioann Vostorgov to Oberprocurator Piotr Izvol'skii on efforts to suppress dissident voters among the clergy in provinces throughout the empire. Vostorov was a prominent missionary who traveled throughout Siberia and Central Asia as a representative of the Synod to inspect religious schooling, missionary work, and living conditions among Orthodox settlers.[64] He was also a prominent right-wing political activist and prolific writer and orator. As an "Orthodox patriot," Vostorgov advocated a close alliance between the Church and the autocracy.[65] In 1907, he undertook another mission on behalf of the Synod to monitor clerical elections to the Third Duma throughout European Russia. Vostorgov collaborated with diocesan bishops and provincial governors to ensure that politically suspect priests were identified and excluded from elections. From Simbirsk, for example, Vostorov reported, "At the last electoral congress there will be no extreme leftists among the priests, even if such make it to the electors: they will all be given missions and summons out of the city."[66] From Tver' he reported an even more elaborate campaign of coercion and intimidation. The chairmen of the clergy's local congresses were called before the bishop, who instructed them to compile lists of loyal and dissident clergymen in their districts. The latter were to be excluded from the electoral process by confining them to their parishes or sending them on errands. Any leftist priests who managed to be chosen as electors would then be excluded from the city of Tver' during the elections.[67] These measures ensured that the three clerical deputies that Tver's electoral assembly sent to the Third Duma, Fathers Gumilin, Troitskii, and Kupriianov, were all reliable conservatives.[68] The parish clergy offered some resistance to these restrictions on their political activity. In 1912, for example, a district police captain in Tambov gubernia reported that "ahead of the elections, several of the superintendents who had been elected gave me their word that those under Nos. 10 and 24 ('unreliable' priests Nikiforov and Krylov) would by no means be elected. Yet they were elected. . . . The clergy unabashedly expressed their dissatisfaction at the narrow boundaries within which they had been placed by the authorities for the Duma elections."[69]

Despite such occasional defiance, the joint supervision of clerical voting by the Synod and provincial governors ensured the election of almost exclusively right-wing clerical deputies after 1907.

The June 3rd system facilitated the election of much larger contingents of clerical deputies to the Third Duma. The disenfranchisement of urban voters gave clerical candidates a particular edge in provinces that were divided between rural, Orthodox populations, on the one hand, and, on the other, non-Orthodox, urban elites, such as Kiev, which elected six priests. Forty-six Orthodox priests and two bishops were sent to the Third Duma, including Metropolitan Evlogii for the second time.[70] After the defrocking of Ognev and Tikhvinskii, Vyatka gubernia elected a third dissident clergyman in 1907, Aleksandr Popov.[71] In December 1907, an article in the Synod's journal reported on a speech by Popov, which was critical of government policy, as a sad exception to the otherwise loyal conduct of the clerical deputies: "In the Third Duma, this was the first and until now, thank God, the only speech to compromise the Orthodox clergy, and may it be the last."[72] Indeed, over the course of the longest of the four Dumas, clerical deputies of the Third Duma (1907–12) generally provided passive support for the right-wing majority. While priests in the first two Dumas had openly engaged in political debate over Russia's social problems, those of the Third Duma were only active in debates directly relevant to church affairs. Evlogii later recalled his growing distaste for political work: "The longer I was there the more strongly I felt that work in the Duma was fundamentally remote from the Church, even hostile to her.... The Church and politics were mutually exclusive."[73] While these deputies avoided involvement in such issues as agrarian and judicial reform, they were heavily involved in debates over religious toleration, parish reform, parish school funding, and the annexation of the province of Kholm from Poland in order to protect its Orthodox population from Catholic influence.[74] In the hope that unobtrusive cooperation with the government would earn them the political and financial sponsorship of the regime, prelates and clerical conservatives declared the Church to be aloof from "partisan politics."

The Duma clergy's turn away from representative democracy, and reversion to reliance on state protection, was epitomized in the controversy over religious toleration. Although it was welcomed by many clergymen, the Edict of Toleration on April 17, 1905, horrified "Orthodox patriots," who saw it as a betrayal of the tsar's responsibility to protect the Church. The edict's most significant consequence was the legalization of conversion from Orthodoxy to other Christian confessions, but it promised further reform by expressing the emperor's "heartfelt aspiration to guarantee each subject freedom of belief and prayer by the dictates of his conscience."[75] Moreover, among the civil rights that were promised by the subsequent October Manifesto was "freedom of conscience." The first two Dumas were unable to pass legislation in fulfillment of this promise before they were dismissed, and it was only by 1909 that the Third Duma had prepared a bill on religious conversion. This bill would have legalized conversion from Orthodoxy into non-Christian faiths, a freedom that had already been granted in the specific case of baptized Tatars. Yet the idea of granting official sanction to apostasy from Christianity was deeply disturbing to conservatives, as were other proposals, such as the legalization of proselytism among the Orthodox population and the legalization of atheism. These efforts to establish freedom of conscience, together with the campaign to transfer control over parish schools from the Church to the Ministry of Education, created a sense among clerical deputies that the Church was under siege in the Duma. In July 1908, Savva Bogdanovich, a priest from Kiev on the extreme right, delivered a speech in which he complained, "Whenever there is a speech about the affairs of the Church, the mother of the largest part of the population, we hear blasphemy and sacrilege, and the majority joins together in a masonic endeavor to more deeply undermine Christianity and further degrade the dignity of faith."[76] He went on to excoriate the Duma for its pandering to the claims of non-Russian subjects, reliance on foreign capital, and resistance to funding the military, and he blamed these evils on divisive, foreign "party politics": "The soul of Christian statehood is being weighed on the false scales of foreigners." Bogdanovich called upon the Russian, Christian majority in the Duma, and especially his "brothers in the priesthood," to abandon "party politics," by which he meant parliamentary debate, in favor of Christian and nationalist unity.[77] The Synod also encouraged clerical deputies to cease collaboration with "anti-Church parties," particularly the Octobrists, in order to exacerbate growing divisions in that party, which formed the centrist majority of the Third Duma.[78]

In order to safeguard the Church's protected status, clerical deputies placed themselves on the side of the enemies of the Duma project. On May 16, 1909, the Duma narrowly voted in favor of amendments to a bill on Old Believers, one of which would have given them the right to proselytize their faith among the mainstream Orthodox. This bill, together with a dispute over the Duma's right to approve the establishment of a new Naval General Staff, precipitated resignations of conservatives from the Octobrists, which would critically weaken their centrist faction. Clerical deputies and other "Right Octobrists" joined a new coalition of monarchists and nationalists in the Russian National Front, which dominated the Third Duma's third, fourth, and fifth sessions from 1909 to 1912.[79] This shift to the right altered the Duma as an institution. As Geoffrey

Hosking observes in his study of the Third Duma, Stolypin was forced to compromise with this new faction in order to pass his agrarian reform, which meant emphasizing nationalist aims at the expense of other political and social reforms: "Almost all the other measures in the government's reform programme were emasculated or rejected outright—in the fields of factory life, education, religious toleration, local government and peasant courts."[80] The bill on legalizing proselytism among the Orthodox was withdrawn. The Duma narrowly passed the bill on legalized conversion to any non-Christian religion, but it was vetoed by the State Council, the Duma's upper chamber, half of whose members were appointed by the tsar. Russian subjects could legally convert to Islam, Buddhism, or other non-Christian religions only if they could demonstrate ancestral ties to their chosen faith and prove that they had never actually practiced Orthodoxy. Illegal converts were now spared severe persecution but continued to endure indignities, such as the inability to register marriages within their own tradition.[81]

The political defeat of freedom of conscience was a blow to the freedom of the parish clergy as well as to the promise of the October Manifesto. Metropolitan Antonii and others had argued in 1905 that the expansion of religious toleration necessitated greater freedom of expression for the Orthodox clergy because the censorship of their speech was predicated upon the insulation of Orthodoxy from religious and ideological competition. Since 1884, this insulation had been enforced by the "diocesan missionaries," officials appointed by the Synod to assume responsibility from the regular clergy for fighting apostasy as well as atheism. These officials, who were often laymen, monitored the social interactions of the Orthodox and non-Orthodox alike in order to prevent the exposure of the faithful to heterodox "propaganda." Just as the non-Orthodox were forbidden from promoting their faith, so were Orthodox priests forbidden from engaging in public debates with representatives of other confessions or with anti-religious activists. The Duma's failure to establish the freedom to proselytize removed justification for the relaxation of this censorship on the parish clergy and strengthened the power of the diocesan missionaries to restrict the interaction of the Orthodox, both clergy and laity, with the non-Orthodox. Parish priests, therefore, remained dependent on these officials to respond to challenges to their religious authority, often with the help of the local police.[82] In 1912, for example, a priest from the town of Mytishchi wrote letters to Moscow's diocesan missionary council, complaining that the meetings of seven Baptists were illegal because they were preaching to his parishioners. The council, in turn, complained to the governor, who dispatched the police to shut down the meetings.[83] In 1914, a priest in Moscow district reported the illegal circulation of Lev Tolstoy's religious writings by a local zemstvo library to the missionary council, which had the material seized.[84] Such cases demonstrate the insecurity of the parish clergy, who felt forced into reliance on state protection by restrictions on their freedom of speech.

The clerical contingent of the Fourth Duma was even larger than the preceding one. With 46 priests and 2 bishops, the clerical share of the last Duma's 462 deputies was grossly inflated beyond their estate's proportion of the population.[85] These clergymen were also even further to the right than their predecessors, many having been hand-picked by the Synod from the conservative clerical elite.[86] Their presence provoked invectives by other electors and deputies against the "attack of the priests."[87] Clerical deputies had faced hostility since the beginning of the Duma experiment. Vostorgov complained that, during opening prayers held in the First Duma, many delegates had turned their backs, smoked, or laughed.[88] Their inflated presence and abandonment of common causes in favor of self-interested collaboration with the state exacerbated such anticlerical sentiment. One archpriest, Nikonovich, who served in the Third Duma, overheard a conversation among peasant deputies in which they declared all priests to be "a great evil in Russia, because they are not servants of the Church, but policemen who work for the government."[89] Such hostility contributed to fierce resistance of clerical priorities in the last two Dumas. Evlogii reported sarcastic rebuttals of his requests for funding for monasteries: "Money for icons? . . . Icons are miraculous works. Let them be painted by miracles."[90] The clergy's most intense political battle took place over the initiative to transfer control of parish schools from the Church to the Ministry of Education. In 1908, Evlogii expressed dismay that representatives of the "Orthodox peasantry, the very people that parish schools were intended to benefit, were leading opponents of their continued existence."[91] When the clerical deputies failed to save the parish school system, they were aided by the State Council, which vetoed the "universal education bill" in 1912. Having alienated moderate and leftist deputies, the Duma clergy became reliant on the autocracy to protect their interests. While this outcome was more reflective of the Synod's machinations than of the will of the average parish priest, it nevertheless reinforced anti-religious propaganda, which depicted the Orthodox clergy as agents of the increasingly unpopular regime.

The Extreme Right

The parish clergy's foray into parliamentary politics, while ultimately deleterious to the credibility of the pastorate, is remarkable for what it did not become. The Synodal leadership did not prohibit the parish clergy from organizing a clerical party on the Right. Indeed, they actively encouraged it. Once the Synod had suppressed leftist, dissident clerical electors in 1907 and established a conservative cohort of clerical deputies to the Third Duma, it provided them with common housing in Saint Petersburg's Mitrofan Monastery so as to encourage their collaboration.[92] Some leading churchmen had more ambitious plans than the formation of a mere voting bloc for the promotion of Church's interests. After new election laws created a separate clerical curia in 1907, Vostorgov wrote an article in which he called upon the clergy to form a mass political movement. He noted that "the clergy" were not merely priests, deacons, and sacristans. Their community encompassed a diverse group of church servants, including retired clergymen and night watchmen, "and these also have the right to vote [in the clerical curia]."[93] If this population could be united ideologically, Vostorgov saw potential for a powerful political force: "In ancestrally Russian cities, such as Moscow, where there are many cathedrals and clergymen, the clergy could comprise an extremely large force . . . if it were completely united in all its members in the election of candidates to the State Duma from the city, it could present such a solid number of votes that is even difficult to estimate."[94] Freed by the new voting laws from interaction with "non-Russians, non-Christians, and petty landowners with revolutionary ideas," the clergy could now form a constituency that was "the most national [*narodnoe*] of all the Russian estates [*soslovie*]."[95] His dream was not to form a political party, which he considered to be a Western import, but to unite clerical voters behind an ultranationalist, monarchist movement. But Vostorgov and his allies in the Synod proved much more successful at suppressing political expression among the clergy than at eliciting it.

The organization for which Vostorgov hoped to win mass support from the clergy, and to which he himself belonged, was the Union of Russian People (URP). This organization was founded in October 1905 by the monarchist and antisemitic politicians Aleksandr Dubrovkin and Vladimir Purishkevich. It commanded the loyalty of nationalist paramilitary groups, organized around anti-Jewish and anti-socialist pogroms, known to themselves and others as Black Hundreds.[96] The URP endorsed a slightly updated version of the slogan "Orthodoxy, Autocracy, and Nationality," the third pillar of which was to be more explicitly associated with Russian ethnicity. Yet it retained the emphasis on Orthodox Christianity as an essential element of Russian nationalism, making the URP a natural ally of "Orthodox patriots" within the Church.[97] Official missionaries were particularly attracted to this organization by the hope that it would aid them in the fight against freedom of conscience. For example, Vladimir Skvortsov, the chief lay missionary in the Synod, called upon the clergy to support the URP through his journal, *Kolokol*, ahead of elections to the Third Duma.[98] In a 1913 letter to Vostorgov, one diocesan missionary identified himself as a "loyal black-hundredist."[99] The URP, moreover, actively courted the Orthodox clergy, as the public endorsements of priests and bishops lent credibility to their ideology of religiously informed nationalism. In addition to its support for the Orthodox Church's exclusive right to proselytism and missionary activity, the URP championed the convening of the Sobor, the restoration of the patriarchate, and reforms to establish free elections of diocesan officials.[100] This presented a powerful attraction to clerical electors and deputies who were experiencing hostility in the Duma, even from the conservative parties.

Although membership figures for the URP do not exist, the organization did not receive the clerical support for which its leaders had hoped. Some diocesan leaders, most notably Metropolitan Vladimir of Moscow, supported and actively campaigned for the organization. Yet, empire-wide, the URP's representatives and press organs repeatedly expressed frustration at the lack of support they received from the clergy in general.[101] In December 1906, for example, lay representatives of the Ufa chapter of the URP wrote to the ober-procurator to complain of opposition to their organization by "influential clerical figures in the diocese" and requested that clergymen be granted formal permission to join the URP and perform the liturgy at their meetings.[102] In January 1907, under pressure from the tsar, the Synod resolved that such petitioners should be informed that "the Holy Synod does not forbid clergymen from participating in lawful gatherings."[103] This ambiguous decree failed to unleash a groundswell of clerical support for the URP. Moreover, even in Moscow, where parish clergymen were encouraged by their prelate to join the URP, the organization attracted only lukewarm support. In March 1909, a merchant who led a local chapter of the URP in Moscow reported to Metropolitan Vladimir that "upon opening the Dmitrovskii section of the Union of Russian People . . . the following clergymen took part in the first assembly: the Archimandrite of the Boris and Gleb Monastery Father Feodosii, the cathedral priests Father Kozlov and Father Felitsyn, and the priest of Borisov, Father Afonskii. All other local clergymen, to our deep sorrow, did not attend although they were invited."[104] The URP achieved greater success in provinces where the clergy felt threatened by non-Orthodox populations, such as Turkestan.[105] Several clerical deputies to each of the last two Dumas were affiliated with the URP, including Vicar Bishop Anatolii (Kamenskii) of Kherson, who served on the URP's Central Council while deputy to the Fourth Duma.[106] Nevertheless, neither the URP nor any other ultranationalist organization achieved the kind of mass following that Vostorgov had hoped to evoke.

The failure of the URP to attract substantial support from the clerical estate can partially be attributed to imperial Russia's idiosyncratic version of nationalism. To their credit, the majority of the Church's prelates refused to endorse black-hundredist violence. The Synod as a whole refused to condone an outright alliance between the ecclesiastical hierarchy and the URP, and Metropolitan Antonii (Vadkovskii) condemned the URP as a terrorist organization.[107] Orthodox intellectual leaders, such as Sergei Bulgakov, also urged the parish clergy to resist the allure of the extreme Right: "The members of that pogrom-terrorist organization, the Union of Russian People, will inundate you (and are already doing so) with masked or direct exhortations that you should go yourselves and lead your flock into the Union of Russian People. Do not believe them, however highly they may be placed, for in them speaks the 'prince of darkness.'"[108] In addition to being morally abhorrent, the ideology of the extreme right proved to be politically ineffective. The goals of the URP included defense of the autocracy, the Russian nation, and the Orthodox Church against the corrupting force of democracy. Its members hoped to mobilize a modern mass movement against modern parliamentary politics per se. It is according to this logic that the aforementioned Father Bogdanovich, himself a member of the URP, called upon his fellow deputies to abandon "party politics" and unite as Orthodox Russians. Although similar ideologies would enjoy unfortunate success later in the twentieth century, this rejection of Russia's first parliament in favor of an uncharismatic dynast failed to resonate on a mass political scale. Only thirty-two deputies elected to the conservative Third Duma were formally affiliated with the URP.[109] Like the general public, the clergy were uninspired by Russia's extreme right.

The fatal flaws of the URP alone cannot account for the failure of the clerical estate to rally behind a conservative party. Even the conservative deputies to the last two Dumas offered passive support to a variety of parties, including the liberal progressives, despite the efforts of the Synod to coral them into a united bloc. Although they did band together in support of specific issues, they presented no united support for issues unrelated to church affairs. Evlogii provides some explanation in his memoirs. During elections for the Fourth Duma in 1912, he reports, Evlogii was visited by Ober-procurator Sabler, who urged him to lead the formation of a clerical faction. Evlogii refused.

> Our humble parish clergy are closely, organically, and practically bound to the people; united with them in thought, feeling, and suffering, they cannot go to the Duma having torn that deep bond asunder. If we isolate the clergy from the people, we will make them odious. "The priests have wormed their way into

the Duma." "The priests are looking out for their own pockets." That is how the people will perceive the formation of a clerical faction in the Duma.... The clergy should work in all parties according to their consciences.[110]

Following this refusal, Evlogii received a letter from the Synod, instructing him not to stand for election to the Fourth Duma. His explanation to Sabler reflected a fundamental idea behind the pastoral movement: that the clerical estate existed for the sake of the Orthodox laity. In 1907, a Moscow priest published an article in which he condemned as parasitic those marginal occupations within the clerical estate that Vostorgov sought to mobilize as a political interest group: "At baptisms the communion bread bakers give [the child] a little shirt and perform little services that no one needs and only cause confusion. There is only one goal here: 'to receive'—and for those who perform the baptism, this is the whole story. Give to the priest, give to the deacon [for registration], give to the watchman, give to the communion bread baker, and to the needy."[111] At all levels of the hierarchy, the clergy were conscious that their estate could not survive as an exclusive interest group, as this would alienate its lay supporters. This awareness informed the clergy's political behavior just as it animated their pastoral work. Once the clergy were prevented from acting as political advocates for their parishioners, they could not be united around a narrower constituency.

Conclusion

The 1905 Revolution placed the parish clergy in a paradoxical situation. Church and state authorities viewed them as potentially useful allies in stemming the tide of revolution and provided the clergy with extended freedom of association to allow them to form pastoral councils, organize parish associations, and vote for political representatives. Initially, these pastoral networks seem to have used their political freedom to advocate for the interests of the Orthodox peasantry. Yet this pastoral political activism was deemed too threatening to the regime. The Synod restored its tight control over clerical expression and packed the Duma with conservative and nationalist priests. The church hierarchy's revocation of their freedom of political expression in the Duma era rendered the clergy dependent on entrenched authorities, from the State Council to the local police, to protect their interests. While the Church gleaned short-term benefits from this appeal to authority, such as budgetary concessions and the fortification of its privileged status, it sacrificed the credibility of the pastorate, which became more closely associated with the oppressive regime. The clerical representation in the Duma was converted into added ballast for the inflated right wing, yet the extreme right was unable to mobilize the clergy's social networks as a support system for an authoritarian movement. The failure of "Orthodox patriotism" to galvanize a right-wing clerical party cannot be attributed to a lack of organizational capacity within the clerical estate, which was experiencing an expansion of pastoral associations at this very time.

Orthodox priests were not "apolitical," as Bulgakov lamented in his exposé of voting manipulation among the clergy. Individually, many priests served as organizers for the All-Russian Peasant Union and contributed to the formation of local sections of this revolutionary organization in multiple provinces, including Tver'.[112] Many other clergymen participated in the meetings and pogroms of black-hundredist groups. Collectively, however, the parish clergy did not play a decisive role in Russia's experiment with representative democracy, especially after 1907. Gregory Freeze attributes their political indecision to divisions within the clerical estate, along lines of wealth, education, and geography: "Perhaps the most striking element in ecclesiastical politics was not the clergy's conservatism or liberalism . . . rather, it was the coexistence of both currents—the inability of churchmen high or low to fight cohesively for the old regime or even for a new one."[113] Yet the parish clergy had proven themselves to be more than capable of overcoming these social and geographical boundaries in their campaigns against poverty, illiteracy, and famine. The ecclesiastical hierarchy paralyzed the political capacity of the clergy's diocesan networks in the context of the June 3rd system, but they did not neutralize the networks themselves. A lasting effect of the clerical experience in the Duma era was an aggravation of the parish clergy's resentment of the monastic hierarchy. When the tsarist regime collapsed in February 1917, this resentment fueled a revolt against the monastic hierarchy within the Church, and the diocesan networks served as ideal conduits for this revolution.

7

Revolution in the Church

IN HIS MEMOIRS, Metropolitan Evlogii of Paris described the 1917 diocesan congress of Volynia, where he served as archbishop from 1917 to 1918. For the previous half century, this institution had been convened at the discretion of the bishop and had been limited to priests and, for the final decade of the Russian Empire, lay church elders as well. This congress was quite different.

> In Volynia (as in many dioceses at that time), there arose agitation among the lower servants of the Church, deacons and sacristans. They were jokingly referred to as "social-deacons" and "social-sacristans" [a pun on "social democrat"]. They demanded that I immediately convene a diocesan congress to discuss pressing matters, and I agreed. The congress convened on Easter. In addition to clergy, it was composed of representatives 1) from the Red Cross . . . 2) from the zemstvo; 3) from the frontline military organizations and hospitals. . . . Before work began a prayer was held in the church. I delivered an address on new life and on the renovation of the life of the Church, as the Church was not removed from the common fate of the Russian people. I concluded with the announcement that I considered my presence at the congress to be superfluous, as the question to be discussed was the desirability or undesirability of my continued leadership of the diocese.[1]

Over the spring and summer of 1917, similar diocesan congresses of clergy and laity assembled in all sixty-seven dioceses of the Russian Empire to discuss church reform, usually without the traditional blessing of the diocesan bishop. Evlogii enjoyed popularity in Volynia, and he was informed by a delegation of a priest, a deacon, a sacristan, and a representative of a women's organization that the accusations against him of being a black-hundredist and agent of the old regime were found to be baseless and that he should remain as bishop.[2] Yet at least fifteen other diocesan congresses would depose their prelates that summer.[3]

Many Orthodox Christians viewed the February Revolution as an opportunity to resolve long-standing grievances that had been suppressed under the tsarist regime. The hierarchy sought administrative independence from the secular bureaucracy. The parish clergy resented the nearly absolute power that the bishops wielded within the dioceses. The laity resented the financial burden of supporting the clergy and their institutions, over which they had limited control. Some politicians and intellectuals demanded the democratization of church administration. In the months after the February Revolution, the Church was convulsed by a general revolt against all forms of ecclesiastical authority. The Church survived this revolt and organized an All-Russian Church Sobor from September 1917 until August 1918, which reestablished the Patriarchate of Moscow and negotiated a comprehensive reform of the Church's authority structure. The ultimate success of the reform process depended on the ability of the Church's various communities to forge a compromise in the midst of a political and ecclesiastical revolution. This compromise developed through the discourse of canon law.

Once the synodal system lost its political sponsorship, different factions emerged with competing visions of ecclesiastical reform. Meanwhile, the Church descended into chaos at the parish level. Throughout the provinces, laypeople deposed their clergy. Some attacked the priests as agents of the old regime, while others simply took the opportunity to seize parish land.[4] In some cases, parishioners deposed their own elected elders in order to seize the parish funds with which the elders had been entrusted.[5] This chaos created anxiety among Orthodox Christians, especially priests, who feared the disintegration of the institutional church, even as they hoped for change. The diocesan congresses came to facilitate broad-based discussions of how the Church could be reformed, while preserving "canonicity," or institutional integrity according to Orthodox Church law. These central institutions of the parish clergy's social networks, which had for so long failed to integrate church and society, now helped the Orthodox population to overcome deep divisions and achieve institutional reform in the midst of a collapsing state.

Little has been written about the Church's revolutionary congresses over the summer of 1917.[6] By far, the most comprehensive study is Pavel Rogoznyi's monograph on the subject, *Tserkovnaia revoliutsiia 1917 goda*. Rogoznyi identifies the solidarity of the episcopate as an important factor in the Church's emergence as the only institution of tsarist Russia to survive the revolutions of 1917.[7] The present chapter highlights another crucial factor, the pastoral movement, as a moderating force in the Church's revolution. For all their efforts to radically reform the ecclesiastical authority structure, the parish clergy depended on the Church's institutional integrity to endorse their status as ordained pastors. In their capacity as leaders and organizers of the diocesan congresses, therefore, the parish clergy resisted overt transgression of canon law. Moreover, the 1917 congresses proposed unprecedented concessions to lay interests. These concessions, had they been realized, would have effectively dismantled the material basis for a separate clerical estate. They were the conclusion of the process of integrating lay participation in the diocesan networks of the parish clergy. Clerical leaders who supported this final relinquishment of control over diocesan resources to parishioners were likely motivated by the urgent necessity of lay support for the Church in its state of revolution. In the short term, these efforts increased they laity's stake in the institutional church and reduced anarchy in the parishes. This move by the parish clergy to achieve social integration within a canonical framework greatly contributed to the preservation of church unity.

This chapter begins by examining the debates over canon law that took place in the late nineteenth century. It focuses on discussions of the parish clergy's representative institutions and their place in the Church's canonical structure. It then examines the continuation of these debates in the context of the 1917 diocesan congresses in Tver' and Moscow. The congress in Tver' was particularly radical, following dramatic revolutionary events in that city, including the brutal execution of the governor, Nikolai von Bünting, on March 2.[8] This congress was also unique in that, after demanding the resignation of the prominent Archbishop Serafim (Chichagov), it recognized his locum tenens, Arsenii (Smolenets), who was vicar bishop of Staritsa.[9] With the help of this member of the hierarchy, Tver's diocesan revolutionaries negotiated with the Synod throughout the summer of 1917 in the hope of achieving recognition of their agenda as canonically legitimate. Moscow's congress also deposed its prelate, and the diocese became the focus of church reform on a national scale. The diocese then hosted the All-Russian Congress of Clergy and Laity, a national gathering of representatives from the revolutionary diocesan congresses. This national congress exerted a powerful influence on the Sobor, which followed it in Moscow.

Canonicity

Orthodox canon law is used to regulate many aspects of church life, such as marriage, conversion, clerical discipline, and the structure of ecclesiastical authority. The main sources of Orthodox canon law are the New Testament, the Apostolic

Canons, rules of the ecumenical councils, and certain statements of the church fathers. Canon law, as derived from this material, was compiled in the *Nomocanon* of Patriarch Photios in the ninth century.[10] This compilation of ecclesiastical and Byzantine civil law was translated into the Slavonic *Kormchaia kniga*, which entered medieval Rus' in multiple versions between the eleventh and thirteenth centuries.[11] This medieval compilation was never recodified for use in Russia. Instead, the tsarist state would step in to guide church administration in the modern world. Under the Synodal Church, there was no clear division between canon, civil, and criminal law. The norms of canon law applied to marriage and divorce, for example, while criminal law was applied to investigations of clerical misconduct.[12] The overlapping and sometimes contradictory application of government decrees, synodal resolutions, and canon law to ecclesiastical administration placed few restraints on the bishop's personal authority within his diocese.[13] Yet it was limitations imposed on the hierarchy's collective independence by the synodal system that first provoked demands for the clarification of canonical norms. The practice of transferring bishops from one diocese to another as a form of punishment, which increased dramatically under Nicholas I, was frequently criticized for being uncanonical.[14] Appeals to canon law were made to argue for the Church's right to administer its own religious and organizational affairs, independently of state interference. Yet the weakness of canon law as a source of authority stemmed from the lack of an independent arbiter of what was and was not canonical.

By the 1850s, high-ranking prelates had begun to call for an all-Church council, or Sobor, to discuss the reform of church administration independently of the Synod.[15] This movement drew inspiration from the concept of "conciliarity," a theory of ecclesiastical authority based on collective decision-making on the model of the Ecumenical Councils.[16] The Slavophiles, lay Orthodox philosopher-theologians, popularized and embellished this concept as *sobornost'*. Taken from the Slavonic translation of the word "catholic" or "universal" in the Nicene Creed as *sobornyi*, the term was used to express an ideal of uncoerced unity among Christians.[17] Orthodox intellectuals called for the freedom of the hierarchy to assemble independently of the closely supervised Synod of twelve prelates and form a new High Church Council with the competence to interpret canon law. Yet the Slavophiles attributed *sobornost'* to other forms of voluntary assembly, including the peasant commune. Thus, the concept of *sobornost'* inspired other visions of ecclesiastical governance, beyond the confines of the monastic hierarchy. For example, in a series of articles published in the Slavophile paper *Rus'* in 1882, the Moscow Archpriest A. M. Ivantsov-Platonov argued that *sobornost'* should serve as the guiding principle of church administration at all levels, from the parish assemblies to the diocesan congresses to the episcopal councils. The convening of the Sobor was to be the culmination of this extensive participatory system.[18] This inclusive understanding of *sobornost'* supported a vision of ecclesiastical reform in which canonical authority would be determined through broad-based participation. It was different from the model espoused by most of the hierarchy.

The study of canon law in Russia was in its infancy in the mid-nineteenth century and was therefore strongly shaped by the polemics surrounding these rival visions of church reform.[19] If the controversy over the proper relationship between state and ecclesiastical authority figured most prominently in the writings of Russia's early scholars of canon law, then the issue of nonepiscopal participation in a more conciliary church administration followed closely thereafter. Many scholars of canon law in late imperial Russia believed that some kind of "electoral principle" (*vybornoe nachalo*) should be introduced into church administration so that the Orthodox community could participate in its own governance through elected representatives. E. E. Golubinskii, professor of canon law at Moscow Theological Academy, for example, argued that the personal authority wielded by the bishops within their dioceses was uncanonical and that "the status of the members of the board with the bishops, now known as the consistories, should have a voice that is not merely consultative, but authoritative, like that of the bishop himself."[20] Vasilii Myshtsyn, another professor at Moscow Theological Academy, went further, arguing that in a reformed church, the apostolic authority of the bishop should be supported by the active participation of the entire diocesan community. His comments reveal the importance of the concept of *sobornost'* in the study of canon law, which Myshtsyn equated with canonicity: "The Soborno-canonical principal demands that the new institution [of diocesan administration] should be an organ not of episcopal power but of the whole diocese."[21] Critics of this version of *sobornost'* argued that canon law had been determined by the apostles and their successors and not through broad-based participation. For example, Nikolai Suvorov, a professor of canon law at Moscow University, pointed out that nonepiscopal participants in the Ecumenical Councils had acted as advisors to the bishops but never as voting members.[22] Defenders of the hierarchy's apostolic authority often viewed the movement for a more participatory church administration as a result of the fetishization of contemporary political ideas of the "zemstvo-constitutionalists."[23] Yet, as George Kosar argues, "the electoral principle was widely viewed as an instrument for achieving *sobornost'*, not as an end unto itself."[24] Many Orthodox intellectuals and members of the clergy sought a reinterpretation of apostolic authority on a more *sobornyi*, or conciliar, basis.

Nikolai Zaozerskii, a prominent scholar of canon law during his lifetime (1851–1919), published his dissertation in 1894 on the canonical basis of hierarchic authority in the Orthodox Church. The primary argument of the 458-page study is that ecclesiastical authority should be independent of state authority, and this study also advocates collaboration between the bishop and the parish clergy and laity in church administration. While acknowledging the views of his opponents in extensive notes, Zaozerskii argued that the Church's authority structure should be parallel to that of the state, neither part of it nor subservient to it. Strict separation is possible, he claimed, because ecclesiastical authority is of a different nature from that of the state: "The All-Wise Lord does not give his disciples, apostles, and their successors the kind of imperious authority and honor that is wielded by *the kings of the gentiles, and they that exercise authority upon them* (Luke 22:25–26). But those who believe in Him are commanded to show unconditional loyalty and obedience to his messengers and disciples."[25] While there is "no greater authority on earth" than that of the successors to the apostles, Zaozerskii argued that bishops are accountable for that authority to both God and the Church. In numerous places, the Apostolic Canons decree that a bishop, found wanting in his duties or conduct, should be deposed.[26] In order to help the bishop live up to this high standard, Zaozerskii argued, Orthodox canon law provides broad leeway for the participation of both laity and the state in the affairs of church administration.[27] The ideal arrangement, according to Zaozerskii, was that of the ancient church, in which the bishop was elected by his followers and maintained close contact with them: "Every manifestation of the Church's governing power was carried out by the bishop publicly and in close collaboration with all his flock. The bishop himself was viewed not only as a church leader and pastor of Christian society but also as her representative—her chosen and beloved face."[28] He acknowledged that the consistorial system of his contemporary church was useful for the administration of the massive dioceses of the Russian Empire. Yet, by strengthening his administrative authority with the help of an appointed consistory, the bishop suffered serious disadvantages as well: "First of all, the bishop is deprived of the essential collaboration and advice of his canonical assistants—presbyters and other clergy, just as the latter are deprived of their ancient, canonical rights of power and honor."[29] Moreover, citing the supervisory role of the consistory's lay secretary, Zaozerskii pointed out that the consistories had so come to dominate church administration that they had begun to infringe on the bishop's own authority.[30]

Zaozerskii proposed that the diocesan congresses, which he saw as a revival of the diocesan *sobory* or *sbory* of ancient Rus', could alleviate the bishop's isolation from his flock. Citing book 2, chapter 47 of the Constitutions of the

Apostles, Zaozerskii proposed that the congresses serve as juries for cases in ecclesiastical courts: "Let deacons and presbyters be present [with the bishop] at court and judge not with bias, but justly as people of God."[31] In actual fact, cases of clerical misconduct or malfeasance were investigated by individual inspectors, whose observations were compiled in a report by a lay bureaucrat, under the supervision of the consistory secretary, for presentation to the bishop. Clerical defendants were thus deprived of a trial by jury, and Zaozerskii cited numerous examples of injustice resulting from careless investigations. Entrusting this process to the diocesan congress, he argued, would facilitate collaboration between bishop and clergy and restore control over the Church's court system to the clergy.[32] In Zaozerskii's view, both the episcopate and the parish clergy had become subjugated to the secular bureaucracy under the synodal system, and only through collaboration could they regain control of the Church and restore dignity to the clerical rank.

Zaozerskii's vision was similar to that of many within the episcopal party, who could not fail to perceive the importance that the diocesan congresses had come to play in church administration. Yet their vision was informed by a more top-down understanding of *sobornost'*, according to which the Church's unity and independence were derived entirely from the individual apostolic authority of the bishop. Such a vision was expressed in an academic thesis, "Diocesan Congresses of the Clergy: Their Work and Significance," submitted to Kazan' Theological Academy in 1900 by a priest, Vasilii Bogoiavlenskii, for the completion of his master's degree. In this thesis, Bogoiavlenskii argued that the critics and opponents of the diocesan congresses and other clerical associations failed to understand the complexity of the modern church, which made such institutions necessary: "The administration, both church and government, despite its best intentions, could not resolve these problems with its own resources and decided to call upon the clergy itself to take an active role."[33] In addition to their practical necessity, Bogoiavlenskii took pains to establish the canonical foundation of the diocesan congress.

> That the active participation of the parish clergy in affairs of faith and of the Church is not a tendency arising from the spirit of the times . . . but has always been a property of the Christian Church, is not difficult to discern in the history of the life of the Church. Turning to the apostolic era, we find presbyters or elders with whom they held council on all important matters in the Church. We see the same thing with the successors of the apostles—the bishops, with whom there were also presbyters, forming a council. This council had the name presbytery. These presbyteries can be called the ancestors of our consistories, or the Latin cathedral chapters, papal chapters, as well as other institutions intended

for the active participation of presbyters in the affairs of faith and the Church, including our diocesan congresses. There is clear indication of the existence of the presbytery in the Apostolic Constitutions, the acts of the councils, and the works of the church fathers.[34]

He went on to enumerate the long list of restrictions imposed on the work of the diocesan congresses by the Synod, officially limiting their activity to financial matters. He looked to the episcopate to free the congresses and the Church from these unreasonable restrictions imposed by the synodal system: "Diocesan congresses, by force of the demands of Russian church life, have expanded the sphere of their activities in the affairs of religious-educational institutions. They have engaged questions of the improvement of conditions for the clergy, especially questions of religious-moral character. Thus, naturally, they came to be guided not by synodal decrees alone, but by the authority given them from the diocesan bishop, and this authority came to be as great and varied as the activity of the diocesan congresses."[35] Yet Bogoiavlenskii's narrative of episcopal authority as the guarantor of freedom for the diocesan congresses from state regulation did not conform to the experience of most parish clergymen. Many perceived "episcopal absolutism" as a greater threat to pastoral freedom than synodal regulations.[36] Diocesan congresses were as likely to appeal to the Synod for protection from this threat as they were to do the reverse.[37] Bogoiavlenskii's subsequent career is telling. He was ordained as a bishop himself in 1909, after the death of his wife, and rose to become a member of the Synod. In 1917, he was expelled from the see of Chernigov by his own diocesan congress.[38]

As preparations for reform began within the Church, divisions between the clerical and episcopal parties continued to widen. When panicked soldiers fired on the workers' procession led by Father Gapon in the streets of the capital in January 1905, the topic of church reform was thrown into the open for public discussion. The Church's immediate reaction to this event came from the parish clergy, the Group of Thirty-Two Saint Petersburg Priests, who had convened in the wake of Bloody Sunday to discuss the appropriate response of the pastorate to the current state of crisis. Their proposal, "On the Necessity of Change in the Russian Church Administration," was published in *Tserkovnyi vestnik* on March 17, 1905. It was the Church's first public call for the convening of a national Sobor to reform the ecclesiastical administration. As the group explained in a subsequent article, their proposed Sobor was to be composed of bishops, parish clergy, and laity, all of whom would be freely elected.[39] This would give the Sobor the necessary independence from the state to "restore canonical freedom in the Russian Church."[40] Ober-procurator Konstantin

Pobedonostsev circulated a questionnaire about church reform among the diocesan bishops in the hope that their replies would express support for the status quo. Instead, the bishops' responses revealed overwhelming support for a Sobor, but one whose membership would be limited to the monastic hierarchy.[41] From January to December 1906, a Pre-Council Commission was held to discuss the anticipated Sobor. The commission's thirty-nine members included nine bishops, seven parish clergymen, and nineteen lay professors from universities and theological academies, many of whom were experts in canon law. These lay experts decisively shifted the balance of the commission away from plans for a more inclusively organized Sobor, on the grounds that voting rights for non-bishops would constitute an uncanonical infringement on apostolic authority.[42]

While the clerical party continued to press for a more inclusive and conciliary model of reform, only rarely did its partisans advocate infringement of canon law. In 1906, the Slavophile and lay theologian N. P. Aksakov argued that Apostolic Canon 39, which declares that the authority of the priest proceeds only from the authority of the bishop, had become "an anachronism."[43] While the parish clergy challenged the authority of the monastic hierarchy, rarely did they challenge canon law itself in this way. The Group of Thirty-Two Saint Petersburg Priests argued that dioceses had grown too large, that the episcopate had become alienated from the people under their authority, and that bishops should be elected by clergy and laity. Other groups of parish clergymen, inspired by "the Thirty Two," published demands for the episcopate to be opened to married priests. These radical challenges to the existing ecclesiastical structure did not contradict canon law, which does not explicitly prohibit the ordination of married bishops.[44] Moreover, despite the opinion expressed in *Tserkovnyi vestnik* in May 1906 that the Church was threatened by "a dangerous Presbyterian movement," the clerical party never challenged the apostolic authority of the episcopate per se.[45] Most among the parish clergy wanted substantial reform of the Church's authority structure but not its dissolution. While few among the laity understood the intricacies of canon law, their respect for the parish clergy and all their institutions was largely contingent on the latter's canonical status as pastors of the Church, ordained through the apostolic authority of their diocesan bishops. Thus, in order to preserve the Church's social and institutional integrity, even the most radical reformers pressed for change within the parameters of "canonicity."

The February Revolution unleashed a general confrontation within the Church, which included the rival visions of canonicity that had developed over the preceding decades. The Provisional Government appointed the former Octobrist deputy Vladimir L'vov to the post of ober-procurator in February

1917. A strong advocate of reform according to the electoral principle, L'vov played a conspicuous role in subsequent events within the Church. Ironically, this revolutionary ober-procurator resorted to the tsarist-era prerogative of dissolving the Synod in April. He replaced the old members, with the exception of Sergei (Starogorodskii) of Finland, with four bishops and four priests who were more amenable to his reform agenda.[46] Over his short tenure, which lasted until August, L'vov took heavy-handed measures to purge the hierarchy of his opponents. Metropolitan Evlogii said of L'vov, "He behaved like a dictator and dismissed no small number of bishops."[47] L'vov's actions and rhetoric encouraged the uprising against the hierarchy at the diocesan level, and he received numerous delegations from the diocesan congresses that subsequently convened to demand reform. For lack of any alternative, the Synod continued to serve as the final arbiter of canonical legitimacy until the convening of the Sobor. In this capacity, it officiated the debates over the Church's canonical structure that would now be carried out at the local level.

Tver'

The diocesan congresses of the spring and summer of 1917 varied in composition and focus. Tver's congress was particularly noteworthy for its radicalism, for the prominence of the archbishop that it deposed, and most of all for the temporary settlement that it reached with the prelate's replacement, the Vicar Bishop of Tver', before the Synod intervened. Once the conflict reached the level of the hierarchy, the Vicar Bishop Arsenii defended his position by arguing for the canonical legitimacy of the diocesan congress that supported him.

Serafim (Chichagov) became Archbishop of Tver' in March 1914. He took an active role in the clergy's war relief effort. In April 1914, he chided parish priests for being "listless, apathetic, and slothful" in their task of organizing parish councils and trusteeships for the relief of soldiers' families.[48] Despite his enthusiasm for the organizational work of the parish clergy, Serafim was wary of granting them autonomy. In 1914, he abolished the election of superintendents by their clerical peers, calling such elections "illegal and harmful."[49] Serafim was also a member of the Synod and of the State Council, and spent much of his tenure as archbishop outside of the diocese, attending to his duties in the capital. This absenteeism, as well as his condescending attitude toward the parish clergy, seems to have generated much of the animosity toward him that would animate the diocesan congress.

Serafim greeted the February Revolution with enthusiasm before returning to his diocese from Petrograd, the new name given to the capital in September to disassociate it from the German enemy. In March, he himself convened the diocesan congress to discuss reform of the ecclesiastical administration, possibly in the hope of depriving more radical elements of the initiative. Nevertheless, when the congress assembled on April 20, it promptly discarded the agenda that Serafim had proposed. Delegates accused Serafim of being, on the one hand, "alien to the diocese, having left it at a difficult time without leadership," and, on the other hand, "despotic . . . that he established a police regime in the diocese . . . always urging the clergy to fight against revolution."[50] The congress delegates voted for Serafim's replacement by an elected candidate from among the white clergy or even laity.[51]

Despite the prominence of radical clergymen within its leadership, Tver's congress did not primarily serve the professional interests of the parish clergy. As chairman, the delegates elected F. V. Tikhvinskii, one of the clerical deputies to the Second Duma who had been defrocked for his leftist politics and had recently been serving in the town of Rzhev as a military doctor. The clerical radicalism of Tikhvinskii and other leftist priests is revealed in proposals to establish elected district (*uezd*) bishops and to abolish the offices of superintendent and clerical inspector, the functions of which would be performed by elected district councils. There were also measures to protect the clergy from popular unrest, such as the resolution that parish priests should only be deposed by an ecclesiastical court. Yet the congress also resolved that all parish clergymen should henceforth be elected by their parishioners. More surprising were the resolutions that the parish should be granted independent legal status and that all emoluments and contributions to clerical and diocesan needs should be made with the express permission of the parish council. The clergy had long resisted these demands by advocates for lay interests. Their fulfillment would have transferred almost complete control over parish property and wealth to the parishioners, who were very likely to use them for parish needs and bankrupt diocesan institutions. The delegates "wishing not to ruin popular education" did resolve that regular contributions to religious schools should be maintained temporarily, until the Constituent Assembly could "decide their fate," and that parishes could only enjoy the services of those diocesan institutions that they agreed to support.[52]

The firm position of the episcopal party had always been that no church assembly could be canonically legitimate without the blessing of its diocesan bishop and his approval of any decision that it took, popular support notwithstanding. Yet Serafim's relentless attacks on the congress's claim to represent the will of the diocese reveal the moral authority that a democratic mandate had come to exert. The official minutes of the congress record sixty-two priests, sixty deacons, sixty-one sacristans, sixty-one church elders, one hundred forty-nine other laypeople, and fifteen seminary and ecclesiastical school teachers.[53] In a letter to the Synod, Serafim claimed that its composition was more chaotic and that people from the street had been wandering into the assembly and dominating the proceedings by aggressively drowning out opposition: "There was a strong smell of alcohol. There is no doubt that sectarians and Bolsheviks had appeared among the deputies. The goal of this assembly was completely clear: to overturn everything."[54] In a subsequent letter, Serafim claimed that a "union of deacons and sacristans" from Rzhev had dominated the congress and that their radical leaders had paid other delegates to appear and dominate proceedings.[55] This latter version is somewhat corroborated in a letter by a lay deputy to the congress from Rzhev, Shchechkin. He claimed that only a portion of the diocesan priesthood had supported the rebellion against Serafim and blamed its success on the radicalization of the lower parish clergy: "This mass of people is attracted to the Church for the sake of a crust of bread and not for any religious feeling or calling. They follow their leaders almost blindly, 'knowing not what they do,' and I consider this venerable institution [of the sacristan] to be entirely superfluous."[56] The goal of this radical grouping of lower parish clergymen, according to Serafim, was to abolish the educational requirements for ordination in order to obtain easier access to the priesthood.[57]

A significant number of petitions to the Synod also attacked the congress's legitimacy on the grounds that it had not been representative of public opinion within the diocese. For example, a letter written on August 10 and signed by more than three hundred residents of the city of Tver' called for Serafim's return to the diocese.[58] The reason for such a backlash may be explained by another letter from the superintendent assembly of Staritsa from July 30, which complained that "the decision regarding Archbishop Serafim came from the members of the congress personally and not from their parishes, because this question was not discussed in the parishes." The petitioners claimed that the possibility of Serafim's ouster was discussed in only three Staritsa parishes ahead of the congress itself.[59] It is likely that the archbishop's departure did come as a great surprise to much of the diocese and that it was particularly shocking to clergymen who were already living in fear of the restive population. Shchechkin expressed his anxiety that this decision would make the situation worse: "By voting for the dismissal of its archpastor, the clergy is sawing off the limb on which it sits. After this, the layman will return home from the congress together with a sacristan and say: 'We overthrew the bishop, the prelate, and we will deal with you, priest, in the same way.'"[60] Other letters submitted to the Synod by groups of laypeople and clergymen in support of Serafim expressed similar concerns about the congress's aftereffects on relations with the laity and argued that the bishop's expulsion had been uncanonical.[61]

It cannot be concluded that the decisions of Tver's April congress were the work of a radical fringe, clerical or otherwise. While certainly radical, the congress reflected the priorities of a large and variegated segment of Tver's Orthodox population. For example, it is clear that the lower parish clergy, deacons and sacristans, made their collective influence felt but did not dominate the congress as Serafim claimed. The congress resolved that lower parish clergymen, "especially those with families," should be given more compensation for their services, but recommended a distribution of parish emoluments of "two parts for the priest, 1½ for the deacon, and 1 for the sacristan."[62] This would have been a substantially more equitable rate than that of the previous decade, which was approximately three parts to the priest, one to the deacon, and one half to the sacristan.[63] Yet this decision also preserved the hierarchic distinctions among these different ranks. The congress agenda also included the proposal to "gradually abolish the diaconate, where this institution is unnecessary."[64] These decisions are not indicative of a coup by the lower clergy.

The congress' decision against Serafim was accepted by many among the laity, as indicated by the removal of the archbishop's name from the liturgy in numerous parishes.[65] In May, two letters, each signed by more than one hundred people, were addressed to L'vov from residents of the town of Kashin in support the congress's decisions. The first signature on both letters expressed hostility to estate distinctions: "Former townsman [*meshchanin*] of the city of Kashin, and now citizen, I. Eshin"; "It is repugnant to an Orthodox Christian standing in church to hear the clergy, on orders from above, publicly deceiving people, proclaiming 'May God first of all remember the Holy Governing Synod.' At that moment one wishes to spit and not pray. Then they say, 'and our most holy Archbishop of Tver' and Kashin Serafim,' Let them pray for their lord in secret, and not in public, so as not to affront the conscience of the believers."[66] In their second letter, these petitioners appealed to L'vov's own Duma speech: "[You spoke] against unworthy government servants from among the higher clergy, who disgrace the Orthodox Church with their actions. We ask that you turn your enlightened attention to the following fact: shortly after congresses of all-city and all-zemstvo organizations in Moscow, Archbishop Serafim of Tver' and Kashin permitted himself, from the church dais in Tver', to insult these congresses, the State Duma, and you, a member of the Duma."[67] The petition reveals that contemporary politics, and L'vov's synodal revolution, had come to influence the religious views of some Orthodox Christians. While the congress had not leveled similar accusations of political reaction against Serafim, which were most likely groundless, it had clearly aligned itself with the conciliar movement by replacing most diocesan offices with representative assemblies, which would include both clergy and laity. The petition's hostility toward estate categories was also echoed in the congress's agenda, which proposed "for clergymen to participate in all institutions with rights equal to those of all other citizens" as well as "the abolition of all clerical awards and privileges."[68] The congress clearly expressed the priorities of an important segment of the Tver' diocese's Orthodox population.

Although many priests were alarmed by the expulsion of Serafim, it cannot be concluded that the priesthood was a negligible force in Tver's diocesan revolution. Priests and archpriests figured prominently in the leadership of Tver's congress and the administration that followed it. While these individuals could be dismissed as a radical fringe, the influence of the priesthood more broadly is apparent in the congress's concern for canonical legitimacy. There are few examples to be found of laypeople appealing to canon law. At the diocesan congress of Rostov-on-Don in May, lay delegates even cried out that "we need to look less at the canons of the Councils!"[69] Yet the pastorate's concern with canonical legitimacy was closely linked with their concern for the legitimacy of the priestly office among the laity. Objections to the congress's "uncanonical" expulsion of Serafim were expressed in conjunction with concerns about the impact of this action on lay-clergy relations. Such an objection was recorded in the minutes of the congress: "It was also pointed out that, according to the canons of the First-Second Council [of Constantinople in 861], removal [of a bishop] is only possible if it is voluntary or carried out by a court, and that the reelection of the prelate would logically demand the reelection of the entire clergy as well, which would lead to the collapse of church life at such a difficult time as the present."[70] Parish priests perceived that, even if most of the laity was uninterested in the esoteric details of canon law, the dignity and social status of the pastorate were inextricably linked with that of the Church and its hierarchy. Tver's diocesan revolutionaries took pains to maintain that dignity by seeking "canonical freedom," which meant freedom within canon law.

The congress's ultimate decision to pursue the election of a new bishop was subtly framed as a request, without explicitly claiming the authority to depose the archbishop: "The congress declares its wish that he leave the episcopal see of Tver', which shall be conveyed to him through an elected delegation."[71] Serafim was thus invited to make the decision himself, and he obliged the congress in this regard. At nine o'clock in the morning on April 22, a delegation headed by an archpriest, Lebedev, was sent to Serafim to inform him of the congress's decision. The congress's official minutes present his response thus:

> "I thank you. Apparently, Tver' diocese does not need such an archpastor whose work is known by all of Russia, including the State Duma and the government. I have served in seven dioceses, and my work was recognized everywhere." (At

this point the bishop indicated two display cases with albums). "I had already decided to leave because my spiritual rift with the diocese occurred on the first day of my return after the revolution. Of course, with such a fracture in my heart, I cannot serve as the spiritual leader [*molitvennikom*] for Tver' diocese. But it is not you who installed me, and it is not by your will that I depart. They will be most surprised at the top [*tam na verkhu*], where I am considered to be needed for Russia, and they will not thank you, the diocese where I served.... I do not consider the congress to be legitimate, and so I am still in power.... It is not a congress, but a representative assembly. At any rate, I will not expound upon this as I have already decided to leave the diocese. I have worked enough. I need no diocese. I will work to prevent divisions among the people and the soldiers." The bishop repeated, "I am very grateful," and blessed all in common.[72]

Arsenii, Tver's Vicar Bishop who would replace Serafim, later claimed that the publication of these comments helped turn public opinion against the archbishop.[73] Serafim's self-importance and indignation are palpable in his own letters to the Synod as well: "Is this not comic? Having led three large monasteries . . . administered four dioceses, in which I accomplished a great deal, as is well known throughout Russia; for a handful of miscreants to write about their distrust of my religious-social work—it is simply insolent and hilarious."[74] He left the diocese on May 4 and then asked L'vov to assign him to some task in the Synod.[75] Serafim's resentful departure from the diocese left it under the control of the congress. His defiant claim that this departure was voluntary would undermine subsequent attacks on the congress's canonical legitimacy.

Immediately after Serafim declared his intention to leave Tver', the congress leaders turned to the Synod to confirm his resignation. Relying on L'vov's sympathy for reform, the congress dispatched a delegation of an archpriest and two seminary teachers to the Synod on April 22 to present its case for the election of a new bishop.[76] They received the ober-procurator's response on April 25. L'vov informed the delegation that Serafim had written a letter declaring his desire to resign from the diocesan see. It was, therefore, possible to elect a new bishop. As for the election of a candidate from among the white clergy, this would have to wait for deliberation at the upcoming Sobor.[77] On April 29, however, Serafim dispatched several frantic telegrams to various members of the Synod in an attempt to reverse his initial resignation: "I ask Synod not to dismiss me without request. Personal letter with various thoughts to procurator cannot substitute request. Entire diocese begs me to wait, indignant, did not grant authority to judge bishop. Possibly I will request inquiry. Intend travel to Petrograd to determine fate."[78] A prominent hierarch, Serafim was able to convert his apparent resignation into official leave.

With Serafim's reversal having thrown their canonical legitimacy into question, the congress leaders found an invaluable ally in his vicar bishop, Arsenii of Staritsa. The congress had originally accused Arsenii of despotism and neglect along with Serafim, but he chose to discuss these charges before the delegates and even apologize. This gesture would garner him support throughout the diocese, even among those who disagreed with the congress's decisions. The congress's official minutes paraphrased Arsenii's speech on April 22.

> Bishop Arsenii, in an extensive speech, explained the difficulties of episcopal service in former times, especially in a populous diocese like Tver', which contains more than 1,000 parishes, while normal relations are only possible in dioceses of no more than 200–300 parishes. Yet he also admitted the possibility of mistakes from his side. In conclusion, the bishop noted that through the close unity among clergy, people, and episcopate that will now be established in a free Russia, those misunderstandings and mistakes that were possible under the old order will no longer take place.[79]

The next day, the congress incorporated Arsenii into a new administrative organ to replace the consistory, the Diocesan Soviet (*eparkhial'nyi sovet*).[80] Arsenii would serve in this body together with two priests, a deacon, a sacristan, two seminary teachers, a seminary inspector, and a peasant. Each member of the council, including Arsenii, would vote on all administrative decisions on an equal basis. Although, in the event of a fundamental disagreement with the rest of the council, the bishop reserved the right to appeal to a higher authority, "Metropolitan, Synod, or Patriarch." All diocesan institutions, trusteeships, candle factories, and so on, which had formerly fallen under the supreme authority of the bishop, would now be administered by the Soviet.[81] On May 10, the Synod granted Serafim's request for leave and recognized Arsenii as his locum tenens.[82] For the moment, the congress had ended "episcopal absolutism" in Tver' diocese, while retaining the apostolic authority of a prelate.

Over the chaotic summer of 1917, the Diocesan Soviet presented itself to the Synod as the recognized authority within the diocese but continued to solicit the latter's confirmation of its canonical legitimacy. In letters to the Synod in May and June, Arsenii reported that some parishes had begun to replace Serafim's name with his own in the liturgy, while others had ceased commemorating any bishop at all. He claimed that these practices were largely determined by the parishioners: "In certain places, priests inclined toward canonical practices are being forced to acquiesce to the demands of the laity."[83] Still other parishioners had begun deposing unpopular clergymen, as so many had feared would happen.[84] In a letter to the Synod on June 26, the Diocesan Soviet claimed that the majority of Tver's parishes were refusing to acknowledge Serafim in their liturgies and that the delay in finalizing the question of Tver's official prelate was harming the Soviet's authority. Further delay, the letter warned, would render it unable to prevent the dissolution of the diocese into anarchy.

> In the eyes of the diocese, the Soviet is the only legitimate, authoritative organ of administration. It can remain so only if its integrity is not called into question. If this were to happen . . . the result of such a loss of confidence in the Soviet would be anarchy in the diocesan administration. In their search for an authoritative institution, the laity would have to turn to some other organ, foreign to the life of the Church, as in the case of the monks of Nilov Monastery, who turned to the Soviet of Workers' Deputies when the diocesan authorities did not respond to their requests. It is obvious how unfortunate another such appeal would be.[85]

This thinly veiled threat was reinforced by another letter to the Synod on July 13 from the Tver' gubernia Soviet of Peasants' Deputies, protesting the "systematic disregard" of the decision of the Diocesan Soviet to remove Serafim: "If the Synod does not satisfy this decision, the Soviet of Peasants' Deputies will consider itself obligated to investigate."[86] These admonitions and threats were, however, considerably mitigated by the Diocesan Soviet's own acknowledgement of its "lacking the right, from a canonical perspective, to sanction the omission of the archbishop's name [from the liturgy]."[87] Despite its radicalism, the Diocesan Soviet never directly claimed that it had lawfully deposed Serafim but rather that the archbishop's initial resignation should be considered binding in order to appease the restless population.

The process of Serafim's restoration revealed the increasing ambiguity of the diocesan congress's status within the church hierarchy. While the Soviet's claim to represent the majority of the diocese failed to convince the Synod to uphold Serafim's resignation, it did assign Bishop Mikhail of Samara to investigate the congress's allegations against him. As these allegations had been vague, it is no surprise that Serafim's fellow-synodal prelate found them groundless.[88] Rather than simply reinstating the archbishop at this point, however, the Synod saw fit to revisit the issue at another diocesan congress on August 8, presided over by Mikhail, and also tasked with electing representatives to the Sobor. A slight majority of the delegates to this congress voted to uphold Serafim's expulsion. On August 9, however, the Synod declared that Serafim was to be reinstated as archbishop of Tver'. The Synod explained its decision on the basis of Mikhail's investigation, Serafim's own desire to return, and "because a majority of only six votes (142 vs. 136) upheld the archbishop's dismissal."[89] The hope was most likely that a more closely monitored congress would be less susceptible to radicalization and would reveal popular support for Serafim. When this gamble failed, the Synod dismissed the results.

Once reinstated, Serafim attacked his vicar bishop for having supported the revolt against him. In a letter to the Synod, he accused Arsenii of attempting to usurp the diocesan see for personal gain and plundering the property that Serafim had left behind. "To spare his own resources, he dined in my home every day and even brought there guests of the female gender."[90] To achieve this goal, Serafim claimed, Arsenii had pandered to the demands of the "drunk peasants" and lower clergymen who had dominated the April congress. He had dignified their radical program by voting in favor of the congress's resolutions. "Bishop Arsenii, in the hope of being chosen to replace me, voted on all issues together with them and became a collaborator in the most illegal, uncanonical, and obscene decisions of the congress."[91] Once a member of the Diocesan Soviet, Serafim claimed, Arsenii had continued to appease the rebellious lower clergy by ordaining uneducated deacons to the priesthood. In order to consolidate his position, Arsenii had spent the summer of 1917 slandering his superior bishop throughout the diocese. Serafim blamed the unfavorable outcome of the August congress on this "agitation" as well as Arsenii's intrigue at the congress itself, including the use of radical soldiers to intimidate the delegates. It is interesting that Serafim justified his demand that Arsenii be transferred to another vicariate with the claim that the latter had lost the popular support of the diocese: "It is necessary for his own personal interest that Bishop Arsenii be transferred to another diocese, to the same position, because he has severely betrayed his office [*uronil svoi san*] and lost all respect from the majority of the clergy and laity."[92] Again, Serafim's intent to discredit the assembly and its claim to represent the diocese revealed that claims that the congress was "illegal and uncanonical" had become insufficient to dismiss the challenge it presented. By accusing Arsenii of leading the congress, Serafim sought to undermine its moral authority as a conciliar institution.

Arsenii's response, submitted to the Synod on September 3, presented an articulate defense of his and the congress's decisions from a canonical perspective. It began with a subtle criticism of his senior bishop.

> Over the course of 3½ years, I have served as ARCHBISHOP SERAFIM's closest colleague. In his personal relations with me, the BISHOP was always straightforward, civil, and courteous; in our profession relations, He consistently adhered to the tactics of "enlightened absolutism." . . . Unfortunately, the ARCHPASTOR was not inclined toward *sobornost'* in the management of affairs, and, left to my

own devises, in April I embarked on the path to which I was guided by my reason and for which, to this day, my conscience does not assail me.[93]

Arsenii's references to Serafim's disinclination from *sobornost'* and his "absolutism" were intended to highlight the archbishop's adherence to the authoritarian practices of the imperial Church, which were already being reformed in the Sobor. Yet, like the Diocesan Soviet in its letter to the Synod in June, Arsenii was careful not to claim that Serafim had been deposed by the decision of the diocesan congress. Instead, he suggested that once Serafim had convened the congress, it had acted within its canonical rights by "asking" him to resign and by exerting popular pressure on Serafim and the Synod to confirm his resignation: "The decision of the congress to ask the ARCHBISHOP to leave the see, and for the HOLY SYNOD to dismiss him from the diocesan administration, I considered to be extremely sad, but not anti-canonical, as it was in accordance with the practices of the Eastern Churches, which have so often changed their archpastors according to the wishes of popular church assemblies. Moreover, the congress was convened by legal authority and was never dismissed by that authority; consequently, my presence there could not have been illegal."[94] Arsenii did not explain which "popular church assemblies" he had in mind. He may have been referring to the seventeenth-century brotherhoods of the Polish-Lithuanian Commonwealth that resisted their bishops' decision to unite with Rome.[95]

In his defense of his conduct over the summer of 1917, Arsenii elaborated upon the Diocesan Soviet's earlier claims to have served as a force of order amid popular unrest. Together with the elected members of the Diocesan Soviet, Arsenii claimed to have mediated compromise among various factions within the diocese, sometimes through hours-long negotiations with parish delegates. These efforts prevented a mass expulsion of parish clergy by the laity in exchange for less educated and less expensive candidates. He also claimed to have discouraged the demands of deacons and sacristans for larger shares of parish resources.[96] Arsenii admitted to having filled some parish vacancies by ordaining twenty-four deacons with only partial seminary educations but noted that the "old regime" had also ordained deacons on occasion.[97] It was this "democratization" of the priesthood, Arsenii acknowledged, that led to discontent among the more educated clergymen. Serafim, he alleged, exploited this discontent by sending "more than 100 letters," agitating for his reinstatement: "The PRELATE's actions accomplished their goal. By August, among the priests of the diocese, especially in the cities, there arose some animosity toward the clerical members of the Diocesan Soviet. They came to be identified with the tendency to democratize the priesthood to the detriment of its intellectual level, and their influence was seen in the appointment of individuals with incomplete educations to priestly positions."[98] Arsenii insisted that he and the Diocesan Soviet had acted as neutral arbiters among the various factions of the diocese while Serafim had sown discord. In conclusion, Arsenii admitted that he had done nothing to help Serafim's cause at the second congress.

> The ARCHBISHOP's return can be such a boon to the diocese, and the diocese's view of the PRELATE can change in the near future, insofar as the HIERARCH can take the path of peace and love. After YOUR HOLINESS's decision, and out of respect for HIS MOST HOLINESS, I do not consider it to be within my rights to explain the reasoning, by no means of an egoistic nature, which prompted me to maintain my former practice of noninterference in the struggle between the BISHOP and the congress. If YOUR HOLINESS or the BISHOPS OF TVER' and SAMARA consider my passivity on August 8 to have been reprehensible, if not criminal, then I can offer no defense.[99]

Arsenii's admission of passivity toward the final congress and his expression of hope that the diocese's view of Serafim would change were mostly likely intended to highlight Serafim's rejection by the congress and his lack of conciliar support.

Subsequent expressions of support for Arsenii lend some credence to his claims to have served as a peacekeeper in the diocese. A petition in protest of his expected dismissal was signed by approximately four hundred parishioners of the city of Tver' and submitted to the Synod on September 3.[100] An article also appeared on September 1 in the liberal newspaper *Tverskaia mysl'*, which expressed outrage that Arsenii's service to the diocese was being punished as a crime. It suggested that Arsenii had demonstrated what Serafim might have accomplished: "It is now clear that if Archbishop Serafim had humbled himself, personally appeared among his flock, and spoken to them in a spirit of fatherly patience and Christian prudence, no one would have dared to touch him." The article went on to predict that "further discord and revolt are surely coming."[101] This prediction proved to be accurate. That same month, Serafim secured Arsenii's transfer to the Priazov and Taganrog Vicariate of Ekaterinoslav diocese but was himself expelled from Tver' in December by order of the Tver' Soviet of Workers' and Soldiers' Deputies.[102] This order was that Serafim should finally obey the decision of the diocesan congress of the previous April.[103] This was not, however, a victory for the "electoral principle" or *sobornost'*. By this time, genuine representative assemblies throughout Tver' gubernia were being dissolved by Bolshevik soldiers.[104]

The details of Tver's diocesan revolution strongly suggest that parish priests were not passive victims of a grassroots uprising against the clergy, resulting in "all power to the parish."[105] The blurring of estate boundaries through the integration of laity into their own social network, while maintaining the integrity of that network, had been a priority of Tver's pastorate for decades. Tver's diocesan congress in April 1917 supported that priority, albeit through far more radical measures than ever before. The congress's plan for a nearly complete transfer of power over diocesan resources to the laity may have been deemed an appropriate response to the gravity of the situation. It was coupled with a strategy of transferring apostolic authority to a conciliar body overseen by the bishop, without overtly violating canon law. Tver's Diocesan Soviet was at least temporarily successful in retaining the allegiance of the rebellious laity by both responding to their demands and maintaining communion with the greater Church. While this diocesan revolution ultimately failed, it demonstrated the importance that the diocesan congress had assumed as a point of contact between the Church's vertical hierarchy and vast horizontal community.

It is, of course, not possible to determine the extent to which Tver's parish clergy was united behind the program of the April congress with certainty. The active participation of lay delegates clearly influenced its program. Yet, for supporters of the pastoral movement, the blurring of estate boundaries through the incorporation of laypeople into the diocesan network was, after all, the point. Parallel events in Moscow strongly suggest that the pastoral movement was the driving force behind other efforts to integrate the Church, as a society, while preserving its canonical integrity.

Moscow

Moscow's diocesan congress received broad public support for its resolution to oust the unpopular Metropolitan Makarii (Nevskii). It also received important political support from Ober-procurator L'vov. Having achieved success against this symbol of episcopal corruption, Moscow diocese and its leadership became the focus of church reform on a national scale. Their "diocesan revolution" attracted leading figures from the Orthodox intelligentsia, who believed that parish clergy and laity should play a more independent and robust role in the public life of the new Russia. These leaders proceeded to organize the All-Russian Congress of Clergy and Laity in June 1917, a national gathering of representatives from diocesan congresses throughout the former empire. A major goal of this congress was to forge a new, democratic alliance of parish clergy and laity that would renew the Church through solidarity. Moscow's diocesan revolution threatened to undermine the authority of the episcopate on the eve of the Sobor, which would also convene in Moscow two months later. Yet diocesan leaders recognized the need to negotiate the restoration of canonical authority with the hierarchy, in order to preserve the unity of the

Church. This was accomplished through the popular election of Archbishop Tikhon (Belavin) as the new archpastor of Moscow, immediately prior to his elevation to the renewed patriarchate.

Moscow's first diocesan congress of 1917 was less radical than that of Tver', but it presented a direct challenge to the authority of the Synod. This was possible because of the unpopularity of the prelate they deposed and the strong support of the ober-procurator. Makarii was widely believed to have been installed in the See of Moscow in 1912 through the intervention of Grigory Rasputin, the obscure and corrupt holy man who had risen to a position of authority in the Church by finding favor with the imperial family. The tsar had rejected all of the Synod's candidates for the position and, at Rasputin's recommendation, unilaterally appointed the eighty-two-year-old archbishop from the diocese of Tomsk and Altai. Makarii was out of place in Moscow. Having completed only a seminary education, he preached to Moscow's cosmopolitan public on how to arrange one's fingers when making the sign of the cross and how to bow to icons properly.[106] His presence exemplified major problems of the synodal system: the episcopate's isolation from the people and its vulnerability to manipulation by the state. Under the organizational leadership of Moscow's newly formed Organization of United Clergy, the diocesan delegates convened in Moscow on March 13, 1917, without Makarii's consent. While a small number of Moscow's most conservative priests, including Ioann Vostorgov, resigned in protest, a majority of the congress delegates voted to dismiss the Metropolitan.[107] The United Clergy announced this decision to the diocese in a printed pamphlet: "Metropolitan Makarii, that pious and devout pastor, apostle of the Altar and renowned missionary, but also an elder 'Ancient of Days,' is in no condition to be the manager and leader that every archpastor must now be."[108] Thus, the congress did not accuse Makarii of any particular misdeeds and made no attempt to justify its decision to the Synod.

When L'vov raised the issue of Makarii's retirement before the old Synod in March, the prelates initially resisted, perceiving the move as an attack on episcopal authority in general.[109] Ultimately, Archbishop Arsenii (Stadnitskii) of Novgorod suggested that Makarii follow the example of Saint George the Theologian by retiring for the good of the Church, and the metropolitan acquiesced.[110] The Synod accepted Makarii's resignation on March 20 and designated Bishop Ioasaf (Kallistov) as the temporary prelate of Moscow.[111] Upon his return to the diocese, however, Makarii became indignant to learn that Moscow's clergy and laity had assembled without his blessing. Citing Apostolic Canons 39 and 55, as well as canons from the Fourth Ecumenical Council and the First-Second Council of Constantinople, all of which pertain to episcopal authority, he declared the suspension of any priest who had removed his name from the liturgy.¹¹² This decree was overturned by Moscow's consistory, under instructions by L'vov, on the grounds that the metropolitan had already resigned.¹¹³ But Makarii withdrew his resignation and retreated to Holy Trinity Monastery, from which he carried on his struggle for the diocese.

Makarii launched a series of attacks on the diocesan revolutionaries. Like Serafim, he attacked the congress's credibility as a representative institution of the diocese: "At these gatherings there are students, soldiers, workers, and individuals of the female gender. They pass judgment on the actions of the bishops and the superintendents while loudly beating the tables with their palms, screaming, and laughing. This is not an assembly in the strictest sense, but a mob."¹¹⁴ With no popular support of his own, however, Makarii's only real weapon was canon law. He used elaborate citations from the Apostolic Canons, ecumenical councils, and church fathers to attack the movement against him. He accused L'vov of threatening him with imprisonment in the Peter and Paul Fortress if he refused to resign: "I hereby ask the Holy Synod not to appoint a prelate to the See of Moscow with the title of Metropolitan, but to reserve that title for me on the basis of the canons (rule 3 of the First-Second Council), as I was compelled to retire under the pressure of a mob and [other] external forces."¹¹⁵ Makarii also argued that L'vov was at the center of a conspiracy to reform the Church over the heads of the monastic hierarchy: he was unilaterally encouraging the involvement of the laity in church affairs, approving the elections of bishops, and proposing to reform the organization of the Church's educational system, all without regard for canon law.¹¹⁶

Makarii's claim that L'vov was abusing his power found corroboration in a report by Bishop Feodor (Pozdeevskii), rector of Moscow Theological Academy and possibly Makarii's only ally. Like Makarii, Feodor enjoyed little popular support. Boris Titlinov, the radical professor of church history at Saint Petersburg Theological Academy, visited Feodor on March 12 on orders from L'vov to investigate administrative abuses, including the dismissal in 1910 of Professor Il'ia Gromoglasov, a member of the diocesan congress. According to Feodor, Titlinov cruelly interrogated the purser, inspector, and inspector's assistant in front of laughing students. When Feodor protested that the Academy did not answer to the ober-procurator but to the Synod, Titlinov answered that "the ober-procurator, as a member of the Provisional Government, is higher than the Synod and could disband the Synod itself."¹¹⁷ Feodor joined Makarii in his campaign of protest at Holy Trinity Monastery. In April, the two were accused of anti-government, monarchist agitation and placed under house arrest by the local military committee. Ultimately, Feodor was sent to Danilov Monastery, and Makarii was sent back to Altai.¹¹⁸ While Makarii's own legitimacy was undermined by the role of Rasputin in his appointment, his removal was carried out with the help of the state—and with short shrift for canon law.

If Moscow's diocesan leaders had not intended to dispense with canon law, they had resolved to seize the authority to interpret it from the Synod. L'vov's political support had made this possible. Archpriest Nikolai Tsvetkov, chairman of Moscow's Organization of United Clergy, publicly named L'vov as a "supporter of [the Church's] emancipation and development on the principles of canonical freedom."[119] This term, "canonical freedom," also used by the Group of Thirty-Two Saint Petersburg Priests in 1905, meant recognition of the parish clergy's assemblies and congresses as autonomous entities within church administration rather than as extensions of the bishop's authority. More specifically, it meant the right of the diocesan community to elect its own metropolitan. The former goal was partially approved on May 5 in Synodal decree No. 2668, "On the More Active Participation of Clergy and Laity in Church Administration," which recognized the clergy's right to organize assemblies at all levels of the diocese without prior approval and without restrictions on the subject matter of discussion.[120] The latter goal was approved on July 5, when the Synod announced the "Common Regulations for the Election of Diocesan Bishops."[121] Yet Moscow's diocesan leaders waited for neither of these resolutions. A new congress convened on March 21. Archpriest Nikolai Bogoliubov argued that the congress should not ask for the Synod's permission to elect a metropolitan but develop their own electoral procedure to serve as a precedent for other dioceses. At the suggestion of Professor Gromoglasov, the delegates resolved to ask for the Synod's "blessing" but not its "permission."[122] They then elected a special committee of forty-six clergy and laity, tasked with developing the rules and procedures for the election.[123] The diocesan leaders then moved to provide a national forum at which representatives of all Russia's diocesan congresses could discuss church reform, independently of the hierarchy. It convened from June 1 to June 9 with 1,268 delegates, according to the representative norm of one clergyman and one layman for every one hundred churches, as well as one monk and one religious school representative from each diocese.[124]

The All-Russian Congress of Clergy and Laity was a moment of culmination for the diocesan revolutions as well as for the pastoral movement. The speeches and resolutions of the congress are, therefore, highly indicative of the goals of these movements. The religious and social unification of the Church, regardless of estate or class, was prominent among them. Father Tsvetkov, the chairman and chief organizer of the congress, expressed his vision for the Church in his interpretation of the diocesan congress in March: "With the understanding that only 'in unity is there strength,' [the diocesan congress] appealed with brotherhood to pastors and laymen to abandon their estate interests, forget their corporate needs, and sincerely extend their hands to one another so as to work in cooperation for the good of the motherland and the Church."[125] This vision was echoed by numerous delegates at the All-Russian Congress. Father Bogoliubskii opened the first session with a speech on unity: "That they may all be one; even as thou, Father, art in me, and I in thee (John 17:21) . . . all turning away from this strength [of unity] is a turning away from the very face of Christ."[126] One Petrograd priest expressed the optimistic view that, while "previously, our Church was divided into sections . . . it almost could not live, as a head cannot live without a body. . . . Now the Church in all its components of clergy and laity is standing before Christ."[127] In order to realize this vision, the delegates agreed on the concession to parishioners that clergymen had long resisted, for fear that it would bankrupt the dioceses. Aleksandr Papkov, the longtime activist for parish renewal, announced on the eighth day of the congress that the parish would now have the rights of a legal entity with ownership over all parish property.[128] Ultimately, this would include the plots of land that had supported the rural parish clergy. On June 12, delegates resolved that "all land and water within our country should belong to those who work on it." The only stipulation was that peasants should not seize the Church's land until it had been legally redistributed by the Constituent Assembly.[129] The only precaution the congress took for the material security of clergymen was the creation of an All-Russian Union of Clergy to organize mutual aid and advocate on behalf of the parish clergy. Delegates stipulated that this union was "professional," specifically rejecting the appellation of "brotherly," so as to minimize the social distinction between clergy and laity.[130] Through these drastic measures, aimed to breathe new life into the Church as a society, representatives of diocesan leaders from across Russia had resolved to dismantle the clergy as a materially and socially distinct estate.

How did the delegates envision the Church's future, which they were entrusting to the Orthodox laity? There was hope that the revolutionary enthusiasm, which had drawn so many laypeople to the diocesan congresses, could be sustained. The delegates resolved that representative bodies of clergy and laity should be introduced at all levels of diocesan administration, presided over by the bishop.[131] They also established a permanent organization, the All-Russian Union of Orthodox Clergy and Laity, to coordinate the work of Russia's diocesan congresses, communicate with the Church leadership on their behalf, and convene future all-Russian congresses. Yet the organizers were aware of the deeply fragmented and volatile state of Orthodox society. Announcing the establishment of the organization, Titlinov explained that "there arises a need for a closer union of clergy and laity. [The Union's] task is to support the

Orthodox Church, strengthening it in the social life of the modern Russian state. Our people are very religious, and only their disunity has created the impression of a lifeless Church."[132] The new alliance of clergy and laity would work to repair broken social bonds by continuing the social activism of the pastoral movement. A lay delegate from Chernigov encouraged this work: "The Church and its servants should go from words to actions. . . . The poor have been forgotten; they are rotting in their cellars without seeing the brotherly care of the more fortunate. Spiritual fathers, be philanthropic! Be our good Samaritans as Christ taught, and others will follow!"[133] Prince Evgenii Trubetskoi also expressed the idea that the Church could cure Russia of "class hatred and rude materialism" through social engagement.:"Patriotism has been extinguished. National ardor is gone. And the task of the Church is to reawaken it and inspire the social organism with the idealism of a higher life."[134] Yet some delegates responded to this exuberant optimism with words of caution. Sergei Bulgakov argued that while the Church was democratic, "democracy" could become an idol for the Church, just as "autocracy" had been: "The earthly trinity of democracy (the Soviet of Peasants', Workers', and Soldiers' Deputies), like the despotism of Roman emperors, can never replace the Trinity of heaven."[135] Other delegates raised similar concerns that the plans to forge a democratic alliance of clergy and laity were driven more by politics than by *sobornost'* and would degrade the canonical authority of the Church.

The All-Russian Congress of Clergy and Laity resembled the Church's version of the Union of Unions, the alliance of professional unions that had organized on the national level during the 1905 Revolution. The 1917 Congress was the first free assembly of Orthodox community leaders to meet on a national level. This fact made the congress inherently political, and many of its organizers had little desire to involve the monastic hierarchy in their revolutionary moment. This politicization of the gathering, however, provoked opposition within the congress itself. Protests erupted when Father Tsvetkov announced that the congress's chairman should hold the rank of presbyter but should not be a bishop, as the workload would be too large for a busy prelate. While Tsvetkov was elected chairman, some delegates complained that he was wrong to limit their freedom of choice by excluding bishops.[136] L'vov supported the effort to limit episcopal participation in the congress, and only seven bishops ended up attending. This would concern Archpriest Nikolai Liubimov, a member of the new Synod, who wrote in his journal that "there cannot be total unity among the members of the Church of Christ at this one-sided congress, because the episcopate here is almost completely absent."[137] In addition to such principled objections to the congress's anti-episcopal tone, delegates also raised concerns that this revolt against the hierarchy could weaken the unity of the Church as a whole. For example, a group of delegates vigorously protested the creation of the All-Russian Union of Orthodox Clergy and Laity on the grounds that such an organization would be "another Church alongside the Church."[138] Most illustrative of the threat that the congress presented to the hierarchy was the speech of Archbishop Platon (Rozhdestvenskii), Exarch of Georgia. Addressing the delegates on behalf of the Synod, he paid respect to the diocesan movement: "All the recent diocesan congresses have been vigorous. The breadth of their views, the depth of their thought, and the strength of their feelings are all features of the free Russian Church. If there were some excesses in certain places, these by no means stand against the path that life has shown from Christ to the people and from the people to Christ." Platon also acknowledged that "from the political revolution, we are moving toward a church revolution." Yet, without making direct reference to the parish clergy's relations with the hierarchy, Platon warned that a divided Church would not survive in the politically unstable environment: "We must believe that the Church, united and organized, can live without the state. Join together, you delegates of our Orthodox, Russian Church! Strengthen your position as a Church. Prove that you can live not only separately but also in one common, moral organization!"[139] Platon's diplomatic circumspection indicated that the congress had succeeded as a collective show of force by the parish clergy. Yet, as had been the case in Tver', participants in this church revolution had come to realize that by weakening the authority of the hierarchy, the movement could degrade the prestige of the Church itself among the population.

Moscow's organizational committee continued preparations for the election of Moscow's new metropolitan with far greater solicitude for the consent of the episcopate than had the first congress when it ousted Makarii, composing meticulous canonical justification for the election before submitting their plans to the Synod for approval.[140] They cited, for example, chapter 1 of the Book of Acts, which describes the election of Matthias as the twelfth apostle to replace Judas: "'Eleven' elected the twelfth with the participation of 'all the brothers,' about one hundred twenty people.'" They also cited the historical precedent of the ancient Church in which bishops were elected by their flock.[141] The committee developed a three-stage electoral procedure, which would give the parish clergy 50 percent of the vote. In the first stage, all parishioners, men and women twenty-one years of age and older, would elect lay representatives corresponding to the number of clergy in their parish. These representatives, together with all the clergy, would then proceed to the superintendent assemblies, at which two priests, a deacon, a sacristan, and four laypeople would be elected. Moscow's monasteries would also send representatives. These delegates, more than eight hundred, would compose Moscow's next diocesan congress, which would elect the new metropolitan. An assembly of bishops would preside over the election and confirm its outcome but would not themselves cast votes. Each stage of this process would be initiated by prayer and treated as a sacred act. The description of this procedure, as reported in Moscow's diocesan journal, concluded with: "The common voice will then be the voice of God."[142] The anonymous author of this report published in the diocesan journal expressed exasperation at the amount of time and effort that had been dedicated to the canonical justification of this election: "The canons of the Church are a sphere that is far from accessible for everyone. This field, moreover, is not so intelligible or rational even for those who are acquainted with it. The ancient canons belong to a distant era. Just try to apply them to the twentieth century."[143] The committee's work was not, of course, for the consumption of the public. It was intended to forge an agreement with the Synod that would find acceptance among the hierarchy. It succeeded in this aim, as the committee's electoral procedure was ultimately adopted by the Synod on July 5.[144]

While the Synod's compliance was a major victory for the Moscow Union of Clergy and Laity, as the diocesan leaders now called themselves, the election itself still posed a risk to church unity. Candidates for the metropolitanate included prominent hierarchs such as Archbishop Sergii (Starogorodskii) of Finland (and future patriarch from 1943 to 1944), Archbishop Andrei (Ukhtomskii) of Ufa, Archbishop Tikhon (Belavin) of Lithuania, Archbishop Platon (Rozhdestvenskii), and Moscow's temporary prelate Bishop Ioasaf (Kallistov).[145] Yet strong support also emerged for the candidacy of the chairman of Moscow's diocesan congress, Aleksandr Samarin. He had served as ober-procurator of the Synod in 1915 before being dismissed at the urging of Rasputin.[146] Samarin was himself a fairly moderate figure, but anti-episcopal sentiment was certainly to be found among his supporters. On the day before the election, a prominent Moscow priest, Father Ioann Kedrov, made a speech in which he recalled that when the monastic clergy, standing at the head of the Church's administration, had not raised their voices against Rasputin's influence over the Church, Samarin had spoken out and was forced to leave his post as a consequence.[147] As a widower, Samarin was technically eligible for the metropolitanate, according to canon law. Yet a layman had never been elevated to the episcopate in the history of the Russian Orthodox Church. The election of Moscow's prelate would be one of eleven such elections to take place in 1917. Of those, only two would result in the election of candidates who did not already hold the rank of bishop. The Synod had rejected the Yekaterinburg congress's election of a seminary inspector in May and would reject the Ryazan' congress's election of an archimandrite in June.[148] If Moscow's influential congress were to elect a layman due to anti-episcopal sentiment, it would almost certainly have led to crisis—and possibly schism within the Church.

The diocesan congress met on June 19 in Moscow's Diocesan Home (*Eparkhial'nyi dom*), the same building in which the Sobor would convene in August. The first votes were cast the next day. Tikhon and Samarin each received an equal number of votes, 297, putting them well ahead of any other candidate.[149] In an article written the following month, the Moscow priest Friazinov described Samarin's supporters: "They broke the boundaries of practicality that were created by the old life of the Church. It would seem that they have earned the great praise of all those who thirst for the renovation of the Church and, in seeking it, step across all boundaries, including those of caste."[150] This camp was driven by the vision expressed at the preceding congress of rejuvenating the Church through the destruction of the old estate boundaries that had kept it divided for so long. Many of Tikhon's supporters also espoused this vision. He was seen as a mild prelate who, in Tsvetkov's words, "always allowed local social forces the broadest autonomy."[151] Yet this faction was also motivated by caution. Friazinov identified Father Bogoliubskii as a leader among supporters of Tikhon and quoted his argument at the preceding debates: "The candidacy of a layman may give rise to temptation among the wide mass of simple Orthodox people. Thus, unless there is great need, we should not forget the old system of election from among the existing episcopate."[152] Thus, Moscow's diocesan revolutionaries were divided by the concern that a drastic break with tradition and with the episcopate would compromise the status of the parish clergy among the laity. Tikhon also drew support from the more conservative clergymen, while Samarin's supporters were predominantly rural clergymen who distrusted the elite priests of Moscow. Friazinov took issue with this animosity: "We were under the yoke of the old diocesan satraps ourselves, and you want to put their deeds on our shoulders."[153] Ultimately, the leadership of Moscow's United Clergy prioritized church unity over the more radical agenda, and it was likely their support that shifted the balance in Tikhon's favor. On June 21, another vote was held in the Cathedral of Christ the Savior. Tikhon was elected, receiving 481 votes against Samarin's 303.[154]

The Church's tumultuous summer of 1917 culminated not in schism but in reconciliation. The process of Tikhon's election by secret ballot was incorporated into the Divine Liturgy. According to an "eyewitness," ballots were cast in silence. When Tikhon's victory was announced, cries of "Thank God!" resounded throughout Russia's largest cathedral.[155] The "document of election" was then taken behind the iconostasis, to the altar, where it was received by the council of bishops: "Then the royal doors were opened, and the archpastors—

there were six—came out to the soleas in their robes, facing the people. The document was again read from the ambon. Archbishop Agafangel pronounced 'ἄξιος' [worthy], which the assembly then chanted thrice. It was the moment of confirmation of the election, which Greek Orthodox antiquity referred to as 'δοκιμασία.'"[156] This moment marked the first popular election of the chief prelate in the history of Russia's Orthodox Church. Yet it was carried out according to the old Byzantine rite of ordination, according to which the hierarch is ordained through "election and examination [Ψήφῳ καὶ δοκιμασίᾳ]."[157] As Zaozerskii had argued, Orthodox canon law permitted the involvement of both state and society in the establishment of apostolic authority. The crucial constant, according to the contemporary scholar of Orthodox canon law Father Alexander Rentel, is that "the divine has the initiative in calling someone for ordination that is made manifest in the election process."[158] Moscow's Union of Clergy and Laity were able to compromise with the episcopate in the organization of this election process. Albeit narrowly, this election elevated a prelate to the see of Moscow who was generally acceptable to episcopate, clergy, and laity. Two days after his election, possibly in acquiescence to Makarii's canonically based protests, the Synod stipulated that Tikhon should be recognized as archbishop until the Sobor recognized his elevation to the metropolitanate.[159] Tikhon's election stood for both canonicity and the broad-based version of *sobornost'* that was demanded by much of the clergy and laity.

While overshadowed by the All-Russian Church Sobor that followed it, Moscow's diocesan revolution profoundly affected the larger council's program of reform. Tsvetkov, Gromoglasov, and other representatives from the All-Russian Congress of Clergy and Laity were admitted to the Pre-Sobor Council.[160] This body, which included representatives from the episcopate, clergy, and laity, had first convened on May 6. On July 5, the Synod approved its Statute on the Convocation of the Sobor, which elevated the role of delegates from the laity and parish clergy far beyond the status they had been assigned by the 1906 Pre-Sobor Commission. Rather than being confirmed by their diocesan bishops and serving in a purely consultative capacity, as the earlier body had decreed, the Pre-Sobor Council resolved that nonepiscopal delegates would be elected by the diocesan congresses alone and vote on an equal basis with the bishops. The bishops' apostolic authority would be preserved through a bicameral structure, according to which a Council of Bishops was given veto power over the decisions of the General Assembly of the Sobor.[161] True to the spirit of reconciliation in which he had been elected, Tikhon upheld this atmosphere of compromise after he was elected chairman of the Sobor in August.[162] While the Sobor involved heated debates, delegates also worked to find common ground on the details of church reform, including the incorporation of clergy and laity into church governance within the parameters of canon law. Bishop Serafim of Cheliabinsk, for example, suggested that the canonical authority of the bishops could be preserved if the authority of the clergy and laity within diocesan administration was considered man-given and not God-given.[163] The final decree of the Sobor was that bishops would henceforth be elected from an approved list by the clergy and laity of the diocese and that they would govern their dioceses "with the conciliar [*sobornyi*] collaboration of its clergy and laity."[164]

One of the most lasting achievements of the Sobor was to provide the Church with a final arbiter of canon law by electing Tikhon to the reestablished Patriarchate of Moscow and All Rus'. After several rounds of voting, three leading candidates for patriarch emerged from a field of twenty-five: Tikhon, Arsenii (Stadnitskii), and Antonii (Khrapovitskii). The final decision was made not by vote but by "divine initiative." On November 2, after the Kremlin had already fallen to the Bolsheviks and amid ongoing street fighting, a massing crowd assembled once again within and around the Cathedral of Christ the Savior, where the names of the three final candidates were placed in a box before the iconostasis. After a lengthy prayer before the Icon of the Mother of God of Vladimir, an aged hieromonk, Father Aleksei, drew a slip from the box and handed it to Metropolitan Vladimir (Bogoiavlenskii), who read Tikhon's name and intoned, "ἄξιος."[165] The Church now had a single figurehead to provide leadership and unity through the coming years of persecution. The ecclesiastical "revolution" of 1917 had resulted in the preservation of the Church's canonical authority structure, but it had also secured a voice for the parish clergy and laity within that structure. The restored patriarchate would be neither monarchic nor democratic but conciliar (*sobornyi*). The Sobor established an All-Russian Church Council of Bishops, Parish Clergy, and Laity as the supreme governing body. "The Patriarch, together with the institutions of ecclesial governance, is accountable before the Council."[166] The plan of the Sobor for an inclusive, conciliar Church in dialogue with the modern world could not be realized under the Soviet dictatorship, but it would serve as a model for the whole of Christendom. The Sobor was the most important Orthodox council in more than one thousand years and a forerunner of the twentieth-century revival of Christian conciliarism that would be taken up by the ecumenical movement and the Second Vatican Council of 1962–65.[167]

Conclusion

The organizers of the 1917 diocesan congresses in Tver' and Moscow found themselves in a position of leadership over a movement for the reform of ecclesiastical administration on a more conciliar and inclusive basis. In this capacity, their prioritization of canon law proved to be a decisive factor in guiding the Church toward reform rather than schism. Orthodox canon law was subjected to broad interpretation in early twentieth-century Russia. It served simultaneously as a symbol of liberation from oppression and of order in the face of anarchy. Vladimir L'vov's prominent role in the Synod from February to August 1917 demonstrated that the secular bureaucracy would continue to influence the arbitration of canon law until the Church was able to reorganize its own authority structure. During the precarious inter-revolutionary period, diocesan congress leaders appealed to canon law as a source of unity. It was used to ensure that their priorities were recognized under the apostolic authority of the Church as a whole. This tendency of the congresses was largely driven by the influence of the parish clergy, who recognized the necessity of church unity for the survival of the pastorate and its associations.

The April congress of Tver' and the All-Russian Congress of Clergy and Laity in Moscow both proposed the transfer of control over diocesan resources to a cooperative union of clergy and parishioners. Behind this decision lay a wager on the willingness of the Orthodox laity to sustain, in some form, the mutual aid networks that the clergy had built. This attempt was not confined to Moscow and Tver', where the pastoral movement had been most active. The project of an All-Russian Union of Orthodox Clergy and Laity was taken up by other diocesan congresses. In August 1917, for example, the diocesan periodical of Tobol'sk proposed that "this brotherly unification of members of the Orthodox Church must take shape freely, in accordance with the wish of parishioners themselves, as a result of their own realization of the necessity and utility of such an organization."[168] Was such a unification realistic? Since the Great Reform era, church leaders had been reluctant to entrust control over diocesan resources to the laity, for fear that they would withdraw these resources for use on purely parish needs. In 1917, however, the continued existence of estate-based institutions for the support of the pastorate was unlikely. For some of its clerical supporters, therefore, this attempt to bring the laity into the diocesan associations as full partners was seen as the best means to preserve those associations and enable the Church to address the social challenges of the modern world. Sadly, the free associations of the Orthodox pastorate could not exist in Soviet Russia. The task of the pastorate would be to serve the remnants of the Orthodox community or accept martyrdom as the Bolshevik regime dismantled the Church's social networks.

Conclusion

JUST AS THE ORTHODOX PARISH lacked a coherent ecclesiological vision to define its diverse functions in the late nineteenth century, so did the increasingly complex work of the parish clergy lack a modern pastoral theology. There was little theological framework for such tasks as the organization of large mutual aid societies or serving the religious needs of itinerant factory workers. The career of Archimandrit Feodor (Bukharev) illustrates this theological stagnation. The son of a deacon from Tver', Feodor received tonsure in 1852 and caused a public controversy with his 1860 work, *On Orthodoxy in Relation to the Modern World*. In this essay, Feodor argued that the Church could address the social and intellectual problems of the modern world without fear of falling into error because Christ would take upon himself any sins of the mind that might result.[1] Because of the controversy that arose as a result of Feodor's ideas, he was relieved of his post as censor, sent to monastic seclusion, and forbidden to publish any more work until he renounced his monastic vows. Most of Feodor's intellectual successors were Orthodox laymen, who could build on his ideas outside of synodal censorship.[2] Meanwhile, however, Feodor's contemporaries among the parish clergy, such as the Saint Petersburg priest A. V. Gumilevskii, were pioneering the practical organization of church-based mutual aid societies.[3] By the early twentieth century, as we have seen, pastoral work was characterized by social engagement at the parish and inter-parish levels. The Church's response to the traumas and dislocations of the modern world was largely formulated from below. It is this response that this book has called "the pastoral movement."

In the absence of an elite leadership, the intellectual foundation of the pastoral movement must be examined in the writings by and for the parish clergy.

In 1901, for example, a short obituary in Moscow's diocesan journal commemorated the exemplary life of a rural pastor. It lauded one Father Vasilii for having "drawn up a broad program for the establishment of a variety of charitable and educational institutions in his community." These institutions included a parish trusteeship, a community library, a parish school, and shelters for orphans and the elderly. For all his social work, the obituary called him "sensitive to the questions of our time [*chutkii k voprosam nashego vremeni*]."[4] The author's clerical readership would have understood the unspecified "questions" to which he referred. The depressed condition of the peasantry forty years after their emancipation, the growth of urban slums, widespread illiteracy, and other social problems occupied the forefront of Russia's cultural discourse. Of more specific concern to clerical readers was for the Orthodox laity to perceive the Church as a source of solutions to these "questions." At the turn of the century, many priests strove to draw parishioners into the Church as a source of social support, beyond the bounds of their immediate community, in the hope that laypeople would become more willing participants in the diocesan social networks that sustained the clerical estate. Yet the obituary also revealed another component of the pastoral ideal. It claimed that Father Vasilii had impoverished himself by making secret charitable donations throughout his pastoral service, which were only revealed after his death. Anonymous care for the poor was not merely a tactic to recruit supporters for church-based mutual aid. It was also personal self-sacrifice for the Christian value of *philanthropia*. The pastoral movement was rooted in both the contemporary social context and ancient Christian tradition.

The parish clergy's practical approach to the pastoral movement was shaped by their struggle with poverty within their own estate. The great importance of mutual aid for the provision of education and social security within the clerical estate profoundly influenced the understanding of religious duty among the pastorate. Parish clergymen typically viewed material assistance as an essential expression of Christian piety. In his speech at the establishment of a charitable society for a girls' gymnasium in 1901, a Moscow priest described the relationship between "material and spiritual charity" (*milost' telesnaia i milost' dukhovnaia*). He emphasized the greater importance of the latter but then explained how the two are connected: "It happens in life that material charity assumes spiritual significance and is transformed into spiritual charity."[5] Moreover, clerical writings emphasized charitable action as important not only for its own sake but also as a means of religious instruction. An article on the "internal mission" of the pastor to the Orthodox laity from 1902 illustrates the connection, in the minds of many clergymen, between material assistance and the Church as a society.

> In the sphere of social life, the internal mission fights against need of all kinds that oppress the poor classes. The mission especially works to organize housing for the impoverished because in most cases the moral life of the population depends on decent housing—not to mention the fact that people's understanding of health is connected with their access to comfortable and healthy housing. . . . The mission, thus, collaborates in the establishment of various associations, organized for different kinds of mutual aid, loan funds, companies for the organization of inexpensive apartments, and consumers' societies. The mission also works to instill into the members of these societies the spirit of true Christian self-sacrifice, on which their success depends.[6]

Parish clergymen thus viewed effective material assistance as important for creating the conditions for Christian life and for instilling mutual aid as a value into the religious consciousness of the laity.

The success of the pastoral movement as an "authorizing discourse" for the inculcation of collective philanthropic care into popular Orthodoxy was contingent upon the integration of laity into the allocation of that care. Despite the use of diocesan resources to serve the needs of their parishioners, the tithe boycotts of 1905–6 demonstrated that laypeople could not identify those networks with their religious lives unless they were directly involved in the management of those resources. Parish reform was a contentious endeavor that only partially integrated parishioners into the diocesan authority structure. Nevertheless, the early twentieth century saw the proliferation of church-based associations for the laity, which allowed parishioners to assume control over the resources they contributed to their religious communities. In a 1908 speech before a gathering of synodal prelates in the ober-procurator's apartment, a parish priest from Orel diocese described his use of a parish council to promote social engagement as a religious practice.

> The council does not limit its activities to religious-moral and educational tasks. As its chairman and administrator, I pursue the following goals. Firstly, the influence of the Church should penetrate all aspects of human life and activity: social, family, and private. Secondly, the entire order of life and all the activities of each of my parishioners should be sanctified by the consciousness of God and penetrated by the spirit of Christian devotion, brotherly love, and mutual aid. Thirdly, the parish church should be the center of parish life, unifying everyone not only in questions of faith and morality but also for purely practical affairs.[7]

Over the final years of the synodal administration, lay organizations assumed responsibility for a growing proportion of religious contributions collected at the parish level. Particularly in urban centers, parish associations provided social support for migrant workers, disaster victims, orphans, and widows. They played an important role in the spread of primary and adult education, especially for women. In the dioceses and parishes where it achieved success, the pastoral movement promoted trust, cooperation, and free association through the religious practice of the empire's largest confession.

The pastoral movement was symptomatic of a broader transition in the Russian Empire's organizational structure, in which the state ceded responsibility for social services to estate societies. As Allison Smith explains, "The responsibilities of *soslovie* societies had shifted from facing outward—from acting as a conduit for the payment of the soul tax to the center—to facing inward, dealing with local taxes and providing services."[8] Clerical associations were also unique in this context because of their deliberate expansion beyond the bounds of their estate. While other societies sought to limit their membership to particular localities in order to conserve resources, clerical networks were organized for the consolidation of mutual aid across distances, communities, and institutions. The state provided financial subsidies and privileges of association to facilitate the pastorate's circulation of resources and information throughout the hinterland, but only to the extent that these efforts were perceived as an extension of the will of the synodal bureaucracy. The synodal authorities were quick to invoke "apostolic authority" to curtail the independence of pastoral initiatives, particularly those of a political nature. Moreover, they were reluctant to sanction church-based associations among the laity, over whom they had less control than the clergy, and these remained largely confined to individual parishes. The legal confinement of the pastorate within the "spiritual domain" thus limited the autonomy of their associations and exacerbated social divisions with their parishioners, as exemplified by the divergence of lay and clerical philanthropic campaigns during World War I. The pastoral movement, therefore, was far from a complete success, even in dioceses such as Moscow and Tver' where it was most active.

The pastoral movement was one "authorizing discourse" among many within Orthodox Christianity, but it played a vital role in preserving the unity of "the Church," in all its diversity. With the fall of the tsarist regime, Orthodox laity, parish clergy, and hierarchy confronted one another, and the result was church reform rather than schism. Over the preceding decades, the pastoral movement had built a conciliar structure that served as a vehicle for dialogue at this moment of crisis. The "electoral principle" facilitated reconciliation of numerous grievances at diocesan congresses throughout the former empire. It also influenced the organization of the Sobor that followed and established a popular mandate for the restoration of the Moscow Patriarchate. The assemblies of parish clergy and laity did not carry out a democratic revolution within the Church. Adherence to canon law throughout the pastorate's conciliar network preserved the Church's apostolic authority and the integrity of its hierarchic structure. The assemblies did, however, ensure that the voices of parish clergy and laity were included in the concept of conciliarity (*sobornost'*), as articulated by participants in the Sobor as the guiding principle of church renewal. This teaching of the Sobor, of unity through collaboration at all levels of the Church, profoundly influenced Orthodox Christian identity in the twentieth century.[9] The contribution of the pastoral movement to the revival of Orthodox conciliarity is, perhaps, its most enduring legacy.

The political oppression and social divisions that plagued the pastoral movement are indicative of the features of imperial Russia that generations of scholars have identified as obstacles to the development of civil society. Boris Chicherin, whose writing on the topic was referenced at the beginning of this book, regarded estate identity as incompatible with civil society: "Thus, with the development of the state, estate service [*soslovnaia sluzhba*] is replaced by the establishment of common rights and obligations for all citizens. . . . The division of civil society into estates contradicts that principle and must, therefore, give way to another order sooner or later."[10] While never entirely realized, it was the tendency of the pastoral movement to replace estate identity with a more universal Orthodox solidarity. In order to secure the support of laypeople for seminaries, brotherhoods, and other institutions of the pastorate, the parish clergy had to blur the estate parameters of pastoral service. In pursuit of this aim, the movement presented a challenge to the cultural and legal boundaries that fragmented society. Diocesan networks connected diverse communities and institutions in pursuit of common aims, including peasant communes, merchant societies, zemstvos, and the Red Cross. While these collaborative initiatives never achieved the legal autonomy that Chicherin and others envisioned for genuine civil society, the parish clergy and their supporters asserted their determination to collaborate at their own initiative and for their own purposes through petitions, delegations, student protests, political campaigns, and the very work they performed. The Bolsheviks did not establish their dictatorship in the absence of a civil society to oppose them, as Antonio Gramsci and others have claimed.[11] Rather, they co-opted Russia's voluntary associations and steadily eroded their autonomy from "the Party."[12]

The early Bolshevik state was too precarious to support an all-out assault on religious belief, and so it confined its efforts to propaganda and harassment. In January 1918, the Soviet of People's Commissars declared the freedom to practice any religion or no religion.[13] Meanwhile, state publications such as *Bednota* (The poor), launched in 1918 for distribution among the rural population, mocked religious practices such as icon veneration and demonized priests as black-hundredists.[14] Vladimir (Bogoiavlenskii), Ioann Vostorov, and other prominent clerics were arrested and executed for various offenses. These, along with the many priests who were massacred in random violence, were later canonized as the first of the "new martyrs."[15] Patriarch Tikhon, however, remained the recognized head of the canonical Church—and a looming threat to the regime's totalitarian ambitions. Without challenging the regime's legitimacy, Tikhon openly condemned its bloody excesses and called for amnesty for its victims.[16] The threat of the "Tikhonite Church" became intolerable after its response to the famine that descended upon the Volga region in 1921–22, the result of systematic expropriation of grain in the Civil War and far more devastating than any of the famines that preceded it. In July 1921, Tikhon delivered an appeal via radio broadcast to the Orthodox population to donate resources for the relief of famine victims, including nonliturgical valuables from parish churches. In its desperation, the Politburo of the Russian Communist Party permitted religious organizations to participate in famine relief, on the condition that they refrain from "religious demonstrations," such as icon processions. Yet the Church's reemergence as a source of philanthropic care was unacceptable to the new regime. Tikhon's receipt of aid from Metropolitan Evlogii, now in charge of the émigré Church in Western Europe, and from the virulently anti-Bolshevik Metropolitan Antonii (Khrapovitskii), in exile in Serbia, was also politically unacceptable.[17] Beginning in 1922, the Church's relief campaign was criticized as superficial in light of the fact that it had not relinquished its valuable liturgical objects, which were already the property of the people. In February, the All-Russian Central Executive Committee announced the forcible confiscation of ecclesiastical valuables from parish churches. Clergy and parishioners, who had been delivering donations and church decorations to the authorities voluntarily, now resisted these confiscations and were punished with arrests and executions. Tikhon condemned the looting of churches as sacrilege. On May 7, five priests were executed in Moscow for distributing Tikhon's printed statement of protest.[18] Two days later, Tikhon was placed under house arrest in Donskoi Monastery.[19]

The regime attacked the Church from another angle when it sponsored a revolt among the clergy against the canonical leadership. The leaders of this movement were mostly Petrograd priests but included some lay figures like Vladimir L'vov and Boris Titlinov, who were driven by the same grievances against the hierarchy that had animated the ecclesiastical revolution during the summer of 1917. These "renovationists," however, rejected the Sobor as a reconciliation with the canonical Church and turned to the Bolsheviks to support their agenda. The renovationists were a relatively obscure group until their overture in 1919 to Grigory Zinoviev, Chairman of the Petrograd Soviet, for an alliance between the revolutionary state and a new, revolutionary Church. It is interesting that these clergymen used a profession of political neutrality as code for their alliance with the state, just as the "Orthodox patriots" had done to indicate their loyalty to the autocracy: "The clergy, as it is, cannot be White or Red: the clergy of Christ is outside of politics."[20] Zinoviev was noncommittal but encouraging.[21] The renovationists were invited to take part in the regime's pretense at freedom of religious expression. In January, *Petrogradskaia pravda* described a debate between a Marxist agitator and Father Aleksandr Vvedenskii, a leading renovationist: "In his fiery, almost hour-long speech, the opponent [Vvedenskii] attempted to deny the speaker's position and show that science does not contradict religion. But he was unable to give one scientific reason. In order to give his speech such a form that would influence the feelings of his listeners (a common device in religious sermons), he employed all possible forms of mysticism and poetry."[22] The debate itself was not recounted. Meanwhile, their political favor began to attract new adherents to the renovationists, some of whom had little to do with their original movement, such as Father Vladimir Krasnitskii, a former member of the Union of Russian People.[23] The Living Church, as the organization came to be known, finally received approval to move against the leadership of the canonical Church over the issue of the confiscation of liturgical objects.

The price of their state-sponsored coup was dissemination of propaganda against the official Church. On March 14, 1922, the leadership of the Living Church published a statement in *Izvestiia* denouncing the church leadership: "We, the undersigned priests of the Orthodox Church, representing a wide circle of people, condemn the actions of those hierarchs and pastors who are guilty of organizing resistance to government authority in its rendering of aid to the hungry and other undertakings for the benefit of workers. The Church, in its very existence, should be a union of love and truth and not a political organization or a counterrevolutionary party."[24] Tikhon conceded to a temporary abdication in favor of Metropolitan Agafangel (Preobrazhenskii) of Yaroslavl', but the Living Church group established a new Supreme Church Administration in Moscow on May 16, which presented a series of reforms, such as adoption of the Gregorian calendar, the shaving of priests' beards, the permission for priests to remarry after the death of a spouse, and the elevation of priests to the episcopacy.[25] In contrast with the dissident movement within the Church in 1917, the Living Church members made no effort to justify their reforms or their seizure of power according to canon law but declared canon law itself to be in need of reform.[26] With the backing of the Politburo, the clergy of the Living Church required neither the support of the laity nor endorsement of other priests in order to seize control of parishes throughout the Soviet Union. They could use political denunciation and threats of arrest. As Edward Roslof demonstrates in his book on the renovationist schism, however, the intention of the regime was never to sponsor an ecclesiastical revolution but rather to provoke conflict within the Church. By the early 1930s, the regime escalated its attack on religious practice, and many "Red priests" were subjected to the same level of persecution as their "Tikhonite" opponents.[27]

The early Bolshevik regime sought to weaken the Orthodox Church by undermining two important elements of the pastoral movement, the Church's social mission and the pastorate's connection with the laity. The clergy's capacity to organize philanthropic aid on a large scale was severely degraded by the seizure of church property, the censorship of religious expression, and the imprisonment and execution of thousands of priests. Yet Orthodox communities remained a potent social force at the local level. In 1920, an article in *Bednota* expressed concern over the potential of parish communities to organize opposition to the regime: "Under the flag of religion, churchmen created a counter-revolutionary society, the Council of United Parishes of Moscow, and through it secretly led a struggle against worker and peasant power, which emancipated the people, by their decrees, from age-old religious obscurity."[28] Parish communities and "parish unions" rejected state-backed renovationist clergy, successfully resisted the Living Church schism, and administered their own dioceses in the absence of canonical bishops and priests.[29] The Stalinist dictatorship finally drove these communities underground in the 1930s through forced collectivization and mass murder. Orthodox Christianity was not a marginalized anachronism in the early twentieth century but rather a prominent and dynamic social force that was suppressed by the most brutal religious persecution that the Christian world had ever seen.

NOTES

Introduction

1. Timothy Samuel Shah, *Faith on Fire: The Global Explosion of Political Religion* (Stanford, CA: Hoover Institution Press, 2011); Kevin D. Smith, "Breaking Faith: Religion, Americanism, and Civil Rights in Postwar Milwaukee," *Religion and American Culture: A Journal of Interpretation* 20, no. 1 (Winter 2010): 57–92; Elna C. Green, "*The Master-Word*: Lily Hardy Hammond and the Social Gospel in the South," *Journal of Southern Religion* 15 (2013).

2. Peter L. Berger, "The Desecularization of the World: A Global Overview," in *The Desecularization of the World: Resurgent Religion and World Politics*, ed. Peter L. Berger (Washington, DC: Eerdmans/Ethics and Public Policy Center, 1999), 1–18.

3. For a discussion of conciliar decision-making throughout the Christian world, see Paul Valliere, *Conciliarism: A History of Decision-Making in the Church* (New York: Cambridge University Press, 2012).

4. Eric Hobsbawm, *The Age of Revolution, 1789–1848* (New York: Vintage Books, 1962).

5. Benedict Anderson, *Imagined Communities: Reflections on the Origin and Spread of Nationalism* (London: Verso, 1983). For a discussion of nationalism in imperial Russia, see Nathaniel Knight, "Ethnicity, Nationality and the Masses: *Narodnost'* and Modernity in Imperial Russia," in *Russian Modernity: Politics, Knowledge, Practices*, ed. Yanni Kotsonis and David Hoffman (New York: St. Martin's, 2000), 41–64.

6. Hobsbawm, *The Age of Revolution*, 220.

7. José Casanova, *Public Religions in the Modern World* (Chicago: University of Chicago Press, 1994); Daniel Philpott, "Has the Study of Global Politics Found Religion?," *Annual Review of Political Science* 12 (2009): 183–202.

8. Margaret Lavinia Anderson, "The Limits of Secularization: On the Problem of the Catholic Revival in Nineteenth-Century Germany," *Historical Journal* 38, no. 3 (September 1995): 648.

9. Laurie Manchester, *Holy Fathers, Secular Sons: Clergy, Intelligentsia, and the Emergence of Modern Selfhood in Revolutionary Russia* (DeKalb: Northern Illinois University Press, 2008).

10. Patrick Lally Michelson, *Beyond the Monastery Walls: The Ascetic Revolution in Russian Orthodox Thought, 1814–1914* (Madison: University of Wisconsin Press, 2017).

11. Lucian Hölscher, "Secularization and Urbanization," in *European Religion in the Age of Great Cities, 1830–1930*, ed. Hugh McLeod (New York: Routledge, 1995), 263–88.

12. Peter van der Veer, *Imperial Encounters: Religion and Modernity in India and Britain* (Princeton, NJ: Princeton University Press, 2001), 15; Carl Strikwerda, "A Resurgent Religion: The Rise of Catholic Social Movements in Nineteenth-Century Belgian Cities," in *European Religion in the Age of Great Cities, 1830–1930*, ed. Hugh McLeod (New York: Routledge, 1995), 59–87.

13. Jordan J. Ballor, ed., *Makers of Modern Christian Social Thought: Leo XIII and Abraham Kuyper on the Social Question* (Grand Rapids, MI: Action Institute, 2016).

14. Harry Liebersohn, *Religion and Industrial Society: The Protestant Social Congress in Wilhelmine Germany* (Philadelphia: American Philosophical Society, 1986), 50.

15. See, for example, Mark Lilla, *The Stillborn God: Religion, Politics, and the Modern West* (New York: Alfred Knopf, 2007), 261.

16. Matthew Bowman, "Sin, Spirituality, and Primitivism: The Theologies of the American Social Gospel, 1885–1917," *Religion and American Culture: A Journal of Interpretation* 17, no. 1 (Winter 2007): 95–126.

17. Walter Rauschenbusch, *A Theology for the Social Gospel* (New York: Abingdon Press, 1960).

18. Talal Asad, "Religion as an Anthropological Category," in *Genealogies of Religion: Discipline and Reasons of Power in Christianity and Islam* (Baltimore: Johns Hopkins University Press, 1993), 27–54.

19. Asad, "Religion as an Anthropological Category," 38. For an analysis of Foucault's concept in Asad's work, see Steven C. Canton, "What Is an 'Authorizing Discourse?,'" in *Powers of the Secular Modern: Talal Asad and His Interlocutors*, ed. David Scott and Charles Hirschkind (Stanford, CA: Stanford University Press, 2006), 31–56.

20. Asad, "Religion as an Anthropological Category," 35.

21. Talal Asad, "The Idea of an Anthropology of Islam," *Qui Parle* 17, no. 2 (Spring/Summer 2009): 21.

22. Asad, "Religion as an Anthropological Category," 28.

23. Asad, "Religion as an Anthropological Category," 29.

24. See, for example, Veer, *Imperial Encounters*, 24.

25. See M. M. Gromyko and A. V. Buganov, *O vozzreniiakh russkogo naroda* (Moscow: Palomnik, 2000), 54–73. Based on surveys and reports that the Imperial Ethnographic and Geographic Societies published on religious observance in the 1890s, Gromyko and Buganov conclude that high levels of piety and respect for the Church prevailed among the Orthodox population at that time. See also B. N. Mironov, "Narod-bogonosets ili narod-ateist? Kak rossiiane verili v Boga nakanune 1917 g.," *Rodina*, no. 3 (2001): 52–58.

26. Patricia Herlihy, *The Alcoholic Empire: Vodka and Politics in Late Imperial Russia* (New York: Oxford University Press, 2002); Robert H. Greene, "Bodies in Motion: Steam-Powered Pilgrimages in Late Imperial Russia," *Russian History* 39, nos. 1–2 (2012): 247–68.

27. John Strickland, *The Making of Holy Russia: The Orthodox Church and Russian Nationalism before the Revolution* (Jordanville, NY: Holy Trinity Publications, 2013).

28. Between 1825 and 1907, the number of tonsured monks in the Empire increased from 5,742 to 24,444. See Scott M. Kenworthy, *The Heart of Russia: Trinity-Sergius, Monasticism, and Society after 1825* (New York: Oxford University Press, 2010), 3.

29. Michelson, *Beyond the Monastery Walls*, 36.

30. Michelson, *Beyond the Monastery Walls*, 125–28.

31. George F. Putnam, *Russian Alternatives to Marxism: Christian Socialism and Idealistic Liberalism in Twentieth-Century Russia* (Knoxville: University of Tennessee Press, 1977). For a discussion of political dissidence within the Church, see Argyrios Pisiotis, "Orthodoxy versus Autocracy" (PhD diss., Georgetown University, 2000).

32. See I. E. Ivanova, *Fol'klor i etnografiia v dukhovnoi periodike XIX veka: Kontekstnye sviazi* (Tver': "Lilia Print," 2006), 94–122.

33. A. Iu. Polunov, *Pod vlast'iu ober-prokurora: Gosudarstvo i tserkov' v epokhu Aleksandra III* (Moscow: Airo-XX, 1996), 12.

34. Jennifer Hedda, *His Kingdom Come: Orthodox Pastorship and Social Activism in Revolutionary Russia* (DeKalb: Northern Illinois University Press, 2008), 17–19.

35. M. A. Babkin, *Dukhovenstvo Russkoi pravoslavnoi tserkvi i sverzhenie monarkhii (nachalo XX v.–konets 1917 g.)* (Moscow: Gosudarstvennaia publichnaia istoricheskaia biblioteka Rossii, 2007), 62.

36. Demetrios J. Constantelos, *Byzantine Philanthropy and Social Welfare* (New Brunswick, NJ: Rutgers University Press, 1968), 30–41.

37. Rodney Stark, *The Rise of Christianity: A Sociologist Reconsiders History* (Princeton, NJ: Princeton University Press, 1996).

38. Stark, *The Rise of Christianity*, 83.

39. Timothy S. Miller, "Byzantine Philanthropic Institutions and Modern Humanitarianism," *Review of Faith and International Affairs* 14, no. 1 (Spring 2016): 18–25.

40. Constantelos, *Byzantine Philanthropy*, 69, 261.

41. Scott Kenworthy, "To Save the World or to Renounce It: Modes of Moral Action in Russian Orthodoxy," in *Religion, Community, and Morality after Communism*, ed. Mark Steinberg and Catherine Wanner (Washington, DC: Woodrow Wilson Center Press; Bloomington: Indiana University Press, 2008), 27.

42. Demetrios J. Constantelos, *Poverty, Society and Philanthropy in the Late Mediaeval Greek World* (New York: Aristide D. Caratzas, 1992); Timothy S. Miller, *The Birth of the Hospital in the Byzantine Empire*, 2nd ed. (Baltimore: Johns Hopkins University Press, 1997).

43. *The Monastic Rule of Iosif Volotsky*, ed. and trans. by David M. Goldfrank, rev. ed. (Kalamazoo, MI: Cistercian Publications, 2000), 150–51.

44. For a discussion of the historiography on Volotsky, see David Goldfrank, "Old and New Perspectives on Iosif Volotsky's Monastic Rules," *Slavic Review* 34, no. 2 (June 1975): 279–301.

45. Goldfrank, *The Monastic Rule*, 32.

46. Alexander Muller, "Introduction," in *The Spiritual Regulation of Peter the Great* (Seattle: University of Washington Press, 1973), xvii. See also Georg Michels, *At War with*

the Church: Religious Dissent in Seventeenth-Century Russia (Stanford, CA: Stanford University Press, 1999).

47. A. V. Kartashev, *Ocherki po istorii russkoi tserkvi* (Paris: YMCA Press, 1959), 2:311–67.

48. Adele Lindenmeyr, *Poverty Is Not a Vice: Charity, Society, and the State in Imperial Russia* (Princeton, NJ: Princeton University Press, 1996), 30–33.

49. Michelson, *Beyond the Monastery Walls*, 28–29.

50. Irina Paert, *Spiritual Elders: Charisma and Tradition in Russian Orthodoxy* (DeKalb: Northern Illinois University Press, 2010), 105.

51. Gregory Freeze, *The Russian Levites: Parish Clergy in the Eighteenth Century* (Cambridge, MA: Harvard University Press, 1977), 114.

52. T. G. Leont'eva, *Vera i progress: Pravoslavnoe sel'skoe dukhovenstvo Rossii vo vtoroi polovine XIX–nachale XX veka* (Moscow: Novyi khronograf, 2002), 18–20.

53. Polunov, *Pod vlast'iu ober-prokurora*, 12.

54. Aileen Friesen, *Colonizing Russia's Promised Land: Orthodoxy and Community on the Siberian Steppe* (Toronto: University of Toronto Press, 2020), 44.

55. Hedda, *His Kingdom Come*, 65.

56. Robert Lee discusses the Anglican clergy's performance of administrative and social services on behalf of the British government and the latter's enforcement of the tithe as a form of private property for the clergy. See Robert Lee, *Rural Society and the Anglican Clergy, 1815–1914: Encountering and Managing the Poor* (Woodbridge, UK: Boydell and Brewer, 2006), 11, 87. For the Habsburg monarchy's payment of salaries to Catholic priests, see William D. Bowman, *Priest and Parish in Vienna, 1780 to 1880* (Boston: Humanities Press, Inc., 1999), 139–40.

57. Father S. Friazinov, "Preds"ezdnye dumy," *Moskovskii tserkovnyi golos*, July 14, 1917, 3.

58. In 1909, the Synod approved the first elections of women to the post of church elder by fellow parishioners in Moscow and Smolensk: "Po voprosu ob utverzhdenii zhenshchin v dolzhnosti tserkovnago starosty," *Turkestanskie eparkhial'nye vedomosti*, August 1, 1909, 395. Aleksandr Papkov, an Orthodox intellectual and advocate for parish reform, argued that more women should take on positions of leadership in Russia's parishes. A. Papkov, *Besedy o pravoslavnom prikhode* (Petrograd: Sinodal'naia tipografiia, 1917), 20.

59. Gregory Freeze, "Critical Dynamic of the Russian Revolution: Irreligion or Religion?," in *Redefining the Sacred: Religion in the French and Russian Revolutions*, ed. Daniel Schönpflug and Martin Schulze Wessel (Frankfurt: Peter Lang, 2012) 52.

60. Antonio Gramsci's well-known statement that "in Russia the state is everything and civil society is primordial and gelatinous" has been widely referenced in scholarship on late imperial Russian society. See, for example, Adele Lindenmeyr, "Primordial and Gelatinous? Civil Society in Imperial Russia," *Kritika: Explorations in Russian and Eurasian History* 12, no. 3 (Summer 2011): 703–20.

61. Alexis de Tocqueville, *Democracy in America* (New York: Vintage, 1990), 1:191–98.

62. Sheri Berman, "Civil Society and the Collapse of the Weimar Republic," *World Politics* 9, no. 3 (April 1997): 401–29; Simone Chambers and Jeffrey Kopstein, "Bad Civil Society," *Political Theory* 29, no. 6 (December 2001): 837–65.

63. See, for example, Andrew J. Ringlee's dissertation on Russia's Red Cross as a "common space" for both educated society and the Romanov regime to organize humanitarian relief. Andrew J. Ringlee, "The Romanov's Militant Charity: The Red Cross and Public Mobilization for War in Tsarist Russia, 1853–1914" (PhD diss., University of North Carolina at Chapel Hill, 2016).

64. Nancy L. Rosenblum and Charles H. T. Lesch, "Civil Society and Government," in *The Oxford Handbook of Civil Society*, ed. Michael Edwards (Oxford: Oxford University Press, 2011), 285.

65. Samuel D. Kassow, "Russia's Unrealized Civil Society," in *Between Tsar and People: Educated Society and the Quest for Public Identity in Late Imperial Russia*, ed. Edith W. Clowes, Samuel D. Kassow, and James L. West (Princeton, NJ: Princeton University Press, 1991), 371.

66. Although Russia's estate system was somewhat fluid and porous, the primary estate (*soslovie*) categories included the peasantry (*krest'iane*), townspeople (*meshchane*), merchantry (*kupechestvo*), nobility (*dvorianstvo*), and clergy (*dukhovenstvo*), each of which entailed different privileges and obligations to the state.

67. David McDonald, "Introduction," in *Russia's Revolutionary Experience, 1905–1917: Two Essays*, by Leopold Haimson (New York: Columbia University Press, 2005), xii.

68. Jo Ann Ruckman, *The Moscow Business Elite: A Social and Cultural Portrait of Two Generations, 1840–1905* (Dekalb: Northern Illinois University Press, 1984); Alfred Rieber, *Merchants and Entrepreneurs in Imperial Russia* (Chapel Hill: University of North Carolina Press, 1982).

69. See, for example, Valeriia Nardova, *Gorodskoe samoupravlenie v Rossii v 60-kh–nachale 90-kh godov XIX v* (Leningrad: Nauka, 1984); Leopold Haimson, "The Problem of Social Identities in Early Twentieth Century Russia," *Slavic Review* 47, no. 1 (Spring 1988): 1–20. For a classic exposition of this view, see I. Martov, *Obshchestvennoe dvizhenie* (Saint Petersburg: tip. t-va "Obshestv. pol'za," 1909), 1:664.

70. Wayne Dowler, *Russia in 1913* (DeKalb: Northern Illinois University Press, 2010), 94.

71. Ernest Gellner, *Conditions of Liberty: Civil Society and Its Rivals* (New York: Penguin Press, 1994), 12.

72. Penelope Ismay, "Trust among Strangers: Securing British Modernity 'by Way of Friendly Society,' 1780s–1870s" (PhD diss., University of California, Berkeley, 2010), 10.

73. In addition to Dowler's previously cited monograph, recent studies on free associations in imperial Russia include Vera Kaplan, "From Soslovie to Voluntary Associations: New Patterns of Collective Identities in Late Imperial Russia," *Cahiers du Monde russe* 51, nos. 2–3 (May 2010): 369–96; Joseph Bradley, *Voluntary Associations in Tsarist Russia: Science, Patriotism, and Civil Society* (Cambridge, MA: Harvard University Press, 2009).

74. Dowler, *Russia in 1913*, 36–37; Eugene Kayden and Alexis N. Antsiferov, *The Cooperative Movement in Russia during the War* (New Haven, CT: Yale University Press, 1929), 14.

75. TsGARKaz, f. 369, op. 1, d. 1065, l. 1280b. (Ustav Omskago obshchestva popecheniia o nuzhdaiushchikhsia pereselentsakh, 1912).

76. P. I. Mel'nikov, *Otchet o sovremennom sostoianii raskola v Nizhegorodskoi gubernii* (Nizhnii Novgorod: Izd. I. M. Mashistova, 1910).

77. Norihiro Naganawa, "A Civil Society in a Confessional State? Muslim Philanthropy in the Volga-Urals Region," in *Russia's Home Front in War and Revolution, 1914–1922*, vol. 2, *The Experience of War and Revolution*, ed. Adele Lindenmeyr, Christopher Read, and Peter Waldron (Bloomington: Slavic, 2016), 59–78.

78. A. S. Tumanova, *Obshchestvennye organizatsii i russkaia publika v nachale XX veka* (Moscow: Novyi khronograf, 2008), 7.

79. Peter Holquist, "'In Accord with State Interests and the People's Wishes': The Technocratic Ideology of Imperial Russia's Resettlement Administration," *Slavic Review* 69, no. 1 (Spring 2010): 151–79.

80. Laura Engelstein, *Slavophile Empire: Imperial Russia's Illiberal Path* (Ithaca, NY: Cornell University Press, 2009), 79.

81. Engelstein, *Slavophile Empire*, 89.

82. Alison K. Smith, *For the Common Good and Their Own Well-Being: Social Estates in Imperial Russia* (New York: Oxford University Press, 2015), 151.

83. TsGARKaz, f. 369, op. 1, d. 1015, l. 13 (Svedeniia o kooperativnykh uchrezhdeniiakh).

84. Boris Chicherin, *Filosofiia prava* (Moscow: Tipo-litografiia Tovarishshestva I.N. Kushnerev i Ko, 1900), 259.

85. Randall Poole, "The Defense of Human Dignity in Nineteenth-Century Russian Thought," in *Iosif Volotskii and Eastern Christianity: Essays across Seventeen Centuries*, ed. David Goldfrank, Nollan Valeria, and Jennifer Spock (Washington, DC: New Academia Publishing, 2017), 271–305.

86. Chicherin, *Filosofiia prava*, 282–83.

87. Gregory Freeze, *The Parish Clergy in Nineteenth-Century Russia: Crisis, Reform, Counter-Reform* (Princeton, NJ: Princeton University Press, 1983).

88. Hedda, *His Kingdom Come*.

89. Hedda, *His Kingdom Come*, 28–29.

90. M. E. Grabko, *Deiatel'nost' Russkoi pravoslavnoi tserkvi v rabochei srede Moskovskoi gubernii v kontse XIX–nachale XX v.* (Moscow: PSTGU, 2017), 6.

91. *Svod otchetov fabrichnykh inspektorov za 1909 g.* (Saint Petersburg: Tipografia V.F. Kirshbauma, 1910), 4.

Chapter 1. The New Kind of Pastor

1. One *desiatina* is about 10,925 square meters.

2. D. A. Begovatov and T. G. Leont'eva, eds., *Iz istorii provintsial'nogo dukhovenstva: Zapiski sviashchennika V. F. Vladislavleva* (Tver': "SFK-ofis," 2012), 30.

3. Begovatov and Leont'eva, *Zapiski sviashchennika Vladislavleva*, 30.

4. S. A. Ikonnikov, "Prikhodskoe dukhovenstvo Voronezhskoi eparkhii vtoroi poloviny XIX–nachala XX veka: Sotsiokul'turnaia kharakteristika" (Kand. diss., Voronezh State University, 2015), 96–97.

5. Iu. I. Belonogova, "Material'noe obespechenie tserkvei v XIX–nachale XX v. na primere khramov Volokolamskogo blagochiniia Moskovskoi eparkhii," *Vestnik PSTGU* 79 (2017): 50.

6. TsIAM, f. 203, op. 475, d. 14, l. 213 (Prosheniia lits dukhovnogo zvaniia o naznachenii na sluzhbu).
7. Mitropolit Evlogii, *Put' moei zhizni* (Moscow: Moskovskii rabochii, 1994), 18.
8. Begovatov and Leont'eva, *Zapiski sviashchennika Vladislavleva*, 29.
9. Ioann S. Belliustin, *Description of the Clergy in Rural Russia: The Memoir of a Nineteenth-Century Parish Priest*, trans. Gregory L. Freeze (Ithaca, NY: Cornell University Press, 1992), 122–23.
10. Belliustin, *Description of the Clergy*, 125. For discussion of the widespread demands for government salaries among parish clergymen in the mid-nineteenth century, see Gregory Freeze, *The Parish Clergy in Nineteenth-Century Russia: Crisis, Reform, Counter-Reform* (Princeton, NJ: Princeton University Press, 1983), 271.
11. There were 38,188 parishes in 1904. Freeze, *The Parish Clergy*, 453.
12. V. A. Fedorov, *Russkaia pravoslavnaia tserkov' i gosudarstvo: Sinodal'nyi period, 1700–1917* (Moscow: Russkaia Panorama, 2003), 42.
13. T. G. Leont'eva, *Vera i progress: Pravoslavnoe sel'skoe dukhovenstvo Rossii vo vtoroi polovine XIX–nachale XX veka* (Moscow: Novyi khronograf, 2002), 29.
14. Protoierei Vladimir Rozhkov, *Tserkovnye voprosy v Gosudarstvennoi Dume* (Moscow: Izd. Krutitskogo Podvor'ia, 2004), 256.
15. S. I. Alekseeva, *Sviateishii Sinod v sisteme vysshikh i tsentral'nykh gosudarstvennykh uchrezhdenii poreformennoi Rossii, 1856–1904* (Saint Petersburg: "Nauka," 2006), 26.
16. Alekseeva, *Sviateishii Sinod*, 46.
17. Gregory Freeze, "Handmaiden of the State? The Church in Imperial Russia Reconsidered," *Journal of Ecclesiastical History* 36 (1985): 82–102.
18. Freeze, "Handmaiden of the State?," 88.
19. Gregory Freeze, "Bringing Order to the Russian Family: Marriage and Divorce in Imperial Russia, 1760–1860," *Journal of Modern History* 62, no. 4 (December 1990): 709–46.
20. Alexander Etkind, *Internal Colonization: Russia's Imperial Experience* (Malden, MA: Polity, 2011), 145–49.
21. Quoted in M. A. Babkin, *Dukhovenstvo Russkoi pravoslavnoi tserkvi i sverzhenie monarkhii (nachalo XX v.–konets 1917 g.)* (Moscow: Gosudarstvennaia publichnaia istoricheskaia biblioteka Rossii, 2007), 88.
22. Alekseeva, *Sviateishii Sinod*, 27–28.
23. A. A. Bogolepov, "Church Reforms in Russia, 1905–1918," *St. Vladimir's Quarterly* 10 (1966): 44–66.
24. Alekseeva, *Sviateishii Sinod*, 45.
25. Alekseeva, *Sviateishii Sinod*, 42.
26. M. E. Grabko, *Deiatel'nost' Russkoi pravoslavnoi tserkvi v rabochei srede Moskovskoi gubernii v kontse XIX–nachale XX v.* (Moscow: PSTGU, 2017), 72.
27. Gregory Freeze, *The Russian Levites: Parish Clergy in the Eighteenth Century* (Cambridge, MA: Harvard University Press, 1977), 72.
28. TsIAM, f. 203, op. 475, d. 14, l. 189.
29. For an example of such an incarceration and its economic effects on the family of a deacon, see GATO, f. 160, op. 1, d. 10188 (Delo o razdele bratskikh dokhodov mezhdu chlenami prichta sela Gubina-Ugla, Korchevskogo Uezda. 1903).

30. Freeze, *The Parish Clergy*, 27–28.
31. N. A. Zaozerskii, *O tserkovnoi vlasti: Osnovopolozheniia, kharakter i sposoby primeneniia tserkovnoi vlasti v razlichnykh formakh ustroistva tserkvi po ucheniiu pravoslavnokanonicheskago prava* (Sergiev Posad: 2-ia tipografiia A.I. Snegirevoi, 1894), 204–205.
32. Leont'eva, *Vera i progress*, 46.
33. Sergei Firsov, *Tserkov' v Imperii: Ocherki iz tserkovnoi istorii epokhi Imperatora Nikolaia II* (Saint Petersburg: Satis Derzhava, 2007), 22.
34. "Spisok blagochinnykh Moskovskoi eparkhii s razpredeleniem blagochinnii goroda Moskvy na otdeleniia, a blagochinii uezdnykh na okruga," *Moskovskie tserkovnye vedomosti. Offitsial'nyi otdel,* September 30, 1907, 270.
35. Fedorov, *Russkaia pravoslavnaia tserkov' i gosudarstvo.* 21.
36. Sir Donald Mackenzie Wallace, *Russia on the Eve of War and Revolution*, ed. Cyril E. Black (Princeton, NJ: Princeton University Press, 1961), 377.
37. See GATO, f. 160, op. 1, d. 34393, ll. 1–157ob. (Svedeniia o sostoianii tserkvei i blagochinnikh okrugov Tverskoi Gub. 1905–06); and GATO, f. 160, op. 1, d. 34398, ll. 1–119 (Svedeniia o sostoianii tserkvei i blagochinnikh okrugov Tverskoi Gub. 1906).
38. TsIAM, f. 203, op. 475, d. 17, l. 140b. (Delo po prosheniiu zashtatnago sviashchennika, Mikhaila Nezhdanova o sniatii s nego sana, 1905).
39. Freeze, *The Russian Levites*, 30–31; Babkin, *Dukhovenstvo Russkoi pravoslavnoi tserkvi*, 62.
40. Freeze, *The Parish Clergy*, 130.
41. Fr. Vasilii Bazhenov, "Zhelatelen-li tip sovremennykh pastyrei, kak obshchestvennykh deiatelei?," *Tverskie eparkhial'nye vedomosti*, April 1914, 310–11.
42. Bazhenov, "Zhelatelen-li tip sovremennykh pastyrei," 311.
43. Bazhenov, "Zhelatelen-li tip sovremennykh pastyrei," 311.
44. Freeze, *The Russian Levites*, 114.
45. Leont'eva, *Vera i progress*, 37.
46. This issue was discussed in the debates over zemstvo taxation of clerical property. See, for example, GATO, f. 160, op. 1, d. 9079, ll. 34–34ob. (O zemskikh nalogakh).
47. GATO, f. 318, op. 1, d. 654, l. 5 (Delo ob otkrytii popechitel'stva o bednykh dukhovnogo zvaniia. 1823).
48. T. Barsov, *Sbornik deistvuiushchikh i rukovodstvennykh tserkovnykh i tserkovnograzhdanskikh postanovlenii po vedomstvu pravoslavnago ispovedaniia* (Saint Petersburg: Sinodal'naia tipografiia, 1885), 179.
49. Barsov, *Sbornik*, 178.
50. Barsov, *Sbornik*, 177–78.
51. Barsov, *Sbornik*, 181.
52. Barsov, *Sbornik*, 183. The scriptural quotation is from 1 Timothy 5:4, which is here rendered in the King James translation. The Slavonic quotation is: "свой дом благочестиво устроити и взаим воздаяти родителям."
53. Barsov, *Sbornik*, 183.
54. GATO, f. 318, op. 1, d. 654, l. 5.
55. See N. G. Koroleva, ed., *Zemskoe samoupravlenie v Rossii, 1864–1918*, 2 vols. (Moscow: Nauka, 2005); Jane Burbank, *Russian Peasants Go to Court: Legal Culture in*

the Countryside, 1905–1917 (Bloomington: Indiana University Press, 2004); Daniel Balmuth, "Origins of the Russian Press Reform of 1864," *Slavonic and East European Review* 47, no. 109 (July 1969): 369–88.

56. Leont'eva, *Vera i progress*, 33.
57. James Cunningham, *A Vanquished Hope* (Crestwood, NY: St. Vladimir's Seminary Press, 1981), 183.
58. Freeze, *The Parish Clergy*, 230–33.
59. *Poluvekovoi iubilei Obshchestva Liubitelei Dukhovnago Prosveshcheniia* (Moscow: Pechatnia A.I. Snegirevoi, 1913), 19–21.
60. "Pastyrskiia sobraniia," *Pribavleniia k tserkovnym vedomostiam*, January 12, 1908, 54.
61. V. Beliaev, A. Viktorov, and M. Mansurov, *Eparkhial'nye s"ezdy. Sbornik deistvuiushchikh zakonopolozhenii ob eparkhia'nykh s"ezdakh. Ikh praktika za 1903–1907 gg. Predstoiashchaia reforma s"ezdov. Prilozheniia* (Saint Petersburg: "Bereg," 1908), 7–8.
62. Fr. Vasilii Bogoiavlenskii, *Eparkhial'nye s"ezdy dukhovenstva: Ikh deiatel'nost' i znachenie. Sochinenie kandidata bogosloviia sviashchennika Vasilliia Bogoiavlenskogo* (Bezplatnoe prilozhenie k Omskim eparkhial'nym vedomostiam za 1902 g.), 103.
63. Bogoiavlenskii, *Eparkhial'nye s"ezdy dukhovenstva*, 111.
64. "Pastyrskiia sobraniia," 53–55.
65. "Ustav emeritel'noi kassy dukhovenstva Moskovskoi eparkhii," *Moskovskie tserkovnye vedomosti. Offitsial'nyi otdel*, August 13, 1906, 71; Leont'eva, *Vera i progress*, 31.
66. "Ustav emeritel'noi kassy," 71.
67. "Soobrazheniia o vozmozhnom rasshirenii i ozhivlenii deiatel'nosti emeritel'noi kassy dukhovenstva Moskovskoi eparkhii," *Moskovskie tserkovnye vedomosti*, April 17, 1905, 192–93.
68. Leont'eva, *Vera i progress*, 32.
69. "Ustav Moskovskago eparkhial'nago tserkovno-svechnogo zavoda," *Moskovskie tserkovnye vedomosti. Offitsial'nyi otdel*, January 16, 1905, 10–12.
70. "Ob utverzhdenii instruktsii nastoiateliam tserkvei," *Moskovskie tserkovnye vedomosti. Offitsial'nyi otdel*, August 19, 1901, 79–80.
71. This point is made in Bogoiavlenskii, *Eparkhial'nye s"ezdy dukhovenstva*, 11.
72. Freeze, *The Parish Clergy*, 334–36.
73. Bogoiavlenskii, Eparkhial'nye s"ezdy dukhovenstva, 113.
74. Barsov, *Sbornik*, 367–84.
75. TsIAM, f. 203, op. 506, d. 292, ll. 1–130b. (Po prosheniiu prikhozhan Nikolaevskoi sela Chashnikova tserkvi, ob otvode ot nikh sviashchennika Ioanna Orlova).
76. Evlogii, *Put' moei zhizni*, 136.
77. GATO, f. 160, op. 1, d. 34382, l. 30b. (Delo s predstavleniem protokolov s"ezda Tverskago Eparkhial'nogo dukhovenstva. 1901–2).
78. For examples of personal donations by clergymen at clerical congresses to make up for funding shortfalls, see TsIAM, f. 203, op. 550, d. 239, l. 12 (Protokol zasedanii obshcheeparkhial'nogo s"ezda blagochinnykh 1908 goda). See also GATO, f. 160, op. 1, d. 9084, ll. 1–20b. (S protokolom s"ezda dukhovenstva 5 okruga Tverskogo uezda o dobrovol'nom ego samooblazhenii sebia sborom v pol'zu vdov i sirot okruga. 1910).

79. TsIAM, f. 203, op. 550, d. 239, ll. 142–44 (Protokoly zasedanii obshcheeparkhial'nogo s"ezda blagochinnykh 1908 goda).

80. Harley Balzer, "Introduction," in *Russia's Missing Middle Class: The Professions in Russian History*, ed. Harley Balzer (New York: M. E. Sharpe, 1996), 12.

81. Adele Lindenmeyr, *Poverty Is Not a Vice: Charity, Society, and the State in Imperial Russia* (Princeton, NJ: Princeton University Press, 1996), 57–60.

82. *Poluvekovoi iubilei Obshchestva Liubitelei Dukhovnago Prosveshcheniia.*

83. Mikhail Koialovich, *Litovskaia tserkovnaia uniia* (Saint Petersburg: Strannik, 1861), 2:84.

84. O. V. Kravchenko, "Tserkovnye bratstva: Istoriia i istoriografiia," in *Provintsial'noe dukhovenstvo dorevoliutsionnoi Rossii: Sbornik nauchnykh trudov vserossiiskoi zaochnoi konferentsii*, ed. T. G. Leont'eva (Tver': Slavianskii Mir, 2006), 248–49.

85. *Obzor deiatel'nosti vedomstva pravoslavnogo ispovedaniia za vremia tsarstvovaniia imperatora Aleksandra III* (Saint Petersburg: Sinodal'naia tipografiia, 1901), 311.

86. A. Papkov, *Tserkovnyia bratstva: Kratkii statisticheskii ocherk o polozhenii tserkovnykh bratstv k nachalu 1893 goda* (Saint Petersburg: Sinodal'naia tipografiia, 1893), 11–12, 44–45.

87. Papkov, *Tserkovnyia bratstva*, 11.

88. For example, see the report of a brotherhood founded in the Moscow diocese in 1884 in TsIAM, f. 1408, op. 1, d. 1, ll. 1–30b. (Sokolovskoe sviato-pokrovskoe pravoslavnoe bratstvo).

89. For an example of this kind of large brotherhood, see GATO, f. 644, op. 1, d. 430 (Zhurnaly soveta bratstva kniazia Mikhaila Iaroslavicha Tverskogo za 1896–97).

90. For example, the provision of financial support for Muslim converts to Orthodoxy. TsGARKaz, f. 358, op. 1, d. 3, l. 54 (Otchet o deiatel'nosti Kazansko-Bogodichnago Bratstva Turkestanskoi eparkhii za 1888 god).

91. See the response of one superintendent to the request of Tver's largest brotherhood for information on local charities and sobriety societies in his district. GATO, f. 644, op. 1, d. 438, l. 2 (Delo ob otkrytii obshchest trezvosti v Tverskoi gub. 1910).

92. TsIAM, f. 1794, op. 1, d. 15, ll. 1–40b. (Zhurnaly zasedanii Soveta bratstva o denezhnykh posobiiakh uchenikam dukhovnykh uchilishch za 1890/91 gody).

93. Such a situation is described in L. A. Egorova, "Blagotvoritel'nost' pravoslavnykh bratstv Kostromskoi gubernii," in *Blagotvoritel'nost' v Rossii: Istoricheskie i sotsial'no-ekonomicheskie issledovaniia*, ed. B. V. Anan'ich, Larisa Viktorovna Badia, and O. L. Leikind (St. Petersburg: Izd. Novikova, 2004), 195.

94. Papkov, *Tserkovnyia bratstva*, 14–45.

95. See A. L. Zhukova, "Vyrabotka konservativnoi kontseptsii mestnogo upravleniia v Rossii: Komissiia M. S. Kakhanova, 1881–1885," in *Zemskoe samoupravlenie v Rossii, 1864–1918*, ed. N. G. Koroleva (Moscow: Nauka, 2005), 1:235–48.

96. Zhukova, "Vyrabotka konservativnoi kontseptsii," 239.

97. A. Iu. Polunov, *Pod vlast'iu ober-prokurora: Gosudarstvo i tserkov' v epokhu Aleksandra III* (Moscow: Airo-XX, 1996), 31.

98. A. Polunov and I. Solov'ev, "Istoricheskoe vvedenie," in *Otzyny eparkhial'nykh arkhiereev po voprosu o tserkovnoi reforme*, ed. A. Polunov and I. Solov'ev (Moscow: Obshchestvo Liubitelei Tserkovnoi Istorii, 2004), 1:11.

99. K. P. Pobedonostsev, "Tserkov' i gosudarstvo," in *K. P. Pobedonostsev, pro et contra: Lichnost', obshchestvenno-politicheskaia deiatel'nost' i mirovozzrenie Konstantina Pobedonostseva v otsenke russkikh myslitelei i issledovatelei. Antologiia*, ed. D. K. Burlaka (Saint Petersburg: Izd. Russkogo Khristianskogo gumanitarnogo instituta, 1996), 86.

100. Polunov, *Pod vlast'iu ober-prokurora*, 26.

101. Pobedonostsev, "Tserkov' i gosudarstvo," 92.

102. Freeze, *The Parish Clergy*, 414.

103. Beliaev, Viktorov, and Mansurov, *Eparkhial'nye s"ezdy*, 8. See also A. I. Mramornov, *Dukhovnaia seminariia v Rossii nachala XX veka: Krizis i vozmozhnosti ego preodoleniia* (Saratov: Nauchnaia kniga, 2007), 47.

104. S. G. Wheatcroft, "The 1891–92 Famine in Russia: Towards a More Detailed Analysis of Its Scale and Demographic Significance," in *Economy and Society in Russia and the Soviet Union, 1860–1930: Essays for Olga Crisp*, ed. Linda Edmondson (New York: St. Martin's, 1992), 44–64.

105. Orlando Figes, *A People's Tragedy: The Russian Revolution 1891–1924* (New York: Penguin Books, 1996), 157–58.

106. Richard G. Robbins Jr., *Famine in Russia, 1891–1892: The Imperial Government Responds to a Crisis* (New York: Columbia University Press, 1975), 173.

107. Robbins, *Famine in Russia*, 24.

108. *Vsepoddaneishii otchet Ober-prokurora Sviateishago sinoda po vedomstvu pravoslavnago ispovedaniia za 1890–1891 gody* (Saint Petersburg: Sinodal'naia tipografiia, 1893), 337, 342, Robbins, *Famine in Russia*, 103.

109. Moscow's diocesan journal reported the formation of famine-relief brotherhoods in Novgorod, Pskov, and Saint Petersburg; see "Vnutrenniia izvestiia," *Moskovskie tserkovnye vedomosti*, July 28, 1891, 418.

110. *Vsepoddaneishii otchet za 1890–1891 gody*, 334–36.

111. "Vnutrenniia izvestiia," *Moskovskie tserkovnye vedomosti*, August 18, 1891, 446.

112. *Vsepoddaneishii otchet za 1890–1891 gody*, 338.

113. "Eparkhial'nye komitety v Moskve i ikh deistviia," *Moskovskie tserkovnye vedomosti*, September 29, 1891, 512–14.

114. *Vsepoddaneishii otchet za 1890–1891 gody*, 337–38; *Moskovskie tserkovnye vedomosti. Offitsial'nyi otdel*, September 8, 1891, 76.

115. Robbins, *Famine in Russia*, 55.

116. GATO, f. 886, op. 1, d. 13, l. 25 (Sbornik bumagam s vedomostiami o postuplenii, otpravke i nalichnosti pozhertvovanii khlebom postupavshikh v sklady Eparkhial'nogo i uezdnykh komitetov Tverskoi eparkhii v pol'zu bedstvuiushchago naseleniia postignutykh neurozhaem gubernii).

117. GATO, f. 886, op. 1, d. 28, ll. 116–170b. (Pravila dlia rukovodstva uezdnym komitetam, blagochinnym i prichtam tserkvei po sboru, khranenie i otsylke pozhertvovanii v pol'zu bedstvuiushchago naseleniia postignutykh neurozhaem gubernii).

118. Robbins, *Famine in Russia*, 52.

119. GATO, f. 886, op. 1, d. 3, ll. 26–27 (Delo po Novotorzhskomu uezdnomu komitetu).

120. GATO, f. 886, op. 1, d. 1, l. 7 (Delo po Bezhetskomu uezdnomu komitetu dlia sbora pozhertvovanii v pol'zu golodaiushchago naseleniia postignutykh neurozhaem gubernii).

121. I am grateful to my colleague John Corcoran for this archival reference, which provides an example of zemstvo corruption during the war.: Gosudarstvennyi arkhiv Penzenskoi oblasti (GAPO), f. 11, op. 1, d. 40, l. 43, l. 115.

122. GATO, f. 886, op. 1, d. 1, l. 25.

123. GATO, f. 886, op. 1, d. 1, ll. 26ob.–27.

124. GATO, f. 886, op. 1, d. 1, ll. 19–21.

125. GATO, f. 886, op. 1, d. 10, ll. 14–16ob. (Delo o postupivshikh pozhertvovaniiakh).

126. GATO, f. 886, op. 1, d. 13, l. 53ob.

127. *Moskovskie tserkovnye vedomosti*, September 8, 1891, 686.

128. "Vnutreniia Izvestiia," *Moskovskie tserkovnye vedomosti*, December 1, 1891, 660.

129. Robbins, *Famine in Russia*, 97–101.

130. GATO, f. 886, op. 1, d. 19, l. 85 (Delo raskhodnye dokumenty).

131. This transition can be observed in GATO, f. 886, op. 1, d. 19, ll. 1–85.

132. Robbins, *Famine in Russia*, 103.

133. A copy of this circular can be found in GATO, f. 886, op. 1, d. 28, l. 107 (Vedomost' o dvizhenii summ).

134. GATO, f. 886, op. 1, d. 13, ll. 83, 103ob.

135. *Moskovskie tserkovnye vedomosti. Offitsial'nyi otdel*, August 23, 1892, 173–75.

136. Robbins, *Famine in Russia*, 108.

137. *Vsepoddaneishii otchet za 1890–1891 gody*, 339.

138. Beliaev, Viktorov, and Mansurov, *Eparkhial'nye s"ezdy*, 15.

Chapter 2. War, Revolution, and Famine

1. A. P. Chekhov, "Koshmar," in *Izbrannye proizvedeniia: Rasskazy i povesti* (Moscow: Gos. Izd. Khudozhestvennoi literatury, 1960), 1:168.

2. Alison K. Smith, *For the Common Good and Their Own Well-Being: Social Estates in Imperial Russia* (New York: Oxford University Press, 2015), 153–54.

3. Victoria E. Bonnell, *Roots of Rebellion: Workers' Politics and Organizations in St. Petersburg and Moscow, 1900–1914* (Berkeley: University of California Press, 1999), 451–54.

4. See, for example, Laura Engelstein, *Moscow, 1905: Working-Class Organization and Political Conflict* (Stanford, CA: Stanford University Press, 1982), 8.

5. M. E. Grabko, *Deiatel'nost' Russkoi pravoslavnoi tserkvi v rabochei srede Moskovskoi gubernii v kontse XIX–nachale XX v.* (Moscow: PSTGU, 2017), 35.

6. Grabko, *Deiatel'nost' Russkoi pravoslavnoi tserkvi*, 27–31.

7. TsIAM, f. 1408, op. 1, d. 1, ll. 1–30b. (Sokolovskoe sviato-pokrovskoe pravoslavnoe prikhodskoe bratstvo).

8. GATO, f. 160, op. 1, d. 34398, l. 21 (Svedeniia o sostoianii tserkvei i blagochinnikh okrugov Tverskoi Gub.).

9. "Fr. E. V. Kremenskii (Nekrolog)," *Moskovskie tserkovnye vedomosti*, August 3, 1903, 404.
10. GATO, f. 160, op. 1, d. 8807, ll. 1–10b. (Po proshenii moskovskikh meshchan Ivana Zaitseva i Evdokii Zhuravlevoi o pozhertvovanii imi Gosud. 4% renty v 1000 rublei v pol'zu bednykh prikhozhan tserkvi sela Krasnogo Kaliazinskogo uezda—1909).
11. GATO, f. 160, op. 1, d. 8186, ll. 1–6 (Delo o bezporiadkakh v Staritskoi Ladyginskoi bogadel'ni).
12. TsIAM, f. 203, op. 551, d. 165, ll. 1–11 (Delo ob utverzhdenii proekta ustava bratstva sviatoi ravnoapostol'noi Marii Magdaliny v g. Ruze).
13. "Protokol s"ezda dukhovenstva Moskovskoi eparkhii 1892 goda," *Moskovskie tserkovnye vedomosti. Offitsial'nyi otdel*, November 29, 1892, 230.
14. Arkhimandrit Mikhail, "Episkop i eparkhial'nye s"ezdy," *Tserkovnyi vestnik*, July 7, 1905, 834.
15. See, for example, TsIAM, f. 203, op. 550, d. 239, ll. 112–13 (Protokoly zasedanii obshcheeparkhial'nogo s"ezda blagochinnykh 1908 goda).
16. This phenomenon is discussed in "Pastyrskiia sobraniia," *Pribavleniia k tserkovnym vedomostiam*, January 12, 1908, 54.
17. TsIAM, f. 203, op. 550, d. 239, l. 142.
18. V. Beliaev, A. Viktorov, and M. Mansurov, *Eparkhial'nye s"ezdy. Sbornik deistvuiushchikh zakonopolozhenii ob eparkhia'nykh s"ezdakh. Ikh praktika za 1903–1907 gg. Predstoiashchaia reforma s"ezdov. Prilozheniia* (Saint Petersburg: "Bereg," 1908), 24–26.
19. Obstructionism was thus characterized in an article written in defense of the congresses. Arkhimandrit Mikhail, "Episkop i eparkhial'nye s"ezdy," *Tserkovnyi vestnik*, July 7, 1905, 835.
20. Beliaev, Viktorov, and Mansurov, *Eparkhial'nye s"ezdy*, 27.
21. "Pastyrskiia sobraniia," *Pribavleniia k tserkovnym vedomostiam*, January 12, 1908, 54–56. For a discussion of the Society for Moral and Religious Enlightenment, see Jennifer Hedda, *His Kingdom Come: Orthodox Pastorship and Social Activism in Revolutionary Russia* (DeKalb: Northern Illinois University Press, 2008), 86–105.
22. "Pastyrskiia sobraniia," 57–59.
23. "Pastyrskiia sobraniia," 57.
24. Sergei Firsov, *Tserkov' v Imperii: Ocherki iz tserkovnoi istorii epokhi Imperatora Nikolaia II* (Saint Petersburg: Satis Derzhava, 2007), 14–15.
25. Firsov, *Tserkov' v Imperii*, 15–31.
26. See, for example, Ts. V. "Nuzhna li tsenzura propovedei?," *Pskovskie eparkhial'nye vedomosti*, October 15–31, 1905, 391.
27. Hedda, *His Kingdom Come*, 157.
28. Hedda, *His Kingdom Come*, 154–58.
29. A. Polunov, "Vvedenie," in *Otzyvy eparkhial'nykh arkhiereev po voprosu o tserkovnoi reforme*, ed. A. Polunov and I. Solov'ev (Moscow: Obshchestvo Liubitelei Tserkovnoi Istorii, 2004), 1:12; James Cunningham, *A Vanquished Hope* (Crestwood, NY: St. Vladimir's Seminary Press, 1981), 133–36.
30. A. Polunov and I. Solov'ev, eds., *Otzyvy eparkhial'nykh arkhiereev po voprosu o tserkovnoi reforme* (Moscow: Obshchestvo Liubitelei Tserkovnoi Istorii, 2004), 2:394.

31. "Opredeleniia Sviateishago Sinoda," *Tserkovnyia vedomosti*, November 26, 1905, 523–25.

32. N. M. Pirumova, *Zemskoe liberal'noe dvizhenie: Sotsial'nye korni i evoliutsiia do nachala XX veka* (Moscow: Nauka, 1977), 48–49.

33. Terence Emmons, "The Beseda Circle, 1899–1905," *Slavic Review* 32, no. 3 (September 1973): 463; Thomas Earl Porter, *The Zemstvo and the Emergence of Civil Society in Late Imperial Russia 1864–1917* (San Francisco: Mellon Research University Press, 1991), 44.

34. Hedda, *His Kingdom Come*, 141–45.

35. Abraham Ascher, *The Revolution of 1905: Russia in Disarray* (Stanford, CA: Stanford University Press, 1988), 90–95; Abraham Ascher, *The Revolution of 1905: Authority Restored* (Stanford, CA: Stanford University Press, 1992), 241–43.

36. Ascher, *Authority Restored*, 170–71.

37. Grabko, *Deiatel'nost' Russkoi pravoslavnoi tserkvi*, 40.

38. Firsov, *Tserkov' v Imperii*, 43–45.

39. Ascher, *Russia in Disarray*, 183; Ian Nish, *The Origins of the Russo-Japanese War* (New York: Longman, 1985), 207.

40. TsIAM, f. 203, op. 546, d. 15, ll. 1–2 (Delo o navedenii spravok o nalichii mest v uchrezhdeniiakh, podvedomstvennykh MDK, dlia ranenykh russko-iaponskoi voiny).

41. TsIAM, f. 203, op. 546, d. 15, l. 1.

42. TsIAM, f. 203, op. 546, d. 15, ll. 9–19.

43. TsIAM, f. 203, op. 546, d. 15, ll. 40–40ob.

44. TsIAM, f. 203, op. 546, d. 15, l. 26.

45. TsIAM, f. 203, op. 546, d. 15, ll. 125–250b.

46. TsIAM, f. 203, op. 546, d. 15, l.125, ll. 139–40.

47. For examples of anti-cholera work by parish clergy in Tver' and Moscow, respectively, see GATO, f. 160, op. 1, d. 9075, ll. 1–5 (Delo po otnosheniiu Tverskogo Gubernatora, o naznachenii predstavitelia dlia uchastiia v zasedaniiakh Gubernskoi Sanitarno-Ispolnitel'noi Komissii, v vidu ob"iavleniia gubernii ugrozhaemoi po kholere—1910); TsIAM, f. 203, op. 550, d. 130, ll. 1–15 (Delo o poriadke rasprostraneniia sredi naseleniia Moskovskoi gub. mer po preduprezhdeniiu epidemii kholery—1908).

48. TsIAM, f. 203, op. 546, d. 15, ll. 119–200b.

49. For reports of violence against clergy and vandalism of churches in Tver', see GATO, f. 160, op. 1, d. 34393, ll. 210b., 137, 157 (Svedeniia o sostoianii tserkvei i blagochinnikh okrugov Tverskoi Gub.—1905–06).

50. GATO, f. 160, op. 1, d. 34393, l. 147.

51. GATO, f. 160, op. 1, d. 34393, l. 146ob.

52. Metropolitan Evlogii describes the burning of a barn belonging to his father, a parish priest. Mitropolit Evlogii, *Put' moei zhizni* (Moscow: Moskovskii rabochii, 1994), 19.

53. TsIAM, f. 203, op. 550, d. 158, ll. 1–3 (Delo o predostavlenii blagochinnym Moskovskoi eparkhii svedenii o nalichii detei nizshikh sluzhashchikh vedomstva pravoslavnogo veroispovedaniia, postradavshikh ot anarkhistov-grabitelei dlia pomeshcheniia ikh v priiut).

54. TsIAM, f. 203, op. 550, d. 158, l. 70.

55. TsIAM, f. 203, op. 550, d. 158, l. 9.
56. TsIAM, f. 203, op. 550, d. 158, ll. 22, 75.
57. TsIAM, f. 431, op. 1, d. 225, ll. 1–900b. (Moskovskii eparkhial'nyi komitet po okazaniiu pomoshchi postradavshim pri bezporiadkakh v Moskve v dekabre 1905 goda). See also TsIAM, f. 203, op. 550, d. 91 (Delo po sboru pozhertvovanii v pol'zu postradavshikh ot besporiadkov v g. Moskve).
58. "O sbore pozhertvovanii v pol'zu postradavshikh ot neurozhaia," *Tserkovnyia vedomosti*, November 26, 1905, 526.
59. "Rasporiazheniia eparkhial'nago nachal'stva. O proizvodstve sbora v pol'zu golodaiushchikh," *Moskovskie tserkovnye vedomosti. Offitsial'nyi otdel*, November 6, 1905, 418.
60. For example, the committee of the town of Ostashkov, in Tver' gubernia, informed the diocesan committee that it had sent twenty-five rubles to Voronezh in April 1907. GATO, f. 886, op. 1, d. 24, l. 15 (Nariad bumag o predstavlenii blagochinnami raznykh uezdov spiski i den'gi sobrannyia v tserkvakh v pol'zu naseleniiu gubernii postradavshikh ot neurozhaia).
61. "Ot komiteta dlia sbora pozhertvovanii v Moskovskoi eparkhii na nuzhdy golodaiushchikh," *Moskovskie tserkovnye vedomosti. Offitsial'nyi otdel*, November 6, 1905, 420.
62. TsIAM, f. 2171, op. 1, d. 1, ll. 1–18, 29–114, 213–425 (Eparkhial'nyi komitet po okazaniiu pomoshchi golodaiushchim, g. Moskvy); GATO, f. 886, op. 1, d. 30, ll. 1–250b. (Otryvok iz prikhodnoi denezhnoi knigi o postuplenii na golodaiushchikh v pol'zu dukhovenstva i mirian denezhnykh summ).
63. TsIAM, f. 2171, op. 1, d. 1, ll. 20–260b.
64. TsIAM, f. 2171, op. 1, d. 1, l. 209.
65. TsIAM, f. 2171, op. 1, d. 1, l. 183.
66. TsIAM, f. 2171, op. 1, d. 4, l. 3 (Delo o sbore pozhertvovanii v pol'zu golodaiushchikh).
67. TsIAM, f. 2171, op. 1, d. 1, ll. 212–120b.
68. TsIAM, f. 2171, op. 1, d. 1, ll. 27–28.
69. TsIAM, f. 2171, op. 1, d. 4, l. 5.
70. Moskovskie tserkovnye vedomosti, May 31, 1908, 561.
71. Fr. I. Kedrov, "Vozzvanie k dukhovenstvu Moskovskoi eparkhii," *Moskovskie tserkovnye vedomosti*, February 18, 1906, 187.
72. TsIAM, f. 2171, op. 1, d. 4, ll. 1–10b.
73. GATO, f. 886, op. 1, d. 24, l. 22.
74. GATO, f. 886, op. 1, d. 30, ll. 1–26.
75. In 1903, there were 105,962 parish clergymen employed throughout the empire and 4,904 retired. Combined with the female and non-ordained members of the clerical *soslovie*, this figure would comprise less than 2 percent of the population that had reached about 126,367,000 by 1897. See *Vsepoddanneishii otchet Ober-prokurora Sviateishago sinoda po vedomstvu pravoslavnago ispovedaniia za 1903–1904 gody* (Saint Petersburg: Sinodal'naia tipografiia, 1909), 24–27. See also B. R. Mitchell, ed., *European Historical Statistics, 1750–1975*, 2nd ed. (New York: Facts on File, 1980), 33.
76. GATO, f. 886, op. 1, d. 30, ll. 1–26.
77. This can be observed by comparing donation submission forms with their corresponding diocesan records: GATO, f. 886, op. 1, d. 24, ll. 29, 33, 37, 43; GATO, f. 886, op. 1, d. 30, ll. 160b.–170b.

78. GATO, f. 886, op. 1, d. 30, ll. 1–26.
79. "Opredeleniia Sviateishago Sinoda," *Tserkovnyia vedomosti*, November 26, 1905, 524.
80. GATO, f. 886, op. 1, d. 30, ll. 1–26.
81. GATO, f. 886, op. 1, d. 30, ll. 1–26.
82. GATO, f. 160, op. 1, d. 8672, ll. 5–16 (Delo s otchetom konsistorskikh summ za 1906 god).
83. Ascher, *Authority Restored*, 319.
84. Konstantin Pobedonostsev, "Velikaia lozh' nashego vremeni," accessed July 19, 2019, http://dugward.ru/library/alexandr3/pobedonoscev_vel_log.html.

Chapter 3. Revolt in the Seminaries

1. TsIAM, f. 234, op. 2, d. 365, ll. 1130b.–140b. (Zhurnaly pedagogicheskago sobraniia pravleniia Moskovskoi Dukhovnoi Seminarii za 1906 god).
2. Laurie Manchester, *Holy Fathers, Secular Sons: Clergy, Intelligentsia, and the Emergence of Modern Selfhood in Revolutionary Russia* (DeKalb: Northern Illinois University Press, 2008), 187.
3. *Vsepoddanneishii otchet Ober-prokurora Sviateishago sinoda po vedomstvu pravoslavnago ispovedaniia za 1905–1907 gody* (Saint Petersburg: Sinodal'naia tipografiia, 1910), appendix, 156–59.
4. Mitropolit Evlogii, *Put' moei zhizni* (Moscow: Moskovskii rabochii, 1994), 17.
5. For an example of this collection of funds for the Tver' seminary in 1909, see GATO, f. 575, op. 1, d. 1287, ll. 1–5 (Tverskaia seminariia).
6. *Vsepoddanneishii otchet za 1905–1907 gody*, appendix, 153–55.
7. Gregory Freeze, *The Parish Clergy in Nineteenth-Century Russia: Crisis, Reform, Counter-Reform* (Princeton, NJ: Princeton University Press, 1983), 146.
8. For discussion of "caste isolation," see "Mneniia i otzyvy," *Tserkovnyi vestnik*, July 7, 1905, 837.
9. "Ustav Pravoslavnykh Dukhovnykh Seminarii 1884 g.," in *Dukhovnaia seminariia v Rossii nachala XX veka: Krizis i vozmozhnosti ego preodoleniia*, A. I. Mramornov (Saratov: Nauchnaia kniga, 2007), 209.
10. A. Gusev, "Polozhenie prepodavatelei dukhovnykh seminarii i uchilishch," *Pravoslavnoe obozrenie*, no. 12, 1885, 707.
11. TsIAM, f. 234, op. 2, d. 401, l. 970b. (Zhurnaly za 1908).
12. TsIAM, f. 234, op. 2, d. 441, l. 300b. (Zhurnaly za 1910); TsIAM, f. 234, op. 2, d. 463, l. 550b. (Zhurnaly za 1911).
13. Aleksandr Mramornov finds that 70 percent of the teachers at Saratov Seminary in the early twentieth century came from the clerical estate. A. I. Mramornov, *Dukhovnaia seminariia v Rossii nachala XX veka: Krizis i vozmozhnosti ego preodoleniia* (Saratov: Nauchnaia kniga, 2007), 62.
14. For example, the charity for poor students of Tver' Seminary contained nineteen clerical members and fifteen lay members in 1901. Some from the latter group were seminary instructors. GATO, f. 575, op. 1, d. 1472, l. 5.
15. See, for example, letters to the administration of Kashin Seminary in 1913, requesting financial aid and reporting family circumstances. GATO, f. 575, op. 1, d. 1541.

16. TsIAM, f. 234, op. 2, d. 365, l. 54.
17. TsIAM, f. 234, op. 2, d. 384, l. 96 (Zhurnaly za 1907).
18. TsIAM, f. 234, op. 2, d. 477, l. 93 (Zhurnaly za 1912).
19. TsIAM, f. 234, op. 2, d. 513, l. 74 (Zhurnaly za 1914).
20. Gregory Freeze, *The Russian Levites: Parish Clergy in the Eighteenth Century* (Cambridge, MA: Harvard University Press, 1977), 34, 114.
21. Freeze, *The Parish Clergy*, 309–10.
22. Freeze, *The Parish Clergy*, 239–45, 309–10, 356–57.
23. T. G. Leont'eva, *Vera i progress: Pravoslavnoe sel'skoe dukhovenstvo Rossii vo vtoroi polovine XIX–nachale XX veka* (Moscow: Novyi khronograf, 2002), 84.
24. Freeze, *The Parish Clergy*, 361.
25. For an example of a peasant seminarian called to the priesthood, see TsIAM, f. 234, op. 2, d. 513, l. 231.
26. "Nekrolog," *Moskovskie tserkovnye vedomosti*, September 2, 1901, 408–9.
27. TsIAM, f. 234, op. 2, d. 401, l. 3.
28. TsIAM, f. 234, op. 2, d. 401, l. 310b.
29. TsIAM, f. 234, op. 2, d. 344, l. 110 (Zhurnaly za 1905).
30. TsIAM, f. 234, op. 2, d. 365, l. 1100b.
31. TsIAM, f. 234, op. 2, d. 384, ll. 28, 480b., 72; TsIAM, f. 234, op. 2, d. 401, l. 1130b.; TsIAM, f. 234, op. 2, d. 423, l. 62 (Zhurnaly za 1909).
32. Freeze, *The Russian Levites*, 79–80.
33. See, for example, GATO, f. 160, op. 1, d. 10280, l. 1 (Sekretno. Po otnosheniiu direktora narodnykh uchilishch o litsakh udalennykh ot ispolneniia uchitel'skikh obiazannostei po politicheskoi neblagonadezhnosti. 1904).
34. V. B. Titlinov, *Molodezh' i revoliutsiia, 1860–1905* (Leningrad: Gosudarstvennoe izdatel'stvo, 1925), 21–23.
35. TsIAM, f. 203, op. 475, d. 1, ll. 1–9 (Delo ob otkaze naznachit' uchitelia Simonovskoi tserkovno-prikhodskoi shkoly Skvortsova N. sviashchennikom).
36. Leont'eva, *Vera i progress*, 72.
37. Freeze, *The Parish Clergy*, 18.
38. Evlogii, *Put' moei zhizni*, 80.
39. Titlinov, *Molodezh' i revoliutsiia*, 51; Evlogii, *Put' moei zhizni*, 70.
40. Freeze, *The Parish Clergy*, 405.
41. A. Iu. Polunov, *Pod vlast'iu ober-prokurora: Gosudarstvo i tserkov' v epokhu Aleksandra III* (Moscow: Airo-XX, 1996), 63–64.
42. GATO, f. 160, op. 1, d. 7933, l. 1 (Po ukazu Sv. Sinoda ob ogranichenii priema v dukhovnye seminarii i uchilishcha detei inososlovnykh roditelei).
43. Freeze, *The Parish Clergy*, 249–50.
44. Mramornov, *Dukhovnaia seminariia*, 47–48.
45. For a description of conditions in Saratov Seminary, see Mramornov, *Dukhovnaia seminariia*, 93.
46. V. Kolosov, *Istoriia Tverskoi dukhovnoi seminarii: Ko dniu 150-letniago iubileia seminarii* (Tver': Tipografiia Gubernskago Pravleniia, 1889), 325.
47. Kolosov, *Istoriia Tverskoi dukhovnoi seminarii*, 319.
48. Titlinov, *Molodezh' i revoliutsiia*, 27.

49. Titlinov, *Molodezh' i revoliutsiia*, 74,
50. Titlinov, *Molodezh' i revoliutsiia*, 82.
51. John D. Morison, "Church Schools and Seminaries in the Revolution of 1905–06," in *Church, Nation and State in Russia and Ukraine*, ed. Geoffrey A. Hosking (New York: St. Martin's, 1991), 204.
52. T. G. Leont'eva, "Vera i bunt: Dukhovenstvo v revoliutsionnom obshchestve Rossii nachala XX veka," *Voprosy istorii* no. 1 (2001): 35.
53. Titlinov, *Molodezh' i revoliutsiia*, 69.
54. GARF, f. 124, op. 10, d. 477, l. 1 (Delo o volneniiakh seminaristov v Tverskoi dukhovnoi seminarii. 1901).
55. Morison, "Church Schools and Seminaries," 205.
56. Mramornov, *Dukhovnaia seminariia*, 113.
57. Morison, "Church Schools and Seminaries," 203–4.
58. Morison, "Church Schools and Seminaries," 203.
59. Titlinov, *Molodezh' i revoliutsiia*, 77.
60. Sergei Golubtsov, *Moskovskaia Dukhovnaia Akademiia v revoliutsionnuiu epokhu: Akademiia v sotsial'nom dvizhenii i sluzhenii v nachale XX veka. Po materialam arkhivov, memuarov i publikatsii* (Moscow: Izd. "Martis," 1999), 5.
61. "Kartinka iz zhizni sel'skogo sviashchennika," in Mramornov, *Dukhovnaia seminariia*, 267.
62. Manchester, *Holy Fathers, Secular Sons*, 55.
63. TsIAM, f. 234, op. 2, d. 344, ll. 105–12.
64. Mramornov, *Dukhovnaia seminariia*, 113.
65. "S chego nachinat' reformu dukh.-uchebnykh zavedenii?," *Tserkovnyi vestnik*, May 5, 1905, 551.
66. TsIAM, f. 234, op. 2, d. 344, ll. 114–15.
67. TsIAM, f. 234, op. 2, d. 344, l. 113ob.
68. TsIAM, f. 234, op. 2, d. 344, l. 112ob.
69. TsIAM, f. 234, op. 2, d. 365, ll. 20ob.–21.
70. TsIAM, f. 234, op. 2, d. 365, ll. 29–30.
71. TsIAM, f. 234, op. 2, d. 401, ll. 5ob., 26.
72. Mramornov, *Dukhovnaia seminariia*, 261.
73. A. Beglov, "Prikhodskii vopros v istorii i v trudakh Sviashchennogo Sobora Pravoslavnoi Rossiiskoi Tserkvi 1917–1918 gg.," in *Dokumenty Sviashchennogo Sobora Pravoslavnoi Rossiiskoi Tserkvi, 1917–1918 godov: Protokoly zasedanii i materialy otdela o blagoustroenii prikhoda*, ed. A. Beglov (Moscow: Izd. Novospasskogo monastyria, 2017), 14:31.
74. TsIAM, f. 234, op. 2, d. 423, l. 5.
75. Mramornov, *Dukhovnaia seminariia*, 54.
76. TsIAM, f. 234, op. 2, d. 495, l. 55 (Zhurnaly za 1913).
77. Mramornov, *Dukhovnaia seminariia*, 113.
78. Manchester, *Holy Fathers, Secular Sons*, 156–61.
79. Golubtsov, *Moskovskaia Dukhovnaia Akademiia*, 4.
80. Golubtsov, *Moskovskaia Dukhovnaia Akademiia*, 6; Titlinov, *Molodezh' i revoliutsiia*, 105.

81. GARF, f. 280, op. 1, d. 3017, l. 22 (Delo Otdeleniia po okhraneniiu obshchestvennoi bezopasnosti i poriadka v Moskve).
82. GARF, f. 1167, op. 4, d. 839, l. 1 (Obrashchenie sotsial-demokraticheskoi organizatsii seminaristov Chernigovskoi seminarii v Tsentral'nyi Komitet Seminarskogo Soiuza).
83. GARF, f. 280, op. 1, d. 3017, l. 56ob.
84. GARF, f. 280, op. 1, d. 3017, ll. 13ob., 74–74ob.
85. GARF, f. 280, op. 1, d. 3017, l. 16.
86. GARF, f. 280, op. 1, d. 3017, l. 16.
87. GARF, f. 280, op. 1, d. 3017, ll. 16ob.–17.
88. GARF, f. 280, op. 1, d. 3017, ll. 16ob.–17.
89. M. A. Adamov, "Stanovlenie i razvitie dukhovnykh seminarii Russkoi pravoslavnoi tserkvi XVIII–nachala XX vekov," *Nauchnye vedomosti* 7 (78), no. 14 (2010): 109.
90. GARF, f. 579, op. 1, d. 2665, l. 4 (Pis'ma P. N. Miliukovu ot vospitanikov Kurskoi, Tverskoi i Nizhegorodskoi dukhovnykh seminarii s pros'boi khodataistvovat' o dopuske seminaristov v universitet, 1908).
91. TsIAM, f. 234, op. 2, d. 384, ll. 55–57ob.
92. GARF, f. 280, op. 1, d. 3017, ll. 56ob.–57.
93. TsIAM, f. 234, op. 2, d. 384, ll. 67–67ob.
94. GARF, f. 280, op. 1, d. 3017, ll. 57–57ob.
95. GARF, f. 280, op. 1, d. 3017, ll. 57–57ob.; TsIAM, f. 234, op. 2, d. 384, l. 67.
96. TsIAM, f. 234, op. 2, d. 384, ll. 87ob.–90ob.
97. GARF, f. 280, op. 1, d. 3017, l. 59.
98. Mramornov, *Dukhovnaia seminariia*, 142–44.
99. GARF, f. 63, op. 31, d. 1127, l. 1 (O predpolagaemom s"ezde 28–30 avgusta 1911 g. seminaristov).
100. GARF, f. 280, op. 1, d. 3017, ll. 116–17.
101. Jennifer Hedda, *His Kingdom Come: Orthodox Pastorship and Social Activism in Revolutionary Russia* (DeKalb: Northern Illinois University Press, 2008), 183.
102. *Vsepoddanneishii otchet za 1905–1907 gody*, appendix, 156–59; *Vsepoddanneishii otchet Ober-prokurora Sviateishago sinoda po vedomstvu pravoslavnago ispovedaniia za 1914 god* (Petrograd: Sinodal'naia tipografiia, 1916), appendix, 68–71.
103. GATO, f. 160, op. 1, d. 34398, l. 7ob. (Svedeniia o sostoianii tserkvei i blagochinnikh okrugov Tverskoi Gub.).
104. GATO, f. 575, op. 1, d. 1299, l. 1 (Doklad pravleniia Tverskoi dukhovnoi seminarii).
105. GATO, f. 575, op. 1, d. 1299, l. 4.
106. GATO, f. 575, op. 1, d. 1299, l. 2ob.

CHAPTER 4. THE CHURCH AS A SCHOOL

1. Nikolai Ostrovskii, *Kak zakalialas' stal'*, accessed August 28, 2019, https://librebook.me/kak_zakalialas_stal/vol1/1.
2. TsGARKaz, f. 115, op. 1, d. 51, ll. 9–9ob. (S protokolami eparkhial'nogo komiteta, 1913).

3. "Tserkovno-prikhodskaia shkola pred Gosudarstvennoi Dumoi," *Moskovskie tserkovnye vedomosti*, March 5, 1906, 105–7.

4. Petr Zaionchkovskii, *Provedenie v zhizn' krest'anskoi reformy, 1861* (Moscow: Izd. Sotsial'no-ekonomicheskoi literaturoi, 1958), 47–49.

5. A. S. Prugavin, *Zaprosy naroda i obiazannosti intelligentsii v oblasti umstvennago razvitiia i prosveshcheniia* (Moscow: "Russkaia Mysl'," 1890), 35.

6. Quoted in Ben Eklof, *Russian Peasant Schools: Officialdom, Village Culture, and Popular Pedagogy, 1861–1914* (Los Angeles: University of California Press, 1986), 85.

7. Eklof, *Russian Peasant Schools*, 157.

8. See TsIAM, f. 203, op. 550, d. 11 (Delo ob utverzhdenii v dolzhnosti zakonouchitelei po Kolomenskomu uezdu); and TsIAM, f. 203, op. 550, d. 48 (Delo ob utverzhdenii v dolzhnosti zakonouchitelei po Moskovskomu uezdu).

9. TsIAM, f. 203, op. 550, d. 64, ll. 1–2 (Delo po prosheniiu psalomshchika Georgievskoi na Krasnoi gorke, tserkvi Protopopova o razreschenii ispolniat' obiazannost' pomoshchnika vospitatelia Lazarevskago Instituta).

10. TsIAM, f. 203, op. 550, d. 159, l. 20b. (Delo o nagrazhdenii Dmitrovskago uezda sela Deumina diakona Vasilia Izmailovskago).

11. Sviashchennik V. O., "Tserkovno-prikhodskaia shkola i zemstvo," *Moskovskie tserkovnye vedomosti*, January 27, 1902, 48.

12. *Istoricheskii ocherk razvitiia tserkovnykh shkol za istekshee dvadtsatipiatiletie (1884–1909)* (Saint Petersburg: Izd. Uchilishchnogo soveta pri Sviateishem Sinode, 1909), 493.

13. N. E. Svetlova, "K. P. Pobedonostsev i tserkovno-prikhodskie shkoly Rossii v nachale XX v.," *Vestnik PSTTU* 49 (2018): 61.

14. Gregory Freeze, *The Parish Clergy in Nineteenth-Century Russia: Crisis, Reform, Counter-Reform* (Princeton, NJ: Princeton University Press, 1983), 429.

15. T. G. Leont'eva, *Vera i progress: Pravoslavnoe sel'skoe dukhovenstvo Rossii vo vtoroi polovine XIX–nachale XX veka* (Moscow: Novyi khronograf, 2002), 106.

16. Eklof, *Russian Peasant Schools*, 162.

17. Quoted in Protoierei Vladimir Rozhkov, *Tserkovnye voprosy v Gosudarstvennoi Dume* (Moscow: Izd. Krutitskogo Podvor'ia, 2004), 123.

18. Leont'eva, *Vera i progress*, 96. Vladimir Fedorov gives an average figure of 1,500 parishioners in the early twentieth century: V. A. Fedorov *Russkaia pravoslavnaia tserkov' i gosudarstvo: Sinodal'nyi period, 1700–1917* (Moscow: Russkaia Panorama, 2003), 28.

19. Eklof, *Russian Peasant Schools*, 164.

20. *Istoricheskii ocherk razvitiia tserkovnykh shkol*, 533–34.

21. *Moskovskie tserkovnye vedomosti. Offitsial'nyi otdel*, November 25, 1901, 122. According to this report, seventy-nine teachers earned between 300 and 400 rubles a year, two hundred nine earned between 200 and 300, two hundred forty-three earned around 200, and seventy-eight earned between 180 and 60 rubles a year. Eighty-seven other teachers worked for free.

22. TsIAM, f. 203, op. 50, d. 239, l. 155 (Protokoly zasedanii obshcheeparkhial'nogo s"ezda blagochinnykh 1908 goda).

23. Gregory Freeze, *The Russian Levites: Parish Clergy in the Eighteenth Century* (Cambridge, MA: Harvard University Press, 1977), 144.

24. For a description of mutual aid among parish school teachers, see *Moskovskie tserkovnye vedomosti. Offitsial'nyi otdel*, December 8, 1902, 112.
25. TsIAM, f. 203, op. 50, d. 239, ll. 155–55ob.
26. TsIAM, f. 234, op. 2, d. 345, ll. 1–20ob. (Protokoly ispytaniia na zvanie uchitelei tserkovno-prikhodskoi shkoly, 1900–1905).
27. TsIAM, f. 234, op. 2, d. 345, ll. 3–195.
28. TsIAM, f. 234, op. 2, d. 401, l. 82ob. (Zhurnaly pedagogicheskikh sobranii za 1908 g.).
29. TsIAM, f. 234, op. 2, d. 401, l. 82ob.
30. TsIAM, f. 2375, op. 1, d. 4, ll. 1–97 (Formuliarnye spiski zakonouchitelei i uchitelei tserkovno-prikhodskikh shkol Bronnitskogo uezda, Moskovskoi eparkhii za 1906–7).
31. Eklof, *Russian Peasant Schools*, 536.
32. TsIAM, f. 203, op. 475, d. 14, ll. 63–64ob. (Prosheniia lits dukhovnogo zvaniia o naznachenii na sluzhbu).
33. *Moskovskie tserkovnye vedomosti. Offitsial'nyi otdel*, October 30, 1905, 413.
34. *Moskovskie tserkovnye vedomosti. Offitsial'nyi otdel*, February 5, 1901, 24.
35. *Moskovskie tserkovnye vedomosti. Offitsial'nyi otdel*, November 25, 1901, 122.
36. Freeze, *The Parish Clergy*, 309.
37. TsIAM, f. 203, op. 475, d. 14, l. 170.
38. O. D. Popova, *V stenakh konvikta—ocherki povsednevnoi zhizni zhenskikh eparkhial'nykh uchilishch* (Ryazan': Izdatel'stvo "Poverennyi," 2006), 25–32.
39. Popova, *V stenakh konvikta*, 34.
40. For an example of such a congress in Moscow, see TsIAM, f. 203, op. 550, d. 193, ll. 2–20ob. (Delo o vvedenii izmenenii v uchebnyi kurs dukhovnykh uchilishch Moskovskoi eparkhii).
41. "Kratkii ocherk deiatel'nosti Obshchestva vspomoshchestvovaniia nastoiashchim i byvshim vospitannitsam Moskovskago Filaretovskago eparkhial'nago zhenskago uchilishcha za 1-e desiatiletie ego sushchestvovaniia (1898–1908 g.)," *Moskovskie tserkovnye vedomosti*, May 24, 1908, 545.
42. Popova, *V stenakh konvikta*, 47.
43. Quoted in Popova, *V stenakh konvikta*, 56, from *Tserkovnye vedomosti*, no. 1, 1897.
44. Laurie Manchester, *Holy Fathers, Secular Sons: Clergy, Intelligentsia, and the Emergence of Modern Selfhood in Revolutionary Russia* (DeKalb: Northern Illinois University Press, 2008), 128.
45. Popova, *V stenakh konvikta*, 60.
46. *Vsepoddanneishii otchet Ober-prokurora Sviateishago sinoda po vedomstvu pravoslavnago ispovedaniia za 1903–1904 gody* (Saint Petersburg: Sinodal'naia tipografiia, 1909), appendix, 114–15.
47. Eklof, *Russian Peasant Schools*, 186–94.
48. Christine Ruane, "Divergent Discourses: The Image of the Russian Woman Schoolteacher in Post-Reform Russia," *Russian History* 20, nos. 1–4 (1993): 109–23.
49. Consistory records indicate that many female teachers shared the last name of the priest in charge of the parish school. TsIAM, f. 2375, op. 1, d. 3, ll. 96–440ob. (Staticheskiia svedeniia).

50. Ruane, "Divergent Discourses," 112.
51. For a description of such a class, see TsIAM, f. 2375, op. 1, d. 3, ll. 225–26.
52. TsIAM, f. 2375, op. 1, d. 3, ll. 22–226.
53. *Vsepoddanneishii otchet Ober-prokurora za 1903–1904 gody*, appendix, 126–29.
54. *Vsepoddanneishii otchet Ober-prokurora Sviateishago sinoda po vedomstvu pravoslavnago ispovedaniia za 1914 god* (Petrograd: Sinodal'naia tipografiia, 1916), appendix, 128–29.
55. Eklof, *Russian Peasant Schools*, 168.
56. GATO, f. 575, op. 1, d. 1541, l. 1270b. (Kashinskaia dukhovnaia seminariia. Spiski i svedeniia o vospitannikakh, prosheniia i perepiska po voprosam uchebnoi i vospitatel'noi raboty, svedeniia o semeinom i ekonomicheskom polozhenii sviashchennikov, d'iakonov, psalomshchikov).
57. Quoted in Rozhkov, *Tserkovnye voprosy*, 128.
58. For examples of such clerical contributions, see TsIAM, f. 2375, op. 1, d. 3, l. 112.
59. *Istoricheskii ocherk razvitiia tserkovnykh shkol*, 516.
60. GATO, f. 160, op. 1, d. 10308, ll. 1–13 (O vzyskanii sbora v pol'zu tserkovno-prikhodskikh shkol s shtatskikh diakonov—1904–6).
61. For fifty-one such nominations, see TsIAM, f. 203, op. 550, d. 267, ll. 1–90b. (Delo o sostavlenii spiskov lits dukhovnago zvaniia, predstavlennykh k nagradam—1908). For an example from the Tver' diocese, see GATO, f. 160, op. 1, d. 34474 (Khodataistva o nagrazhdenii tserkovnykh sluzhitelei po Tverskoi gubernii—1916).
62. TsIAM, f. 203, op. 551, d. 18, l. 470b. (Predstavleniia raznykh lits Moskovskomu i Kolomenskomu mitropolitu Vladimiru o nagrazhdenii sviashchennotserkovnosluzhitelei tserkvei Moskovskoi eparkhii).
63. A. Italinskii, *Iz zhizni tserkovno-prikhodskoi shkoly* (Moscow: Sinodal'naia tipografiia, 1906), 16–18.
64. *Istoricheskii ocherk razvitiia tserkovnykh shkol*, 515.
65. Leont'eva, *Vera i progress*, 110.
66. *Moskovskie tserkovnye vedomosti. Offitsial'nyi otdel*, January 21, 1901, 8.
67. In his obituary, one priest is described as an avid beekeeper. "Sviashchennik A. A. Lebedev (Nekrolog)," *Moskovskie tserkovnye vedomosti*, February 3, 1902, 68.
68. *Istoricheskii ocherk razvitiia tserkovnykh shkol*, 371–74.
69. Italinskii, *Iz zhizni*, 27–30.
70. *Istoricheskii ocherk razvitiia tserkovnykh shkol*, 401, 404.
71. Italinskii, *Iz zhizni*, 61.
72. *Moskovskie tserkovnye vedomosti. Offitsial'nyi otdel*, November 30, 1903, 94.
73. GATO, f. 160, op. 1, d. 34398, ll. 44–44ob. (Svedeniia o sostoianii tserkvei, 1906).
74. GATO, f. 160, op. 1, d. 34393, l. 36ob.
75. GATO, f. 160, op. 1, d. 34393, l. 36ob.
76. GATO, f. 160, op. 1, d. 34398, l. 14ob.
77. For the concept of the "internal mission," see John Strickland, *The Making of Holy Russia the Orthodox Church and Russian Nationalism before the Revolution* (Jordanville, NY: Holy Trinity Publications, 2013), 46–52.

78. "Metody i zadachi 'vnutrennei missii' pastyrei Tserkve v sovremennom russkom obshchestve," *Moskovskie tserkovnye vedomosti*, January 22, 1906, 28.

79. T. Barsov, *Sbornik deistvuiushchikh i rukovodstvennykh tserkovnykh i tserkovno-grazhdanskikh postanovlenii po vedomstvu pravoslavnago ispovedaniia* (Saint Petersburg: Sinodal'naia tipografiia, 1885), 259.

80. Barsov, *Sbornik postanovlenii*, 260.

81. GATO, f. 160, op. 1, d. 34398, l. 49.

82. GATO, f. 160, op. 1, d. 34398, l. 49.

83. *Istoricheskii ocherk razvitiia tserkovnykh shkol*, 407.

84. GATO, f. 160, op. 1, d. 34393, l. 93.

85. In 1903, Moscow's diocesan school inspector mentioned two priests by name and ridiculed their poor excuses for not holding readings. *Moskovskie tserkovnye vedomosti. Offitsial'nyi otdel*, January 26, 1903, 15.

86. GATO, f. 160, op. 1, d. 34393, l. 93.

87. "Okonchanie shestogo goda chtenii dlia rabochikh," *Moskovskie tserkovnye vedomosti*, May 31, 1908, 561.

88. Leont'eva estimates distances of six to twelve versts (four to eight miles) between rural parishes. Leont'eva, *Vera i progress*, 112.

89. TsIAM, f. 203, op. 542, d. 2, ll. 1–2 (Delo o razreshenii sviashchenniku Khristorozhdestvenskoi tserkvi osnovat' obshchestvo trezvosti, 1900). See also, TsIAM, f. 203, op. 542, d. 9 (Delo o razreshenii otkryt' obshchestvo trezvosti, 1900).

90. GATO, f. 160, op. 1, d. 10383, l. 6 (O prichislenii sluzhashchikh i rabochikh vagonostroitel'nago zavoda, zhivushchikh v slobode pri zavode v sostav prikhoda voennoi tserkvi 1-go leib dragunskago Moskovskago polka. 1905).

91. GATO, f. 160, op. 1, d. 10383, ll. 1–10b.

92. GATO, f. 160, op. 1, d. 34393, l. 73.

93. GATO, f. 160, op. 1, d. 34398, l. 11.

94. GATO, f. 160, op. 1, d. 34398, l. 130b.

95. GATO, f. 644, op. 1, d. 409, l. 1 (Zhurnaly soveta bratstva kniazia Mikhaila Iaroslavicha Tverskogo za 1900).

96. Italinskii, *Iz zhizni*, 37–38.

97. GATO, f. 160, op. 1, d. 34398, l. 200b. See also GATO, f. 160, op. 1, d. 34398, l. 320b.

98. GATO, f. 160, op. 1, d. 34398, l. 430b.

99. Eklof, *Russian Peasant Schools*, 155.

100. Rozhkov, *Tserkovnye voprosy*, 136.

101. Quoted in Rozhkov, *Tserkovnye voprosy*, 137.

102. See, for example, Thomas Sorenson, "Pobedonostsev's Parish Schools: A Bastion against Secularism," in *Religious and Secular Forces in Late Tsarist Russia: Essays in Honor of Donald W. Treadgold*, ed. Charles E. Timberlake (Seattle: University of Washington Press, 1992), 192. See also Orlando Figes, *A People's Tragedy: The Russian Revolution, 1891–1924* (New York: Penguin Books, 1998), 63.

103. Eklof, *Russian Peasant Schools*, 170.

104. Quoted in Rozhkov, *Tserkovnye voprosy*, 159.

105. Rozhkov, *Tserkovnye voprosy*, 132.

106. Charles Timberlake describes a case in 1874, when the school inspector closed down a school in Tver' gubernia for impiety, while the priest had made no such accusation. Charles Timberlake, "Tver Zemstvo's Technical School in Rzhev: A Case Study in the Dissemination of Revolutionary and Secular Ideas," in *Religious and Secular Forces in Late Tsarist Russia: Essays in Honor of Donald W. Treadgold*, ed. Charles Timberlake (Seattle: University of Washington Press, 1992).

107. N. V. K-vich, "Tserkovno-shkol'noe delo v Rossii," *Vestnik Evropy* 36, no. 5 (September 1901): 218–47.

108. Eklof, *Russian Peasant Schools*, 91–93.

109. Rozhkov, *Tserkovnye voprosy*, 128.

110. Leont'eva, *Vera i progress*, 112.

111. Eklof, *Russian Peasant Schools*, 174.

112. *Moskovskie tserkovnye vedomosti. Offitsial'nyi otdel*, November 8, 1914, 572.

113. "Iz Bronnitskago uezda: Otkrytie tserkovno-prikhodskoi shkoly," *Moskovskie tserkovnye vedomosti*, January 14, 1901, 22–23.

114. *Vsepoddanneishii otchet Ober-prokurora Sviateishago sinoda po vedomstvu pravoslavnago ispovedaniia za 1910 god* (Saint Petersburg: Sinodal'naia tipografiia, 1913), appendix, 110–15; *Vsepoddanneishii otchet za 1911–12 gody* (Saint Petersburg: Sinodal'naia tipografiia, 1913), appendix, 176–81.

115. *Vsepoddanneishii otchet Ober-prokurora Sviateishago sinoda po vedomstvu pravoslavnago ispovedaniia za 1913 god* (Saint Petersburg: Sinodal'naia tipografiia, 1915), appendix, 120–25; *Vsepoddanneishii otchet Ober-prokurora za 1914 god*, appendix, 122–27.

116. A. Troshin, *Moskovskii obshchezemskii s"ezd po narodnomu obrazovaniiu i tserkovnyia shkoly rossiiskoi imperii* (Saint Petersburg: Sinodal'naia tipografiia, 1911), 1–2.

117. Quoted in Sviashchennik N. Speranskii, "Otkrytoe pis'mo g.g. uchashchim zemskikh shkol Dmitrovskago uezda," *Moskovskie tserkovnye vedomosti*, June 12, 1905, 263.

118. Eklof, *Russian Peasant Schools*, 168.

119. Eklof, *Russian Peasant Schools*, 116–17.

120. Rozhkov, *Tserkovnye voprosy*, 185.

121. GATO, f. 160, op. 1, d. 34398, l. 70b.

122. GATO, f. 160, op. 1, d. 34398, l. 140b.

123. A. I. Mramornov, ed., *Sviashchennik A. P. Mramornov: Sochineniia 1896–1919 gg.* (Saratov: Nauchnaia Kniga, 2005), 31.

Chapter 5. The Parish Crisis

1. Sviashch. N. Vinogradov, "Ob ustroenii tserkovno-prikhodskoi zhizni," *Moskovskie tserkovnye vedomosti*, January 29, 1906, 46–47.

2. A. Beglov, "Prikhodskii vopros v istorii i v trudakh Sviashchennogo Sobora Pravoslavnoi Rossiiskoi Tserkvi 1917–1918 gg.," in *Dokumenty Sviashchennogo Sobora Pravoslavnoi Rossiiskoi Tserkvi, 1917–1918 godov: Protokoly zasedanii i materialy otdela o blagoustroenii prikhoda*, ed. A. Beglov (Moscow: Izd. Novospasskogo monastyria, 2017), 14:14–15.

3. Gregory Freeze, *The Parish Clergy in Nineteenth-Century Russia: Crisis, Reform, Counter-Reform* (Princeton, NJ: Princeton University Press, 1983), 289–91.

4. Gregory Freeze, *The Russian Levites: Parish Clergy in the Eighteenth Century* (Cambridge, MA: Harvard University Press, 1977), 148–50.

5. Beglov, "Prikhodskii vopros," 10.

6. A. Papkov, *Tserkovno-Obshchestvennye voprosy v epokhu tsaria-osvoboditelia (1855–1870)* (Saint Petersburg: Tip. A. P. Lopukhina, 1902), 165–66.

7. A. Beglov, "Kommentarii," in *Dokumenty Sviashchennogo Sobora Pravoslavnoi Rossiiskoi Tserkvi, 1917–1918 godov: Protokoly zasedanii i materialy otdela o blagoustroenii prikhoda*, ed. A. Beglov (Moscow: Izd. Novospasskogo monastyria, 2017), 14:750–51.

8. Quoted in A. Beglov, "'Obshchina, uchrezhdenie, bratstvo . . .': Poisk identichnosti pravoslavnogo prikhoda v proektakh i diskussiiakh kontsa XIX–nachala XX v.," *Dialog so vremenem: Al'manakh intellektual'noi istorii*, no. 48 (2014): 243.

9. Beglov, "'Obshchina, uchrezhdenie, bratstvo,'" 245.

10. Freeze, *The Parish Clergy*, 240.

11. Freeze, *The Parish Clergy*, 255.

12. T. Barsov, *Sbornik deistvuiushchikh i rukovodstvennykh tserkovnykh i tserkovnograzhdanskikh postanovlenii po vedomstvu pravoslavnago ispovedaniia* (Saint Petersburg: Sinodal'naia tipografiia, 1885), 384.

13. In 1864, only 5,327 out of 28,785 parishes had established trusteeships. Galina Ul'ianova, "Tserkovnoprikhodskie popechitel'stva kak strukturnaia edinitsa blagotvoritel'nosti vnutri mestnogo soobshchestva v pozdneimperskoi Rossii," in *Blagotvoritel'nost' v Rossii: Istoricheskie i sotsial'no-ekonomicheskie issledovaniia*, ed. B. V. Anan'ich, S. A. Basov, and V. M. Voronkov (Saint Petersburg: Izd. Novikova, 2004), 168.

14. Papkov, *Tserkovno-Obshchestvennye voprosy*, 149–50.

15. Freeze, *The Parish Clergy*, 294.

16. Vera Shevzov, *Russian Orthodoxy on the Eve of Revolution* (New York: Oxford University Press, 2004), 35.

17. TsIAM, f. 203, op. 550, d. 130, ll. 1–15 (Delo o poriadke rasprostraneniia sredi Moskovskoi gub. mer po preduprezhdeniiu epidemii kholery, 1908); GATO, f. 160, op. 1, d. 9075, ll. 1–5 (Delo po otnosheniiu Tverskogo Gubernatora, o naznachenii predstavitelia dlia uchastiia v zasedaniiakh Gubernskoi Sanitarno-Ispolnitel'noi Komissii, v vidu ob"iavleniia gubernii ugrozhaemoi po kholere, 1910).

18. "Ob utverzhdenii instruktsii nastoiateliam tserkvei," *Moskovskie tserkovnye vedomosti. Offitsial'nyi otdel*, August 19, 1901, 79–81.

19. GATO, f. 160, op. 1, d. 34393, ll. 9–90b. (Svedeniia o sostoianii tserkvei i blagochinnikh okrugov Tverskoi gub).

20. Papkov, *Tserkovno-Obshchestvennye voprosy*, 175.

21. A. Beglov, "Zemskie proekty pereustroistva pravoslavnogo prikhoda, 1860–1890," *Gosudarstvo, religiia, Tserkov' v Rossii i za rubezhom* 32, no. 1 (2014): 170–96.

22. T. G. Leont'eva, *Vera i progress: Pravoslavnoe sel'skoe dukhovenstvo Rossii vo vtoroi polovine XIX–nachale XX veka* (Moscow: Novyi khronograf, 2002), 105.

23. Quoted in Beglov, "Zemskie proekty pereustroistva," 189.

24. GATO, f. 160, op. 1, d. 9079, l. 20 (O zemskikh nalogakh).

25. TsIAM, f. 203, op. 551, d. 18, l. 34 (Predstavleniia raznykh lits Moskovskomu i Kolomenskomu Mitropolitu Vladimiru o nagrazhdenii sviashchennotserkovnosluzhitelei tserkvei Moskovskoi eparkhii. 1909).

26. Beglov, "Zemskie proekty pereustroistva," 189.
27. Beglov, "Zemskie proekty pereustroistva," 185–88.
28. "Ob oblozhenii tserkovnykh zemel' zemskimi sborami," *Pribavleniia k tserkovnym vedomostiam*, November 5, 1905, 1929–30.
29. Shevzov, *Orthodoxy on the Eve of Revolution*, 35–53.
30. Beglov, "'Obshchina, uchrezhdenie, bratstvo,'" 248.
31. For a study of peasant relations with the zemstvos, see Dorothy Atkinson, "The Zemstvo and the Peasantry," in *The Zemstvo in Russia: An Experiment in Local Self-Government*, ed. Terence Emmons and Wayne S. Vucinich (Cambridge: Cambridge University Press, 1982), 79–132.
32. A. Papkov, *Besedy o pravoslavnom prikhode* (Petrograd: Sinodal'naia tipografiia, 1917), 4.
33. Shevzov, *Orthodoxy on the Eve of Revolution*, 39.
34. A. Papkov, *Drevnerusskii prikhod: Kratkii ocherk tserkovno-prikhodskoi zhizni v Vostochnoi Rossii do XVIII v. i v Zapadnoi Rossii do XVII v.* (Sergiev Posad: 2-ia tip. A.I. Snegirevoi, 1897).
35. Papkov, *Besedy o pravoslavnom prikhode*, 20.
36. Papkov, *Besedy o pravoslavnom prikhode*, 14.
37. Shevzov, *Orthodoxy on the Eve of Revolution*, 35–45.
38. A. Polunov and I. Solov'ev, eds., *Otzyvy eparkhial'nykh arkhiereev po voprosu o tserkovnoi reforme* (Moscow: Obshchestvo Liubitelei Tserkovnoi Istorii, 2004), 2:385.
39. Polunov and Solov'ev, *Otzyvy eparkhial'nykh arkhiereev*, 2:385.
40. Polunov and Solov'ev, *Otzyvy eparkhial'nykh arkhiereev*, 2:385.
41. Papkov, *Tserkovno-Obshchestvennye voprosy*, 179.
42. GATO, f. 160, op. 1, d. 8820, l. 3 (Po prosheniiu prikhodskago popechitel'stva pri tserkvi sela Ivanovskago, Korchevskago uezda, ob ukreplenii za nim zemli).
43. GATO, f. 160, op. 1, d. 8820, l. 4.
44. Beglov, "Prikhodskii vopros," 33–42.
45. Protoierei Vladimir Rozhkov, *Tserkovnye voprosy v Gosudarstvennoi Dume* (Moscow: Izd. Krutitskogo Podvor'ia, 2004), 256–57.
46. Beglov, "Prikhodskii vopros," 44.
47. "Chto pishut o pastyrskom vozdeistvii na pasomykh," *Moskovskie tserkovnye vedomosti*, October 22, 1906, 592.
48. O. V. Kravchenko, "Tserkovnye bratstva: Istoriia i istoriografiia," in *Provintsial'noe dukhovenstvo dorevoliutsionnoi Rossii: Sbornik nauchnykh trudov vserossiiskoi zaochnoi konferentsii*, ed. T. G. Leont'eva (Tver': Slavianskii Mir, 2006), 248–49.
49. Quoted in Papkov, *Tserkovno-Obshchestvennye voprosy*, 75.
50. Papkov, *Tserkovno-Obshchestvennye voprosy*, 77–79.
51. GATO, f. 160, op. 1, d. 34393, ll. 1–157ob. (Svedeniia o sostoianii tserkvei i blagochinnikh okrugov Tverskoi Gub. 1905–06). See also GATO, f. 160, op. 1, d. 34398, ll. 1–119 (Svedeniia o sostoianii tserkvei i blagochinnikh okrugov Tverskoi Gub. 1906).
52. For example, see GATO, f. 160, op. 1, d. 34393, l. 114ob.
53. GATO, f. 160, op. 1, d. 34398, ll. 118–118ob.

54. "Popytka k ustroistvu popechitel'stva (iz vospominanii sel'skago sviashchennika. Prodolzhenie)," *Moskovskie tserkovnye vedomosti*, October 7, 1907, 1239.
55. For a discussion of religious observance in late imperial Russia, see M. M. Gromyko and A. V. Buganov, *O vozzreniiakh russkogo naroda* (Moscow: Palomnik, 2000).
56. For some examples, see TsIAM, f. 203, op. 550, d. 267, ll. 24–25, 27–35ob. (Delo o sostavlenii spiskov lits dukhovnago zvaniia, predstavlennykh k nagradam. 1908); TsIAM, f. 203, op. 551, d. 71, ll. 1–90b. (Delo o nagrazhdenii dukhovnykh lits za zaslugi po eparkhial'nomu vedomstvu, 1909); GATO, f. 160, op. 1, d. 34457, l. 2 (Khodataistva o nagrazhdenii dukhovnykh lits. 1914–1916).
57. This letter was included in the papers of Moscow's 1908 diocesan congress, where it was presumably discussed. TsIAM, f. 203, op. 550, d. 239, ll. 71–72 (Protokoly zasedanii obshcheeparkhial'nogo s"ezda blagochinnikh 1908 goda).
58. TsIAM, f. 203, op. 550, d. 267, l. 24.
59. GATO, f. 160, op. 1, d. 34398, ll. 44–44ob.
60. GATO, f. 160, op. 1, d. 34393, l. 22ob.
61. Patricia Herlihy, *The Alcoholic Empire: Vodka and Politics in Late Imperial Russia* (New York: Oxford University Press, 2002), 69–89.
62. For a full list of these regulations and activities, see GATO, f. 644, op. 1, d. 438, ll. 5–130b. (Delo ob otkrytii obshchestv trezvosti v Tverskoi gub).
63. GATO, f. 160, op. 1, d. 34398, l. 64ob.
64. GATO, f. 160, op. 1, d. 34398, l. 67.
65. GATO, f. 160, op. 1, d. 34398, l. 62ob.
66. GATO, f. 160, op. 1, d. 34398, l. 64ob.
67. For some membership statistics, see GATO, f. 160, op. 1, d. 34398, ll. 62, 67.
68. T. Barsov, *Sbornik deistvuiushchikh i rukovodstvennykh tserkovnykh i tserkovnograzhdanskikh postanovlenii po vedomstvu pravoslavnago ispovedaniia* (Saint Petersburg: Sinodal'naia tipografiia, 1885), 384; Freeze, *The Parish Clergy*, 253.
69. T. V. Pankrat, *Blagotvoritel'naia deiatel'nost' prikhodskikh popechitel'stv Moskvy, vtoraia polovina XIX–nachalo XX stoletiia* (Moscow: Izd. PSTGU, 2011), 29.
70. "Popytka k ustroistvu popechitel'stva (iz vospominanii sel'skago sviashchennika)," *Moskovskie tserkovnye vedomosti*, October 7, 1907, 1239–43.
71. "Iz g. Kolomny (Otkrytie tserkovno-prikhodskago popechitel'stva)," *Moskovskie tserkovnye vedomosti*, December 22–29, 1902, 619.
72. Gregory Freeze, "All Power to the Parish? The Problems and Politics of Church Reform in Late Imperial Russia," in *Social Identities in Revolutionary Russia*, ed. Madhavan K. Palat (New York: Palgrave Macmillan, 2001), 176.
73. In 1902, 19,450 out of 37,465 parishes had established trusteeships. Ul'ianova, "Tserkovnoprikhodskie popechitel'stva," 168.
74. Ul'ianova, "Tserkovnoprikhodskie popechitel'stva," 169.
75. Adele Lindenmeyr, *Poverty Is Not a Vice: Charity, Society, and the State in Imperial Russia* (Princeton, NJ: Princeton University Press, 1996), 54.
76. *Vsepoddanneishii otchet Ober-prokurora Sviateishago sinoda po vedomstvu pravoslavnago ispovedaniia za 1913 god* (Saint Petersburg: Sinodal'naia tipografiia, 1915), appendix, 16–19.

77. Boris Veselovskii, *Istoricheskii ocherk deiatel'nosti zemskikh uchrezhdenii Tverskoi gubernii, 1864–1913 gg.* (Tver': Tip. Gubernskago Zemstva, 1914), 400.

78. "Stranichka iz prikhodskoi zhizni," *Moskovskie tserkovnye vedomosti*, May 31, 1908, 567–68.

79. GATO, f. 160, op.1, d. 34393, l. 2.

80. TsIAM, f. 203, op. 545, d. 31, l. 47 (Delo o sbore svedenii o nalichii i deiatel'nosti tserkovnoprikhodskikh popechitel'stv. 1903–1904).

81. TsIAM, f. 203, op. 545, d. 31, l. 110.

82. GATO, f. 160, op. 1, d. 34393, l. 77.

83. "Doklad Ioanna Netsvetaeva," *Pribavleniia k tserkovnym vedomostiam*, May 31, 1908, 1006.

84. For example, the income for 1903 of one trusteeship in the city of Moscow was listed as follows: "Member dues—190 rubles. Rent collected from church land—150 rubles. Rent collected from apartments—583.33 rubles. Interest from invested capital—98.80 rubles. Taken from the collection box—20.48 rubles." See TsIAM, f. 203, op. 545, d. 31, l. 67.

85. TsIAM, f. 203, op. 545, d. 31, l. 230ob.

86. Ul'ianova, "Tserkovnoprikhodskie popechitel'stva," 173.

87. For example, see the large contributions by Moscow's urban clergymen, announced at Moscow's 1908 diocesan congress, to fund the clerical school system for the rest of the diocese. TsIAM, f. 203, op. 550, d. 239, l. 17 (Protokoly zasedanii obshcheeparkhial'nogo s"ezda blagochinnykh 1908 goda).

88. GATO, f. 160, op. 1, d. 34393, ll. 145–145ob.

89. See, for example, GATO, f. 160, op. 1, d. 34393, l. 21.

90. Pankrat, Blagotvoritel'naia deiatel'nost' prikhodskikh popechitel'stv, 36.

91. "Otchet o deiatel'nosti prikhodskago popechitel'stva o bednykh pri Moskovskoi Smolenskoi, na Arbate, tserkvi za g.g. 1900–1901," *Moskovskie tserkovnye vedomosti*, November 4, 1901, 539.

92. GATO, f. 160, op. 1, d. 34457, ll. 1–2 (Perepiska s popechitel'nym sovetom Novotorzhskoi Tetiukhinskoi bogadel'ni o prichislenii Tetiukhinskoi bogadel'ni k Novotorzhskoi Klimentovskoi tserkvi).

93. M. E. Grabko, *Deiatel'nost' Russkoi pravoslavnoi tserkvi v rabochei srede Moskovskoi gubernii v kontse XIX–nachale xx v.* (Moscow: Izd. PSTGU, 2017), 179.

94. TsIAM, f. 203, op. 545, d. 31, ll. 73–73ob.

95. Grabko, *Deiatel'nost' Russkoi pravoslavnoi tserkvi*, 184.

96. Grabko, *Deiatel'nost' Russkoi pravoslavnoi tserkvi*, 180–81.

97. These priorities were expressed in the charters of numerous parish trusteeships in Moscow. See Pankrat, *Blagotvoritel'naia deiatel'nost' prikhodskikh popechitel'stv*, 50.

98. GATO, f. 160, op. 1, d. 8807, l. 1 (Po proshenii moskovskikh meshchan Ivana Zaitseva i Evdokii Zhuravlevoi o pozhertvovanii imi Gosud. 4% renty v 1000 rublei v pol'zu bednykh prikhozhan tserkvi sela Krasnogo Kaliazinskogo uezda—1909).

99. In the same year, Tver' contained 221 trusteeships. See *Vsepoddanneishii otchet Ober-prokurora Sviateishago sinoda po vedomstvu pravoslavnago ispovedaniia za 1914 god* (Petrograd: Sinodal'naia tipografiia, 1916), appendix, 7.

100. Pankrat, *Blagotvoritel'naia deiatel'nost' prikhodskikh popechitel'stv*, 35.

101. For the number of parish churches, see *Vsepoddanneishii otchet Ober-prokurora za 1914 god*, appendix, 3.
102. "Opredeleniia Sviateishago Sinoda ot 18-go noiabria 1905 g., za no. 5900, po voprosu ob ustroenii tserkovno-prikhodskoi zhizni i pastyrskikh sobranii," *Tserkovnyia vedomosti*, November 26, 1905, 523–25, 524.
103. "Opredeleniia ot 18-go noiabria," 523–24.
104. "Opredeleniia ot 18-go noiabria," 523–24.
105. Freeze, "All Power to the Parish?," 182.
106. TsIAM, f. 203, op. 550, d. 239, l. 1420b.
107. TsIAM, f. 203, op. 551, d. 207, l. 8 (Ukaz Moskovskoi dukhovnoi konsistorii. 1909).
108. "Eparkhial'nyi s"ezd dukhovenstva," *Moskovskie tserkovnye vedomosti*, October 24, 1909, 746.
109. "O blagochinnicheskikh s"ezdakh," *Tverskie eparkhia'nye vedomost*, February 24, 1914, 137.
110. For example, see the community-focused goals of the members of one rural Moscow parish in their establishment of a parish soviet that attracted widespread participation in 1908. TsIAM, f. 203, op. 550, d. 244, ll. 1–20b. (Delo po prosheniiu sviashchennika Pokrovskoi, sela Teshilova, tserkvi, Dmitrovskago uezda, o razreshenii uchredit' pri oznachennoi tserkvi tserkovno-prikhodskoi sovet. 1908).
111. GATO, f. 886, op. 1, d. 30, ll. 1–26 (Otryvok iz prikhodnoi denezhnoi knigi o postuplenii na golodaiushchikh v pol'zu dukhovenstva i mirian denezhnykh summ).
112. "Protokoly s"ezda o.o. deputatov dukhovenstva Bezhetskago uchilishchnago okruga 4 iiunia 1914 goda," *Tverskie eparkhial'nye vedomosti, chast' offitsial'naia*, July 28, 1914, 528–30.
113. Those figures, in 1913, were 5,647,424.47 and 341,892,119.15 rubles, respectively. *Vsepoddanneishii otchet Ober-prokurora za 1913 god*, appendix, 46–49.
114. Freeze, *The Parish Clergy*, 290.
115. *Vsepoddanneishii otchet Ober-prokurora za 1913*, appendix, 16–19.
116. William Gleason, "The All-Russian Union of Zemstvos and World War I," in *The Zemstvo in Russia: an Experiment in Local Self-Government*, ed. Terence Emmons and Wayne S. Vucinich (Cambridge: Cambridge University Press, 1982), 365–78.
117. "Opredeleniia Sviateishago Sinoda. I. Ot 20 iiulia 1914 g. za No. 6502, Vysochaishii Manifest o voine s Germaniei," *Tserkovnye vedomosti*, July 26, 1914, 348–49.
118. "Opredeleniia Sviateishago Sinoda.," 349–50.
119. "Opredeleniia Sviateishago Sinoda," *Tserkovnyia vedomosti*, September 6, 1914, 423.
120. GATO, f. 160, op. 1, d. 34461, l. 128 (Otchety blagochinnykh ob okazanii pomoshchi sem'iam prizvannykh v armiiu. 1915).
121. GATO, f. 160, op. 1, d. 34461, l. 128.
122. GATO, f. 160, op. 1, d. 34461, l. 18.
123. GATO, f. 160, op. 1, d. 34461, l. 128.
124. For one such example, see GATO, f. 160, op. 1, d. 34461, l. 14.
125. Lindenmeyr, *Poverty Is Not a Vice*, 53.
126. GATO, f. 160, op. 1, d. 34461, l. 121.

127. GATO, f. 160, op. 1, d. 34461, ll. 61, 85, 1290b.
128. GATO, f. 160, op. 1, d. 34461, l. 121.
129. GATO, f. 160, op. 1, d. 34461, l. 1240b.
130. GATO, f. 160, op. 1, d. 34461, l. 1210b.
131. GATO, f. 160, op. 1, d. 34461, l. 5.
132. "Zhurnal zasedaniia Moskovskago Stolichnago Soveta o.o. Blagochinnykh," *Moskovskie tserkovnye vedomosti. Offitsial'nyi otdel*, August 15, 1914, 495–504.
133. Ioann Vostorgov, "Ot voenno-blagotvoritel'noi komissii Moskovskago dukhovenstva," *Moskovskie tserkovnye vedomosti*, September 6, 1914, 684.
134. "Zhurnal zasedaniia Moskovskago Stolichnago Soveta," 501.
135. "Zhurnal zasedaniia Moskovskago Stolichnago Soveta," 600.
136. "Uchrezhdeniia dukhovnago vedomstva v okazanii pomoshchi ranenym i bol'nym voinam i ikh semeistvam," *Pribavleniia k tserkovnym vedomostiam*, October 18, 1914, 1787–89.
137. This was the case in Tver' and Volynia, among other dioceses. See "Uchrezhdeniia dukhovnago vedomstva," 1717.
138. Students of the Mozhaisk ecclesiastical school, for example. See "Zhurnal No. 5. Moskovskago eparkhia'nago komiteta o bol'nykh i ranenykh voinakh," *Moskovskie tserkovnye vedomosti. Offitsial'nyi otdel*, December 5, 1914, 600.
139. See, for example, GATO, f. 160, op. 1, d. 34477, ll. 1–8 (Delo o naznachenii sviashchennika tserkvi sela Rogaleva Rzhevskago uezda, Nevskago v deistvuiushchuiu armiiu. 1916).
140. "Uchrezhdeniia dukhovnago vedomstva," 1788–89.
141. "Zhurnal zasedaniia Moskovskago Stolichnago Soveta," 497.
142. GATO, f. 160, op. 1, d. 34461, ll. 1–2, 61–85.
143. For a discussion of the comparative reactions to the war among the peasantry and the educated classes, see Leonid Heretz, *Russia on the Eve of Modernity: Popular Religion and Traditional Culture under the Last Tsars* (Cambridge: Cambridge University Press, 2008), 191–233.
144. Peter Gatrell, *Russia's First World War: A Social and Economic History* (London: Pearson Education Limited, 2005), 1–14, 169.
145. "Zhurnal zasedaniia Moskovskago Stolichnago Soveta," 501.
146. Patrick Brown, "The Orthodox Church in Revolutionary Cheliabinsk: Reform, Counter-Reform, and Popular Revolution in 1917," *Canadian Slavonic Papers* 59, nos. 1–2 (2017): 83.

Chapter 6. The Pastor as a Political Actor

1. Sergei Bulgakov, "Na vyborakh (Iz dnevnika)," *Russkaia mysl'*, no. 11 (1912): 187–88.
2. Catherine Evtuhov, *The Cross and the Sickle: Sergei Bulgakov and the Fate of Russian Religious Philosophy, 1890–1920* (Ithaca, NY: Cornell University Press, 1997), 112.
3. For discussions of clerical parties in Italy, Germany, and Austria, see Richard Webster, *The Cross and the Fasces: Christian Democracy in Italy* (Stanford, CA: Stanford University Press, 1960); Margaret Lavinia Anderson, *Windthorst: A Political Biography* (Oxford: Clarendon, 1981); and John Boyer, *Political Radicalism in Late Imperial Vienna:*

Origins of the Christian Social Movement, 1848–1897 (Chicago: University of Chicago Press, 1981).

4. David T. Koyzis, "Imaging God and His Kingdom: Eastern Orthodoxy's Iconic Political Ethic," *Review of Politics* 55, no. 2 (Spring 1993): 278.

5. John Strickland, *The Making of Holy Russia: The Orthodox Church and Russian Nationalism before the Revolution* (Jordanville, NY: Holy Trinity Publications, 2013), 32–34.

6. Protoierei Vladimir Rozhkov, *Tserkovnye voprosy v Gosudarstvennoi Dume* (Moscow: Izd. Krutitskogo Podvor'ia, 2004), 17–19.

7. M. A. Babkin, *Dukhovenstvo Russkoi pravoslavnoi tserkvi i sverzhenie monarkhii (nachalo XX v.–konets 1917 g.)* (Moscow: Gosudarstvennaia publichnaia istoricheskaia biblioteka Rossii, 2007), 75.

8. For an example of denied ordination because of political speech, see TsIAM, f. 203, op. 475, d. 1, ll. 1–9 (Delo ob otkaze naznachit' uchitelia Simonovskoi tserkovno-prikhodskoi shkoly Skvortsova N. sviashchennika). For an example of defrocking for "revolutionary activity," see TsIAM, f. 203, op. 475, d. 14, l. 245 (Prosheniia lits dukhovnogo zvaniia o naznachenii na sluzhbu).

9. See, for example, GATO, f. 160, op. 1, d. 10280, l. 1 (Sekretno. Po otnosheniiu direktora narodnykh uchilishch o litsakh udalennykh ot ispolneniia uchitel'skikh obiazannostei po politicheskoi neblagonadezhnosti. 1904).

10. "Eshche po povodu fel'etona 'Pervyi Den'," *Moskovskie tserkovnye vedomosti*, September 18, 1905, 398.

11. A. Stebler, "Posledniaia entsiklika papy L'va XIII-go," *Moskovskie tserkovnye vedomosti*, March 4, 1901, 105.

12. Ukaz, "O prednachertaniiakh k usovershenstvovaniiu gosudarstennogo poriadka," December 12, 1904, Sait Konstitutsii Rossiiskoi Federatsii, accessed June 10, 2020, https://constitution.garant.ru/history/act1600-1918/3080/.

13. Prot. Georgii Florovskii, *Puti russkago bogosloviia* (Paris: YMCA Press, 1983), 476.

14. James Cunningham, *A Vanquished Hope: The Movement for Church Renewal in Russia, 1905–1906* (Crestwood, NY: St. Vladimir's Seminary Press, 1981), 79.

15. M. E. Grabko, *Deiatel'nost' Russkoi pravoslavnoi tserkvi v rabochei srede Moskovskoi gubernii v kontse XIX–nachale XX v.* (Moscow: PSTGU, 2017), 40.

16. "O neobkhodimosti peremen v russkom tserkovnom upravlenii. Mnenie gruppy stolichnykh sviashchennikov," *Tserkovnyi vestnik*, no. 11 (March 1905): 321–25.

17. Ot gruppy Peterburgskikh sviashchennikov, "Gosudarsvennaia Duma i pastyr' tserkvi," *Pskovskie eparkhial'nye vedomosti*, December 15–31, 1905, 495.

18. Jennifer Hedda, *His Kingdom Come: Orthodox Pastorship and Social Activism in Revolutionary Russia* (DeKalb: Northern Illinois University Press, 2008), 183.

19. "Bog i Tsar'," *Moskovskie tserkovnye vedomosti*, February 12, 1906, 65–66.

20. Strickland, *The Making of Holy Russia*, xviii.

21. John H. M. Geekie, "The Church and Politics in Russia, 1905–1917: A Study of Political Behavior of Russian Orthodox Clergy in the Reign of Nicholas II" (PhD diss., University of East Anglica, 1976), 21.

22. Grabko, *Deiatel'nost' Russkoi pravoslavnoi tserkvi*, 63–64.

23. "K bogatym i bednym (Slovo Mitropolita Moskovskago Vladimira)," *Pribavleniia k tserkovnym vedomostiam*, December 24, 1905, 2277.
24. Babkin, *Dukhovenstvo Russkoi pravoslavnoi tserkvi*, 62.
25. "Pochva dlia ob"edineniia pravoslavnago dukhovenstva," *Moskovskie tserkovnye vedomosti*, February 12, 1906, 72.
26. "Pochva dlia ob"edineniia," 72.
27. "Pochva dlia ob"edineniia," 73.
28. V. Lisiunin, "Uchastie tambovskogo dukhovenstva v parlamentskikh vyborakh i deiatel'nosti Gosudarstvennoi dumy I–IV sozyvov (1906–1917)," *Vestnik Tambovskogo universiteta* 23, no. 174 (2018): 172.
29. Cunningham, *A Vanquished Hope*, 183. See also Babkin, *Dukhovenstvo Russkoi pravoslavnoi tserkvi*, 70.
30. Scott Kenworthy, *The Heart of Russia: Trinity-Sergius, Monasticism, and Society after 1825* (Washington, DC: Woodrow Wilson Center Press, 2010), 257; "Golos iz obiteli prepodobnago Sergiia po sluchaiu Manifesta 6 avgusta," *Moskovskie tserkovnye vedomosti*, September 4, 1905, 369–71.
31. RGIA, f. 796, op. 187, d. 775, l. 8 (K voprosu o tom, mogut li dukhovnye litsa vstupat' v chleny politicheskikh partii).
32. RGIA, f. 796, op. 187, d. 775, l. 9.
33. "Golos pastyrei k narodu," *Moskovskie tserkovnye vedomosti*, October 30, 1905, 456.
34. GATO, f. 160, op. 1, d. 34398, l. 49 (Svedeniia o sostoianii tserkvei i blagochinnikh okrugov Tverskoi Gub. 1906).
35. GATO, f. 160, op. 1, d. 34398, l. 86ob.
36. GATO, f. 160, op. 1, d. 34398, l. 86.
37. "Pochva dlia ob"edineniia pravoslavnago dukhovenstva," 73.
38. GATO, f. 160, op. 1, d. 34398, ll. 118–19.
39. In 1907, for example, there were 9 priests out of 183 electors on Tambov's assembly of the landowners' curia. Lisiunin, "Uchastie tambovskogo dukhovenstva," 174.
40. GATO, f. 160, op. 1, d. 34398, l. 118.
41. Argyrios Pisiotis, "Orthodoxy versus Autocracy" (PhD diss., Georgetown University, 2000), 335–60.
42. A notable exception was the Zealots for Church Renovation, a political association of priests and laymen that grew out of the Group of Thirty-Two Saint Petersburg Priests. See Hedda, *His Kingdom Come*, 160–75.
43. "Konstitutsionno-demokraticheskaia partiia i otnoshenie k nei dukhovenstva," *Moskovskie tserkovnye vedomosti*, April 23, 1906, 192. For other examples of invectives against clerical support for the Kadets, see "Iz inoeparkhial'noi zhizni: My ne poidem za vami!," *Moskovskie tserkovnye vedomosti*, May 21, 1906, 60; and "Obrashchenie k s"ezdu tambovskago dukhovenstva Preosviashchennago Innokentiia, Episkopa Tambovskago," *Pribavleniia k tserkovnym vedomostiam*, February 16, 1908, 305.
44. M. A. Davydov, V. A. Demin, N. A. Ivanova, and K. I. Mogilevskii, eds., *Rossiia nakanune velikikh potriasenii: Sotsial'no-ekonomicheskii atlas, 1906–1914* (Moscow: Kuchkovo pole, 2017), 108.
45. Pisiotis, "Orthodoxy versus Autocracy," 602.

46. For a discussion of the origins of the Kadet Party within this movement, see Shmuel Galai, *The Liberation Movement in Russia, 1900–1905* (Cambridge: Cambridge University Press, 1973).

47. Aleksandr Fedoseev, *Sviashchenniki v Gosudarstvennoi Dume Rossiiskoi Imperii, 1906–1917* (Moscow: "Strannik," 2019), 11.

48. Fedoseev, *Sviashchenniki v Gosudarstvennoi Dume*, 12.

49. Fedoseev, *Sviashchenniki v Gosudarstvennoi Dume*, 15.

50. RGIA, f. 796, op. 187, d. 775, ll. 11–12.

51. "Tsirkuliarnyi ukaz Sviateishego Sinoda ot 12 dekabria 1906 g., za No. 11, po povodu vyborov v Gosudarstvennuiu Dumu v 1907 godu," *Tserkovnye vedomosti*, December 16, 1906, 530–31.

52. Father Nikolai Gepetskii, "K svedeniiu dukhovenstva," *Tserkovnye vedomosti*, July 28, 1907, 1230–32; I. A. Vasil'ev, "Pravoslavnoe dukhovenstvo v II Gosudarstvennoi Dume Rossiiskoi imperii," *Vestnik Sankt-Peterburgskogo universiteta. Pravo*, no. 4 (2012): 4.

53. In 1917, as Exarch of Georgia, Platon would act as a representative of the hierarchy to the All-Russian Congress of Clergy and Laity in Moscow. See chapter 7.

54. The Trudoviks had split from the Socialist Revolutionaries in 1906, defying that party's boycott of the First Duma. The majority of Trudovik deputies were peasants.

55. Fedoseev, *Sviashchenniki v Gosudarstvennoi Dume*, 25–45. Pisiotis attributes slightly different party affiliations to these clerical deputies and omits Fedor Vladimirskii of Nizhni Novgorod, a Kadet Pisiotis, "Orthodoxy versus Autocracy," 604–5.

56. Mitropolit Evlogii, *Put' moei zhizni* (Moscow: Moskovskii rabochii, 1994), 164.

57. Pisiotis, "Orthodoxy versus Autocracy," 395.

58. Fedoseev, *Sviashchenniki v Gosudarstvennoi Dume*, 45.

59. Pisiotis, "Orthodoxy versus Autocracy," 397; Abraham Ascher, *The Revolution of 1905: Authority Restored* (Stanford, CA: Stanford University Press, 1992), 333–34.

60. Fedoseev, *Sviashchenniki v Gosudarstvennoi Dume*, 39.

61. Fedoseev, *Sviashchenniki v Gosudarstvennoi Dume*, 39.

62. See chapter 7.

63. Ascher, *Authority Restored*, 198–204.

64. Aileen Friesen, "Building an Orthodox Empire: Archpriest Ioann Vostorgov and Russian Missionary Aspirations in Asia," *Canadian Slavonic Papers* 57, nos. 1–2 (2015): 56–75.

65. Strickland, *The Making of Holy Russia*, 114–15.

66. Pisiotis, "Orthodoxy versus Autocracy," 411.

67. Pisiotis, "Orthodoxy versus Autocracy," 415.

68. Fedoseev, *Sviashchenniki v Gosudarstvennoi Dume*, 71; Pisiotis, "Orthodoxy versus Autocracy," 608–9.

69. Quoted in Lisiunin, "Uchastie tambovskogo dukhovenstva," 175.

70. Pisiotis, "Orthodoxy versus Autocracy," 608–9.

71. Fedoseev, *Sviashchenniki v Gosudarstvennoi Dume*, 71.

72. A. Volynets, "Tret'ia Gosudarstvennaia Duma i dukhovenstvo," *Tserkovnye vedomosti*, December 1, 1907, 2122.

73. Evlogii, *Put' moei zhizni*, 172.

74. For the annexation of Kholm, see Abraham Ascher, *P. A. Stolypin: The Search for Stability of Late Imperial Russia* (Stanford, CA: Stanford University Press, 2001), 320–22. All church issues debated in the Duma are outlined in Rozhkov, *Tserkovnye voprosy*.

75. Quoted in Paul W. Werth, *The Tsar's Foreign Faiths: Toleration and the Fate of Religious Freedom in Imperial Russia* (Oxford: Oxford University Press, 2014), 205.

76. Fedoseev, *Sviashchenniki v Gosudarstvennoi Dume*, 68–69; A. Volynets, "Gosudarstvennaia Duma i dukhovenstvo," *Tserkovnye vedomosti*, July 26, 1908, 1426.

77. Volynets, "Gosudarstvennaia Duma i dukhovenstvo," 1426.

78. I. A. Vasil'ev, "Pravoslavnoe dukhovenstvo v III Gosudarstvennoi Dume Rossiiskoi imperii," *Vestnik Sankt-Peterburgskogo universiteta. Pravo*, no. 1 (2013): 5.

79. For a full account of the "Naval Staffs crisis," which led to the disintegration of the Octobrist faction, see Geoffrey Hosking, *The Russian Constitutional Experiment: Government and Duma, 1907–1914* (Cambridge: Cambridge University Press, 1973), 74–105.

80. Hosking, *The Russian Constitutional Experiment*, 245.

81. For a complete account of the attempts to legislate freedom of conscience in the Duma era, see Werth, *The Tsar's Foreign Faiths*, 207–44.

82. Daniel Scarborough, "Missionaries of Official Orthodoxy," in *Religious Freedom in Modern Russia*, ed. Randall Poole and Paul Werth (Pittsburgh, PA: University of Pittsburgh Press, 2018), 142–59.

83. TsIAM, f. 1381, op. 1, d. 9, ll. 6–11 (Doklady i pis'ma v eparkhial'nom missionerskom sovete).

84. TsIAM, f. 1381, op. 1, d. 11, l. 20b. (Donesenie Moskovskago uezdnago missionera Alekseia Zvereva Moskovskomu eparkhial'nomu protivosektantskomu misssioneru).

85. By 1912, the clerical estate made up 0.4 percent of the empire's population. *Rossiia nakanune velikikh potriasenii*, 57.

86. Pisiotis, "Orthodoxy versus Autocracy," 421–22.

87. Lisiunin, "Uchastie tambovskogo dukhovenstva," 176.

88. Ioann Vostorgov, "Gosudarstvennaia Duma i pravoslavno-russkaia Tserkov'," *Moskovskie tserkovnye vedomosti*, June 25, 1906, 163.

89. Rozhkov, *Tserkovnye voprosy*, 135.

90. Evlogii, *Put' moei zhizni*, 179.

91. Rozhkov, *Tserkovnye voprosy*, 136.

92. Vasil'ev, "Pravoslavnoe dukhovenstvo v III Gosudarstvennoi Dume Rossiiskoi imperii," 4.

93. Prot. I. Vostorgov, "Novyi vybornyi zakon i dukhovenstvo," *Moskovskie tserkovnye vedomosti*, July 8, 1907, 856.

94. Vostorgov, "Novyi vybornyi zakon," 856.

95. Vostorgov, "Novyi vybornyi zakon," 858–60.

96. Walter Laqueur, *Black Hundred: The Rise of the Extreme Right in Russia* (New York: Edward Burlingame Books, 1993), 7–14.

97. Strickland, *The Making of Holy Russia*, 141–42.

98. Pisiotis, "Orthodoxy versus Autocracy," 400.

99. TsIAM, f. 1381, op. 1, d. 10, l. 13 (Pis'ma Moskovskoi dukhovnoi konsistorii).

100. Pisiotis, "Orthodoxy versus Autocracy," 521.
101. Pisiotis, "Orthodoxy versus Autocracy," 532.
102. RGIA, f. 796, op. 187, d. 775, ll. 18–19.
103. RGIA, f. 796, op. 187, d. 775, l. 20.
104. TsIAM, f. 203, op. 551, d. 71, l. 2 (Delo o nagrazhdenii dukhovnykh lits za zaslugi po eparkhial'nomu vedomstvu).
105. "K otkrytiiu Semirechenskago Preobrazhenskago otdela Soiuza russkago naroda," *Turkestanskie eparkhial'nye vedomosti*, January 1, 1910, 10.
106. Fedoseev, *Sviashchenniki v Gosudarstvennoi Dume*, 100–101.
107. Fedoseev, *Sviashchenniki v Gosudarstvennoi Dume*, 523–25.
108. Quoted in Evtuhov, *The Cross and the Sickle*, 119.
109. Hans Rogger, "Was There a Russian Fascism? The Union of Russian People," *Journal of Modern History* 36, no. 4 (December 1964): 408.
110. Evlogii, *Put' moei zhizni*, 213.
111. Sviashch. Vvedenskii, "K voprosu o moskovskikh trapeznikakh i prosfornitsakh," *Moskovskie tserkovnye vedomosti*, March 4, 1907, 329.
112. Geekie, "The Church and Politics in Russia," 71.
113. Gregory Freeze, *The Parish Clergy in Nineteenth-Century Russia: Crisis, Reform, Counter-Reform* (Princeton, NJ: Princeton University Press, 1983), 473.

CHAPTER 7. REVOLUTION IN THE CHURCH

1. Mitropolit Evlogii, *Put' moei zhizni* (Moscow: Moskovskii rabochii, 1994), 264.
2. Evlogii, *Put' moei zhizni*, 264.
3. P. G. Rogoznyi, *Tserkovnaia revoliutsiia 1917 goda: Vysshee dukhovenstvo Rossiiskoi Tserkvi v bor'be za vlast' v eparkhiiakh posle Fevral'skoi revoliutsii* (Saint Petersburg: "Liki Rossii," 2008), 139.
4. RGIA, f. 796, op. 204, d. 122 (Po telegrammu upolnomochennykh sel'skago skhoda s. Mechislavki Baltskago uezda ob udalenii Sviashchennika Mel'nitskago i psalomshchika Marchenko i naznachenii novuiu); RGIA, f. 796, op. 204, d. 133 (Po Prosheniiu prikhozhan tserkvi sela Kuz'kina, ob udalenii iz ikh prikhoda Sviashchennika Leonida Malinovskago).
5. RGIA, f. 796, op. 204, d. 202 (O samovol'nom udalenii prikhozhanami tserkovnykh starost Spasskoi tserkvi s. Khokhla, Nizhnedevitskago uezda). This report to the ober-procurator from May 10, 1917, describes two such cases.
6. For an examination of the congresses in Tobol'sk and Nizhni Novgorod, see Catherine Evtuhov, "The Church's Revolutionary Moment: Diocesan Congresses and Grassroots Politics in 1917," in *Russian Culture in War and Revolution, 1914–22*, ed. Murray Frame, Boris Kolonitskii, Steven G. Marks, and Melissa K. Stockdale, book 1, *Popular Culture, the Arts, and Institutions* (Bloomington, IN: Slavica Publishers, 2014), 377–402.
7. Rogoznyi, *Tserkovnaia revoliutsiia*, 214–15.
8. RGIA, f. 796, op. 204, d. 154, l. 730b. (Po povodu postanovleniia Tverskogo eparkhial'nogo s"ezda ob udalenii arkhiepiskopa Serafima).
9. Staritsa's monastery was home to Russia's first patriarch, Iov.

10. Scott Kenworthy, "Canon Law," in *The Supplement to the Modern Encyclopedia of Russian, Soviet, and Eurasian History*, ed. Bruce F. Adams (Gulf Breeze, FL: Academic International Press, 2004), 5:91–96.

11. L. V. Moshkova, "Sozdanie novykh tipov Kormchikh na vostochnoslavianskikh zemliakh v XV–XVI vekakh," in *Kormchaia kniga: Ot rukopisnoi traditsii k pervomu pechatnomu izdaniiu*, ed. E. V. Beliakova, L. V. Moshkova, and T. A. Oparina (Moscow: Tsentr gumanitarnykh initsiativ, 2017), 92–106.

12. Gregory Freeze, "Bringing Order to the Russian Family: Marriage and Divorce in Imperial Russia, 1760–1860," *Journal of Modern History* 62, no. 4 (December 1990): 709–46.

13. Gregory Freeze, *The Russian Levites: Parish Clergy in the Eighteenth Century* (Cambridge, MA: Harvard University Press, 1977), 72.

14. Gregory Freeze, *The Parish Clergy in Nineteenth-Century Russia: Crisis, Reform, Counter-Reform* (Princeton, NJ: Princeton University Press, 1983), 27.

15. John D. Basil, *Church and State in Late Imperial Russia: Critics of the Synodal System of Church Government (1861–1914)* (Minneapolis: University of Minnesota Press, 2005), 10.

16. Paul Valliere, *Conciliarism: A History of Decision-Making in the Church* (New York: Cambridge University Press, 2012), 7.

17. As Hyacinthe Destivelle explains, the term was unique to Slavonic Orthodoxy, as the original Greek Καθολικῆς does not carry the same connotation. Hyacinthe Destivelle, O. P., *The Moscow Council (1917–1918): The Creation of the Conciliar Institutions of the Russian Orthodox Church*, ed. and trans. Jerry Ryan (Notre Dame, IN: University of Notre Dame Press, 2015), 18–19.

18. George T. Kosar, "Russian Orthodoxy in Crisis and Revolution: The Church Council of 1917–1918" (PhD diss., Brandeis University, 2003), 10–11.

19. Basil, *Church and State*, 35–36.
20. Igumen Savva (Tutunov), *Eparkhial'nye reformy* (Moscow: "Nauka," 2011), 81.
21. Savva, *Eparkhial'nye reformy*, 80.
22. Destivelle, *The Moscow Council*, 38.
23. Savva, *Eparkhial'nye reformy*, 80.
24. Kosar, "Russian Orthodoxy in Crisis and Revolution," 36.
25. N. A. Zaozerskii, *O tserkovnoi vlasti: Osnovopolozheniia, kharakter i sposoby primeneniia tserkovnoi vlasti v razlichnykh formakh ustroistva tserkvi po ucheniiu pravoslavno-kanonicheskago prava* (Sergiev Posad: 2-ia tipografiia A.I. Snegirevoi, 1894), 3–4.
26. Zaozerskii, *O tserkovnoi vlasti*, 21.
27. Zaozerskii, *O tserkovnoi vlasti*, ix.
28. Zaozerskii, *O tserkovnoi vlasti*, xi–xii.
29. Zaozerskii, *O tserkovnoi vlasti*, 195.
30. Zaozerskii, *O tserkovnoi vlasti*, 201.
31. Zaozerskii, *O tserkovnoi vlasti*, 215.
32. Zaozerskii, *O tserkovnoi vlasti*, 216–18.
33. Vasilii Bogoiavlenskii, *Eparkhial'nye s"ezdy dukhovenstva: Ikh deiatel'nost' i znachenie. Sochinenie kandidata bogosloviia sviashchennika Vasilliia Bogoiavlenskogo* (Bezplatnoe prilozhenie k Omskim eparkhial'nym vedomostiam za 1902 g.), 3.

34. Bogoiavlenskii, *Eparkhial'nye s"ezdy dukhovenstva*, 11–12.
35. Bogoiavlenskii, *Eparkhial'nye s"ezdy dukhovenstva*, 111.
36. John H. M. Geekie, "The Church and Politics in Russia, 1905–1917: A Study of Political Behavior of Russian Orthodox Clergy in the Reign of Nicholas II" (PhD diss., University of East Anglia, 1976), 62.
37. V. Beliaev, A. Viktorov, and M. Mansurov, *Eparkhial'nye s"ezdy. Sbornik deistvuiushchikh zakonopolozhenii ob eparkhia'nykh s"ezdakh. Ikh praktika za 1903–1907 gg. Predstoiashchaia reforma s"ezdov. Prilozheniia* (Saint Petersburg: "Bereg," 1908), 26.
38. Rogoznyi, *Tserkovnaia revoliutsiia*, 157–60.
39. Jennifer Hedda, *His Kingdom Come: Orthodox Pastorship and Social Activism in Revolutionary Russia* (DeKalb: Northern Illinois University Press, 2008), 154–60.
40. Destivelle, *The Moscow Council*, 22–23.
41. Savva, *Eparkhial'nye reformy*, 83–85.
42. Destivelle, *The Moscow Council*, 35–37.
43. Quoted in Savva, *Eparkhial'nye reformy*, 81.
44. Scott Kenworthy, "Russian Reformation? The Program for Religious Renovation in the Orthodox Church, 1922–1925," *Modern Greek Studies Yearbook* 16/17 (2000/2001): 94, 100.
45. Quoted in Geekie, "The Church and Politics in Russia," 61.
46. Destivelle, *The Moscow Council*, 46–47.
47. Evlogii, *Put' moei zhizni*, 267.
48. GATO, f. 64, op. 1, d. 236, ll. 1–10b. (Predpisanie Tverskogo Arkhiepiskopa Serafima blagochinnym o nepravil'nom ispolnenii imi obrashcheniia arkhipiskopa ob otkrytii prikhodskikh sovetov, 1914).
49. Rogoznyi, *Tserkovnaia revoliutsiia*, 99.
50. RGIA, f. 796, op. 204, d. 154, l. 72a.
51. RGIA, f. 796, op. 204, d. 154, l. 74ob.
52. RGIA, f. 796, op. 204, d. 154, ll. 73a–74a.
53. RGIA, f. 796, op. 204, d. 154, l. 71aob.
54. RGIA, f. 796, op. 204, d. 154, l. 19ob.
55. RGIA, f. 796, op. 204, d. 154, ll. 38–38ob.
56. RGIA, f. 796, op. 204, d. 154, l. 16.
57. RGIA, f. 796, op. 204, d. 154, l. 69ob.
58. RGIA, f. 796, op. 204, d. 154, l. 65.
59. RGIA, f. 796, op. 204, d. 154, ll. 59–60.
60. RGIA, f. 796, op. 204, d. 154, l. 16.
61. RGIA, f. 796, op. 204, d. 154, ll. 55, 59.
62. RGIA, f. 796, op. 204, d. 154, l. 75a.
63. GATO, f. 160, op. 1, d. 34398, l. 43ob. (Svedeniia o sostoianii tserkvei i blagochinnikh okrugov Tverskoi Gub., 1906); GATO, f. 160, op. 1, d. 10188, ll. 1–3ob. (Delo o razdele bratskikh dokhodov mezhdu chlenami prichta sela Gubina-Ugla, Korchevskago Uezda, 1903).
64. RGIA, f. 796, op. 204, d. 154, l. 21.
65. RGIA, f. 796, op. 204, d. 154, l. 38.
66. RGIA, f. 796, op. 204, d. 154, l. 62.

67. RGIA, f. 796, op. 204, d. 154, l. 63.
68. RGIA, f. 796, op. 204, d. 154, l. 21.
69. Kosar, "Russian Orthodoxy in Crisis and Revolution," 53.
70. RGIA, f. 796, op. 204, d. 154, l. 72aob.
71. RGIA, f. 796, op. 204, d. 154, l. 72aob.
72. RGIA, f. 796, op. 204, d. 154, l. 72aob.
73. RGIA, f. 796, op. 204, d. 154, l. 75ob.
74. RGIA, f. 796, op. 204, d. 154, l. 19ob.
75. RGIA, f. 796, op. 204, d. 154, l. 3.
76. RGIA, f. 796, op. 204, d. 154, l.o, 72a.
77. RGIA, f. 796, op. 204, d. 154, ll. 74a–74aob.
78. RGIA, f. 796, op. 204, d. 154, l. 6.
79. RGIA, f. 796, op. 204, d. 154, ll. 72aob.–73a.
80. While the name of this administrative body could be translated as "diocesan council," the term "soviet" more accurately conveys its revolutionary context.
81. RGIA, f. 796, op. 204, d. 154, ll. 73aob.–74a.
82. RGIA, f. 796, op. 204, d. 154, ll. 26–27.
83. RGIA, f. 796, op. 204, d. 154, l. 34.
84. RGIA, f. 796, op. 204, d. 154, ll. 17–17ob.
85. RGIA, f. 796, op. 204, d. 154, l. 36.
86. RGIA, f. 796, op. 204, d. 154, l. 39.
87. RGIA, f. 796, op. 204, d. 154, l. 35ob.
88. RGIA, f. 796, op. 204, d. 154, ll. 46–48.
89. GATO, f. 64, op. 1, d. 126, l. 52 (Ukazy iz sinoda Tverskomu arkhiepiskopu, 1917).
90. RGIA, f. 796, op. 204, d. 154, l. 69ob.
91. RGIA, f. 796, op. 204, d. 154, l. 69ob.
92. RGIA, f. 796, op. 204, d. 154, l. 69.
93. RGIA, f. 796, op. 204, d. 154, ll. 73–73ob.
94. RGIA, f. 796, op. 204, d. 154, l. 74.
95. Georgii Florovskii would later refer to these brotherhoods as a prime example of Orthodox *sobornost'*. Georgii Florovskii, *Puti russkago bogosloviia*, 3rd ed. (Paris: YMCA Press, 1983), 38.
96. RGIA, f. 796, op. 204, d. 154, ll. 75–75ob.
97. RGIA, f. 796, op. 204, d. 154, l. 75ob.
98. RGIA, f. 796, op. 204, d. 154, l. 76.
99. RGIA, f. 796, op. 204, d. 154, l. 77.
100. RGIA, f. 796, op. 204, d. 154, ll. 105–112.
101. RGIA, f. 796, op. 204, d. 154, l. 116.
102. RGIA, f. 796, op. 204, d. 154, l. 104.
103. Rogoznyi, *Tserkovnaia revoliutsiia*, 107.
104. K. I. Sokolov, *Plamia nad Volgoi: Krest'ianskie vosstaniia i vystupleniia v Tverskoi gubernii v kontse 1917–1922 gg.* (Moscow: Tsentrpoligraf, 2017), 12.
105. Gregory Freeze, "All Power to the Parish? The Problems and Politics of Church Reform in Late Imperial Russia," in *Social Identities in Revolutionary Russia*, ed. Madhavan K. Palat (New York: Palgrave Macmillan, 2001), 174–208.

106. Rogoznyi, *Tserkovnaia revoliutsiia*, 65–66.
107. "Proshenie v Moskovskuiu dukhovnuiu konsistoriiu 10 blagochinnykh Moskvy, 24 marta 1917 g.," in *Rossiiskoe dukhovenstvo i sverzhenie monarkhii v 1917 godu: Materialy i arkhivnye dokumenty po istorii Russkoi Pravoslavnoi Tserkvi, ed. M. A. Babkin*, 2nd ed. (Moscow: Izd. "Inark," 2008), 482–83.
108. RGIA, f. 796, op. 204, d. 72, l. 9 (Ob uvol'nenii Mitropolita Moskovskago Makariia na pokoi).
109. Rogoznyi, *Tserkovnaia revoliutsiia*, 65.
110. Sergei Golubtsov, *Moskovskoe dukhovenstvo v preddverii i nachale gonenii, 1917–1922* (Moscow: Izd-vo Pravoslavnogo bratstva Sporuchnitsy greshnykh, 1999), 33.
111. RGIA, f. 796, op. 204, d. 72, ll. 1–20b.
112. RGIA, f. 796, op. 204, d. 72, l. 6.
113. Golubtsov, *Moskovskoe dukhovenstvo*, 32–33.
114. RGIA, f. 796, op. 204, d. 72, l. 1.
115. RGIA, f. 796, op. 204, d. 72, ll. 6–70b.
116. RGIA, f. 796, op. 204, d. 72, l. 60b.
117. RGIA, f. 796, op. 204, d. 72, ll. 8–180b.
118. RGIA, f. 796, op. 204, d. 72, ll. 21–40.
119. RGIA, f. 796, op. 204, d. 72, l. 9.
120. "Iz opredeleniia Sv. sinoda No. 2668 'O privlechenii dukhovenstva i pastvy k bole aktivnomu uchastiiu v tserkovnom upravlenii,'" in *Rossiiskoe dukhovenstvo i sverzhenie monarkhii v 1917 godu: Materialy i arkhivnye dokumenty po istorii Russkoi Pravoslavnoi Tserkvi*, 2nd ed., ed. M. A. Babkin (Moscow: Izd. "Inark," 2008), 47–48.
121. "Obshchie pravila ob izbranii eparkhial'nykh episkopov," in *Eparkhial'nye reform*, by Igumen Savva (Tutunov) (Moscow: "Nauka," 2011), 398–400.
122. Savva, *Eparkhial'nye reformy*, 258.
123. Golubtsov, *Moskovskoe dukhovenstvo*, 34.
124. Golubtsov, *Moskovskoe dukhovenstvo*, 19.
125. RGIA, f. 796, op. 204, d. 72, l. 9. The Soviet-era church historian Protodeacon Sergei Golubtsov credits Tsvetkov with initiating the congress. Golubtsov, *Moskovskoe dukhovenstvo*, 19.
126. "Vserossiiskii s"ezd dukhovenstva i mirian," *Moskovskii tserkovnyi golos*, June 14, 1917, 2.
127. "Vserossiiskii s"ezd dukhovenstva i mirian," 3.
128. "Vserossiiskii s"ezd dukhovenstva i mirian," 10.
129. "'Deklaratsiia' Vserossiiskogo s"ezda pravoslavnogo dukhovenstva i mirian," in *Rossiiskoe dukhovenstvo i sverzhenie monarkhii v 1917 godu: Materialy i arkhivnye dokumenty po istorii Russkoi Pravoslavnoi Tserkvi*, 2nd ed., ed. M. A. Babkin (Moscow: Izd. "Inark," 2008), 186.
130. "Vserossiiskii s"ezd dukhovenstva i mirian," 6–7.
131. Savva, *Eparkhial'nye reformy*, 267.
132. "Vserossiiskii s"ezd dukhovenstva i mirian," 6.
133. "Vserossiiskii s"ezd dukhovenstva i mirian," 5.
134. "Vserossiiskii s"ezd dukhovenstva i mirian," 4.
135. "Vserossiiskii s"ezd dukhovenstva i mirian," 4.

136. Golubtsov, *Moskovskoe dukhovenstvo*, 22.
137. Quoted in Kosar, "Russian Orthodoxy in Crisis and Revolution," 27.
138. "Vserossiiskii s"ezd dukhovenstva i mirian," 7.
139. "Vserossiiskii s"ezd dukhovenstva i mirian," 2.
140. This process is described in "Po povodu rabot Organizatsionnago Komiteta po voprosu ob izbranii budushchago mitropolita Moskovskago," *Moskovskii tserkovnyi golos*, June 4, 1917, 1–4.
141. "Izbranie pervosviatitelia tserkvi Moskovskoi," *Moskovskii tserkovnyi golos*, July 5, 1917, 3.
142. "Po povodu rabot Organizatsionnago Komiteta," 1–2.
143. "Po povodu rabot Organizatsionnago Komiteta," 1.
144. In Petrograd, by contrast, all delegates had been elected in the parishes, producing a diocesan congress of about 1,600 on May 21. The Synod adopted the three-stage procedure developed in Moscow. See Savva, *Eparkhial'nye reformy*, 277–79.
145. This list is presented in "Po povodu rabot Organizatsionnago Komiteta," 2–4.
146. Golubtsov, *Moskovskoe dukhovenstvo*, 19.
147. Golubtsov, *Moskovskoe dukhovenstvo*, 34.
148. Rogoznyi, *Tserkovnaia revoliutsiia*, 172, 191.
149. "Izbranie pervosviatitelia tserkvi Moskovskoi," 3.
150. Fr. S. Friazinov, "Preds"ezdnye dumy," *Moskovskii tserkovnyi golos*, July 14, 1917, 3.
151. Prot. N. Tsvetkov, "Sobranie ob"edinennago dukhovenstva i mirian," *Moskovskii tserkovnyi golos*, June 29, 1917, 2.
152. Friazinov, "Preds"ezdnye dumy," 3.
153. Friazinov, "Preds"ezdnye dumy," 3.
154. "Izbranie pervosviatitelia tserkvi Moskovskoi," 4.
155. The Cathedral of Christ the Savior would be demolished in December 1931.
156. "Izbranie pervosviatitelia tserkvi Moskovskoi," 4.
157. Alexander Rentel, "A Comparison of the Liturgical Rite of Ordination and the Canonical Act of Deposition," *St. Vladimir's Theological Quarterly* 55, no. 1 (2011): 48.
158. Rentel, "A Comparison of the Liturgical Rite," 48.
159. "Ukaz iz sinoda vremenno upravliaiushchemu moskovskoi eparkhiei episkopu Ioasafu ob utverzhdenii arkhiepiskopa Tikhona na Moskovskoi Kafedre (23 iiunia 1917 g.)," in *Pravoslavnaia Moskva v 1917–1921 godakh: Sbornik dokumentov i materialov*, ed. A. N. Kazakevich (Moscow: Izd. Glavarkhiva Moskvy, 2004).
160. Savva, *Eparkhial'nye reformy*, 281–83.
161. Destivelle, *The Moscow Council*, 53–58.
162. Tikhon worked to calm tensions between delegates who were in extreme disagreement. "S Sobora," *Moskovskii tserkovnyi golos*, October 19, 1917, 2.
163. Kosar, "Russian Orthodoxy in Crisis and Revolution," 106.
164. Destivelle, *The Moscow Council*, 206.
165. Sergei Firsov, *Russkaia Tserkov' nakanune peremen: Konets 1890-kh–1918 gg.* (Moscow: Dukhovnaia biblioteka, 2002), 541–42.
166. Destivelle, *The Moscow Council*, 192.

167. Valliere, *Conciliarism*, 11–12.
168. Quoted in Evtuhov, "The Church's Revolutionary Moment," 386.

CONCLUSION

1. Paul Valliere, *Modern Russian Theology: Bukharev, Soloviev, Bulgakov: Orthodoxy in a New Key* (Grand Rapids, MI: William B. Eerdmans, 2000), 19–106.

2. A notable exception was the priest and scholar Aleksandr Ivantsov-Platonov, whose 1882 work on church governance discussed the importance of conciliar participation in parish life and diocesan administration to support charity, education, and moral development. Aleksandr Ivantsov-Platonov, *O russkom tserkovnom upravlenii* (Saint Petersburg: Tip. A.A. Porokhovshchikova, 1898).

3. P. V. Znamenskii, "Sviashchennik A. V. Gumilevskii, osnovatel' prikhodskoi blagotvoritel'nosti v S.-Peterburge," *Pribavleniia k tserkovnym vedomostiam*, December 10, 1905, 2193–98.

4. "Sviashchennik V. V. Bulgakov (Nekrolog)," *Moskovskie tserkovnye vedomosti*, February 11, 1901, 74–75.

5. "Milost' telesnaia s znacheniem dukhovnym," *Moskovskie tserkovnye vedomosti*, May 6, 1901, 225–26.

6. "O vnutrennei missii," *Moskovskie tserkovnye vedomosti*, September 1, 1902, 564.

7. "Doklad Ioanna Netsvetaeva," *Pribavleniia k tserkovnym vedomostiam*, May 31, 1908, 1006.

8. Alison K. Smith, *For the Common Good and Their Own Well-Being: Social Estates in Imperial Russia* (New York: Oxford University Press, 2015), 151.

9. John Meyendorff, *The Vision of Unity* (Crestwood, NY: St. Vladimir's Seminar Press, 1987), 113–18; Cyril Hovorun, "Conciliarity and the Holy and Great Council," in *Synodality: A Forgotten and Misapprehended Vision: Reflections on the Holy and Great Council 2016*, ed. Maksim Vasiljević and Andrej Jeftic (Alhambra, CA: Sebastian Press, 2017), 81–98.

10. Boris Chicherin, *Filosofiia prava* (Moscow: Tipo-litografiia Tovarishshestva I.N. Kushnerev i Ko, 1900), 286.

11. Laura Engelstein, *Slavophile Empire: Imperial Russia's Illiberal Path* (Ithaca, NY: Cornell University Press, 2009), 79–80.

12. For a Soviet study of the incorporation of cooperative associations into the Soviet state, see B. B. Kabanov, *Oktiabr'skaia revoliutsiia i kooperatsiia (1917–mart 1919)* (Moscow: Nauka, 1973).

13. "Ob otdelenii tserkvi ot gosudarstva i shkoly ot tserkvi: Dekret soveta narodnykh Komissarov, 23 iavaria, 1918," in *O religii i tserkvi: Sbornik vyskazyvanii klassikov Marksizma-Leninizma, dokumentov KPSS i sovetskogo gosudarstva*, ed. A. M. Zalesskii and T. G. Kupchenia (Minsk: Politizdat, 1983), 79.

14. Altaev, "Idoly," *Bednota*, April 20, 1918, 4.

15. For a catalog of Orthodox victims of the Soviet regime, see the database compiled by Saint Tikhon's Orthodox University in Moscow, accessed April 4, 2021, http://213.171.53.29/bin/code.exe/frames/m/ind_oem.html/charset/ans?notextdecor.

16. Anatolii Levitin and Vadim Shavrov, *Ocherki po istorii russkoi tserkovnoi smuty* (Küsnacht, Switzerland: Institut Glaube in der 2. Welt, 1977), 49.

17. Anna Uriadova, *Golod 1920-x gg. v Rossii i russkoe zarubezh'e* (Saint Petersburg: Aleteiia, 2010), 65.
18. Levitin and Shavrov, *Ocherki po istorii russkoi tserkovnoi smuty*, 76.
19. Arto Luukkanen, *The Party of Unbelief: The Religious Policy of The Bolshevik Party 1917–1929* (Helsinki: Studia Historica, 1994), 103–15.
20. A. Vvedenskii, N. Syrenskii, M. Sergeeva, and V. Belousov, "Obrashchenie Petrogradskogo Mitropolita Veniamina i delegatsii ot dukhovenstva i mirian Petrogradskoi eparkhii k tov. Zinov'evu," *Petrogradskaia pravda*, September 18, 1919, 2.
21. Levitin and Shavrov, *Ocherki po istorii russkoi tserkovnoi smuty*, 54.
22. A. A., "Mozhet li kommunist byt' veruiushchim," *Petrogradskaia pravda*, January 7, 1920, 5.
23. Levitin and Shavrov, *Ocherki po istorii russkoi tserkovnoi smuty*, 64.
24. Levitin and Shavrov, *Ocherki po istorii russkoi tserkovnoi smuty*, 83.
25. Edward Roslof, *Red Priests* (Bloomington: Indiana University Press, 2002), 53–59.
26. Levitin and Shavrov, *Ocherki po istorii russkoi tserkovnoi smuty*, 90–91.
27. Roslof, *Red Priests*, 60–61, 167–90.
28. A. L., "Sud nad tserkovnikami," *Bednota*, January 27, 1920, 3.
29. Gregory Freeze, "Counter-Reformation in Russian Orthodoxy: Popular Response to Religious Innovation, 1922–1925," *Slavic Review* 54, no. 2 (Summer 1995): 305–39; Liliia A. Kleimenova, "Sozdanie v Turkestanskoi eparkhii pravoslavnogo bratstva i soiuza prikhodov kak otvet tserkvi na goneniia 1918 i 1923 godov," in *Pravoslavnye bratstva v istorii Rossii k 100-letiiu vozzvaniia patriarkha Tikhona ob obrazovanii dukhovnykh soiuzov: Sbornik nauchnykh trudov*, ed. Iuliia Balakshina and Sergei Smirnov (Moscow: Preobrazhenie, 2018), 1:135–57.

SELECTED BIBLIOGRAPHY

Primary Sources
Archival Material

The Russian State Historical Archive (RGIA, Rossiiskii gosudarstvennyi istoricheskii arkhiv)
    Fond 796, Archive of the Chancellery of the Holy Synod

The State Archive of the Russian Federation (GARF, Gosudarstvennyi arkhiv Rossiiskoi Federatsii)
    Fond 63, Archive of the Department of Public Security and Order in Moscow
    Fond 124, Archive of the Penal Sections of the First Department of the Ministry of Justice
    Fond 280, Archive of Moscow's Central Regional Security Department
    Fond 579, Archive of Pavel Nikolaevich Miliukov
    Fond 1167, Archive of Evidence Acquired by Gendarme Institutions during Searches of Publications, Newspapers, and Individuals

The Central State Historical Archive of the City of Moscow (TsIAM, Tsentral'nyi istoricheskii arkhiv goroda Moskvy)
    Fond 203, Archive of the Moscow Diocesan Consistory
    Fond 234, Archive of Moscow Seminary
    Fond 431, Archive of the Moscow Diocesan Committee for the Provision of Aid to Victims of the Disorders of December, 1905, in the City of Moscow
    Fond 1381, Archive of the Moscow Missionary Council
    Fond 1408, Archive of the Holy Pokrovskoe Orthodox Brotherhood of the City of Sokolov, Sedletsk Gubernia
    Fond 1794, Archive of the Brotherhood of Holy Sergei
    Fond 2171, Archive of the Moscow Diocesan Committee for the Provision of Aid to the Hungry, 1906–8
    Fond 2375, Archive of the Bronnitsy District Branch of the Moscow Diocesan School Council of the Cyril and Methodius Orthodox Brotherhood

The State Archive of Tver' Oblast (GATO, Gosudarstvenyi arkhiv Tverskoi oblasti)
  Fond 64, Archive of the Chancellery of the Archbishop of Tver'
  Fond 160, Archive of the Tver' Diocesan Consistory
  Fond 318, Archive of the Tver' Diocesan Trusteeship for Poor Clergy
  Fond 575, Archive of Tver' Seminary
  Fond 644, Archive of the Council of the Tver' Orthodox Brotherhood of Prince Mikhail Iaroslavich Tverskoi
  Fond 886, Archive of the Tver' Diocesan Committee for the Collection of Donations for Victims of the Famine of 1891–92
The Central State Archive of the Republic of Kazakhstan (TsGARKaz, Tsentral'nyi gosudarstvennyi arkhiv respubliki Kazakhstan)
  Fond 115, Archive of the Turkestan Diocesan Committee for the Organization of Church Life for Settlers
  Fond 358, Archive of the Superintendents of the Churches of the City of Verny
  Fond 369, Archive of the Akmolinsk Oblast Administration of the Ministry of Internal Affairs

Periodicals

Bednota
Moskovskie tserkovnye vedomosti
Moskovskii tserkovnyi golos
Petrogradskaia pravda
Pravoslavnoe obozrenie
Pribavleniia k tserkovnym vedomostiam
Pskovskie eparkhial'nye vedomosti
Tserkovnye vedomosti
Tserkovnyi vestnik
Turkestanskie eparkhial'nye vedomosti
Tverskie eparkhial'nye vedomosti
Vestnik Evropy

Published Sources

Barsov, T. *Sbornik deistvuiushchikh i rukovodstvennykh tserkovnykh i tserkovno-grazhdanskikh postanovlenii po vedomstvu pravoslavnago ispovedaniia*. Saint Petersburg: Sinodal'naia tipografiia, 1885.

Begovatov, D. A., and T. G. Leont'eva, eds. *Iz istorii provintsial'nogo dukhovenstva: Zapiski sviashchennika V. F. Vladislavleva*. Tver': "SFK-ofis," 2012.

Beliaev, V., A. Viktorov, and M. Mansurov. *Eparkhial'nye s"ezdy. Sbornik deistvuiushchikh zakonopolozhenii ob eparkhial'nykh s"ezdakh. Ikh praktika za 1903–1907 gg. Predstoiashchaia reforma s"ezdov. Prilozheniia*. Saint Petersburg: "Bereg," 1908.

Belliustin, Ioann S. *Description of the Clergy in Rural Russia: The Memoir of a Nineteenth-Century Parish Priest*. Translated by Gregory L. Freeze. Ithaca, NY: Cornell University Press, 1992.

Bogoiavlenskii, Fr. Vasilii. *Eparkhial'nye s"ezdy dukhovenstva: Ikh deiatel'nost' i znachenie. Sochinenie kandidata bogosloviia sviashchennika Vasilliia Bogoiavlenskogo*. Bezplatnoe prilozhenie k *Omskim eparkhial'nym vedomostiam* za 1902 g.

Burlaka, D. K., ed. *K. P. Pobedonostsev, pro et contra: Lichnost', obshchestvenno-politicheskaia deiatel'nost' i mirovozzrenie Konstantina Pobedonostseva v otsenke russkikh myslitelei i issledovatelei. Antologiia.* Saint Petersburg: Izd. Russkogo Khristianskogo gumanitarnogo instituta, 1996.

Chekhov, A. P. *Izbrannye proizvedeniia: Rasskazy i povesti.* Moscow: Gos. Izd. Khudozhestvennoi literatury, 1960.

Chicherin, Boris. *Filosofiia prava.* Moscow: Tipo-litografiia Tovarishshestva I.N. Kushnerev i Ko, 1900.

Evlogii, Mitropolit. *Put' moei zhizni.* Moscow: Moskovskii rabochii, 1994.

Goldfrank, David, ed. and trans. *The Monastic Rule of Iosif Volotsky.* Rev. ed. Kalamazoo, MI: Cistercian Publications, 2000.

Istoricheskii ocherk razvitiia tserkovnykh shkol za istekshee dvadtsatipiatiletie (1884–1909). Saint Petersburg: Izd. Uchilishchnogo Soveta pri Sviateishem Sinode, 1909.

Italinskii, A. *Iz zhizni tserkovno-prikhodskoi shkoly.* Moscow: Sinodal'naia tipografiia, 1906.

Ivantsov-Platonov, Aleksandr. *O russkom tserkovnom upravlenii.* Saint Petersburg: Tip. A.A. Porokhovshchikova, 1898.

Kazakevich, A. N., ed. *Pravoslavnaia Moskva v 1917–1921 godakh: Sbornik dokumentov i materialov.* Moscow: Izd. Glavarkhiva Moskvy, 2004.

Koialovich, Mikhail. *Litovskaia tserkovnaia uniia.* 2 vols. Saint Petersburg: Strannik, 1861.

Kolosov, V. *Istoriia Tverskoi dukhovnoi seminarii: Ko dniu 150-letniago iubileia seminarii.* Tver': Tipografiia Gubernskago Pravleniia, 1889.

Martov, I. *Obshchestvennoe dvizhenie.* Saint Petersburg: tip. t-va "Obshestv. pol'za," 1909.

Mramornov, A. I., ed. *Sviashchennik A. P. Mramornov: Sochineniia 1896–1919 gg.* Saratov: Nauchnaia Kniga, 2005.

Nardova, Valeriia. *Gorodskoe samoupravlenie v Rossii v 60-kh–nachale 90-kh godov XIX v.* Leningrad: Nauka, 1984.

"Ob otdelenii tserkvi ot gosudarstva i shkoly ot tserkvi: Dekret soveta narodnykh Komissarov, 23 iavaria, 1918." In *O religii i tserkvi: Sbornik vyskazyvanii klassikov Marksizma-Leninizma, dokumentov KPSS i sovetskogo gosudarstva,* edited by A. M. Zalesskii and T. G. Kupchenia, 79. Minsk: Politizdat, 1983.

Obzor deiatel'nosti vedomstva pravoslavnogo ispovedaniia za vremia tsarstvovaniia imperatora Aleksandra III. Saint Petersburg: Sinodal'naia tipografiia, 1901.

Papkov, A. *Besedy o pravoslavnom prikhode.* Petrograd: Sinodal'naia tipografiia, 1917.

———. *Drevnerusskii prikhod: Kratkii ocherk tserkovno-prikhodskoi zhizni v Vostochnoi Rossii do XVIII v. i v Zapadnoi Rossii do XVII v.* Sergiev Posad: 2-ia tip. A.I. Snegirevoi, 1897.

———. *Tserkovno-Obshchestvennye voprosy v epokhu tsaria-osvoboditelia (1855–1870).* Saint Petersburg: Tip. A. P. Lopukhina, 1902.

———. *Tserkovnyia bratstva: Kratkii statisticheskii ocherk o polozhenii tserkovnykh bratstv k nachalu 1893 goda.* Saint Petersburg: Sinodal'naia tipografiia, 1893.

Poluvekovoi iubilei Obshchestva Liubitelei Dukhovnago Prosveshcheniia. Moscow: Pechatnia A.I. Snegirevoi, 1913.

Polunov, A., and I. Solov'ev, eds. *Otzyny eparkhial'nykh arkhiereev po voprosu o tserkovnoi reforme*. 2 vols. Moscow: Obshchestvo Liubitelei Tserkovnoi Istorii, 2004.
"Proshenie v Moskovskuiu dukhovnuiu konsistoriiu 10 blagochinnykh Moskvy, 24 marta 1917 g." In *Rossiiskoe dukhovenstvo i sverzhenie monarkhii v 1917 godu: Materialy i arkhivnye dokumenty po istorii Russkoi Pravoslavnoi Tserkvi*, 2nd ed., edited by M. A. Babkin, 482–83. Moscow: Izd. "Inark," 2008.
Prugavin, A. S. *Zaprosy naroda i obiazannosti intelligentsii v oblasti umstvennago razvitiia i prosveshcheniia*. Moscow: "Russkaia Mysl'," 1890.
Svod otchetov fabrichnykh inspektorov za 1909 g. Saint Petersburg: Tipografia V.F. Kirshbauma, 1910.
Titlinov, B. V. *Molodezh' i revoliutsiia, 1860–1905*. Leningrad: Gosudarstvennoe izdatel'stvo, 1925.
Troshin, A. *Moskovskii obshchezemskii s"ezd po narodnomu obrazovaniiu i tserkovnyia shkoly rossiiskoi imperii*. Saint Petersburg: Sinodal'naia tipografiia, 1911.
Veselovskii, Boris. *Istoricheskii ocherk deiatel'nosti zemskikh uchrezhdenii Tverskoi gubernii, 1864–1913 gg*. Tver': Tip. Gubernskago Zemstva, 1914
Vsepoddanneishii otchet Ober-prokurora Sviateishago sinoda po vedomstvu pravoslavnago ispovedaniia za 1890–1891 gody. Saint Petersburg: Sinodal'naia tipografiia, 1893.
Vsepoddanneishii otchet Ober-prokurora Sviateishago sinoda po vedomstvu pravoslavnago ispovedaniia za 1892–1893 gody. Saint Petersburg: Sinodal'naia tipografiia, 1894.
Vsepoddanneishii otchet Ober-prokurora Sviateishago sinoda po vedomstvu pravoslavnago ispovedaniia za 1902 god. Saint Petersburg: Sinodal'naia tipografiia, 1905.
Vsepoddanneishii otchet Ober-prokurora Sviateishago sinoda po vedomstvu pravoslavnago ispovedaniia za 1903–1904 gody. Saint Petersburg: Sinodal'naia tipografiia, 1909.
Vsepoddanneishii otchet Ober-prokurora Sviateishago sinoda po vedomstvu pravoslavnago ispovedaniia za 1905–1907 gody. Saint Petersburg: Sinodal'naia tipografiia, 1910.
Vsepoddanneishii otchet Ober-prokurora Sviateishago sinoda po vedomstvu pravoslavnago ispovedaniia za 1908–1909 gody. Saint Petersburg: Sinodal'naia tipografiia, 1911.
Vsepoddanneishii otchet Ober-prokurora Sviateishago sinoda po vedomstvu pravoslavnago ispovedaniia za 1910 god. Saint Petersburg: Sinodal'naia tipografiia, 1913.
Vsepoddanneishii otchet Ober-prokurora Sviateishago sinoda po vedomstvu pravoslavnago ispovedaniia za 1911–12 gody. Saint Petersburg: Sinodal'naia tipografiia, 1913.
Vsepoddanneishii otchet Ober-prokurora Sviateishago sinoda po vedomstvu pravoslavnago ispovedaniia za 1913 god. Petrograd: Sinodal'naia tipografiia, 1915.
Vsepoddanneishii otchet Ober-prokurora Sviateishago Sinoda po vedomstvu pravoslavnago ispovedaniia za 1914 god. Petrograd: Sinodal'naia tipografiia, 1916.
Wallace, Sir Donald Mackenzie. *Russia on the Eve of War and Revolution*. Edited by Cyril E. Black. Princeton, NJ: Princeton University Press, 1961.
Zaozerskii, N. A. *O tserkovnoi vlasti: Osnovopolozheniia, kharakter i sposoby primeneniia tserkovnoi vlasti v razlichnykh formakh ustroistva tserkvi po ucheniiu pravoslavno-kanonicheskago prava*. Sergiev Posad: 2-ia tipografiia A.I. Snegirevoi, 1894.

Secondary Works

Adamov, M. A. "Stanovlenie i razvitie dukhovnykh seminarii Russkoi pravoslavnoi tserkvi XVIII–nachala XX vekov." *Nauchnye vedomosti* 7 (78), no. 14 (2010): 103–10.

Selected Bibliography

Alekseeva, S. I. *Sviateishii Sinod v sisteme vysshikh i tsentral'nykh gosudarstvennykh uchrezhdenii poreformennoi Rossii, 1856–1904.* Saint Petersburg: "Nauka," 2006.
Anderson, Benedict. *Imagined Communities: Reflections on the Origin and Spread of Nationalism.* London: Verso, 1983.
Anderson, Margaret Lavinia. "The Limits of Secularization: On the Problem of the Catholic Revival in Nineteenth-Century Germany." *Historical Journal* 38, no. 3 (September 1995): 647–70.
——. *Windthorst: A Political Biography.* Oxford: Clarendon, 1981.
Asad, Talal. *Genealogies of Religion: Discipline and Reasons of Power in Christianity and Islam.* Baltimore: Johns Hopkins University Press, 1993.
——. "The Idea of an Anthropology of Islam." *Qui Parle* 17, no. 2 (Spring/Summer 2009): 1–30.
——. "Religion as an Anthropological Category." In *Genealogies of Religion: Discipline and Reasons of Power in Christianity and Islam*, 27–54. Baltimore: Johns Hopkins University Press, 1993.
Ascher, Abraham. *P. A. Stolypin: The Search for Stability of Late Imperial Russia.* Stanford, CA: Stanford University Press, 2001.
——. *The Revolution of 1905: Authority Restored.* Stanford, CA: Stanford University Press, 1992.
——. *The Revolution of 1905: Russia in Disarray.* Stanford, CA: Stanford University Press, 1988.
Atkinson, Dorothy. "The Zemstvo and the Peasantry." In *The Zemstvo in Russia: An Experiment in Local Self-Government*, edited by Terence Emmons and Wayne S. Vucinich, 79–132. Cambridge: Cambridge University Press, 1982.
Babkin, M. A. *Dukhovenstvo Russkoi pravoslavnoi tserkvi i sverzhenie monarkhii (nachalo XX v.–konets 1917 g.).* Moscow: Gosudarstvennaia publichnaia istoricheskaia biblioteka Rossii, 2007.
Ballor, Jordan J., ed. *Makers of Modern Christian Social Thought: Leo XIII and Abraham Kuyper on the Social Question.* Grand Rapids, MI: Action Institute, 2016.
Balmuth, Daniel. "Origins of the Russian Press Reform of 1864." *Slavonic and East European Review* 47, no. 109 (July 1969): 369–88.
Balzer, Harley, ed. *Russia's Missing Middle Class: The Professions in Russian History.* New York: M. E. Sharpe, 1996.
Basil, John D. *Church and State in Late Imperial Russia: Critics of the Synodal System of Church Government (1861–1914).* Minneapolis: University of Minnesota Press, 2005.
Beglov, A. "'Obshchina, uchrezhdenie, bratstvo . . .': Poisk identichnosti pravoslavnogo prikhoda v proektakh i diskussiiakh kontsa XIX–nachala XX v." *Dialog so vremenem: Al'manakh intellektual'noi istorii*, no. 48 (2014): 241–64.
——. "Prikhodskii vopros v istorii i v trudakh Sviashchennogo Sobora Pravoslavnoi Rossiiskoi Tserkvi 1917–1918 gg." In *Dokumenty Sviashchennogo Sobora Pravoslavnoi Rossiiskoi Tserkvi, 1917–1918 godov: Protokoly zasedanii i materialy otdela o blagoustroenii prikhoda*, edited by A. Beglov, 5–81. Moscow: Izd. Novospasskogo monastyria, 2017.
——. "Zemskie proekty pereustroistva pravoslavnogo prikhoda, 1860–1890." *Gosudarstvo, religiia, Tserkov' v Rossii i za rubezhom* 32, no. 1 (2014): 170–96.

Belonogova, Iu. I. "Material'noe obespechenie tserkvei v XIX–nachale XX v. na primere khramov Volokolamskogo blagochiniia Moskovskoi eparkhiiю." *Vestnik PSTGU* 79 (2017): 54–78.

Berger, Peter L. "The Desecularization of the World: A Global Overview." In *The Desecularization of the World: Resurgent Religion and World Politics*, edited by Peter L. Berger, 1–18. Washington, DC: Eerdmans/Ethics and Public Policy Center, 1999.

Berman, Sheri. "Civil Society and the Collapse of the Weimar Republic." *World Politics* 9, no. 3 (April 1997): 401–29.

Bogolepov, A. A. "Church Reforms in Russia, 1905–1918." *St. Vladimir's Quarterly* 10 (1966): 44–66.

Bonnell, Victoria E. *Roots of Rebellion: Workers' Politics and Organizations in St. Petersburg and Moscow, 1900–1914*. Berkeley: University of California Press, 1999.

Bowman, Matthew. "Sin, Spirituality, and Primitivism: The Theologies of the American Social Gospel, 1885–1917." *Religion and American Culture: A Journal of Interpretation* 17, no. 1 (Winter 2007): 95–126.

Bowman, William D. *Priest and Parish in Vienna, 1780 to 1880*. Boston: Humanities Press, 1999.

Boyer, John. *Political Radicalism in Late Imperial Vienna: Origins of the Christian Social Movement, 1848–1897*. Chicago: University of Chicago Press, 1981.

Bradley, Joseph. *Voluntary Associations in Tsarist Russia: Science, Patriotism, and Civil Society*. Cambridge, MA: Harvard University Press, 2009.

Burbank, Jane. *Russian Peasants Go to Court: Legal Culture in the Countryside, 1905–1917*. Bloomington: Indiana University Press, 2004.

Canton, Steven C. "What Is an 'Authorizing Discourse?'" In *Powers of the Secular Modern: Talal Asad and His Interlocutors*, edited by David Scott and Charles Hirschkind, 31–56. Stanford, CA: Stanford University Press, 2006.

Casanova, José. *Public Religions in the Modern World*. Chicago: University of Chicago Press, 1994.

Chambers, Simone, and Jeffrey Kopstein. "Bad Civil Society." *Political Theory* 29, no. 6 (December 2001): 837–65.

Constantelos, Demetrios J. *Byzantine Philanthropy and Social Welfare*. New Brunswick, NJ: Rutgers University Press, 1968.

———. *Poverty, Society and Philanthropy in the Late Mediaeval Greek World*. New York: Aristide D. Caratzas, 1992.

Cunningham, James. *A Vanquished Hope*. Crestwood, NY: St. Vladimir's Seminary Press, 1981.

Davydov, M. A., V. A. Demin, N. A. Ivanova, and K. I. Mogilevskii, eds. *Rossiia nakanune velikikh potriasenii: Sotsial'no-ekonomicheskii atlas, 1906–1914*. Moscow: Kuchkovo pole, 2017.

Destivelle, Hyacinthe, O. P. *The Moscow Council (1917–1918): The Creation of the Conciliar Institutions of the Russian Orthodox Church*. Edited and translated by Jerry Ryan. Notre Dame, IN: University of Notre Dame Press, 2015.

Dowler, Wayne. *Russia in 1913*. DeKalb: Northern Illinois University Press, 2010.

Egorova, L. A. "Blagotvoritel'nost' pravoslavnykh bratstv Kostromskoi gubernii." In *Blagotvoritel'nost' v Rossii: Istoricheskie i sotsial'no-ekonomicheskie issledovaniia*, edited

by B V Anan'ich, Larisa Viktorovna Badia, and O L Leikind, 191–205. Saint Petersburg: Izd. Novikova, 2004.
Eklof, Ben. *Russian Peasant Schools: Officialdom, Village Culture, and Popular Pedagogy, 1861–1914.* Los Angeles: University of California Press, 1986.
Emmons, Terence. "The Beseda Circle, 1899–1905." *Slavic Review* 32, no. 3 (September 1973): 461–90.
Engelstein, Laura. *Moscow, 1905: Working-Class Organization and Political Conflict.* Stanford, CA: Stanford University Press, 1982.
———. *Slavophile Empire: Imperial Russia's Illiberal Path.* Ithaca, NY: Cornell University Press, 2009.
Etkind, Alexander. *Internal Colonization: Russia's Imperial Experience.* Malden, MA: Polity, 2011.
Evtuhov, Catherine. "The Church's Revolutionary Moment: Diocesan Congresses and Grassroots Politics in 1917." In *Russian Culture in War and Revolution, 1914–22,* edited by Murray Frame, Boris Kolonitskii, Steven G. Marks, and Melissa K. Stockdale, book 1, *Popular Culture, the Arts, and Institutions,* 377–402. Bloomington, IN: Slavica Publishers, 2014.
———. *The Cross and the Sickle: Sergei Bulgakov and the Fate of Russian Religious Philosophy, 1890–1920.* Ithaca, NY: Cornell University Press, 1997.
Fedorov, V. A. *Russkaia pravoslavnaia tserkov' i gosudarstvo: Sinodal'nyi period, 1700–1917.* Moscow: Russkaia Panorama, 2003.
Fedoseev, Aleksandr. *Sviashchenniki v Gosudarstvennoi Dume Rossiiskoi Imperii, 1906–1917.* Moscow: "Strannik," 2019.
Figes, Orlando. *A People's Tragedy: The Russian Revolution, 1891–1924.* New York: Penguin Books, 1996.
Firsov, Sergei. *Russkaia Tserkov' nakanune peremen: Konets 1890-kh–1918 gg.* Moscow: Dukhovnaia biblioteka, 2002.
———. *Tserkov' v Imperii: Ocherki iz tserkovnoi istorii epokhi Imperatora Nikolaia II.* Saint Petersburg: Satis Derzhava, 2007.
Florovskii, Prot. Georgii. *Puti russkago bogosloviia.* Paris: YMCA Press, 1983.
Freeze, Gregory. "All Power to the Parish? The Problems and Politics of Church Reform in Late Imperial Russia." In *Social Identities in Revolutionary Russia,* edited by Madhavan K. Palat, 174–208. New York: Palgrave Macmillan, 2001.
———. "Bringing Order to the Russian Family: Marriage and Divorce in Imperial Russia, 1760–1860." *Journal of Modern History* 62, no. 4 (December 1990): 709–46.
———. "Counter-Reformation in Russian Orthodoxy: Popular Response to Religious Innovation, 1922–1925." *Slavic Review* 54, no. 2 (Summer 1995): 305–39.
———. "Critical Dynamic of the Russian Revolution: Irreligion or Religion?" In *Redefining the Sacred: Religion in the French and Russian Revolutions,* edited by Daniel Schönpflug and Martin Schulze Wessel, 51–82. Frankfurt: Peter Lang, 2012.
———. "Handmaiden of the State? The Church in Imperial Russia Reconsidered." *Journal of Ecclesiastical History* 36 (1985): 82–102.
———. *The Parish Clergy in Nineteenth-Century Russia: Crisis, Reform, Counter-Reform.* Princeton, NJ: Princeton University Press, 1983.

———. *The Russian Levites: Parish Clergy in the Eighteenth Century.* Cambridge, MA: Harvard University Press, 1977.
Friesen, Aileen. "Building an Orthodox Empire: Archpriest Ioann Vostorgov and Russian Missionary Aspirations in Asia." *Canadian Slavonic Papers* 57, nos. 1–2 (2015): 56–75.
———. *Colonizing Russia's Promised Land: Orthodoxy and Community on the Siberian Steppe.* Toronto: University of Toronto Press, 2020.
Galai, Shmuel. *The Liberation Movement in Russia, 1900–1905.* Cambridge: Cambridge University Press, 1973.
Gatrell, Peter. *Russia's First World War: A Social and Economic History.* London: Pearson Education Limited, 2005.
Geekie, John H. M. "The Church and Politics in Russia, 1905–1917: A Study of Political Behavior of Russian Orthodox Clergy in the Reign of Nicholas II." PhD diss., University of East Anglica, 1976.
Gellner, Ernest. *Conditions of Liberty: Civil Society and Its Rivals.* New York: Penguin, 1994.
Gleason, William. "The All-Russian Union of Zemstvos and World War I." In *The Zemstvo in Russia: An Experiment in Local Self-Government,* edited by Terence Emmons and Wayne S. Vucinich, 365–78. Cambridge: Cambridge University Press, 1982.
Goldfrank, David. "Old and New Perspectives on Iosif Volotsky's Monastic Rules." *Slavic Review* 34, no. 2 (June 1975): 279–301.
Golubtsov, Sergei. *Moskovskaia Dukhovnaia Akademiia v revoliutsionnuiu epokhu: Akademiia v sotsial'nom dvizhenii i sluzhenii v nachale XX veka. Po materialam arkhivov, memuarov i publikatsii.* Moscow: Izd. "Martis," 1999.
———. *Moskovskoe dukhovenstvo v preddverii i nachale gonenii, 1917–1922.* Moscow: Izd-vo Pravoslavnogo bratstva Sporuchnitsy greshnykh, 1999.
Grabko, M. E. *Deiatel'nost' Russkoi pravoslavnoi tserkvi v rabochei srede Moskovskoi gubernii v kontse XIX–nachale XX v.* Moscow: PSTGU, 2017.
Green, Elna C. "*The Master-Word*: Lily Hardy Hammond and the Social Gospel in the South." *Journal of Southern Religion* 15 (2013).
Greene, Robert H. "Bodies in Motion: Steam-Powered Pilgrimages in Late Imperial Russia." *Russian History* 39, nos. 1–2 (2012): 247–68.
Gromyko, M. M., and A. V. Buganov. *O vozzreniiakh russkogo naroda.* Moscow: Palomnik, 2000.
Haimson, Leopold. "The Problem of Social Identities in Early Twentieth Century Russia." *Slavic Review* 47, no. 1 (Spring 1988): 1–20.
———. *Russia's Revolutionary Experience, 1905–1917: Two Essays.* New York: Columbia University Press, 2005.
Hedda, Jennifer. *His Kingdom Come: Orthodox Pastorship and Social Activism in Revolutionary Russia.* DeKalb: Northern Illinois University Press, 2008.
Heretz, Leonid. *Russia on the Eve of Modernity: Popular Religion and Traditional Culture under the Last Tsars.* Cambridge: Cambridge University Press, 2008.
Herlihy, Patricia. *The Alcoholic Empire: Vodka and Politics in Late Imperial Russia.* New York: Oxford University Press, 2002.

Hobsbawm, Eric. *The Age of Revolution, 1789–1848*. New York: Vintage Books, 1962.

Holquist, Peter. "'In Accord with State Interests and the People's Wishes': The Technocratic Ideology of Imperial Russia's Resettlement Administration." *Slavic Review* 69, no. 1 (Spring 2010): 151–79.

Hölscher, Lucian. "Secularization and Urbanization." In *European Religion in the Age of Great Cities, 1830–1930*, edited by Hugh McLeod, 263–88. New York: Routledge, 1995.

Hosking, Geoffrey. *The Russian Constitutional Experiment: Government and Duma, 1907–1914*. Cambridge: Cambridge University Press, 1973.

Hovorun, Cyril. "Conciliarity and the Holy and Great Council." In *Synodality: A Forgotten and Misapprehended Vision. Reflections on the Holy and Great Council 2016*, edited by Maksim Vasiljević and Andrej Jeftic, 81–98. Alhambra, CA: Sebastian Press, 2017.

Ikonnikov, S. A. "Prikhodskoe dukhovenstvo Voronezhskoi eparkhii vtoroi poloviny XIX–nachala XX veka: Sotsiokul'turnaia kharakteristika." Kand. diss., Voronezh State University, 2015.

Ismay, Penelope. "Trust among Strangers: Securing British Modernity 'by Way of Friendly Society,' 1780s–1870s." PhD diss., University of California, Berkeley, 2010.

Ivanova, I. E. *Fol'klor i etnografiia v dukhovnoi periodike XIX veka: Kontekstnye sviazi*. Tver': "Lilia Print," 2006.

Kabanov, B. B. *Oktiabr'skaia revoliutsiia i kooperatsiia (1917–mart 1919)*. Moscow: Nauka, 1973.

Kaplan, Vera. "From Soslovie to Voluntary Associations: New Patterns of Collective Identities in Late Imperial Russia." *Cahiers du Monde russe* 51, nos. 2–3 (May 2010): 369–96.

Kartashev, A. V. *Ocherki po istorii russkoi tserkvi*. Paris: YMCA Press, 1959.

Kassow, Samuel D. "Russia's Unrealized Civil Society." In *Between Tsar and People: Educated Society and the Quest for Public Identity in Late Imperial Russia*, edited by Edith W. Clowes, Samuel D. Kassow, and James L. West, 367–72. Princeton, NJ: Princeton University Press, 1991.

Kayden, Eugene M., and Alexis N. Antsiferov. *The Cooperative Movement in Russia during the War*. New Haven, CT: Yale University Press, 1929.

Kenworthy, Scott. "Canon Law." In *The Supplement to the Modern Encyclopedia of Russian, Soviet, and Eurasian History*, edited by Bruce F. Adams, 5:91–96. Gulf Breeze, FL: Academic International Press, 2004.

———. *The Heart of Russia: Trinity-Sergius, Monasticism, and Society after 1825*. New York: Oxford University Press, 2010.

———. "Russian Reformation? The Program for Religious Renovation in the Orthodox Church, 1922–1925." *Modern Greek Studies Yearbook* 16/17 (2000/2001): 89–130.

———. "To Save the World or to Renounce It: Modes of Moral Action in Russian Orthodoxy." In *Religion, Community, and Morality after Communism*, edited by Mark Steinberg and Catherine Wanner, 21–54. Washington, DC: Woodrow Wilson Center Press; Bloomington: Indiana University Press, 2008.

Kleimenova, Liliia A. "Sozdanie v Turkestanskoi eparkhii pravoslavnogo bratstva i soiuza prikhodov kak otvet tserkvi na goneniia 1918 i 1923 godov." In *Pravoslavnye bratstva v istorii Rossii k 100-letiiu vozzvaniia patriarkha Tikhona ob obrazovanii dukhovnykh soiuzov: Sbornik nauchnykh trudov*, edited by Iuliia Balakshina and Sergei Smirnov, 1:135–57. Moscow: Preobrazhenie, 2018.

Knight, Nathaniel. "Ethnicity, Nationality and the Masses: *Narodnost'* and Modernity in Imperial Russia." In *Russian Modernity: Politics, Knowledge, Practices*, edited by Yanni Kotsonis and David Hoffman, 41–64. New York: St. Martin's, 2000.

Koroleva, N. G., ed. *Zemskoe samoupravlenie v Rossii, 1864–1918*. 2 vols. Moscow: Nauka, 2005.

Kosar, George T. "Russian Orthodoxy in Crisis and Revolution: The Church Council of 1917–1918." PhD diss., Brandeis University, 2003.

Koyzis, David T. "Imaging God and His Kingdom: Eastern Orthodoxy's Iconic Political Ethic." *Review of Politics* 55, no. 2 (Spring 1993): 267–89.

Kravchenko, O. V. "Tserkovnye bratstva: Istoriia i istoriografiia." In *Provintsial'noe dukhovenstvo dorevoliutsionnoi Rossii: Sbornik nauchnykh trudov vserossiiskoi zaochnoi konferentsii*, edited by T. G. Leont'eva, 245–56. Tver': Slavianskii Mir, 2006.

Laqueur, Walter. *Black Hundred: The Rise of the Extreme Right in Russia*. New York: Edward Burlingame Books, 1993.

Lee, Robert. *Rural Society and the Anglican Clergy, 1815–1914: Encountering and Managing the Poor*. Woodbridge, UK: Boydell and Brewer, 2006.

Leont'eva, T. G. "Vera i bunt: Dukhovenstvo v revoliutsionnom obshchestve Rossii nachala XX veka." *Voprosy istorii*, no. 1 (2001): 29–43.

———. *Vera i progress: Pravoslavnoe sel'skoe dukhovenstvo Rossii vo vtoroi polovine XIX–nachale XX veka*. Moscow: Novyi khronograf, 2002.

Levitin, Anatolii, and Vadim Shavrov. *Ocherki po istorii russkoi tserkovnoi smuty*. Küsnacht, Switzerland: Institut Glaube in der 2. Welt, 1977.

Liebersohn, Harry. *Religion and Industrial Society: The Protestant Social Congress in Wilhelmine Germany*. Philadelphia: American Philosophical Society, 1986.

Lilla, Mark. *The Stillborn God: Religion, Politics, and the Modern West*. New York: Alfred Knopf, 2007.

Lindenmeyr, Adele. *Poverty Is Not a Vice: Charity, Society, and the State in Imperial Russia*. Princeton, NJ: Princeton University Press, 1996.

———. "Primordial and Gelatinous? Civil Society in Imperial Russia." *Kritika: Explorations in Russian and Eurasian History* 12, no. 3 (Summer 2011): 703–20.

Lisiunin, V. "Uchastie tambovskogo dukhovenstva v parlamentskikh vyborakh i deiatel'nosti Gosudarstvennoi dumy I–IV sozyvov (1906–1917)." *Vestnik Tambovskogo universiteta* 23, no. 174 (2018): 171–80.

Luukkanen, Arto. *The Party of Unbelief: The Religious Policy of the Bolshevik Party, 1917–1929*. Helsinki: Studia Historica, 1994.

Manchester, Laurie. *Holy Fathers, Secular Sons: Clergy, Intelligentsia, and the Emergence of Modern Selfhood in Revolutionary Russia*. DeKalb: Northern Illinois University Press, 2008.

Mel'nikov, P. I. *Otchet o sovremennom sostoianii raskola v Nizhegorodskoi gubernii*. Nizhnii Novgorod: Izd. I. M. Mashistova, 1910.

Meyendorff, John. *The Vision of Unity*. Crestwood, NY: St. Vladimir's Seminar Press, 1987.

Michels, Georg. *At War with the Church: Religious Dissent in Seventeenth-Century Russia.* Stanford, CA: Stanford University Press, 1999.

Michelson, Patrick Lally. *Beyond the Monastery Walls: The Ascetic Revolution in Russian Orthodox Thought, 1814–1914.* Madison: University of Wisconsin Press, 2017.

Miller, Timothy S. *The Birth of the Hospital in the Byzantine Empire.* 2nd ed. Baltimore: Johns Hopkins University Press, 1997.

———. "Byzantine Philanthropic Institutions and Modern Humanitarianism." *Review of Faith and International Affairs* 14, no. 1 (Spring 2016): 18–25.

Mironov, B. N. "Narod-bogonosets ili narod-ateist? Kak rossiiane verili v Boga nakanune 1917 g." *Rodina*, no. 3 (2001): 52–58.

Mitchell, B. R., ed. *European Historical Statistics, 1750–1975.* 2nd ed. New York: Facts on File, 1980.

Morison, John D. "Church Schools and Seminaries in the Revolution of 1905–06." In *Church, Nation and State in Russia and Ukraine*, edited by Geoffrey A. Hosking, 193–209. New York: St. Martin's, 1991.

Moshkova, L. V. "Sozdanie novykh tipov Kormchikh na vostochnoslavianskikh zemliakh v XV–XVI vekakh." In *Kormchaia kniga: Ot rukopisnoi traditsii k pervomu pechatnomu izdaniiu*, edited by E. V. Beliakova, L. V. Moshkova, and T. A. Oparina, 92–106. Moscow: Tsentr gumanitarnykh initsiativ, 2017.

Mramornov, A. I. *Dukhovnaia seminariia v Rossii nachala XX veka: Krizis i vozmozhnosti ego preodoleniia.* Saratov: Nauchnaia kniga, 2007.

Muller, Alexander. *The Spiritual Regulation of Peter the Great.* Seattle: University of Washington Press, 1973.

Naganawa, Norihiro. "A Civil Society in a Confessional State? Muslim Philanthropy in the Volga-Urals Region." In *Russia's Home Front in War and Revolution, 1914–1922*, vol. 2, *The Experience of War and Revolution*, edited by Adele Lindenmeyr, Christopher Read, and Peter Waldron, 59–78. Bloomington, IN: Slavic, 2016.

Nish, Ian. *The Origins of the Russo-Japanese War.* New York: Longman, 1985.

Paert, Irina. *Spiritual Elders: Charisma and Tradition in Russian Orthodoxy.* DeKalb: Northern Illinois University Press, 2010.

Pankrat, T. V. *Blagotvoritel'naia deiatel'nost' prikhodskikh popechitel'stv Moskvy, vtoraia polovina XIX–nachalo XX stoletiia.* Moscow: Izd. PSTGU, 2011.

Philpott, Daniel. "Has the Study of Global Politics Found Religion?" *Annual Review of Political Science* 12 (2009): 183–202.

Pirumova, N. M. *Zemskoe liberal'noe dvizhenie: Sotsial'nye korni i evoliutsiia do nachala XX veka.* Moscow: Nauka, 1977.

Pisiotis, Argyrios. "Orthodoxy versus Autocracy." PhD diss., Georgetown University, 2000.

Polunov, A. Iu. *Pod vlast'iu ober-prokurora: Gosudarstvo i tserkov' v epokhu Aleksandra III.* Moscow: Airo-XX, 1996.

Poole, Randall. "The Defense of Human Dignity in Nineteenth-Century Russian Thought." In *Iosif Volotskii and Eastern Christianity: Essays across Seventeen Centuries*, edited by David Goldfrank, Nollan Valeria, and Jennifer Spock, 271–305. Washington, DC: New Academia Publishing, 2017.

Popova, O. D. *V stenakh konvikta—ocherki povsednevnoi zhizni zhenskikh eparkhial'nykh uchilishch.* Ryazan': Izdatel'stvo "Poverennyi," 2006.

Porter, Thomas Earl. *The Zemstvo and the Emergence of Civil Society in Late Imperial Russia 1864–1917.* San Francisco: Mellon Research University Press, 1991.

Putnam, George F. *Russian Alternatives to Marxism: Christian Socialism and Idealistic Liberalism in Twentieth-Century Russia.* Knoxville: University of Tennessee Press, 1977.

Rauschenbusch, Walter. *A Theology for the Social Gospel.* New York: Abingdon Press, 1960.

Rentel, Alexander. "A Comparison of the Liturgical Rite of Ordination and the Canonical Act of Deposition." *St. Vladimir's Theological Quarterly* 55, no. 1 (2011): 27–57.

Rieber, Alfred. *Merchants and Entrepreneurs in Imperial Russia.* Chapel Hill: University of North Carolina Press, 1982.

Ringlee, Andrew J. "The Romanov's Militant Charity: The Red Cross and Public Mobilization for War in Tsarist Russia, 1853–1914." PhD diss., University of North Carolina at Chapel Hill, 2016.

Robbins, Richard G., Jr. *Famine in Russia, 1891–1892: The Imperial Government Responds to a Crisis.* New York: Columbia University Press, 1975.

Rogoznyi, P. G. *Tserkovnaia revoliutsiia 1917 goda: Vysshee dukhovenstvo Rossiiskoi Tserkvi v bor'be za vlast' v eparkhiiakh posle Fevral'skoi revoliutsii.* Saint Petersburg: "Liki Rossii," 2008.

Rosenblum Nancy L., and Charles H. T. Lesch. "Civil Society and Government." In *The Oxford Handbook of Civil Society*, edited by Michael Edwards, 285–97. Oxford: Oxford University Press, 2011.

Roslof, Edward. *Red Priests.* Bloomington: Indiana University Press, 2002.

Rozhkov, Protoierei Vladimir. *Tserkovnye voprosy v Gosudarstvennoi Dume.* Moscow: Izd. Krutitskogo Podvor'ia, 2004.

Ruane, Christine. "Divergent Discourses: The Image of the Russian Woman Schoolteacher in Post-Reform Russia." *Russian History* 20, nos. 1–4 (1993): 109–23.

Ruckman, Jo Ann. *The Moscow Business Elite: A Social and Cultural Portrait of Two Generations, 1840–1905.* Dekalb: Northern Illinois University Press, 1984.

Savva, Igumen (Tutunov). *Eparkhial'nye reformy.* Moscow: "Nauka," 2011.

Scarborough, Daniel. "Missionaries of Official Orthodoxy." In *Religious Freedom in Modern Russia*, edited by Randall Poole and Paul Werth, 142–59. Pittsburgh, PA: University of Pittsburgh Press, 2018.

Shah, Timothy Samuel. *Faith on Fire: The Global Explosion of Political Religion.* Stanford, CA: Hoover Institution Press, 2011.

Shevzov, Vera. *Russian Orthodoxy on the Eve of Revolution.* New York: Oxford University Press, 2004.

Smith, Alison K. *For the Common Good and Their Own Well-Being: Social Estates in Imperial Russia.* New York: Oxford University Press, 2015.

Smith, Kevin D. "Breaking Faith: Religion, Americanism, and Civil Rights in Postwar Milwaukee." *Religion and American Culture: A Journal of Interpretation* 20, no. 1 (Winter 2010): 57–92.

Sokolov, K. I. *Plamia nad Volgoi: Krest'ianskie vosstaniia i vystupleniia v Tverskoi gubernii v kontse 1917–1922 gg.* Moscow: Tsentrpoligraf, 2017.
Sorenson, Thomas. "Pobedonostsev's Parish Schools: A Bastion against Secularism." In *Religious and Secular Forces in Late Tsarist Russia: Essays in Honor of Donald W. Treadgold*, edited by Charles E. Timberlake, 185–205. Seattle: University of Washington Press, 1992.
Stark, Rodney. *The Rise of Christianity: A Sociologist Reconsiders History.* Princeton, NJ: Princeton University Press, 1996.
Strickland, John. *The Making of Holy Russia: The Orthodox Church and Russian Nationalism before the Revolution.* Jordanville, NY: Holy Trinity Publications, 2013.
Strikwerda, Carl. "A Resurgent Religion: The Rise of Catholic Social Movements in Nineteenth-Century Belgian Cities." In *European Religion in the Age of Great Cities, 1830–1930*, edited by Hugh McLeod, 59–87. New York: Routledge, 1995.
Svetlova, N. E. "K. P. Pobedonostsev i tserkovno-prikhodskie shkoly Rossii v nachale XX v." *Vestnik PSTTU* 49 (2018): 59–68.
Timberlake, Charles. "Tver Zemstvo's Technical School in Rzhev: A Case Study in the Dissemination of Revolutionary and Secular Ideas." In *Religious and Secular Forces in Late Tsarist Russia: Essays in Honor of Donald W. Treadgold*, edited by Charles Timberlake, 128–44. Seattle: University of Washington Press, 1992.
Tocqueville, Alexis de. *Democracy in America.* New York: Vintage, 1990.
Tumanova, A. S. *Obshchestvennye organizatsii i russkaia publika v nachale XX veka.* Moscow: Novyi khronograf, 2008.
Ul'ianova, Galina. "Tserkovnoprikhodskie popechitel'stva kak strukturnaia edinitsa blagotvoritel'nosti vnutri mestnogo soobshchestva v pozdneimperskoi Rossii." In *Blagotvoritel'nost' v Rossii: Istoricheskie i sotsial'no-ekonomicheskie issledovaniia*, edited by B. V. Anan'ich, S. A. Basov, and V. M. Voronkov, 166–76. Saint Petersburg: Izd. Novikova, 2004.
Uriadova, Anna. *Golod 1920-x gg. v Rossii i russkoe zarubezh'e.* Saint Petersburg: Aleteiia, 2010.
Valliere, Paul. *Conciliarism: A History of Decision-Making in the Church.* New York: Cambridge University Press, 2012.
———. *Modern Russian Theology: Bukharev, Soloviev, Bulgakov; Orthodoxy in a New Key.* Grand Rapids, MI: William B. Eerdmans, 2000.
Vasil'ev, I. A. "Pravoslavnoe dukhovenstvo v II Gosudarstvennoi Dume Rossiiskoi imperii." *Vestnik Sankt-Peterburgskogo universiteta. Pravo*, no. 4 (2012): 3–8.
———. "Pravoslavnoe dukhovenstvo v III Gosudarstvennoi Dume Rossiiskoi imperii." *Vestnik Sankt-Peterburgskogo universiteta. Pravo*, no. 1 (2013): 3–8.
Veer, Peter van der. *Imperial Encounters: Religion and Modernity in India and Britain.* Princeton, NJ: Princeton University Press, 2001.
Webster, Richard. *The Cross and the Fasces: Christian Democracy in Italy.* Stanford, CA: Stanford University Press, 1960.
Werth, Paul W. *The Tsar's Foreign Faiths: Toleration and the Fate of Religious Freedom in Imperial Russia.* Oxford: Oxford University Press, 2014.
Wheatcroft, S. G. "The 1891–92 Famine in Russia: Towards a More Detailed Analysis of Its Scale and Demographic Significance." In *Economy and Society in Russia and*

the Soviet Union, 1860–1930: Essays for Olga Crisp, edited by Linda Edmondson, 44–64. New York: St. Martin's, 1992.

Zaionchkovskii, Petr. *Provedenie v zhizn' krest'anskoi reformy, 1861*. Moscow: Izd-vo sotsial'no-ekonomicheskoi literatury, 1958.

Zhukova, A. L. "Vyrabotka konservativnoi kontseptsii mestnogo upravleniia v Rossii: Komissiia M. S. Kakhanova, 1881–1885." In *Zemskoe samoupravlenie v Rossii, 1864–1918*, edited by N. G. Koroleva, 1:235–48. Moscow: Nauka, 2005.

INDEX

Note: Page numbers in italics refer to illustrations.

Agafangel, Archbishop, 187, 196
Aksakov, N. P., 166
Alexander I, Emperor, 28
Alexander II, Emperor, 36, 86
Alexander III, Emperor, 86
Alexandrovna, Empress Maria, 90
All-Russian Central Executive Committee, 195
All-Russian Church Council of Bishops, Parish Clergy, and Laity, 188
All-Russian Church Sobor, 12, 50–51, 115, 143, 154, 159–66, 172–78, 187–88, 193–95
All-Russian Congress of Clergy and Laity, 12, 160, 178, 181–83, 189, 231n53
All-Russian Peasant Union, 157
All-Russian Union of Clergy, 182
All-Russian Union of Orthodox Clergy and Laity, 182–84, 189
All-Seminarian Union, 78–80
Amvrosii, Bishop (Kliucharev), 50
Anatoli, Vicar Bishop (Kamenskii), 154
Anderson, Margaret, 4
Andrei, Archbishop (Ukhtomskii), 185
antisemitism, 153, 157
Antonii, Metropolitan (Khrapovitskii), 188, 195

Antonii, Metropolitan (Vadkovskii), 50–51, 139, 147, 151, 155
apostolic authority, 11–12, 24, 47–49, 113–14, 137, 162–66, 173, 178, 193–94
Apostolic Canon 39, 166
Arkadii, Bishop (Karpinskii), 57–58
Arkhipov, Father, 147
Arsenii, Archbishop (Stadnitskii), 179, 188
Arsenii, Metropolitan (Moskvin), 33
Arsenii, Vicar Bishop (Smolenets), 160, 167, 172–73, 175–77
Asad, Talal, 5–6, 116
August manifesto, 142
authorizing discourse, 5–8, 116, 192
autocracy, 6, 52, 63, 67, 83, 103, 140, 144. *See also* tsarism

Bazhenov, Father, 26–27
Bednota (The poor), 194–95, 197
Beglov, Aleksei, 107
Belliustin, I. S., 21–22, 29, 43, 48, 109
Bethlehem Seminary, 66, 69, 75
the bible, 7–8, 106, 160–61, 163, 184, 206n52
bishops. *See* apostolic authority
black clergy, 11, 50
Black Hundreds, 153, 155, 157, 159, 195

Bloody Sunday, 52, 139, 165
Bogdanovich, Savva, 150, 155
Bogoiavlenskii, Father, 30, 164–65
Bogoliubskii, Father, 181–82, 186
Bolshevik Revolution, 3, 77, 177, 188–89, 194–97
Brilliantov, Father, 147
Brown, Patrick, 134–35
Buddhism, 151
Bulgakov, Sergei, 136–37, 148, 155, 157, 183
Bünting, Nikolai von, 160
bureaucracy, 23–29, 32, 36, 39, 47, 50, 125, 189, 193
Byzantine church. *See* Eastern Church

canonical freedom, 165, 171, 181
canon law, 8, 24, 159–67, 169–75, 178–81, 184, 187–89, 194, 196. *See also* law
caste isolation, 67, 74, 76
Catherine II, Empress, 9
Catholic Church, 4–6, 16, 112, 137–38
censorship, 18, 29–30, 50, 71–72, 97, 119, 138–40, 144–48, 151–52, 190. *See also* surveillance
Central Committee of the All-Seminarian Union, 77–78, 80, 131
Chancellery of the Ober-Procurator, 24
charity. *See* mutual aid networks; *philanthropia*
Chekhov, Anton, 44
Chetvernikov, Father, 58–59
Chicherin, Boris, 15, 194
church and state: and canon law, 162–63; and censorship, 138–39; and church reform, 69; and the laity, 36; and the pastoral mission, 9–12, 45, 50, 53–54; and politics, 140–57; reform and, 159; and the renovationists, 195–97; and state intervention, 47, 101, 137–38; and the synodal system, 23–24
"Church and State" (Pobedonostsev), 36
church procession (*krestnyi khod*), 52
church publications, 29–31, 48, 50, 60, 67, 93, 138–41, 145, 185

church reform, 162–64; and the diocesan congresses, 158–60, 167–78, 180–82, 185–86; and the electoral principle, 162; liberalism and, 111–12; and the Living Church, 195, 196; and the Orthodox laity, 11, 17, 107–17, 125–29, 134–35, 160, 168, 178, 182, 189, 192; and the parish clergy, 18, 116–17, 119; and party division, 165–66; in the seminary, 63–64, 66, 68–72, 75–76, 81; and the Sobor, 115, 161, 187–88; social, 29; and the state, 109–11. *See also* apostolic authority; counter-reform
church resources, 11, 14, 107–16, 121, *122, 123*–27, *128*, 129–31, *132*, 133–35, 160, 189, 192. *See also* parish trusteeship (*prikhodskoe popechitel'stvo*)
church unity, 112–13, 145, 160–61, 164, 173, 178–86, 189, 193
Circular 3542, 51, 76
City of God, 8
civil liberties, 32
civil society (*grazhdanskoe obshchestvo*), 12–15, 29–30, 43, 45, 111, 129, 194. *See also* social networks
clerical associations. *See* free association; mutual aid networks; voluntary associations
clerical estate. *See* parish clergy
clerical schools for women, 90–92
clerical teaching, 83–94, 97–98, 104, 218n21. *See also* parish clergy
clerical women, 89–93, 219n49. *See also* women
Commissariat of Popular Education, 82
common charter (*ustav*), 90
"Common Regulations for the Election of Diocesan Bishops," 181
conciliarity, 161–62, 170, 175, 177–78, 188, 193–94, 239n2. *See also sobornost'*
conservatism, 6, 19, 104, 137, 140–46, 148–57
Constituent Assembly, 182
Constitutional Democratic Party, 126, 144–46

Constitutions of the Apostles, 163–64
Council of Bishops, 187
Council of Chalcedon, 8
Council of Ministers, 24, 86, 95, 115, 139
Council of United Parishes of Moscow, 197
counter-reform, 17, 35, 66, 72. *See also* church reform
cultural reconfiguration, 4

decree (*ukaz*): and the Apostolic Canons, 163; imperial, 24, 45, 108, 139, 142, 161; and the parish clergy, 7; Rome, 8; and the Sobor, 187–88; Synodal, 25, 30–31, 38–40, 49–53, 65, 72, 76, 89, 97–98, 125–29, 134, 140, 145, 154, 179–81
Decree No. 11, 145
defrocking, 147, 149
democracy, 12, 18–19, 25, 29, 63, 149, 176–78, 183, 194. *See also* parliamentarianism (*parlamentarizm*)
Destivelle, Hyacinthe, 234n17
diocesan committees, 39–40, 42, 57, 61
diocesan congresses: and canon law, 159–60, 164–65; and church reform, 11–12, 19, 31–32, 126, 158–59, 163, 181; and funding, 30, 48, 72, 90–91; of Moscow, 16, 178–89, 226n87; and the Synod, 43, 49, 51; of Tver, 16, 166–77, 188–89; and war, 134
"Diocesan Congresses of the Clergy" (Bogoiavlenskii), 164–65
diocesan districts (*okruga*), 133
Diocesan Home (*Eparkhial'nyi dom*), 186
Diocesan Journals (*Eparkhial'nye vedomosti*), 30
Diocesan Soviet (*eparkhial'nyi sovet*), 173–78, 236n80
diocesan trusteeship for poor clergy (*popechitel'stvo o bednykh dukhovnogo zvaniia*), 28–29, 39. *See also* funding
discursive traditions, 7

dissent. *See* petition movement; political activism; radicalism; terrorism
district (*okrug*), 25, 30
district congresses (*okruzhnye s"ezdy*), 30, 43, 48
Dowler, Wayne, 13
Druzhinin, Aleksandr, 65
Dubrovkin, Aleksandr, 153
dukhovnaia komanda. *See* spiritual domain (*dukhovnaia komanda*)
the Dumas, 18, 22, 63, 77, 100–102, 115–16, 126, 136–37, 142–57, 231n54. *See also* parliamentarianism (*parlamentarizm*)

Eastern Church, 8–9
Eastern Roman Empire, 137
ecclesiastical reform. *See* church reform
ecclesiastical schools (*dukhovnye uchilishcha*), 67
Economic Administration, 24
economics, 105, 134
Ecumenical Councils, 161–62, 179–80
ecumenical movement, 188
Edict of Emancipation, 29
Edict of Toleration, 139, 149–51
educated society (*obshchestvennost'*), 14
education. *See* clerical teaching; clerical women; parish schools; the seminary; urban teaching
Eklof, Ben, 101–3
electoral principle (*vyborne nachalo*), 12, 31–32, 36, 162, 167, 177, 193
emancipation reform, 7
Engelstein, Laura, 14
Eparkhial'nye vedomosti. See *Diocesan Journals* (*Eparkhial'nye vedomosti*)
episcopal absolutism, 165, 168, 173, 176, 178–79
episcopate, 23–24, 159, 164–66, 178–79, 183–87
estate isolation, 45, 67–68, 74, 76
estates (*sosloviia*), 13–17, 19, 33, 45, 68, 74–76, 170–71, 178, 194, 203n66
Eusebius of Caesarea, 8

Evlogii, Metropolitan (Georgievskii), 21, 67, 71, 146, 149, 152, 155–59, 167, 195, 212n52

February Revolution, 135, 157, 159, 166–67
Feodor, Archimandrite, 75, 190
Feodor, Bishop (Pozdeevskii), 180
Filaret, Bishop (Nikol'skii), 142
Filaret, Metropolitan (Drozdov), 29
Filosofiia prava (Chicherin), 15
First All-Russian Missionary Congress, 24
First Council of Nicaea, 8
First Russian Revolution. *See* 1905 Revolution
Flavian, Metropolitan (Gorodetskii), 49–50
Florovskii, Georgii, 236n95
Foucault, Michel, 5
free association: and the 1905 Revolution, 32, 51, 63, 156; and charity, 22, 116; and the Great Reforms, 29; and the laity, 33, 42–43, 189, 193; restrictions on, 36, 48, 51, 98; and rural isolation, 100, 130. 131; and the seminary, 81; and Soviet Russia, 189, 194; and the state, 15, 22, 35; and the Synod, 11, 27, 36, 45; theories of, 13. *See also* mutual aid networks; voluntary associations
freedom of conscience, 139, 143, 149–51, 153
Freeze, Gregory, 11, 15–16, 23, 121, 128, 157
Friazinov, 186
Fundamental Rules, 33
funding: and clerical women, 90, 93; and diocesan trusteeships, 28, 38–39, 107, 109–10, 134; and the Duma, 150, 152; and education, 30, 98, 101–4, 149, 226n87; humanitarian relief, 41–43, 54–62, 126, 130–31, *132*, 133–34; and the laity, 20–22, 108–10, 159; and the parish clergy, 22, 31–32, 47–48, 126, 207n78; seminary, 10, 32, 67, 69, 81–82; state, 22, 69, 83–87, 93, 102, 109–10, 126, 193. *See also* church resources; poverty

Gapon, Father Georgii, 52, 138–39, 165
Gellner, Ernest, 13
General Assembly of the Sobor, 187
Gepetskii of Bessarabia, 145–46
Germogen, Bishop (Dolganev), 59
Gogol, Nikolay, 65
Golubinskii, E. E., 162
Golubtsov, Sergei, 237n125
Government Inspector (Gogol), 65
Grabko, M. E., 24
Gramsci, Antonio, 194, 202n60
Graves de communi re (Pope Leo XIII), 138
grazhdanskoe obshchestvo. *See* civil society (*grazhdanskoe obshchestvo*)
Great Reforms, 29, 33. *See also* church reform
Grinevich, Father, 147
Gromoglasov, Il'ia, 180–81, 187
Group of Thirty-Two Saint Petersburg Priests, 50–51, 139, 146, 165–66, 181, 230n42
Gumilevskii, Father, 116–17, 190
Gumilin, Father, 148

Harnack, Adolf, 5
Hedda, Jennifer, 10, 16
Hobsbawm, Eric, 4
Holquist, Peter, 14
Hölscher, Lucian, 4
Holy Governing Synod, 23
home schools, 84
Hosking, Geoffrey, 150–51
How the Steel Was Tempered (Ostrovskii), 83
humanitarian relief: and collaboration, 129–30, 133–35; and estates, 14–15; and famine, 22, 37–38, 195; and the laity, 107, 110, 134–35; and mutual aid networks, 11, 17, 37, 131; and the parish clergy, 38–43, 46, 53–64, 130–31, 133–35,

167, 213n75; and the state, 37, 133; and the Synod, 38–43, 55–57, 61–62, 69–70, 129–31, 135; and World War I, 18, 129–31, *132*, 133–35

Iakubovich, Viacheslav, 146
Imperial Manifesto of War, 129
indirect rule, 23–24
Industrial Revolution, 4, 119
industrial workers, 125
Innokentii, Bishop (Beliaev), 58
Instructions to Church Elders, 108
intelligentsia, 14–15, 178
internal mission, 96–99, 191–92
inter-seminarian congresses, 74, 77
Ioannikii, Metropolitan (Moscow), 72
Ioasaf, Bishop (Kallistov), 179, 185
Iranian Revolution, 3
Isidor, Metropolitan, 109
Islam, 5, 151
Ismay, Penelope, 13–14
Ivantsov-Platonov, Archpriest A.M., 161–62, 239n2
Izvol'skii, Piotr, 148

Julian the Apostate, 8
June 3rd system, 147–49, 157
Justinian, Emperor, 137

Kadet Party, 126, 144–46
Kazan's Academy for Women, 61
Kedrov, Father Ioann, 185
Khomiakov, Aleksei, 112
Kingdom of Heaven, 8
Kliuchevskii, Vasilii, 71
Kolokol, 154
Kolokol'nikov, Konstantin, 146–47
Kolosov, Vladimir, 75, 81
Kormchaia kniga, 161
Kosar, George, 160
Krasnitskii, Father Vladimir, 196
krestnyi khod. *See* church procession (*krestnyi khod*)
Kulturkampf, 112
Kupriianov, Father, 148

Kuropatkin, General, 71
Kuyper, Abraham, 4–5

laity. *See* church reform; church resources; church unity; funding; humanitarian relief; mutual aid networks
land ownership, 20–22, 27–28, 32, 58, 95, 117, 124, 142–47, 182, 230n39
Lavrentii, Bishop (Nekrasov), 58
law, 15, 29, 35, 67, 114–15, 147. *See also* canon law
Lebedev, Sergei, 78, 171
Lee, Robert, 202n56
Leo, Pope XIII, 138
Leont'eva, Tat'iana, 111
Leontii, Metropolitan (Lebedinskii), 48
liberalism, 15, 18–19, 104, 111, 137, 139, 144, 146–47
Liberation Movement, 77, 144
Lindenmeyr, Adele, 33
literacy, 83, 94–95, 99–100, 102–4, 118
Liubimov, Nikolai, 183
Living Church, 196–97
L'vov, Vladimir, 166–67, 170, 172, 178–81, 183, 189, 195

macroecclesial, 113
Makarii, Metropolitan (Nevskii), 178–81, 184
Manchester, Laurie, 76
martyrs, 195
Maslov, Aleksandr, 78
Michelson, Patrick Lally, 4, 6–7
migrant workers, 124
Mikhail, Archbishop (Golubovich), 31
Mikhail, Bishop, 174
Miliukov, Pavel, 101, 111, 135
Ministry of Education, 92, 103, 152
Ministry of Internal Affairs, 14–15, 39–41, 111, 119
Ministry of State Domains, 41
Mitrofan, Bishop, 101
monasteries, 6–7, 9–10, 53–54, 85, 96
Monastic Rule (Volotsky), 9

Moscow Church Journal (*Moskovskie tserkovnye vedomosti*), 30
Moscow consistory, 53–56, 88
Moscow Filaret School for Girls, 91
Moscow pedagogical committee, 67–68
Moscow Seminary, 66–70, 75, 79–80, 88
Moscow's Society for Lovers of Religious Enlightenment, 33
Moscow Theological Academy, 66, 77, 162
Moscow Union of Clergy and Laity, 185, 187
Moskovskie tserkovnye vedomosti. See *Moscow Church Journal* (*Moskovskie tserkovnye vedomosti*)
Mramornov, Aleksandr, 76, 214n13
Muscovite monarchy, 9
Muslim philanthropy, 14
mutual aid networks: and clergy poverty, 26–27; and famine, 37–43; introduction to, 17–18; and the Orthodox laity, 44–47, 69–70, 76–77, 82, 85, 95–96, 117–20, 123, 135, 189; and the parish community, 22, 117–20; and parish schools, 83–85, 87, 89, 93, 95–96, 105; and parish trusteeships, 28–29, 33, 121–23, 125; and pastoral assemblies, 50; and philanthropy, 46–47; restrictions to, 48–49; and the seminary, 67–69, 74–76, 81, 89; and sobriety societies, 119–20. *See also* free association; *philanthropia*; social networks; voluntary associations
Myshtsyn, Vasilii, 162

nationalism, 6, 155
Naumann, Friedrich, 5
Nicholas I, 161
Nicholas II, 42, 52, 100, 115, 139, 142, 145–47, 149–50
"The Nightmare" (Chekhov), 44
Nikolaevna, Grand Princess Ol'ga, 90
Nikon, Archbishop (Rozhdestvenskii), 68
Nikon, Patriarch, 9

Nikonovich, Archpriest, 152
1905 Revolution, 17, 32, 45–46, 51–58, 63–66, 117, 135, 156, 183
1917 Revolution, 135
Nomocanon, 161
Notes on the History of Russian Culture (Miliukov), 111

ober-procurator, 24–26, 35–36, 45, 148, 172, 179–80. *See also* Pobedonostsev, Konstantin
obshchestvennost'. *See* educated society (*obshchestvennost'*)
October Manifesto, 100, 139–40, 142, 150–51
Octobrist Party, 144, 146–47, 150, 232n79
official registry (*shtat*), 27
Ognev, Father, 145–46, 149
okrug. *See* district (*okrug*)
okruzhnye s"ezdy. *See* district congresses (*okruzhnye s"ezdy*)
Old Believers, 14, 26, 139, 150
On Orthodoxy in Relation to the Modern World (Feodor), 190
"On Plans for the Improvement of Public Order" (Nicholas II), 139
"On Priests, Acting as Members of the State Duma, Who Belong to Extremist Revolutionary Parties," 147
"On Strengthening the Principles of Religious Toleration" (Nicholas II), 139
"On the More Active Participation of Clergy and Laity in Church Administration," 181
"On the Necessity of Change in the Russian Church Administration," 165
Organization of Tver' Seminarians, 79
Organization of United Clergy, 179, 181
Orthodox brotherhoods, 33–37, 43, 46–48, 134, 209n109
Orthodox Church, 3–9, 190, 194, 196–97. *See also* apostolic authority; authorizing discourse; censorship; church

and state; church resources; decree (*ukaz*); social mission
Orthodox ideology, 6–7
Orthodox patriotism, 140, 148–51, 153, 157, 196
"Orthodoxy, Autocracy, and Nationality," 6, 52, 140, 153
"Orthodoxy versus Autocracy" (Pisiotis), 148
Ostrovskii, Nikolai, 83
Otroch Monastery, 98

Paladii, Metropolitan (Raev), 49
palata gosudarstvennykh imushchestv. *See* state domains (*palata gosudarstvennykh imushchestv*)
Pankrat, Tat'iana, 121
Papkov, Aleksandr, 34, 113–15, 182, 202n58
parish assembly (*prikhodskoe sobranie*), 108, 127
parish churches, 107–11, 119, 121, 128
parish clergy, 31; and corruption, 32–33, 100; criticisms of the, 100–103, 117–18, 134; dismantling of the, 182; and dissent, 138, 145–48, 166; duties of the, 10, 21–22, 26–27, 30, 45, 48, 54–55, 110–11, 116–19, 126; and elections, 143–46, 148–49, 153, 156, 184–87; numbers of, 213n75; persecution of the, 194–95, 197; and politics, 136–38, 140–57, 170; and self-determination, 48–49, 56–57, 86, 114; solidarity of the, 25–26, 32, 60; and the state, 136–37, 149–52. *See also* clerical teaching; estates (*sosloviia*); free association; humanitarian relief; mutual aid networks; social networks; voluntary associations
parish council (*tserkovno-prikhodskii sovet*), 51, 62–63, 125–27, 168, 192
parish schools, 83–99, 101–4, 152, 168
parish trusteeship (*prikhodskoe popechitel'stvo*), 109–11, 114–15, 117–18, 120–31, 135, 223n13, 226n84. *See also* church resources

parliamentarianism (*parlamentarizm*), 52, 63, 137, 142, 152, 155. *See also* democracy; the Dumas
Party of Legal Order (*partiia pravovogo poriadka*), 142
Pashkob, Vasilii, 49
pastoral activism, 3, 7, 11, 16–17, 36, 45, 64, 76, 156
pastoral assemblies, 31, 49–51, 53, 62–63, 126–27, 143, 181
pastoral movement: definition of the, 7; intellectual foundation of the, 190–91. *See also* authorizing discourse; church reform; church unity; mutual aid networks
pastoral office (*san*), 46
patriarchate, 9, 51, 115, 154, 159, 179, 188, 193
pension funds, 31
Persönlichkeit, 5
Peter I, 9, 23, 27, 68, 70, 84, 108, 110
petition movement, 17, 73–77
Petrov, Grigorii, 146–47
philanthropia, 8–9, 191–92. *See also* poverty
Photios, Patriarch, 161
Pirskii, Nikolai, 146
Pisiotis, Argyrios, 148
Platon, Vicar Bishop (Rozhdestvenskii), 146, 184–85, 231n53
Pobedonostsev, Konstantin, 35–39, 42–43, 45–54, 63–64, 71–72, 76, 86, 95, 165–66. *See also* ober-procurator
Pogodin, Mikhail, 113
Polish-Lithuanian Commonwealth, 33–34
Politburo of the Russian Communist Party, 195
political activism, 18–19, 81, 143, 146–47, 156
Poole, Randall, 15
popechitel'stvo o bednykh dukhovnogo zvaniia. *See* diocesan trusteeship for poor clergy (*popechitel'stvo o bednykh dukhovnogo zvaniia*)

Pope Leo XIII, 4–5
Popov, Aleksandr, 149
Populist movement, 66
poverty: and clerical women, 89–90; and education, 69–70, 87–88, 91–93; and mutual aid networks, 27–29, 67–70, 120, 140, 191; and the parish clergy, 16, 20–22, 44–45, 141, 144–45, 191; and parishioners, 106; and parish trusteeships, 123–25; and the Synod, 140–41
Pravoslavnoe obozrenie, 67
Pre-Sobor Commission (*predsobornoe prisutsvie*), 76, 115, 166, 187
priest-educator. *See* clerical teaching
propaganda, 196–97
Protasov, Count Nikolai, 26, 71
Provisional Government, 166–67
"Provisions for the Improvement of Conditions among the Clergy," 20
Purishkevich, Vladimir, 153

Rachinskii, Sergei, 86
radicalism: and the diocesan congresses, 167–71, 175, 178; and the Dumas, 136–37, 145–46; and the June 3rd system, 147–48; and the parish clergy, 16, 19, 81, 100, 136–37, 141; and parishioners, 81, 96, 99, 104, 113, 117; and scholarship, 14, 45; and the seminary, 17, 66, 70–71, 73, 75, 77–80, 138
Rasputin, Grigory, 179, 181, 185
Rauschenbusch, Walter, 5
readings, 97–98
Red Cross, 42, 56, 129–31, 133–34, 158, 194, 203n63
Regulations for Church Parish Schools, 86
Religious-Educational Administration, 24
religious life, 3–5, 11, 18, 96, 107, 112, 117–19, 121, 124, 200n25
renovationists, 195–97
Rentel, Father Alexander, 187
Rerum novarum (Pope Leo XIII), 4–5
Resettlement Administration, 10
resources. *See* church resources
revolution. *See* 1905 Revolution; 1917 Revolution; Bolshevik Revolution; church reform
Right Octobrists, 150
The Rise of Christianity (Stark), 8
Robbins, Richard, 37, 42
Rogoznyi, Pavel, 159
Roman Catholic Church. *See* Catholic Church
Roman Empire, 8, 137
Romanov regime, 51, 103–4, 203n63
Roslof, Edward, 197
Ruane, Christine, 92
ruga, 20–21
rural commune (*obshchina*), 108, 130
rural parishes, 41, 43, 123–24, 227n110
Rus', 161
Russian Empire, 51–52, 105, 129, 137, 163
Russian National Front, 150
Russkaia mysl', 136
Russkoe slovo, 103

Sabler (Ober-procurator), 155–56
sacralization, 4, 137
Saint Augustine, 8
Saint Petersburg conferences, 49
Saint Petersburg Theological Academy, 16, 180
Sakharov, Viktor, 53
salaries. *See* funding
Samarin, Aledsandr, 185–86
Samarin, Dmitrii, 112
Samarin, Iurii, 112
scholarship, 4, 12, 14–15, 107
School Council, 86–87
Second Duma, 63
Second Vatican Council, 188
secular domain (*svetskaia komanda*), 23, 27, 51
See of Moscow, 179–80
segmentary society, 13
the seminary, 17–18, 27, 65–82, 84, 87–89. *See also* petition movement
seminary charters, 36, 49, 68–69, 72, 75

Serafim, Archbishop (Chichagov), 160, 167–77, 188
Serafim, Vicar Bishop (Golubiatnikov), 57–58
serfdom, 17, 84, 108
Sergei, Archbishop (Stragorodskii), 115
Sergii, Archbishop (Starogorodskii), 185
service reports (*posluzhnye spiski*), 85
sexism, 92
Shchechkin, Rzhev, 169
Shevzov, Vera, 113
Shipova, Elizaveta, 90
shtat. *See* official registry (*shtat*); synodal roster (*shtat*)
Shultz, Nadezhda, 90
Skvortsov, Vladimir, 153–54
Slavophile movement, 112–13, 161
Smith, Allison, 193
Sobor. *See* All-Russian Church Sobor
sobornost', 161–62, 164–66, 176–77, 183, 187, 194, 236n95
sobornyi, 161–62, 188, 234n17
sobriety society, 119–20, 124, 208n91
social activism, 3–8, 16, 54, 64, 118–20, 183
social gospel movement, 5
socialism, 45, 71, 75–81, 96, 109, 136, 146–47
social mission, 7–11, 16–18, 37, 46, 51, 64, 81, 85, 107, 125
social networks, 10–17, 28–29, 43–45, 63–64, 87, 99, 124–37, 143, 148, 156–60, 189–91. *See also* civil society (*grazhdanskoe obshchestvo*); free association; mutual aid networks; voluntary associations
"The Social Question and the Christian Religion" (Kuyper), 4–5
Society for Lovers of Spiritual Enlightenment, 29–30
Society for Moral and Religious Enlightenment, 49
solidarity (*soslovnost'*), 13
sosloviia. *See* estates (*sosloviia*)
soslovnost'. *See* solidarity (*soslovnost'*)

Soviet of Peasants' Deputies, 174
Soviet of People's Commissars, 194
Spasskii Convent, 90
Special Commission, 117, 121. *See also* parish trusteeship (*prikhodskoe popechitel'stvo*)
Special Committee, 42
Speranskii, Mikhail, 68
The Spirit of a Christian (journal), 116–17
spiritual domain (*dukhovnaia komanda*), 23–24, 40, 65, 109, 126, 138, 193
Spiritual Regulation, 9, 23, 70, 108
Stalin, Joseph, 197
staritsy, 92
Stark, Rodney, 8
State Council, 24, 151–52
state domains (*palata gosudarstvennykh imushchestv*), 20–21, 41
Statute on the Convocation of the Sobor, 187
Stolypin, Piotr, 147, 151
Strickland, John, 137, 140
The Student Paper (*Uchenicheskii listok*), 78–79
superintendent assemblies, 148, 169, 184
superintendent congresses (*blagochinicheskie s"ezdy*), 31
superintendent districts, 39, 50–51, 56, 62, 127, 131, 132, 184
superintendents (*blagochinnyi*), 25–26, 28, 32, 36, 38, 41, 57–58, 118, 180
Supreme Church Administration, 196
surveillance, 15, 137. *See also* censorship
Suvorov, Nikolai, 162
svetskaia komanda. *See* secular domain (*svetskaia komanda*)
Svod Zakonov, 23–24
symphonia, 8, 137
Synod. *See* apostolic authority; censorship; church and state; church resources; decree (*ukaz*); social mission; synodal system
Synodal oppression, 47, 65, 71–72, 137, 141, 144–45, 147–49, 153, 156
synodal roster (*shtat*), 23

synodal system, 23–29, 47, 50–53, 115, 125, 139, 159–61, 164–65, 179, 192–93

terrorism, 66, 73, 77–80, 119, 155. *See also* radicalism

A Theology for the Social Gospel (Rauschenbusch), 5

Tikhon, Archbishop (Belavin), 179, 185–88, 195–96, 238n162

Tikhvinskii, Fedor, 146–47, 149, 168

Timberlake, Charles, 222n106

Time of Troubles, 9

Titlinov, Boris, 180, 182–83, 195

Tocqueville, Alexis de, 12

Tolstoi, Count Aleksandr, 35, 71

Tolstoy, Lev, 71, 152

"To the Rich and to the Poor" (Metropolitan Vladimir), 140

Trans-Siberian Railway, 53

Troitskii, Father, 148

Trubetskoi, Prince Evgenii, 183

Trudoviks, 145–46, 231n54

trusteeship councils, 129–31, 134

tsarism, 137–38, 140, 142. *See also* autocracy

Tserkovnaia revoliutsiia 1917 goda (Rogoznyi), 159

tserkovno-prikhodskii sovet. *See* parish council (*tserkovno-prikhodskii sovet*)

Tserkovnyi vestnik, 139, 165

Tsvetkov, Archpriest Nikolai, 181, 183, 187, 237n125

Tver' Seminary, 66–67, 73, 75, 78–79, 81–82, 93, 133

Tverskaia mysl', 177

Tver' Soviet Workers' and Soldiers' Deputies, 177

Union of Russian People (URP), 153–55

Union of Teachers in Church Educational Establishments, 75

Union of Unions, 183

United Organization, 133

unity. *See* church unity

urban parishes, 124–25, 226n87

urban teaching, 98–100

URP. *See* Union of Russian People (URP)

Uvarov, Sergie, 6

Valuev, P. A., 33, 68, 109

Vera i razum, 50

Veselovskii, Boris, 84–85

Vestnik Europy, 101–2

village council (*sel'skii skhod*), 85, 108

violence. *See* radicalism; terrorism

Vladimir, Metropolitan (Bogoiavlenskii), 48, 51, 56–57, 70, 98, 114, 140–42, 154, 188, 195

Vladislavlev, Father V. F., 21

Volotsky, Iosif, 9

voluntary associations, 12–14, 29–30, 32–33, 43, 49, 66, 107, 109, 120, 194. *See also* civil society (*grazhdanskoe obshchestvo*); free association; mutual aid networks; social networks

Voronezh Seminary, 73

Vostorgov, Ioann, 131, 148, 152–54, 156, 179, 195

Vozdvizhenskii, Father, 144–45

Vvedenskii, Father Aleksandr, 196

Waldegrade, Granville, 49

Wallace, Sir Donald Mackenzie, 26

war, 52–54, 129–35

War-Charity Commission, 131–34

white clergy, 11, 23, 50, 168, 172, 196

Witte, Count Sergey, 50–51, 53

women, 18, 83, 89–93, 102–3, 113, 193, 202n58. *See also* clerical women

Zaozerskii, Nikolai, 163–64, 187

Zealots for Church Renovation, 230n42

zemstvo, 29, 37–40, 52, 77, 84, 100–103, 111–12, 130, 206n46

Zemstvo Congress on Popular Education, 103

zemstvo-constitutionalists, 160

Zinoviev, Grigory, 196

Zvenigorod ecclesiastical school, 54

www.ingramcontent.com/pod-product-compliance
Lightning Source LLC
Chambersburg PA
CBHW051050230426
43666CB00012B/2635